Lecture Notes in Computer Science 10629

Commenced Publication in 1973
Founding and Former Series Editors:
Gerhard Goos, Juris Hartmanis, and Jan van Leeuwen

More information about this series at http://www.springer.com/series/7408

Ofer Strichman · Rachel Tzoref-Brill (Eds.)

Hardware and Software: Verification and Testing

13th International
Haifa Verification Conference, HVC 2017
Haifa, Israel, November 13–15, 2017
Proceedings

 Springer

Editors
Ofer Strichman
Technion - Israel Institute of Technology
Haifa
Israel

Rachel Tzoref-Brill
IBM Research Lab
Haifa
Israel

ISSN 0302-9743 ISSN 1611-3349 (electronic)
Lecture Notes in Computer Science
ISBN 978-3-319-70388-6 ISBN 978-3-319-70389-3 (eBook)
https://doi.org/10.1007/978-3-319-70389-3

Library of Congress Control Number: 2017959620

LNCS Sublibrary: SL2 – Programming and Software Engineering

This Springer imprint is published by Springer Nature
The registered company is Springer International Publishing AG
The registered company address is: Gewerbestrasse 11, 6330 Cham, Switzerland

Preface

These are the conference proceedings of the 13th Haifa Verification Conference (HVC), held on the IBM Research campus in Haifa (HRL), Israel, during November 13–15, 2017. HVC is an annual conference dedicated to advancing the state of the art in verification and testing. The conference provides a forum for researchers and practitioners from academia and industry to share their work, exchange ideas, and discuss the future directions of testing and verification for hardware, software, and complex hybrid systems. It is also an opportunity to view tool demos that are related to the scope of the conference.

The first day of HVC 2017 was dedicated to tutorials. The conference itself was shortened to two days this year, which improved the acceptance ratio and raised the overall quality. This year, 34 full papers were submitted, out of which 13 were accepted. Further, six tool papers were submitted, out of which five were accepted, and five posters were submitted, out of which four were accepted.

Each of the papers and posters was reviewed by three Program Committee members or sub-reviewers of their choice. The reviewing process included a discussion between the reviewers and an attempt to reach a consensus. The posters and tool demos were presented in a dedicated session in the lobby of IBM-HRL.

In addition to the aforementioned papers, HVC 2017 hosted several high-quality keynote talks: Prof. Eli Ben-Sasson from the Technion in Haifa, Prof. Dino Distefano from Queen Mary University of London, Prof. Subhasish Mitra from Stanford University in California, and finally Kedar Namjoshi from Nokia Bell Labs in New Jersey.

The conference also held the annual HVC award ceremony. The award was given to Prof. Cristian Cadar from Imperial College in London for "his contributions to dynamic symbolic execution and the KLEE symbolic execution infrastructure" and more generally for "his outstanding contributions to program verification, bug finding, test generation and, more generally, to software reliability." The members of the HVC Award Committee were:

Andrey Rybalchenko, Chair (Microsoft Research), Hana Chockler (King's College London), Kerstin Eder (University of Bristol), Marta Kwiatkowska (University of Oxford), and Leonardo Mariani (University of Milano-Bicocca). We thank them all.

HVC 2017 received sponsorship from IBM, Cadence Design Systems, Mellanox Technologies, Qualcomm, and Annapurna. Many thanks to all of them.

We would like to extend our appreciation and sincere thanks to the local organization team from IBM Research Haifa Laboratory: Revivit Yankovich, the local coordinator, Tali Rabetti, the publicity chair, Tom Kolan, the tutorials chair, Niva Bar-Shimon, the Web master, and the Organizing Committee, which consisted of Eli Arbel, Laurent Fournier, Sharon Keidar-Barner, Moshe Levinger, Karen Yorav, and Avi Ziv.

We thank the Program Committee and the sub-reviewers that joined them in selecting such high-quality articles for the HVC program. We also thank IBM-HRL for hosting the conference without any registration fees, including the facility and the meals, and providing administrative support before, during, and after the conference. Let us not forget to thank our sponsors, Mellanox and Cadence, and the fabulous conference management system EasyChair, which made our life as conference chairs so simple.

Finally, we thank the participants for coming and engaging in fruitful discussions — we hope to see you next year as well!

September 2017

Ofer Strichman, Program Chair
Rachel Tzoref-Brill, General Chair

Organization

Program Committee

Nikolaj Bjorner	Microsoft Research, USA
Hana Chockler	King's College London, UK
Alessandro Cimatti	FBK-IRST, Italy
Rayna Dimitrova	UT Austin, USA
Adrian Evans	iRoC Technologies, France
Franco Fummi	University of Verona, Italy
Alberto Griggio	FBK-IRST, Italy
Alan J. Hu	University of British Columbia, Canada
Warren Hunt	University of Texas, USA
Alexander Ivrii	IBM, Israel
Laura Kovacs	Vienna University of Technology, Austria
Akash Lal	Microsoft Research, India
Annalisa Massini	Sapienza University of Rome, Italy
Ziv Nevo	IBM Haifa Research Lab, Israel
Shaz Qadeer	Microsoft, USA
Martina Seidl	Johannes Kepler University Linz, Austria
Natasha Sharygina	Università della Svizzera italiana (USI Lugano, Switzerland)
Carsten Sinz	Karlsruhe Institute of Technology (KIT), Germany
Ofer Strichman	Technion, Israel
Mattias Ulbrich	Karlsruhe Institute of Technology, Germany
Willem Visser	Stellenbosch University, South Africa
Greta Yorsh	Queen Mary University of London, UK

Additional Reviewers

Arbel, Eli	Marescotti, Matteo
Asadi, Sepideh	Mari, Federico
Bayless, Sam	Melatti, Igor
Botha, Heila	Morad, Ronny
Desai, Ankush	Roveri, Marco
Fedyukovich, Grigory	Santhiar, Anirudh
Herda, Mihai	Sumners, Rob
Hyvärinen, Antti	Tonetta, Stefano
Jangda, Abhinav	Tronci, Enrico
Kilhamn, Jonatan	Tzevelekos, Nikos
Koyfman, Anatoly	Veksler, Tatyana
Maiya, Pallavi	Weigl, Alexander
Mancini, Toni	

Tutorials

SeaHorn: Software Model Checking with SMT and AI

Arie Gurfinkel

Abstract. Software Model Checking (SMC) is one of the most effective automated program verification techniques available today. SMC is applicable to a large range of programs and properties and is capable of producing both counterexamples (i.e., program executions that show how the property is violated by the program) and certificates (i.e., inductive proofs that justify how the property is satisfied in all program executions). In this tutorial, I will demonstrate a Software Model Checker SeaHorn, currently developed in a collaboration between University of Waterloo and SRI International. SeaHorn provides a verification environment build on top of LLVM – an industrial compiler infrastructure. SeaHorn combines traditional and advanced Software Model Checking algorithms based on Satisfiability Modulo Theory (SMT) with Abstract Interpretation and many unique abstract domains. While being state-of-the-art SMC, SeaHorn provides infrastructure for conducting research in automated program analysis.

Combinatorial Security Testing: Quo Vandis?

Dimitris E. Simos

Abstract. Combinatorial methods have attracted attention as a means of providing strong assurance at reduced cost, but when are these methods practical and cost-effective? This tutorial comprises of two parts. The first introductory part will briefly explain the background, process, and tools available for combinatorial testing, with illustrations from industry experience with the method.

The main part, explains combinatorial testing-based techniques for effective security testing of software components and large-scale software systems. It will develop quality assurance and effective re-verification for security testing of web applications and security testing of operating systems. It will further address how combinatorial testing can be applied to ensure proper error-handling of network security protocols and provide the theoretical guarantees for exciting Trojans injected in cryptographic hardware. Procedures and techniques, as well as workaround will be presented and captured as guidelines for a broader audience. The tutorial is concluded with our vision for combinatorial security testing together with some current open research problems.

Machine Learning in Practice - How to Build and Deploy ML Projects

Litan Ilany

Abstract. Machine Learning projects have already shown significant value in variety of areas, including design and validation fields.

However, in practice, the process of bringing a valuable ML project into production can come across many hurdles, thus It is extremely difficult to truly embed them in the core processes of the organization. In this tutorial we will present some best practices in working on ML projects, deploying them in core processes, and maximizing the value they create.

We will focus on CRISP-DM methodology, Agile ML development process and others topics, as well as present some examples from projects conducted for Intels validation teams.

Invited Talks

Self-Certifying and Secure Compilation

Kedar S. Namjoshi

Bell Labs, Nokia
kedar.namjoshi@nokia-bell-labs.com

Abstract. An optimizing compiler improves the performance of a program by modifying its instructions, control flow, and data representations. How can one be sure that such changes are implemented correctly? Testing is difficult, as it requires producing programs as test data. A mechanized correctness proof is infeasible for a production compiler such as GCC or LLVM. This talk explores a third alternative, self-certification, where a compiler generates a proof of correctness with each compilation run. As the compiler is untrusted, generated proofs have to be independently validated by automated methods. I will lay out the theoretical basis behind this technique, discuss why proof generation and proof checking are feasible in practice, and sketch our implementation for the LLVM compiler. A compiler transformation may be correct and yet be insecure. The possibility of an information leak being silently introduced during compilation is troubling, as such leaks can be hard to detect. I will present a notion of secure compilation, show that some commonly applied optimizations can be insecure, and describe how they may be secured. The end goal is fully verified and secure compilation: through-out the talk, I will highlight important implementation challenges and intriguing open questions.

QED and Symbolic QED: Dramatic Improvements in Pre-silicon and Post-silicon Validation of Digital Systems

Subhasish Mitra

Abstract. Ensuring the correctness of integrated circuits (ICs) is essential for ensuring correctness, safety and security of electronic systems we rely on. As ICs continue to grow in size and complexity, the cost and effort required to validate them are growing at an unsustainable rate. To make matters worse, difficult bugs escape into post-silicon and even production systems.

We present the Quick Error Detection (QED) technique which targets post-silicon validation and debug challenges. QED drastically reduces error detection latency, the time elapsed between the occurrence of an error caused by a bug and its manifestation as an observable failure. Inspired by QED, we also present Symbolic QED which combines QED principles with a formal engine to detect and localize bugs during both pre- and post-silicon validation.

Experimental results collected from several commercial designs as well as hardware platforms demonstrate the effectiveness and practicality of QED and Symbolic QED:

1. For billion transistor-scale industrial multi-core IC designs, Symbolic QED detects and localizes difficult logic design bugs (that may escape traditional simulation-based pre-silicon verification) automatically (without requiring design-specific assertions or properties) in only a few hours (~ 3 hours on average) during pre-silicon verification. In contrast, traditional model checking generally requires specially-crafted design-specific properties and cannot scale to large designs.
2. Results from multiple commercial hardware platforms show that QED improves error detection latencies of post-silicon validation tests by up to 9 orders of magnitude, from billions of clock cycles to very few clock cycles. QED also improves bug coverage during post-silicon validation 4-fold.
3. With drastically improved error detection latencies, QED (together with a formal engine) automatically localizes logic and electrical bugs in billion transistor-scale designs during post-silicon debug. For example, we can now automatically narrow the locations of electrical bugs to a handful of candidate flip-flops (18 flip-flops on average for a design with 1 Million flip-flops) in only a few hours (9 hours on average). In contrast, traditional post-silicon debug techniques might take weeks (or even months) of manual work.

QED and Symbolic QED are effective for logic design bugs and electrical bugs inside processor cores, hardware accelerators, and uncore components such as cache controllers, memory controllers and interconnection networks. QED-based validation and debug techniques have been successfully used in industry.

Joint with Prof. Clark Barrett (Stanford), Prof. Deming Chen (UIUC), several graduate students and industrial collaborators.

Scalable, Transparent and Post-quantum Secure Computational Integrity, with applications to Crypto-Currencies

Eli Ben-Sasson

Abstract. Scalable Zero Knowledge (ZK) are currently used to enhance privacy and fungibility in the ZCash cryptocurrency, and could potentially be used to solve Bitcoin's scalability problems.

This talk describes recent progress towards, and applications of, *transparent* zero knowledge proofs, whose setup requires only a public random string.

Joint work with Iddo Bentov, Ynon Horesh and Michael Riabzev.

Contents

Tool Papers

Posters

Full Papers

A Framework for Asynchronous Circuit Modeling and Verification in ACL2

Cuong Chau[1], Warren A. Hunt, Jr.[1], Marly Roncken[2], and Ivan Sutherland[2]

[1] Department of Computer Science
The University of Texas at Austin
Austin, TX, USA

[2] Maseeh College of Engineering and Computer Science
Portland State University
Portland, OR, USA

{ckcuong,hunt}@cs.utexas.edu, marly.roncken@gmail.com, ivans@cecs.pdx.edu

Abstract. Formal verification of asynchronous circuits is known to be challenging due to highly non-deterministic behavior exhibited in these systems. One of the main challenges is that it is very difficult to come up with a systematic approach to establishing invariance properties, which are crucial in proving the correctness of circuit behavior. Non-determinism also results in asynchronous circuits having a complex state space, and hence makes the verification task much more difficult than in synchronous circuits. To ease the verification task by reducing non-determinism, and consequently reducing the complexity of the set of execution paths, we impose design restrictions to prevent communication between a module M and other modules while computations are still taking place that are internal to M. These restrictions enable our verification framework to verify loop invariants efficiently via induction and subsequently verify the functional correctness of asynchronous circuit designs. We apply a link-joint paradigm to model asynchronous circuits. Our framework applies a hierarchical verification approach to support scalability. We demonstrate our framework by modeling and verifying the functional correctness of a 32-bit asynchronous serial adder.

Keywords: asynchronous circuit modeling, asynchronous circuit verification, non-deterministic behavior, hierarchical verification, link-joint model, mechanical theorem proving, self-timed serial adder

1 Introduction

Asynchronous (or self-timed) circuits have shown their potential advantages over synchronous (or clock-driven) circuits for low power consumption, high operating speed, low electromagnetic interference, elimination of clock skew problems, better composability and modularity in large systems, etc [10,15]. Nonetheless, the asynchronous paradigm exposes great challenges in both design and verification that are not found in the clocked paradigm. It is still a daunting challenge

© Springer International Publishing AG 2017
O. Strichman and R. Tzoref-Brill (Eds.): HVC 2017, LNCS 10629, pp. 3–18, 2017.
https://doi.org/10.1007/978-3-319-70389-3_1

to verify the correctness of asynchronous systems at large scale, mainly due to the high degree of non-determinism for event ordering inherent in such systems. Since verification is a critical component of any complex digital design, *scalable* methods for asynchronous system verification are highly desirable.

Our effort is complementary to the work introduced by Park et al. [11] to validate timing constraints for delay-insensitive handshake components. The authors used model-checking to perform timing verification on handshake components, to validate the correctness of local communication or handshake protocols with respect to delays in gates and wires. Our approach relies on such analysis to justify our abstraction of self-timed circuits to finite-state-machine representations of networks of communication channels, thus ignoring circuit-level timing constraints. Using the ACL2 theorem-proving system [7], we present a framework for specifying and verifying the functional correctness of those networks.

Our work focuses on developing scalable methods for reasoning about the functional correctness of self-timed systems. Our approach applies induction reasoning to establishing loop invariants of self-timed systems. We use the DE (Dual-Eval) system [3], which is built using the ACL2 theorem-proving system, to specify and verify self-timed circuit designs. DE is a formal hardware description language that permits the hierarchical definition of finite-state machines. It has shown its capabilities to specify and verify synchronous microprocessor designs [1,4]. A key feature of the DE system is that it supports *hierarchical verification*, which is critical in verifying the correctness of circuit behavior at large scale. It also provides a library of verified hardware circuit generators that can be used to build and analyze more complex hardware systems [1].

We use DE to model self-timed circuits as networks of communication and computation primitives that operate with each other locally via the *link-joint model* proposed by Roncken et al. [13], a universal model for various self-timed circuit families. To our knowledge, we are the first to model self-timed circuits using the link-joint model in a theorem-proving system. We also develop a method for verifying functional properties of self-timed circuits constructed via the link-joint model.

We model the non-determinism of self-timed circuit behavior by consulting an *oracle* field — an external field we inject into the circuit model. The challenge in reasoning about the correctness of non-deterministic systems is that their state space is not only large as compared to synchronous systems, but also ill-structured in such a way that computing invariants in those systems becomes highly complicated. Since invariants are crucial properties for proving the correctness of circuit behavior, we are interested in developing a method for computing invariants of self-timed circuits systematically, thus ultimately making the verification of these systems tractable. Our approach attempts to reduce non-determinism, consequently reducing the complexity of the set of execution paths, by imposing design restrictions to prevent communication between a module M and other modules while computations are still taking place that are internal to M. These design restrictions enable our verification approach to verify loop invariants efficiently via induction and subsequently verify the functional correctness of self-timed circuit designs. We demonstrate our framework by modeling and verifying the functional correctness of a 32-bit self-timed serial adder [3]. This provides a significant first step towards the formal verification of arbitrary asynchronous designs.

The rest of the paper is organized as follows. Related work is given in Section 2. An overview of the DE system is presented in Section 3. Section 4 describes our self-timed circuit modeling and verification approach. Section 5 demonstrates our approach by describing our modeling and verification of a 32-bit self-timed serial adder. Possible future work and concluding remarks are given in Sections 6 and 7, respectively.

2 Related Work

Asynchronous circuit verification is an active research area in the hardware community. Many efforts in this area have focused on verifying properties of asynchronous circuits by applying timing verification techniques [6,8,9,11]. Park et al. [11] presented their framework, called ARCtimer, for modeling, generating, verifying, and enforcing timing constraints for individual delay-insensitive handshake components. ARCtimer uses the general-purpose model checker NuSMV to perform timing verification of handshake components. The authors' main goal was to verify that the network of logic gates and wires and their delays meet the component's communication protocol specification. Our goal is complementary: to verify that the network of handshake components and their protocols meets its functional specification, while ignoring circuit-level timing constraints that can be handled by tools like ARCtimer.

Verbeek and Schmaltz [17] formalized and verified with the ACL2 theorem prover *blocking* (not transmitting data) and *idle* (not receiving data) conditions over delay-insensitive primitives in the Click library. These conditions were then used to derive SAT/SMT instances from asynchronous circuits built out of these primitives for checking deadlock freedom in those circuits. While our approach also uses ACL2 to model and verify self-timed circuits, we verify the functional correctness of self-timed circuit models.

Clarke and Mishra [2] employed model checking to automatically verify some safety and liveness properties of a self-timed FIFO queue element specified in Computation Tree Logic (CTL). The authors also presented a hierarchical method for verifying large and complex circuits. Nevertheless, their approach imposed an unrealistic assumption on self-timed circuits that each gate has one unit delay. Our approach, on the other hand, does not restrict gate delays except that they are finite.

Other previous work on asynchronous circuit verification attempted to reduce non-determinism by adding restrictions to circuit designs, as presented by Srinivasan and Katti [16] and Wijayasekara et al. [18]. Srinivasan and Katti [16]

---

[3] The source code for this work is available at https://github.com/acl2/acl2/tree/master/books/projects/async/serial-adder

applied a refinement-based method for verifying safety properties of desynchronized pipelined circuits, while Wijayasekara et al. [18] applied the same method for verifying the functional equivalence of NULL Convention Logic (NCL) circuits against their synchronous counterparts. While their verification frameworks are highly automated by using decision procedures, both provided quite limited scalability and no liveness properties were verified. Although we also impose design restrictions to reduce non-determinism, our approach is capable of verifying liveness properties as described in Section 5 in our account of the verification of a 32-bit self-timed serial adder. Our approach exploits hierarchical verification and induction reasoning to support scalability.

3   The DE System

DE is a formal occurrence-oriented hardware description language developed in ACL2 for describing Mealy machines [3]. It has been shown to be a valuable tool in formal specification and verification of hardware designs [14,5]. The operational semantics for the DE language is implemented as an output "wire" evaluator, se, and a state evaluator, de. The se function evaluates a module and returns its outputs as a function of its inputs and its current state. The de function evaluates a module and returns its next state; this state will be structurally identical to the module's current state, but with updated values. The interested reader may refer to Hunt's paper [3] for details about the se and de functions.

In synchronous circuits, storage elements update their values simultaneously at every global clock tick, where the clock rate is fixed. Hence the duration represented by two consecutive de evaluations of a synchronous module is fixed and exactly one clock cycle. In self-timed circuits, however, storage elements update their values whenever their local communication conditions are met; and hence the duration represented by two consecutive de evaluations of a self-timed module varies.

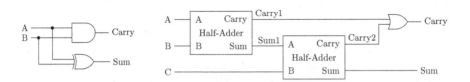

Fig. 1. Half-adder (left) and full-adder (right)

A DE description is an ACL2 constant containing an ordered list of modules, which we call a *netlist*. Each module consists of five elements in the following order: a netlist-unique module name, inputs, outputs, internal states represented by a list of occurrence names identifying those occurrences that contain state-holding devices, and occurrences. Each occurrence consists of four elements in the following order: a module-unique occurrence name, outputs, a reference to a primitive or defined module, and inputs. For instance, the DE descriptions of the half-adder and full-adder netlists shown in Figure 1 are described below. Note that these adders are purely combinational-logic circuits; they do not contain any internal state.

```
(defconst *half-adder*
  '((half-adder
      (a b)
      (sum carry)
      ()    ;; No internal state
      ((g0 (sum)   xor (a b))
       (g1 (carry) and (a b))))))

(defconst *full-adder*
  (cons '(full-adder
          (c a b)
          (sum carry)
          ()    ;; No internal state
          ((t0 (sum1 carry1) half-adder (a b))
           (t1 (sum  carry2) half-adder (sum1 c))
           (t2 (carry)       or         (carry1 carry2))))
        *half-adder*))
```

A key feature of the DE system is that it supports hierarchical verification, which is critical in verifying the correctness of large circuit descriptions. The idea is to verify the correctness of a larger module by composing verified submodules without delving into details about the submodules. More specifically, each time a module is specified, we prove a *value lemma* specifying the module's outputs and a *state lemma* specifying the module's next state. If a module does not have an internal state (purely combinational), only the value lemma need be proven. These lemmas are used to prove the correctness of yet larger modules containing these submodules, without the need to dig into any details about the submodules. Such an approach can scale to very large systems, as has been shown on contemporary x86 designs at Centaur Technology [14]. We refer the interested reader to Hunt's paper [3] for an example of the value lemma of the full-adder mentioned above.

4 Modeling and Verification Approach

We model self-timed circuits by (1) adding local signaling to state-holding devices, (2) establishing local communication protocols, and (3) employing an oracle, which we call a collection of *go* signals, for modeling non-deterministic circuit behavior due to variable delays in wires and gates. The details of our modeling approach are described below.

In the clock-driven design paradigm, state-holding devices are all governed by a global clock signal such that their internal states are updated at the same time when the clock "ticks", which is simulated by a **de** evaluation in the DE system. There is no such global clock signal in the self-timed design paradigm.

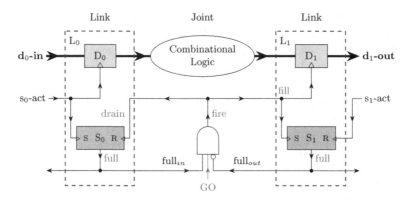

Fig. 2. Simple self-timed communication circuit using the link-joint model from Roncken et al. [13]

Thus, when a self-timed circuit is simulated by a de evaluation, its state-holding
elements will update their states based on their inputs.

For establishing local communication protocols, we model the link-joint model
introduced by Roncken et al. [13]. Our rationale for formalizing this model is the
authors' demonstration that it is a universal communication model for various
circuit families. In this model, links are communication channels in which data
and full/empty states are stored, while joints are handshake components that
implement flow control and data operations. Roughly speaking, joints are the
meeting points for links to coordinate states and exchange data. Figure 2 shows
an example of a simple self-timed communication circuit using the link-joint
model. This circuit consists of a joint associated with an incoming link L_0 and
an outgoing link L_1. In general, a joint can have several incoming and outgoing
links connected to it, as depicted in Figure 3.

Links receive *fill* or *drain* commands from and report their full/empty states
and data to their connected joints. A *full* link carries valid data, while an *empty*
link carries data that are no longer or not yet valid. When a link receives a fill
command, it changes its state to full. A link will change to the empty state if it
receives a drain command. We use a set-reset (SR) latch to model the full/empty
state of a link, as illustrated by the lower box in each link shown in Figure 2 [4].
The interested reader may refer to Roncken et al.'s paper [13] for other options
of link control circuitry.

Joints receive the full/empty states of their links and issue the fill and drain
commands when their communication conditions are satisfied. The control logic
of a joint is an AND function of the conditions necessary for it to act. To enable a
joint-action, all incoming links of a joint must be full and all outgoing links must

---

[4] Using SR latches in this manner requires an implementation to assure sufficient delay
in the AND function to prevent overlap in the S and R inputs. This is handled at
the circuit level by Park et al. [11].

be empty (see the AND gates in Figures 2 and 3). Due to arbitrary delays in wires and gates, enabled joints may fire in any order. We model the non-deterministic circuit behavior by associating each joint with a so-called *go* signal as an extra input to the AND function in the control logic of that joint. The value of the *go* signal will indicate whether the corresponding joint will fire when it is enabled. The idea of using *go* signals to model non-determinism was presented in a paper by Roncken et al. [12]. In our framework, when applying the **de** function that computes the next state of a self-timed circuit, only enabled joints with high values of the *go* signals will fire. When a joint fires, the following three actions will be executed in parallel [5]:

- transfer data computed from the incoming links to the outgoing links,
- fill the outgoing links, make them full,
- drain the incoming links, make them empty.

Below is our DE description of the self-timed module shown in Figure 2, where D_0 and D_1 are one-bit latches, and the combinational logic (Comb. Logic) representing the data operation of the joint is simply a one-bit buffer. This module contains state-holding devices S_0, D_0, S_1, and D_1.

```
'(link-joint
  (s0-act s1-act d0-in go)
  (d1-out)
  (s0 d0 s1 d1)    ;; Internal states
  (;; Link L0
   (s0 (s0-status)        sr     (s0-act fire))
   (d0 (d0-out d0-out-) latch (s0-act d0-in))
   ;; Link L1
   (s1 (s1-status)        sr     (fire s1-act))
   (d1 (d1-out d1-out-) latch (fire d1-in))
   ;; Joint
   (j (fire)   joint-cntl (s0-status s1-status go))
   (h (d1-in) buffer      (d0-out))))
```

We consider all possible interleavings of the *go* signals' values when reasoning about the correctness of circuit behavior. The only requirement is that when applying the **de** function to compute the next state of a module, the go signals are high for at least one enabled joint (if any such joint exists). We call this restriction the *single-step-progress* requirement.

Our framework exploits a hierarchical verification approach to formalizing single transitions of circuit behavior (simulated by **se** and **de** functions), as described in Section 3. The verification process at the module level requires us to show how several asynchronous blocks can be interconnected to provide provably correct, higher level functions. Our framework currently treats modules

---

[5] The work done by Park et al. [11] used ARCtimer to generate and validate timing constraints in joints. Their framework added sufficient delay to the control logic of each joint to guarantee that the clock pulse is wide enough for the three mentioned actions to be properly executed when the joint fires. Our work assumes that we have a valid circuit that satisfies necessary circuit-level timing constraints, as guaranteed by ARCtimer.

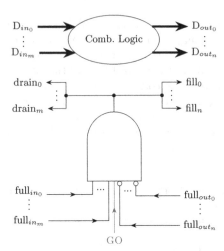

Fig. 3. Sketch of a joint with m incoming and n outgoing links [13]

as "complex" links that communicate with each other via local communication protocols. Hence, self-timed modules report both data and communication states to the joints connecting those modules. In the future, we plan to explore a notion of modules being treated as "complex" joints [6].

The communication state of a self-timed module is more complicated than that of a primitive link in the sense that it can be ready to send and receive data at the same time, or "not ready" to communicate with its connected modules. For this reason, self-timed modules use separate incoming and outgoing communication signals, whereas primitive links only need one full/empty signal for both incoming and outgoing communications. For example, the *ready-in-* (active low) and *ready-out* (active high) output signals of the module in Figure 4 are both active at the same time when the two links on the left side are empty and the three links on the right side are full. This module is in the not-ready state when the two links on the left side are full and the three links on the right side are empty.

In arbitrarily non-deterministic systems, the state space may not exhibit a clear structure for computing invariants effectively. Verification of such systems may require exploring the entire state space. To simplify the verification task by reducing non-determinism, and consequently reducing the complexity of the set of execution paths, we impose restrictions on circuit designs such that a module is ready to communicate with other modules only when it finishes all of its

---

[6] We choose to model modules as links for the purpose of storage-free connections between modules, since they are connected via storage-free joints in this setting. However, this modeling does not keep to the spirit of the link-joint paradigm in which computation is supposed to be done entirely in joints and links serve only to store data [13].

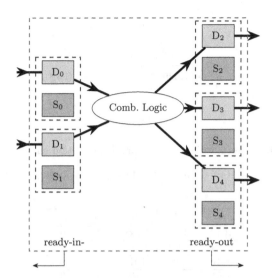

Fig. 4. Example of a self-timed module containing one joint with two incoming and three outgoing primitive links. The flow control of the joint is not shown in the figure for the sake of simplicity. Note that a self-timed module can contain several links and joints. We use this simple example for pedagogical purposes.

internal operations and becomes *quiescent*. By adding these restrictions, the state space is not only reduced but, more importantly, it also exhibits a structure for establishing loop invariants efficiently via induction. These restrictions guarantee that every module will reach a fixed point before it can communicate with other modules, and thus enable our framework to establish invariants and subsequently verify the functional correctness of circuit designs.

5   32-Bit Self-Timed Serial Adder Verification

In this section we demonstrate our framework by describing our modeling and verification of a 32-bit self-timed serial adder. This relatively simple example is sufficiently complex to demonstrate the generality of our approach. First let us introduce the *shift register* concept, which is used in constructing a serial adder. A shift register is a state-holding device that shifts in the data present at its input and shifts out the *least significant bit* (LSB) in the bit-vector whenever the register's advance ("clock") input transitions from low to high. Shift registers can have both parallel (bit-vector) and serial (single-bit) inputs and outputs. Figure 5 illustrates an example of a serial-in, serial-out, and parallel-out *n*-bit shift register. The figure shows that the shift register outputs both the LSB (serial-out) and the entire *n*-bit vector (parallel-out), but it only accepts single-bit inputs (serial-in). When the *write/shift* signal is high, the value of *Shift-Reg* will be shifted right by one position and the *bit-in* will be stored in *Shift-Reg* at the *most-significant-bit* (MSB) position.

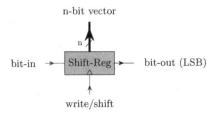

Fig. 5. Serial-in, serial-out, and parallel-out n-bit shift register

Table 1. 4-bit serial addition example. The bit-in is 0 for both shift registers A and B in this example.

A	B	S	s_i	c_{i+1}
1010	0011	1xxx	1	0
0101	0001	01xx	0	1
0010	0000	101x	1	0
0001	0000	1101	1	0

A serial adder is a digital circuit that performs binary addition via bit additions, from the LSB to MSB, one at a time. Bit additions are performed using a 1-bit full-adder to generate a sum bit and a carry bit, and two input operands and the accumulated sum are stored in the shift registers. Table 1 shows a 4-bit serial addition example.

We construct a 32-bit self-timed serial adder using the link-joint model, i.e., the communications between state-holding elements in the circuit are established via the link-joint model. Figure 6 shows the datapath of a 32-bit self-timed serial adder; the control path is elided for the sake of simplicity [7]. In terms of the link-joint model, the figure displays only the data operations of the joints (circles) and the link data (rectangles) [8]; it abstracts both the flow control of the joints and the link states. To model non-determinism, we associate each joint with a *go* signal. In Figure 6, we see that the *go* signals point to the data operations of their corresponding joints, and we also refer to joints by their *go* signals' names. But note that these *go* signals are indeed provided as inputs to the AND gates in the control logic of their corresponding joints, which are omitted from the figure. The roles of the storage elements (the rectangles in Figure 6) used in the serial adder are described below.

- Two 32-bit input operands are stored in *Shift-Reg$_0$* and *Shift-Reg$_1$*, and the 32-bit sum is stored in *Shift-Reg$_2$*. The final 33-bit sum (including the carry-out) is stored in the regular register *Result*.

---

[7] The dotted lines emanating from the *Done-* latch represent the fact that the output of *Done-* is used in the control path, not in the datapath.

[8] Our approach currently declares shift registers as primitive state-holding devices and uses them to store link data. In the future, we plan to be faithful to the link-joint methodology by replacing the shift registers by links and joints.

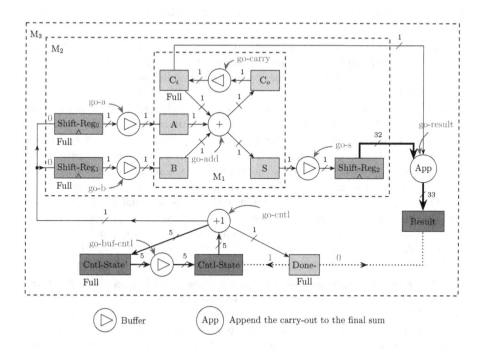

Fig. 6. Data flow of a 32-bit self-timed serial adder, M_3. Circles represent joints, rectangles represent links.

- *Cntl-State* and *Cntl-State'* are 5-bit registers that hold the current and next control states of the serial adder, respectively. The current control state acts as a counter that counts the number of times the bit addition has been executed. Since the adder performs 32-bit additions, the control states are 5 bits long.
- The output of the *Done-* latch indicates whether the circuit will write the final 33-bit result into the *Result* register when the corresponding communication is ready, or the circuit keeps updating the current control state *Cntl-State*.
- Latches A and B contain two 1-bit operands for the full-adder; latch C_i contains the carry-in. The 1-bit sum and the carry-out produced from the full-adder are stored in latches S and C_o, respectively.

We prove that the self-timed serial adder indeed performs the addition under an appropriate initial condition. Initially, *Shift-Reg$_0$*, *Shift-Reg$_1$*, C_i, *Cntl-State'*, and *Done-* are full; other state-holding elements are empty. The initial values stored in *Shift-Reg$_0$*, *Shift-Reg$_1$*, and C_i represent two 32-bit input operands and the carry-in, respectively. The initial value of *Cntl-State'* is the zero vector, and the initial value of *Done-* is high (or 1). We prove that *Result* eventually becomes full and its value at that point is the sum of the two 32-bit input operands and the carry-in.

Our approach applies the hierarchical verification method as described in Section 3 to verifying the correctness of the self-timed serial adder. Specifically, we first construct module M_1 that performs bit additions using a 1-bit full-adder (the innermost dashed-line box in Figure 6). We place a constraint when constructing M_1 so that its *ready-out* signal is active (i.e., ready to send data) if the condition $\left(full(S) \wedge full(C_i)\right)$ is satisfied, and its *ready-in-* signal is active (i.e., ready to receive data) if the condition $\left((empty(A) \vee empty(B)) \wedge full(C_i)\right)$ is satisfied. This constraint guarantees that M_1 is ready to communicate with other modules only when it is quiescent. For example, consider the scenario when A and B and C_i are empty, S and C_o are full. Since the *ready-out* condition for M_1 is not satisfied, the joint associated with the *go-s* signal (henceforth, we refer to this joint simply as *go-s*) is not ready to act even if *Shift-Reg$_2$* is empty. Likewise, neither *go-a* nor *go-b* is ready to act even if *Shift-Reg$_0$* and *Shift-Reg$_1$* are full, since the *ready-in-* condition for M_1 is not satisfied. Note that M_1 is still active in this case; it is not quiescent because *go-carry* is now ready to act.

After constructing module M_1, we prove an **se** value lemma and a **de** state lemma for this module. We then move on to construct module M_2 that performs serial additions without control states (the middle dashed-line box in Figure 6). We also place a constraint on M_2's design to guarantee that M_2 is ready to communicate with other modules only when it is quiescent: its *ready-out* signal is active when $full(Shift\text{-}Reg_2)$ is satisfied, and its *ready-in-* signal is active when $\left(empty(Shift\text{-}Reg_0) \wedge empty(Shift\text{-}Reg_1) \wedge full(Shift\text{-}Reg_2)\right)$ is satisfied. Since M_2 contains M_1 as a submodule, the two lemmas we already proved for M_1 are used in proving the value and state lemmas for M_2, without knowing any further details about M_1. These two lemmas about M_2 are then used in proving the value and state lemmas for circuit M_3, i.e., the serial adder with control states.

A key step in our verification of the self-timed serial adder is to establish the loop invariant of this circuit model via induction. Given the initial state of the circuit as mentioned earlier, we prove that *the full/empty state of every link in this circuit is preserved after each iteration of the circuit execution*, as long as the value of *Done-* before each iteration is 1. Each iteration performs one bit-addition and the orders of operations to be executed in one iteration are displayed by the dependency paths of the *go* signals in Figure 7. Each relation $go_i \rightarrow go_j$ shown in this figure indicates that go_j will not be ready if go_i is not executed. For instance, the two arrows from *go-a* and *go-b* to *go-add* indicate that *go-add* is ready only if *go-a* and *go-b* were executed. At the initial state, only *go-a*, *go-b*, and *go-buf-cntl* are ready to act: *go-a* is ready because *Shift-Reg$_0$* is full, A is empty, and M_1 is ready to receive data (i.e., the *ready-in-* condition for M_1 is satisfied); *go-b* is ready because *Shift-Reg$_1$* is full, B is empty, and M_1 is ready to receive data; *go-buf-cntl* is ready because *Cntl-State'* and *Done-* are full, *Cntl-State* is empty, and the value of *Done-* is 1. Each iteration except the last is finished when *go-cntl* is executed (Figure 7(a)). The last iteration (the value of *Done-* at the beginning of this iteration is 0) is finished when *go-result* is executed

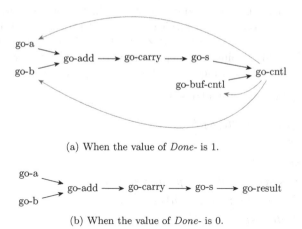

(a) When the value of *Done-* is 1.

(b) When the value of *Done-* is 0.

Fig. 7. Dependency paths of the *go* signals displayed in Figure 6

(Figure 7(b)). Our correctness theorems include the interleaving specification hypotheses, which consider all possible interleavings of the *go* signals' values conforming to the single-step-progress requirement as well as the dependency paths in Figure 7. It is easy to check manually that these dependency paths cover all possible execution paths of M_3. We plan to formalize this claim in the future.

The following two theorems, both proved with ACL2, state correctness of our self-timed circuit. Theorem 1 (partial correctness) states that given the initial state *st* of the serial adder as mentioned previously (Hypothesis 2), and the input sequence *input_seq* satisfying the interleavings of the *go* signals specified by the dependency paths shown in Figure 7 (Hypothesis 4, note that the *go* signals are part of the inputs); if the *Result* register becomes full (Hypothesis 6) after running the serial adder *n* de steps from the initial state (Hypothesis 5), then the value of the *Result* register at that point is the sum of the two 32-bit input operands and the carry-in initially stored in two shift registers $Shift\text{-}Reg_0$ and $Shift\text{-}Reg_1$, and latch C_i, respectively. Theorem 2 (termination) states that the *Result* register will become full if *n* is large enough (Hypothesis 6'; Hypotheses 1-5 are the same as in Theorem 1).

In our verification effort, we automate the verification process for the serial adder by defining macros that help prove automatically the base case of the loop invariant for all possible execution paths. We prove about 230 supporting lemmas (not including other supporting lemmas imported from libraries from the ACL2 Community Books) that help discharge automatically proof obligations required to prove the two main theorems mentioned above. One of the main challenges in verifying the serial adder is to prove the loop invariant by induction: ACL2 fails to discover automatically the correct induction scheme to prove this loop invariant. We have to provide an induction scheme to ACL2. In spite of that, our induction scheme is general enough to be applied to proving loop invariants of other self-timed circuits. The verification time of the 32-bit self-timed serial adder is about 80 seconds on a 2.9 GHz Intel Core i7 processor with 4MB L3 cache and 8GB memory. Since the loop invariant of the serial adder is established by induction, our proof technique can scale to any size of the adder.

Theorem 1 (Partial correctness).

$$async\_serial\_adder(netlist) \land \qquad\qquad (1)$$
$$init\_state(st) \land \qquad\qquad (2)$$
$$(operand\_size = 32) \land \qquad\qquad (3)$$
$$interleavings\_spec(input\_seq, operand\_size) \land \qquad\qquad (4)$$
$$(st' = run(netlist, input\_seq, st, n)) \land \qquad\qquad (5)$$
$$\boldsymbol{full(result\_status(st'))} \qquad\qquad (6)$$
$$\Rightarrow (result\_value(st') = shift\_reg\_0\_value(st) +$$
$$shift\_reg\_1\_value(st) +$$
$$ci\_value(st))$$

Theorem 2 (Termination).

$$async\_serial\_adder(netlist) \land \qquad\qquad (1)$$
$$init\_state(st) \land \qquad\qquad (2)$$
$$(operand\_size = 32) \land \qquad\qquad (3)$$
$$interleavings\_spec(input\_seq, operand\_size) \land \qquad\qquad (4)$$
$$(st' = run(netlist, input\_seq, st, n)) \land \qquad\qquad (5)$$
$$\boldsymbol{(n \geq num\_steps(input\_seq, operand\_size))} \qquad\qquad (6')$$
$$\Rightarrow full(result\_status(st'))$$

6   Future Work

In the future, we plan to prove the partial correctness of the self-timed serial adder without specifying the interleavings of the *go* signals' values. In other words, we aim to remove Hypothesis 4 from Theorem 1. A possible approach is that we can use Theorem 1 as a supporting lemma and also prove that for any interleaving i, there always exists a specified interleaving i' such that the orderings of operations when executing the circuit under i and i' are identical. From these two lemmas, we can derive the desired partial correctness theorem that does not specify the interleavings.

For the termination theorem (Theorem 2), simply removing Hypothesis 4 will make the theorem invalid. We need to add a constraint guaranteeing that delays are bounded in order to prove Theorem 2 without having Hypothesis 4.

We also plan to investigate a notion of modules with joints at the interfaces instead of links, where two modules are connected by one or more external links.

Another possibility for future work is to develop a better compositional reasoning method that improves scalability when the number of interleavings increases. The high-level idea is to verify the correctness of a larger module by composing verified submodules without delving into details about the submodules as well as the interleavings of their internal operations.

Our existing design restrictions may reduce the performance of self-timed implementations. Our purpose of imposing these restrictions in the design stage is to establish loop invariants for iterative circuits. For circuits that have no feedback loops, we are developing a method for verifying these systems without imposing the aforementioned restrictions.

7   Conclusion

This paper presents a framework for modeling and verifying self-timed circuits using the DE system. We model a self-timed system as a network of links communicating with each other locally via handshake components, which are called joints, using the link-joint model. To our knowledge, this is the first time self-timed circuits are modeled using the link-joint model in a theorem-proving system. We also model the non-determinism of event-ordering in self-timed circuits by associating each joint with an external *go* signal. In addition, presenting self-timed modules as complex links is also new in our paper. Another contribution of our work is our verification procedure to self-timed circuits as described. We show that the existing DE system already proven to be successful for synchronous circuits is adaptable for handling self-timed systems by reasoning with *go* signals as well as state-holding elements that have their own gating. Our verification approach is able to establish loop invariants using induction when the circuit behavior obeys the design restrictions we propose. Hierarchical verification is essential in our verification method and critical to circuit verification at large scale.

Acknowledgements

The authors would like to thank Matt Kaufmann for his encouragement, great discussions and feedback. We also thank Anna Slobodova for her useful comments and corrections on this paper. This material is based upon work supported by DARPA under Contract No. FA8650-17-1-7704.

References

1. C. Chau. Extended Abstract: Formal Specification and Verification of the FM9001 Microprocessor Using the DE System. In *Proc of the Fourteenth International Workshop on the ACL2 Theorem Prover and Its Applications (ACL2-2017)*, pages 112–114, 2017.
2. E. Clarke and B. Mishra. Automatic Verification of Asynchronous Circuits. In *Proc of the Workshop on Logic of Programs*, pages 101–115, 1983.

3. W. Hunt. The DE Language. In M. Kaufmann, P. Manolios, and J S. Moore, editors, *Computer-Aided Reasoning: ACL2 Case Studies*, chapter 10, pages 151–166. Springer US, 2000.

4. W. Hunt and E. Reeber. Applications of the DE2 Language. In *Proc of the Sixth International Workshop on Designing Correct Circuits (DCC-2006)*, 2006.

5. W. Hunt and S. Swords. Use of the E Language. In *Hardware Design and Functional Languages*, 2009.

6. P. Joshi, P. Beerel, M. Roncken, and I. Sutherland. Timing Verification of GasP Asynchronous Circuits: Predicted Delay Variations Observed by Experiment. In D. Dams, U. Hannemann, and M. Steffen, editors, *Lecture Notes in Computer Science*, chapter 17, pages 260–276. Springer Berlin Heidelberg, 2010.

7. M. Kaufmann and J. Moore. ACL2 Home Page. `http://www.cs.utexas.edu/users/moore/acl2/`, 2017.

8. H. Kim, P. Beerel, and K. Stevens. Relative Timing Based Verification of Timed Circuits and Systems. In *Proc of the Eighth International Symposium on Asynchronous Circuits and Systems (ASYNC-2002)*, pages 115–124, 2002.

9. A. Kondratyev, L. Neukom, O. Roig, A. Taubin, and K. Fant. Checking Delay-Insensitivity: 10^4 Gates and Beyond. In *Proc of the Eighth International Symposium on Asynchronous Circuits and Systems (ASYNC-2002)*, pages 149–157, 2002.

10. C. Myers. *Asynchronous Circuit Design*. Wiley, 2001.

11. H. Park, A. He, M. Roncken, X. Song, and I. Sutherland. Modular Timing Constraints for Delay-Insensitive Systems. *Journal of Computer Science and Technology*, 31(1):77–106, 2016.

12. M. Roncken, C. Cowan, B. Massey, S. Gilla, H. Park, R. Daasch, A. He, Y. Hei, W. Hunt, X. Song, and I. Sutherland. Beyond Carrying Coal To Newcastle: Dual Citizen Circuits. In A. Mokhov, editor, *This Asynchronous World Essays dedicated to Alex Yakovlev on the occasion of his 60th birthday*, pages 241–261. Newcastle University, 2016.

13. M. Roncken, S. Gilla, H. Park, N. Jamadagni, C. Cowan, and I. Sutherland. Naturalized Communication and Testing. In *Proc of the Twenty First IEEE International Symposium on Asynchronous Circuits and Systems (ASYNC-2015)*, pages 77–84, 2015.

14. A. Slobodova, J. Davis, S. Swords, and W. Hunt. A Flexible Formal Verification Framework for Industrial Scale Validation. In *Proc of the Ninth ACM/IEEE International Conference on Formal Methods and Models for Codesign (MEMOCODE-2011)*, pages 89–97, 2011.

15. J. Sparso and S. Furber. *Principles of Asynchronous Circuit Design - A Systems Perspective*. Springer US, 2001.

16. S. Srinivasan and R. Katti. Desynchronization: Design for Verification. In *Proc of the Eleventh International Conference on Formal Methods in Computer-Aided Design (FMCAD-2011)*, pages 215–222, 2011.

17. F. Verbeek and J. Schmaltz. Verification of Building Blocks for Asynchronous Circuits. In *Proc of the Eleventh International Workshop on the ACL2 Theorem Prover and Its Applications (ACL2-2013)*, pages 70–84, 2013.

18. V. Wijayasekara, S. Srinivasan, and S. Smith. Equivalence Verification for NULL Convention Logic (NCL) Circuits. In *Proc of the Thirty Second IEEE International Conference on Computer Design (ICCD-2014)*, pages 195–201, 2014.

Modeling undefined behaviour semantics for checking equivalence across compiler optimizations

Manjeet Dahiya and Sorav Bansal

Indian Institute of Technology Delhi,
{dahiya, sbansal}@cse.iitd.ac.in

Abstract. Previous work on equivalence checking for synthesis and translation validation has usually verified programs across selected optimizations, disabling the ones that exploit undefined behaviour. On the other hand, modern compilers extensively exploit language level undefined behaviour for optimization. Previous work on equivalence checking for translation validation and synthesis yields poor results, when such optimizations relying on undefined behaviour are enabled.

We extend previous work on simulation-based equivalence checking, by adding a framework for reasoning about language level undefined behaviour. We implement our ideas in a tool to compare equivalence across compiler optimizations produced by GCC and LLVM. Testing these compiler optimizations on programs taken from the SPEC integer benchmark suite, we find that modeling undefined behaviour semantics improves success rates for equivalence checking by 31 percentage points (from 50% to 81%) on average, almost uniformly across the two compilers. This significant difference in success rates confirms the widespread impact of undefined behaviour on compiler optimization, something that has been ignored by previous work on equivalence checking. Further, our work brings insight into the relative significance of the different types of C undefined behaviour on compiler optimization.

1 Introduction

Programming languages have erroneous conditions in the form of erroneous program constructs and erroneous data. Language standards do not impose requirements on all such erroneous conditions. The erroneous conditions on which no requirements have been imposed by the standard, i.e., whose semantics have not been defined are called *undefined behaviour* (UB). Since the standard does not impose any requirements on UB, compilers are permitted to generate code of their choice in presence of the same. In other words, compilers can assume the absence of UB in the target program, and are free to produce code without the checks for UB conditions. Further, they can produce more aggressive optimizations under such assumptions. For example, the C language standard states that writing to an array past its size is undefined. Hence, C compiler writers do not need to check the sanity of the array index during an array access. Moreover,

© Springer International Publishing AG 2017
O. Strichman and R. Tzoref-Brill (Eds.): HVC 2017, LNCS 10629, pp. 19–34, 2017.
https://doi.org/10.1007/978-3-319-70389-3_2

aggressive compilers may even remove a sanity check if the same has been added by the programmer in her C program.

C language contains hundreds of undefined behaviours [14]. All modern compilers like GCC, LLVM and ICC are known to extensively exploit UB while generating optimized code (we provide some evidence in this paper). Further, previous work on *optimization-unstable* code detection [26] reported that 40% of the 8575 C/C++ Debian Wheezy packages they tested, contain unstable code: unstable code refers to code that may get discarded during optimization due to the presence of UB. Undefined behaviour is clearly widespread. The need for UB has also been widely debated. On one hand, many textbook optimizations rely on UB semantics. For example, consider a simple for loop in C: for (int i=0; i<=n; ++i). Now if n equals INT_MAX, then this loop would never terminate, and it would be possible for i to be negative inside the loop body (because i would wrap around after INT_MAX). However, several optimizations would like to depend on the loop termination property, and the loop invariant that i >= 0 inside the loop body. Fortunately, these invariants are valid, because signed integer overflow is undefined in C (thus yielding the assumption that ++i can never wrap around, indirectly implying that it is illegal for n to be equal to INT_MAX). On the other hand, programmers are often annoyed by these "counter-intuitive" optimizations, and some of them go to the extent of disabling certain types of UB through flags provided by the compiler. For example, the Linux kernel build process disables signed integer overflow and type based strict aliasing UB assumptions in GCC [23, 24].

Undefined behaviour semantics and their exploitation by compilers for optimization means that the compiler verification tools (e.g., translation validation) must model these semantics for more precise results. Similarly, synthesis tools and superoptimizers (e.g., [2]) must model such semantics, while comparing equivalence of the target program with the candidate synthesized program, for better optimization opportunity. An equivalence checking algorithm results in a *false negative*, i.e., incorrect equivalence failure if it does not model the UB. Previous work on simulation-based equivalence checking across compiler optimizations has primarily been done in the context of translation validation [11, 17, 18, 21, 25, 27] across selected compiler optimizations, disabling the ones that exploit language level UB. This prior work yields poor results when equivalence checks are performed across the optimizations that exploit UB. This paper addresses this issue and makes the following contributions:

- We extend the simulation relation by adding *assumptions* at each row of the simulation relation table, to model language level UB semantics. Equivalence is now computed under these assumptions, i.e., the original program and the transformed program need to be equivalent only if the corresponding assumptions are *true*. If the assumptions are *false*, the programs are still considered equivalent even if their implementations diverge. We call this the *extended simulation relation*.

```
int A[256];
int sum1 = 0; long* sum2;
void sum(int n) {
    int* p = A;
    for(int i=1;i<n+1;++i) {
        sum1 = sum1 + *p;
        *sum2 = *sum2 + *p;
        p++;
    }
}
```

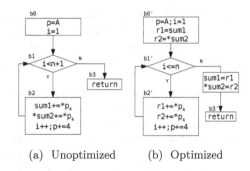

(a) Unoptimized   (b) Optimized

Fig. 1: An example function. sum2 is allocated by the caller.

Fig. 2: Unoptimized and optimized, abstracted versions of the program in Fig. 1.

- We discuss the assumptions produced by different types of UB semantics and experimentally determine the types of UB that are most consequential to compiler-based optimization.
- To model aliasing based UB, which we find is heavily exploited by compilers for optimization, we present an algorithm to compute aliasing information at the IR/assembly level. Computation of aliasing information at the assembly level is necessary because the programs emitted by the compilers are in assembly. The aliasing information computed through this algorithm is used for generating UB assumptions for the extended simulation relation.

We test our ideas by comparing equivalence across unoptimized and optimized implementations of programs derived from the SPEC CPU Integer benchmark suite. The equivalence tests are performed at function granularity, i.e., an unoptimized implementation of a C function (treated as the program specification) is compared against an optimized implementation of a C function. The optimized implementations are generated using GCC and LLVM with -O2 flag. The optimizations enabled by -O2, are commonly enabled by almost all software. Our overall success rate for equivalence checking across these optimizations is 81%, i.e., we successfully generate an equivalence proof, in the form of a provable simulation relation, for 81% of the equivalence checks. The success rate drops to 50% if the UB modeling is removed. Our results emphatically confirm the importance of modeling UB for checking equivalence for validation and synthesis of compiler optimizations.

2   Motivating example

Fig. 1 shows a C program which computes the sum of the first n elements of a global array A and stores the result in a global variable sum1 and at an address sum2. We have deliberately used two different types of accumulators (sum1 and *sum2) and i<n+1 in the for loop, to demonstrate three different types of C undefined behaviour in the same example. Fig. 2a, 2b show the abstracted

unoptimized and optimized versions of the same program compiled by gcc -O0 and -O2 respectively. The original programs are in x86 assembly, and many other optimizations are present in the optimized version; for exposition and brevity, we have abstracted them into a C like syntax and only the UB related optimizations are shown.

The first optimization we discuss through this example, is a peephole optimization involving substitution of the check i<n+1 by a faster check i<=n, avoiding the need to compute n+1. However, as such, the substitution may not seem correct because the two programs are not equivalent when n=INT_MAX. For n=INT_MAX, the loop of unoptimized program takes zero iterations (INT_MAX+1 wraps around to a negative number INT_MIN), while that of the optimized program loops forever (because i will always be ≤INT_MAX). Interestingly however, it is legal and common for C compilers to perform this optimization. This transformation is legal due to the *signed integer overflow* (SIO) assumption, that forms a part of the C undefined behaviour semantics. As per this assumption, signed integer arithmetic *shall not*[1] overflow (i.e., it is an illegal program if it causes signed integer arithmetic to overflow), and hence, the compiler need not worry about the case when overflow takes place.

The second interesting optimization in this example is the register allocation of sum1 and *sum2 to registers r1 and r2 respectively, throughout the execution of the loop. These registers containing the accumulated sum values, are written back to their respective memory locations at loop exit. Again, as such, these transformations may not seem correct: it is possible for the pointer p, which can belong to [A,A+4*n) to alias with either (or both) of &sum1 and sum2, in which case, the values stored at p may get modified as the loop executes, making register allocation of sum1 and *sum2 incorrect. It is however legal (and common) for C compilers to perform such register allocations. This is due to UB related to the following aliasing assumptions: 1) *Type based strict aliasing assumptions* (TBSA): Pointers of different types (e.g., long* and int*) shall not alias with each other (with the exception of char*). 2) *Out-of-bounds variable access assumptions* (OBVA): A program shall not access a memory location beyond the region of an object (variable). In our example, the TBSA assumptions guarantee that sum2 (of type long*) and p (of type int*) cannot alias. Similarly, sum2 cannot alias with &sum1 (of type int*). Further, the OBVA assumptions guarantee that p cannot point beyond the object A, i.e., p must belong to [A, A+4*256). This implies that p cannot alias with &sum1, as sum1 and A are distinct regions. With these assumptions, it is indeed legal to register-allocate sum1 and *sum2 throughout the loop execution.

The programs in Fig. 2a, 2b can be shown to be equivalent only if the UB assumptions are modeled and used in the simulation-based proof. In this paper, we contribute algorithms to model and use these UB assumptions in a simulation-based proof, and show their effectiveness for computing equivalence across compiler transformations on a general purpose code. Sec. 3 discusses the notion of the extended simulation relation that uses undefined behaviour as-

---

[1] Phrasing is taken from the C standard.

sumptions to correctly decide equivalence in the presence of UB. Sec. 4 discusses algorithms to generate these UB assumptions, for use in the extended simulation relation.

3   Extended simulation relation (with assumptions)

A simulation relation [17, 18] between two programs can be used to establish equivalence across the two programs. It has been used extensively in previous work on equivalence checking and translation validation [11, 17, 18, 20, 27]. A simulation relation is a witness of the equivalence between two programs. Given a valid simulation relation, proving equivalence is straight-forward; however the construction of a simulation relation is undecidable in general. We leverage previous work on automatic construction of a simulation relation across two programs, where the second program is the compiler-optimized version of the first program. In addition, we extend previous work to model and use UB assumptions, to allow equivalence computation in the presence of UB semantics. Equivalence is now conditional on these assumptions, i.e., the equivalence proof may fail if these assumptions are discounted.

The relevant assumptions are computed at each program location of the unoptimized program specification. These assumptions are based on a best-effort static analysis of the program: for example, if the program involves arithmetic on a signed integer variable, then the corresponding SIO assumption is inferred at that program location. Some assumptions can be inferred directly from program syntax, while others may require a deeper static analysis. In general, the sophistication of the static analysis required to infer the undefined behaviour assumptions, ought to match the sophistication of the analyses used by the optimizer. SIO and TBSA assumptions are examples of assumptions that can be inferred through straight-forward syntactic analysis of the program, while the OBVA assumptions usually require a deeper alias analysis, the kind used by modern compilers for optimization. We discuss this latter analysis in Sec. 4. In this section, we assume that such assumptions are already available at the respective program locations, and we discuss their effect on the required simulation relation.

Let $Prog_A$ be the unoptimized program specification and $Prog_B$ be the optimized implementation. $Prog_A$ specification also includes a map from the program locations to the corresponding UB assumptions ($Assum$). An extended simulation relation is represented as a table, where each row is a tuple ((L_A, L_B), $Assum[L_A]$, P) such that L_A and L_B are program locations in $Prog_A$ and $Prog_B$ respectively, $Assum[L_A]$ is the set of assumptions in $Prog_A$ at location L_A, and P is a set of invariants on the live program variables at locations L_A and L_B. A tuple ((L_A, L_B), $Assum[L_A]$, P) represents that the invariants P hold whenever the two programs are at L_A and L_B respectively, *assuming* all the UB assumptions at *all* $Prog_A$ program locations ($Assum$) hold.

An extended simulation relation is valid if the invariants at each location pair are inductively provable from invariants and UB assumptions at the predecessor

Location	Assumption	Invariants (P)
(b0,b0')	True	$n_A = n_B, A_A = A_B, \&sum1_A = \&sum1_B, sum2_A = sum2_B, M_A =_\Delta M_B$
(b1,b1')	$(n_A \neq INT\_MAX) \wedge$ $(\&sum1_A \neq p_A) \wedge$ $(sum2_A \neq p_A) \wedge$ $(sum2_A \neq \&sum1_A)$	$sl_4(M_A, \&sum1_A) = r1_B,$ $sl_4(M_A, sum2_A) = r2_B, n_A = n_B, i_A = i_B,$ $A_A = A_B, p_A = p_B, \&sum1_A = \&sum1_B,$ $sum2_A = sum2_B, M_A =_{\Delta \cup \{\&sum1_A, sum2_A\}} M_B$
(b3,b3')	True	$M_A =_\Delta M_B$

Init: $n_A = n_B, A_A = A_B, \&sum1_A = \&sum1_B, sum2_A = sum2_B, M_A =_\Delta M_B$

Fig. 3: Extended simulation relation for the programs in Fig. 2. (b0, b0') and (b3, b3') are the entry and exit rows respectively. A_A and $\&sum1_A$ are the base addresses of the globals A and sum1 respectively in $Prog_A$. $sl_4(M, addr)$ represents 4 bytes of data read in memory (M) at address $addr$. $=_\Delta$ represents equivalent memory states except at Δ; Δ represents the stack region. Init represents equivalence of inputs.

location pairs. Notice that the UB assumptions do not need to be proven. Invariants at the entry location (pair of entry locations of the two programs) represent the equivalence of program inputs $(Init)$; the base case of this inductive proof. Finally, if we can thus inductively prove equivalence of the return values at exit location (pair of exits of the two programs), we have established the programs to be equivalent. For C functions, the return values include the state of the heap and global variables. Formally, an extended simulation relation is valid if:

$$Init \Leftrightarrow invariants_{(Entry_A, Entry_B)}$$

$$\underset{(L'_A, L'_B) \to (L_A, L_B)}{\forall} Assum[L'_A] \wedge invariants_{(L'_A, L'_B)} \Rightarrow_{(L'_A, L'_B) \to (L_A, L_B)} invariants_{(L_A, L_B)}$$

Here $invariants_{(L_A, L_B)}$ represents the conjunction of invariants in the extended simulation relation for the location pair (L_A, L_B), $Init$ is the input equivalence condition at the entry of the two programs, L'_A and L'_B are predecessors of L_A and L_B in programs $Prog_A$ and $Prog_B$ respectively, and $\Rightarrow_{(L'_A, L'_B) \to (L_A, L_B)}$ represents implication over the paths $L'_A \to L_A$ and $L'_B \to L_B$ in programs $Prog_A$ and $Prog_B$ respectively.

Fig. 3 shows an extended simulation relation which establishes the equivalence across the programs in Fig. 2a and 2b. The exit row of this extended simulation relation denotes equivalence of memory states (modulo stack and local variables) at exit, representing the equivalence of globals variables {sum1, A} and values at pointer sum2 and the remaining unused heap. This simulation relation is only provable when the UB assumptions are used in the inductive proof. For example, without the assumptions, the invariant $sl_4(M_A, \&sum1_A) = r1_B$ of the second row is not provable on edge (b1, b1') $\to$ (b1, b1') (sl_4 represents the memory-read of four bytes; see Fig. 3 caption).

Type of undefined behaviour	Description
Signed integer overflow (SIO)	Signed integer arithmetic cannot overflow
Type based strict aliasing (TBSA)	Pointers of different types cannot alias (barring exceptions like char *)
Dereferenced addresses not null	An address that has been dereference cannot be zero
Shift operand bounds	If a value X is shifted left/right by another value S, then $S \geq 0$ and $S < numbits(X)$ ($numbits(X)$ is the number of bits used to represent X)
Type alignment	A value X of type T must be aligned to the size of T
No divide by zero	The divisor of a division operation cannot be zero

Table 1: Examples of types of C undefined behaviour that can be modeled through syntactic analysis of the program.

4   Modeling undefined behaviour assumptions

We now discuss how to obtain the UB assumptions for the simulation relation. We first generate these assumptions on the unoptimized program specification $Prog_A$, for each location, through static analysis of the program. At the time of the construction of the simulation relation, for every row (L_A, L_B), the assumptions corresponding to L_A are added in the simulation relation. In other words, the UB assumptions are inferred for the unoptimized program, and used during the construction and proof of the simulation relation.

The algorithm to infer the UB assumptions, depends on the type of the UB. For example, the assumptions for many types of UB can be inferred purely syntactically — see Table 1 for some examples. Such syntactic analysis and modeling of UB has also been used previously for the verification of manually written peephole optimizations in LLVM [16].

The OBVA undefined behaviour assumptions are an example of UB that require a relatively deeper static alias analysis. This is because the production quality compilers typically implement a similar alias analysis for better optimization opportunity. The static alias analysis provides a *may-alias* relation between program pointers and program *variables*. The program variables include all the global and local variables defined by the programmer. Further, to model aliasing in heap and stack, we include two special "variables", called "stack" and "heap". Thus, a pointer value in the program may alias with one or more of the user-defined variables, and/or with the stack/heap[2]. Based on this analysis, we infer assumptions indicating that a program pointer must point within the memory regions belonging to the variables with which it may alias:

$$aliasing\_assumptions_p \Leftrightarrow \bigvee_{v \in \{u:may\_alias(p,u)\}} (p \geq v_{begin} \land p < v_{end})$$

---

[2] While a stack is not a part of the program's language level semantics, it gets introduced by the compiler in the assembly implementation.

Here p represents a pointer value, v is a program variable p, and $[v_{begin}, v_{end})$ represents the region of memory occupied by variable v. Further, invariants encoding the mutual-disjointness of regions associated with each program variable, and for the stack and heap, are added through conditions on the respective v_{begin} and v_{end} values.

In our running example of Fig. 1, the alias analysis infers that p may alias with only the array variable A. Further, because A and sum1 are different variables, their memory regions are mutually disjoint, thus implying that p cannot alias with sum1.

This alias analysis, to infer the variables with which a program pointer may alias, is similar to the previous work on alias analysis for assembly code [4]. The alias analysis need not be precise, but needs to be sound, i.e., the may-alias relation for a pointer p must be include all variables that a pointer may actually alias with (over-approximation). We next describe the two analyses used by us to infer the may-alias relation.

4.1   May-alias analysis

To compute the may-alias relation, we first compute two relations, *linearly-related* (*lr*) and *may-depend-on* (*dep*) between program pointers and program variables (including stack and heap). The *lr* relation indicates the variable with which a program pointer is linearly-related, i.e., *based-on*. In other words, if a program pointer is at an offset from the address of a program variable then it is *lr* with that program variable. For example, a pointer p=v+10 or p=v+i (for some arbitrary variable i) are both *lr* with the variable address v. On the other hand, p=*v is *not lr* with v (even though p *may depend on* v, as we discuss later). In our running example of Fig. 1, p is *lr* with A. The C type system guarantees that a pointer may be *lr* with at most one program variable[3]. Also, if a program pointer p is *lr* with a program variable A, then p may alias with A, and *cannot* alias with any other variable (including stack/heap). A pointer can at most be *lr* with one variable.

In addition to the *lr* relation, we compute another relation called "may-depend-on" *dep*. This relation indicates the variables on which a program pointer may depend on, i.e., the variables whose address may potentially influence the value of this program pointer. If the address of a variable may not influence the value of a pointer, then that pointer may be assumed to not alias with the aforementioned variable. Note that $lr(p, v)$ implies $dep(p, v)$.

The may-alias relation between a pointer p and program variable v is computed in terms of the linearly-related and may-depend-on relations as follows:

$$may\_alias(p, v) \Leftrightarrow dep(p, v) \wedge \bigwedge_{w \in (V-v)} (\neg lr(p, w))$$

---

[3] A violation of this type-system, through type-punning for example, falls into the realm of UB.

Here V is the set of all program variables. In other words, we assume that a pointer p may alias with a variable v if it may depend on v, *and* it is not linearly-related to any other variable $w \neq v$ in V^4.

4.2   Computing linearly-related and may-depend-on relations

Computing both lr and dep relations involves a forward dataflow analysis on the program's control flow graph. These relations are initialized at program entry with conservative assumptions, and they are computed at each intermediate program location by analyzing transfer functions of the incoming control-flow edges. In our setting, each program represents a C function body, and the calling conventions of the compiler are used to initialize the relations at the entry node, i.e., we assume that the function arguments *may depend on* any of the global variables and/or the heap, but are independent of the stack and local variables of the function. Further, we assume that the function arguments are *not lr* with any global variable. Together, these assumptions at program entry specify that the function arguments may alias with all the program's global variables and the heap, but cannot alias with the function's stack/local variables.

The lr analysis across a control-flow edge involves a simple syntactic analysis of the expression trees of the transfer function on that edge. This syntactic analysis involves inference rules of the type: $lr(p, v) \Rightarrow lr(p \oplus X, v)$. i.e., if p is known to be lr with v, then $p \oplus X$ (for any expression X that may potentially depend on other variables $w \neq v$) is also lr with v. "$\oplus$" represents the addition and subtraction operators; we further generalize these rules to operations involving bitwise masking of lower-order bits of a pointer (a common operation in compiled code). If these inference rules cannot decide a pointer p to be lr with a variable v, then we conservatively assume that p is *not lr* with v (over-approximation). At all internal nodes (except the start node), we initially assume all pointers to be lr with all variables ($\top$), and refine the relations iteratively till a fixed point is reached. As discussed earlier, at the start node, we assume that none of the function arguments are lr with any of the variables. This information on lr relations flows from the program entry to all intermediate program locations, through transfer functions. The meet operator for this lr dataflow analysis is *intersection*, i.e., a pointer is lr with a variable only if it is lr on *all* possible program paths.

Similarly, the dep analysis across a control-flow edge also involves a syntactic analysis on the expression trees of the corresponding transfer function. The syntactic analysis involves inference rules of the type: $dep(p, v) \Rightarrow dep(OP(\ldots, p, \ldots), v)$. i.e., if p may depend on v, then any value derived from p (through any operation OP that uses p as an argument) may also depend on v. At the entry node, we conservatively assume that the function arguments may depend on any of the global variables or on the heap. At all intermediate nodes, we initialize by assuming that the pointers do not depend on any of the variables ($\top$). At

---

[4] As discussed earlier, the C type system ensures that if p is linearly-related to a variable w, then p cannot alias with any other variable $v \neq w$.

each iteration, we refine this may-depend-on relation at every node by analyzing the expression trees of the transfer function of each incoming edge. The meet operator for the *dep* relation is *union*, i.e., a pointer may depend on a variable if it depends on that variable on *any* program path.

Unlike compilers, our alias analysis needs to work for assembly code where pointer arithmetic is much more common. The *lr* relation is intended to capture such pointer arithmetic. Also, the modeling of stack is unique to assembly code. Our algorithm, which over-approximately computes the may-alias relation through *lr* and *dep* relations, is sound and efficient (polynomial in the size of the program and quite fast in practice), and captures the common patterns in compiled code. A more expensive analysis can potentially yield more precise may-alias relations.

5   Inferring the simulation relation

Automatic construction of the simulation relation has been well studied in prior work [5, 11, 17, 18, 20, 27]. Much previous work attempts to first discover a correspondence between program locations across the two programs (correlation (L_A, L_B)) in a first pass, and then attempts to find invariants (P) over the locations in a best-effort second pass. In contrast, our algorithm searches for the correlation simultaneously with the search for the invariants, resulting in a more flexible and robust system. We succinctly outline here, our correlation algorithm to automatically construct a provable simulation; a more detailed discussion is available in [3].

Our algorithm incrementally constructs a *joint transfer function graph* (JTFG) representing the partial simulation relation computed so far. A JTFG is a graph with nodes and edges. A JTFG node (L_A, L_B) represents a pair of program nodes L_A and L_B (indicating that $Prog_A$ is at L_A and $Prog_B$ is at L_B). Similarly, a JTFG edge $(L'_A, L'_B) \rightarrow (L_A, L_B)$, represents a pair of transitions $L'_A \rightarrow L_A$ and $L'_B \rightarrow L_B$ in $Prog_A$ and $Prog_B$ respectively. Thus, a transition across a JTFG edge encodes transitions in the two programs respectively. Each JTFG node (L_A, L_B) contains invariants relating the live variables at locations L_A and L_B in the two programs respectively. To model UB, the JTFG nodes further encode the UB assumptions. Recall that these assumptions have already been computed through static analysis for locations in $Prog_A$; the assumptions at location L_A in $Prog_A$ appear in all JTFG nodes containing L_A. Further, for each JTFG edge, *edge conditions* (*edgecond*) of its two individual constituent program control-flow edges (belonging to $Prog_A$ and $Prog_B$ resp.) should be equivalent. An edge condition represents the condition under which that edge is taken, as a function of the live variables at the source location of that edge.

The algorithm for constructing a JTFG is presented in Algorithm 1. The JTFG is initialized with a single node, representing the pair of entry locations of the two programs. The `CorrelateEdges()` function picks one $Prog_B$ edge, say $edge_B$, at a time and tries to identify paths in the unoptimized program ($Prog_A$) that have an equivalent *path condition* to $edge_B$'s edge condition. Several candi-

Function *CorrelateEdges(jtfg, edges$_B$)*

   if *edges$_B$ is empty* **then**

     | **return** LiveValuesAtExitAreEquivalent(jtfg)

   end

   edge$_B$ ← RemoveFirst(edges$_B$)

   edges$_A$ ← GetEdgesTillUnroll(Prog$_A$,edge$_B$,μ)

   foreach *edge$_A$ in edges$_A$* **do**

     jtfg' = AddEdge(jtfg, edge$_A$, edge$_B$)

     PredicatesGuessAndCheck(jtfg')

     if *IsEqualEdgeConditions(jtfg')* ∧ *CorrelateEdges(jtfg', edges$_B$)* **then**

     | **return** true

     end

   end

   return false

Algorithm 1: Algorithm to construct the JTFG (simulation relation). *edges$_B$* is a list of edges in *Prog$_B$* in depth-first search order. The AddEdge() function returns a new JTFG jtfg', formed by adding the edge to the old JTFG jtfg.

date paths are attempted up to an unroll factor μ (GetEdgesTillUnroll()). All candidate paths must originate from a *Prog$_A$* location that has already been correlated with the source location of *edge$_B$*. The path condition of a path is formed by appropriately composing the edge conditions of the edges belonging to that path. The edge *edge$_B$* is chosen in depth-first search order from *Prog$_B$*, and also dictates the order of incremental construction of the JTFG. The equivalence of the edge condition of *Prog$_B$* with the path condition of *Prog$_A$* is computed based on the invariants inferred so far at the already correlated JTFG nodes (IsEqualEdgeConditions()). These invariants, inferred at each step of the algorithm, are computed through a Houdini-style [7] guess-and-check procedure. The guesses are synthesized from a grammar, through syntax-guided synthesis of invariants [1] (PredicatesGuessAndCheck). The unroll factor μ allows equivalence computation across transformations involving loop unrolling.

These correlations for each edge (*edge$_B$*) are determined recursively to allow backtracking (see the recursive call to CorrelateEdges()). If at any stage, an edge (*edge$_B$*) cannot be correlated with a path in *Prog$_A$*, the function returns with a failure, prompting the caller frame in this recursion stack, to try another correlation for a previously correlated edge. In theory, this backtracking can be exponential in the number of edges, but in practice, backtracking is rare, especially because we prioritize the candidate source paths for correlation, in increasing order of their unrolling factor. Because most compiler transformations do not involve unrolling, backtracking is rare in this scenario.

PredicatesGuessAndCheck() synthesizes invariants through the following grammar of guessing: $\mathbb{G} = \{ \star_A \oplus \star_B, M_A =_{\star_A \cup \star_B} M_B \}$, where operator $\oplus \in \{<, >, =, \leq, \geq\}$ and $\star_A$ and $\star_B$ represent the program values (represented as symbolic expressions) appearing in *Prog$_A$* and *Prog$_B$* respectively. The guesses are formed through a Cartesian product of values in *Prog$_A$* and *Prog$_B$* using the patterns in $\mathbb{G}$. Our checking procedure is a fixed point computation which keeps eliminating the unprovable predicates, until only provable predicates remain (similar to Houdini). At each step, for each guessed predicate at each node, we try to prove it from every predecessor node using the current invariants and assumptions at the predecessor node (as also described in Sec. 3).

For our running example in Fig. 2a, 2b, the JTFG nodes and edges determined through our algorithm are {(b0,b0'), (b1,b1'), (b3,b3')} and {(b0,b0') → (b1,b1'), (b1,b1') → (b1,b1'), (b1,b1') → (b3,b3')} respectively. Further, the algorithm is able to infer the required invariants (shown in the last column of Fig. 3) to complete the equivalence proof.

6   Implementation and Experiments

To demonstrate the impact of undefined behaviour assumptions on compiler optimization, we compute equivalence of C functions across unoptimized (-O0) and optimized (-O2) x86 binaries produced by compiling C programs through production compilers, GCC and LLVM with and without UB models. We disable function inlining during compilation, as our prototype implementation cannot reason about inter-procedural optimizations. Even after disabling inlining, the average speedup across the compiler optimizations on these programs is 1.72x over clang-O0. To be able to reconstruct the C-level information, required for modeling UB and equivalence checking, we enable a few additional flags during the compilation (namely -g and -reloc) to generate debug information and relocation headers respectively. We assume that the binaries contain the symbol table (i.e., are unstripped), which along with relocation headers allow accurate renaming of memory addresses to global variable symbols. Further the debug information provides the signature and types of the variables and functions. Both GCC and LLVM support these compile-time options, and these options have no impact on the runtime of the executable.

The functions are drawn from four SPEC benchmarks: bzip2 (compression utility), gzip (compression utility), mcf (combinatorial optimization) and parser (word processing). The number of global variables in these benchmarks is 100, 212, 43 and 223 respectively. We compiled each program with both compilers to produce 16 binaries (8 unoptimized and 8 optimized), representing a total of 1058 pairs of unoptimized and optimized assembly functions (ignoring the identical glibc functions). Among these pairs, 714 functions had at least one loop in them (cyclic functions). The average number of assembly LOC and C-LOC for these functions is 112 and 35 respectively. We ignored the functions containing floating point operations (14 functions), as our semantic model for x86 floating point instructions is incomplete.

We performed experiments to demonstrate the significance of the three types of UB discussed in Sec 2, namely SIO, TBSA, and OBVA assumptions. We estimate the presence of UB based optimizations for each benchmark and compiler option, by performing the equivalence check twice, for each function, with and without using the UB assumption. If an equivalence check for a function pair

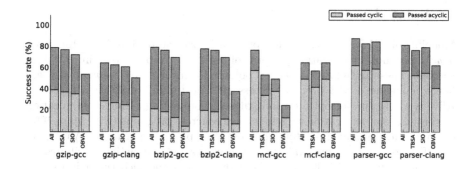

Fig. 4: For every benchmark-compiler option, the first bar shows the success rates when we model all three UB. The remaining three bars show the success rates when a particular type of UB among three (TBSA, SIO, OBVA) is not modeled. Each bar individually shows the contribution to the success rates by cyclic and acyclic functions.

passes with the UB assumption but fails without the assumption, then we assume that the compiler has exploited the respective undefined behaviour towards optimizing the function. The plot in Fig. 4 shows the success rates for each compiler and each benchmark for four different cases: the first bar represents the success rate when all three undefined behaviours are modeled; the second, third and fourth bars represent the cases when TBSA, SIO and OBVA assumptions are not modeled respectively. For SIO and TBSA, we employ the compiler flags `fno-strict-overflow` and `fno-strict-aliasing` to differentially estimate the impact of these assumptions. These flags enable/disable the SIO and TBSA assumptions while performing optimizations. If our equivalence check passes when these assumptions are disabled by the compiler, but fails when these assumptions are enabled by the compiler, we assume that the compiler is leveraging these assumptions for optimization. For OBVA, we simply turn on/off our alias analysis (Sec. 4) to determine the effect of OBVA assumptions.

The overall average success rates for equivalence checking across the four cases are 81%, 76%, 77% and 50%. As expected, the success rates are lower when a certain type of UB is not modeled. The drop in success rates, when a UB is not modeled with respect to the first bar (where all three types of UB are modeled), indicates the impact of the respective type of UB on compiler optimization. The drop in success rates due to non-modeling of OBVA assumptions is 31 percentage points. In contrast, the drop due to non-modeling of SIO and TBSA assumptions is only 4 and 5 percentage points respectively. These experiments confirm (a) the widespread impact of undefined behaviours on compiler optimizations and (b) throw light on the relative impact of different types of C undefined behaviour on optimization.

Our experiments also led to the discovery of a bug in GCC-4.1.0 related to the semantics of `fno-strict-aliasing` [8]. This flag is used to disable the optimizations related to TBSA. However, for certain functions, GCC-4.1.0 was using TBSA assumptions even while compiling with this flag.

7   Related Work

Modeling of UB for verification has previously been studied in Alive [16], where *acyclic* peephole optimization patterns of the `InstCombine` pass in LLVM are verified. These optimizations could potentially involve UB assumptions, and hence modeling of UB becomes necessary. The typical verification target for Alive is a few lines of optimization pattern representing a single optimization. In contrast, our verification targets involve concrete programs (with up to 1000s of lines) and containing *multiple* composed compiler optimizations. Alive models UB involving undefined values, poison values and instruction attributes like `nsw` (signed integer overflow), the kind that can be modeled through a simple syntactic analysis of the LLVM peephole optimization pattern. For example, the presence of UB attributes like `nsw`, `undef`, etc., in the optimization pattern directly indicates the UB assumptions. Aliasing based UB involving OBVA requires an alias analysis, and Alive did not consider this in their work. Our work is directed towards studying the common transformations in end-to-end compiler optimization, and we find that UB involving OBVA is the most commonly exploited for optimization in both GCC and LLVM. We believe that our alias analysis can also benefit Alive interested in capturing aliasing based UB assumptions. Another major difference between Alive and our work is that Alive verifies acyclic optimization patterns, while we generalize the ideas to simulation-based equivalence across programs containing loops.

   Our work overlaps with previous work on detection of *unstable* code, STACK [26]. STACK classifies unstable code as the code whose semantics are sensitive to UB. The underlying assumption of this work is that if an optimizer discards/modifies the (unstable) code due to the presence of UB, the resulting logic may behave differently from what the programmer intended. While STACK identifies certain important types of unstable code through static pattern-matching on LLVM IR, it also leaves out many. Aliasing based UB stands out as an example of UB not considered by STACK. It should be straight-forward to extend STACK by employing an alias analysis similar to our work. Our simulation-based equivalence proof construction approach is in contrast with the largely syntactic pattern matching approach adopted by STACK. It would be instructive to study the merits of applying a semantic procedure like ours, to the detection of unstable code.

   Our *lr* and *dep* analyses, resemble previous work on alias analysis for executable code by Debray et. al. [4]. The authors of this work noted that alias analysis for executable code requires reasoning about pointer arithmetic, and hence proposed special modeling for the `add` and `mult` opcodes, as these were the most commonly encountered opcodes for pointer manipulation on the RISC architecture they considered. However, because their analysis is syntactic in nature, it introduces imprecisions in common situations involving store and subsequent load of a pointer to/from memory. In such situations where a syntactic analysis does not provide enough information, the alias information would be conservatively widened to ⊥ in their approach. Their empirical evaluations reflect these imprecisions. Our approach works on de-sugared expressions obtained from machine opcodes, involving standard bitvector and boolean operators. Also, our memory model allows reasoning about stores followed by loads to identical locations (without other intervening conflicting stores), thus capturing the common pattern of pointers getting saved to stack slots for future reference. This semantic treatment lends robustness to our analysis, and makes it independent of the underlying machine ISA. In another related work on alias analysis, Fernandez and Espasa [6] attempted to remove the imprecisions discussed in [4], by sacrificing soundness guarantees. Sacrificing soundness is not acceptable in our setting. The authors of both these previous works on alias analysis for executable code were interested in link-time optimizations; unlike us, they do not describe a model for reasoning about UB using this obtained aliasing information.

Translation validation infrastructure (TVI) [17] verified five IR passes of compilation of gcc-2.91 and Linux-2.2 by GCC. The passes verified were branch optimization, common-subexpression elimination (CSE), loop unrolling and inversion, register allocation, and instruction scheduling. Similarly, value-graph translation validation for LLVM has been performed in at least two independent efforts [21, 25], albeit only across a known set of nine selected transformations, namely, dead-code elimination, global value numbering, constant propagation, loop-invariant code motion, loop deletion, loop unswitching, dead-store elimination, partial-redundancy elimination, and basic block placement. Neither of these approaches model UB, or study their significance on compiler optimization. Overall, our success rates for equivalence checking are comparable (and often better) to all these previous efforts, albeit in a much more generalized setting (with almost no assumptions on the transformations that are enabled). To our knowledge, our experiments are the first to demonstrate the significance of UB on compiler optimization.

There are more approaches to translation validation and equivalence checking with different settings and goals (e.g., [5, 9, 10, 12, 13, 15, 19, 20, 22, 27, 28]). All previous simulation-based equivalence checkers can also be extended with UB assumptions, to capture a larger set of compiler transformations.

There are hundreds of types of UB in C, and some of them have been bitterly debated in the past [23, 24]. We believe that this approach to quantifying the impact of different types of UB on compiler optimization, can bring some insight and basis for such debates. For example, our limited investigations in this work indicate the overwhelming relative significance of out-of-bounds variable access assumptions (for optimization), compared to other types of UB like signed integer overflow and type based strict aliasing assumptions. We hope that this work triggers more such studies across a wider variety of UB in future.

References

1. Alur, R., Bodik, R., Juniwal, G., Martin, M.M.K., Raghothaman, M., Seshia, S., Singh, R., Solar-Lezama, A., Torlak, E., Udupa, A.: Syntax-guided synthesis. In: FMCAD, 2013
2. Bansal, S., Aiken, A.: Automatic generation of peephole superoptimizers. ASPLOS XII (2006)

3. Dahiya, M., Bansal, S.: Black-box equivalence checking across compiler optimizations. In: APLAS '17 (2017)
4. Debray, S., Muth, R., Weippert, M.: Alias analysis of executable code. POPL '98
5. Felsing, D., Grebing, S., Klebanov, V., Rümmer, P., Ulbrich, M.: Automating regression verification. ASE '14 (2014)
6. Fernández, M., Espasa, R.: Speculative alias analysis for executable code. PACT '02
7. Flanagan, C., Leino, K.: Houdini, an annotation assistant for esc/java. In: FME 2001: Formal Methods for Increasing Software Productivity. LNCS (2001)
8. GCC Bugzilla - Bug 68480, https://gcc.gnu.org/bugzilla/show_bug.cgi?id=68480
9. Hawblitzel, C., Lahiri, S.K., Pawar, K., Hashmi, H., Gokbulut, S., Fernando, L., Detlefs, D., Wadsworth, S.: Will you still compile me tomorrow? static cross-version compiler validation. ESEC/FSE 2013
10. Kanade, A., Sanyal, A., Khedker, U.P.: Validation of gcc optimizers through trace generation. Softw. Pract. Exper. (2009)
11. Kundu, S., Tatlock, Z., Lerner, S.: Proving optimizations correct using parameterized program equivalence. PLDI '09 (2009)
12. Lahiri, S., Hawblitzel, C., Kawaguchi, M., Rebelo, H.: Symdiff: A language-agnostic semantic diff tool for imperative programs. In: CAV '12 (2012)
13. Lahiri, S., Sinha, R., Hawblitzel, C.: Automatic rootcausing for program equivalence failures in binaries. In: Computer Aided Verification (CAV'15) (2015)
14. Lee, J., Kim, Y., Song, Y., Hur, C.K., Das, S., Majnemer, D., Regehr, J., Lopes, N.P.: Taming undefined behavior in llvm. PLDI 2017 (2017)
15. Leung, A., Bounov, D., Lerner, S.: C-to-verilog translation validation. In: MEMOCODE (2015)
16. Lopes, N.P., Menendez, D., Nagarakatte, S., Regehr, J.: Provably correct peephole optimizations with alive. PLDI 2015
17. Necula, G.C.: Translation validation for an optimizing compiler. PLDI '00 (2000)
18. Pnueli, A., Siegel, M., Singerman, E.: Translation validation. TACAS '98 (1998)
19. Poetzsch-Heffter, A., Gawkowski, M.: Towards proof generating compilers. Electron. Notes Theor. Comput. Sci. (2005)
20. Sharma, R., Schkufza, E., Churchill, B., Aiken, A.: Data-driven equivalence checking. OOPSLA '13 (2013)
21. Stepp, M., Tate, R., Lerner, S.: Equality-based translation validator for llvm. CAV'11 (2011)
22. Strichman, O., Godlin, B.: Regression verification - a practical way to verify programs. In: Verified Software: Theories, Tools, Experiments, vol. 4171 (2008)
23. Torvalds, L.: https://lkml.org/lkml/2007/5/7/213
24. Torvalds, L.: https://gcc.gnu.org/ml/gcc/2002-01/msg00395.html
25. Tristan, J.B., Govereau, P., Morrisett, G.: Evaluating value-graph translation validation for llvm. PLDI '11
26. Wang, X., Zeldovich, N., Kaashoek, M.F., Solar-Lezama, A.: Towards optimization-safe systems. SOSP '13 (2013)
27. Zaks, A., Pnueli, A.: Covac: Compiler validation by program analysis of the cross-product. FM '08 (2008)
28. Zuck, L., Pnueli, A., Fang, Y., Goldberg, B.: Voc: A methodology for the translation validation of optimizing compilers 9(3) (2003)

Deferrability Analysis for JavaScript

Johannes Kloos[1], Rupak Majumdar[1], and Frank McCabe[2]

[1] MPI-SWS
[2] Instart Logic

Abstract. Modern web browsers allow asynchronous loading of JavaScript scripts in order to speed up parsing a web page. Instead of blocking until a script has been downloaded and evaluated, the *async* and *defer* tags in a script allow the browser to download the script in a background task, and either evaluate it as soon as it is available (for async) or evaluate it in load-order at the end of parsing (for defer). While asynchronous loading can significantly speed up the time-to-render, i.e., the time that passes until the first page elements are displayed on-screen, the specification for correct loading is complex and the programmer is responsible for understanding the circumstances under which a script can be loaded asynchronously in either mode without breaking page functionality. As a result, many complex web applications do not take full advantage of asynchronous loading. We present an automatic analysis of web pages which identifies which scripts may be safely deferred, that is, deferred without any observable behavior on the page. Our analysis defers a script if every other script that has a transitive read or modification dependency does not access the DOM. We approximate access and modification sets using a dynamic analysis. On a corpus of 462 professionally developed web pages from Fortune 500 companies, we show that on average, we can identify two or three scripts to defer (mean; median: 1). On 18 pages, we find at least 11 deferrable scripts. Deferring these scripts can have notable impact on time-to-render: in 49 pages, we could show that the median improvement in time-to-render was at least 100ms, with improvements up to 890ms.

1 Introduction

Modern web applications use sophisticated client-side JavaScript programs and dynamic HTML to provide a low-latency, feature-rich user experience on the browser. As the scope and complexity of these applications grow, so do the size and complexity of the client-side JavaScript used by these applications. Indeed, web applications download an average of 24 JavaScript files with about 346kB of compressed JavaScript[3]. In network-bound settings, such as the mobile web or some international contexts, optimizing the size and download time of the web page —which is correlated with user satisfaction— is a key challenge.

One particular difficulty is the loading of JavaScript. The browser standards provide a complicated specification for parsing an HTML5 page with scripts [28].

---

[3] See http://httparchive.org/trends.php, as of June 2017

O. Strichman and R. Tzoref-Brill (Eds.): HVC 2017, LNCS 10629, pp. 35–50, 2017.
https://doi.org/10.1007/978-3-319-70389-3_3

Normally, parsing the page stops while the script is downloaded, and continues again after the downloaded script has been run. With tens of scripts and thousands of lines of code, this can significantly slow down page rendering. To address this, HTML5 added "async" and "defer" loading modes. A script marked async is loaded in parallel with parsing and run as soon as it is loaded. Scripts marked defer are also loaded in parallel with parsing, but are evaluated only when parsing is complete, in the order in which they were scheduled for download.

The HTML5 specification notes that the exact processing details for script-loading attributes are non-trivial, and involve a number of aspects of HTML5. Indeed, online forums such as Stack Overflow contain many discussions on the use of defer and async tags for page performance, but most end with unchecked rules of thumb ("make sure there are no dependencies") and philosophical comments such as: "[I]t depends upon you and your scripts."

At the same time, industrial users are interested in having a simple way to use these attributes. In this paper, we define an automatic *deferring transform*, which takes a page and marks some scripts deferred without changing observable behavior. We start by defining the notion of a *safe deferrable set*, comprising a set of scripts on a given page. If all the scripts in this set are loaded using the `defer` loading mode, the user visible behavior of the page does not change. To make the idea of safe deferrable sets usable, we characterize the safe deferrable set using event traces [23]. In particular, we can use event traces to define a dependency order between scripts, and the notion of DOM-accessing scripts, which have user-visible behavior. A safe deferral set is contains no DOM-accessing scripts and is upward-closed under the dependency order. We also show that if a set contains only deterministic scripts, it is sufficient to check a single trace to characterize a safe deferral set, and describe a dynamic analysis based on this criterion.

We evaluate our work by applying JSDefer to a corpus of 462 websites of Fortune 500 companies. We find that 295 (64%) of these web pages contain at least one deferrable script, with 65 (14%) containing at least 6 deferrable scripts. Furthermore, we find that while race conditions and non-determinism are widespread on web pages, we can easily identify a sufficient number of scripts that do not participate in races nor have non-deterministic behavior and are thus candidates for deferral. Finally, actually deferring scripts on these pages shows reasonable improvement in time-to-render (TTR) for 59 pages, where the median improvement of time-to-render was 198.5ms, where the median load time of a page is 3097ms.

We summarize the contributions of this paper.

1. We describe a deferrability analysis, which checks which scripts can be marked as deferred without changing the observable behavior on the page.
2. We provide an extensive evaluation on a large corpus of professionally developed web sites to show that a significant portion of scripts can be deferred. We show the potential for improving the load performance for these pages: in our experiments, the median loading time improvement was 198.5 ms.

2   Background: Loading JavaScript

We briefly recall the WHATWG specification for loading HTML5 documents by a browser. A browser parses an HTML5 page into a data structure called the *document object model* (DOM) before rendering it on the user's screen. Parsing the document may require downloading additional content, such as images or scripts, linked in the document. The browser downloads images asynchronously, while continuing to parse the document. In contrast, it downloads scripts synchronously by default, making the parser wait for the download, and evaluates the script before continuing to parse the page. This puts script download and parsing on the critical path. Since network latency can be quite high (on the order of tens or hundreds of milliseconds) and script execution time may be non-negligible, this may cause noticeable delays in page loading. To allow asynchronous loading of scripts, the WHATWG specification ([28], sec. 4.12) allows two Boolean attributes in a `script` element, *async* and *defer*. In summary, there are three loading strategies for scripts:

- Synchronous loading. When encountering a `script` tag with no special attributes, the browser suspends parsing, downloads the script synchronously, and evaluates it after download is complete. Parsing continues after the evaluation of the script.
- Asynchronous loading. When encountering a `<script src="..."async>` tag, the browser starts an asynchronous download task for the script in the background but continues parsing the page until the script has been loaded. Then, parsing is suspended and the script is evaluated before continuing with parsing.
- Deferred loading. When encountering a `<script src="..."defer>` tag, the browser starts a download task for the script background but continues parsing the page. Once parsing has finished and the script has been downloaded, it is evaluated. Moreover, scripts are evaluated in the order that their corresponding script tags were parsed in the HTML, even though a later script may have finished downloading earlier.

While asynchronous or deferred loading is desirable from a performance perspective, it can lead to *race conditions*, i.e., the output of the page may depend on the order in which scripts are executed [23]. Consider the following example:

```
<html><body><script src="http://www.foo.com/script1.js"></script>
<script>if (!script1executed) { alert("Error!"); }</script></body></html>
```

where `script1.js` is simply `script1executed = true;`. As the script is loaded synchronously, the code has no race (yet): the `alert` function will never be called.

If we annotate the first script with the `async` tag, we introduce a race condition. Depending on how fast the script is loaded, it may get executed before or after the inline script. In case it gets executed later, an alert will pop up, noting that the external script has not been loaded yet. Changing the loading mode to defer does not cause a race, but now the alert always pops up; thus deferred loading of the script changes the observable behavior from the original version.

Another kind of race condition is incurred by scripts that perform certain forms of DOM accesses. For instance, consider the following page:

```
<html><body><script src="http://www.foo.com/script2.js"></script>
<span id="marker">Something</span></body></html>
```

where `script2.js` uses the DOM API to check if a tag with id `marker` exists. Loaded synchronously, the outcome of this check will always be negative. Asynchronous loading would make it non-deterministic, while deferred loading will remain deterministic but the check will always be positive.

Our goal is to analyze a web page and add `defer` tags to scripts, wherever possible. To ensure we can load scripts safely in a deferred way, we need to make certain that deferred loading does not introduce races through program variables or the DOM and does not change the observable behavior. Next, we make this precise.

3   Deferrability analysis

In the following, suppose we are given a web page with scripts $s_1, \ldots, s_n$ (in order of appearance). For this exposition, we assume that all the scripts are loaded synchronously; the extension to pages with mixed loading modes and inline scripts is straightforward.

On a high level, our goal is to produce a modified version of the page where some of the scripts are loaded deferred instead of synchronously, but the visible behavior of the page is the same. Concretely, when loading and displaying the page, the browser constructs a view of the page by way of building a DOM tree, containing both the visible elements of the page and the association of certain event sources (e.g., form fields or `onload` properties of images) with handler functions. Concretely, the DOM tree is the object graph reachable from `document.root` which consists of objects whose type is a subtype of `Node`; compare [28]. This DOM tree is built in stages, adding nodes to the tree, modifying subtrees and attaching event handlers. This can be due to parsing an element in the HTML document, receiving a resource, user interaction, or script execution.

Definition 1. *A DOM trace consists of the sequence of DOM trees that are generated during the parsing of a page. The DOM behavior of a page is the set of DOM traces that executing this page may generate.*

Note that even simple pages may have multiple DOM traces; for instance, if a page contains multiple images, any of these images can be loaded before the others, leading to different intermediate views.

Definition 2. *For a page p with scripts $s_1, \ldots, s_n$, and a set $D \subseteq \{s_1, \ldots, s_n\}$ let p' be the page where the members of D are loaded deferred instead of synchronously. We say that D is a safe deferral set if the DOM behavior of p' is a subset of the DOM behavior of p.*

3.1   Background: Event traces and races in web pages

We recall an event-based semantics of JavaScript [22,23,1] on which we build our analysis; we follow the simplified presentation from [1]. For a given execution of a web page, fix a set of events E; each event models one parsing action, user interaction event or script execution (compare also the event model of HTML in [28]). Our semantics will be based on the following operations:

- $rd(e, x)$ and $wr(e, x)$: These operations describe that during the execution of event $e \in E$, some shared object x (which may be a global variable, a JavaScript object, or some browser object, such as a DOM node) is read from or written to.
- $post(e, e')$: This operation states that during the execution of event $e \in E$, a new event $e' \in E$ is created, to be dispatched later (e.g., by setting a timer or directly posting to an event queue).
- $begin(e)$ and $end(e)$: These operations function as brackets, describing that the execution of event $e \in E$ starts or ends.

A *trace* of an event-based program is a sequence of *event executions*. An event execution for an event e is a sequence of *operations* such that the sequence starts with a begin operation $begin(e)$, the sequence ends with an end operation $end(e)$, and otherwise consists of operations of the form $rd(e, x)$, $wr(e, x)$, and $post(e, e')$ for some event $e' \in E$. For a trace of a program consisting of event executions of events $e_1, e_2, \ldots, e_n$, by abuse of notation, we write $t = e_1 \ldots e_k$.

Furthermore, we define a *happens-before relation*, denoted hb, between the events of a trace. It is a pre-order (i.e., reflexive, transitive, and anti-symmetric) and e_i hb e_j holds in two cases: if there is an operation $post(e_i, e_j)$ in the trace, or if e_i and e_j are events created externally by user interaction and the interaction creating e_i happens before that for e_j.

Two events e_i and e_j are *unordered* if neither e_i hb e_j nor e_j hb e_i. They have a race if they are unordered, access the same shared object, and at least one access is a write.

3.2   When is a set of scripts deferrable?

To make the deferrability criterion given above more tractable, we give a sufficient condition in terms of events. We first define several notions on events, culminating in the notion of the *dependency order* and the *DOM-modifying script*. We use these two notions to give the sufficient condition. Consider a page with scripts $s_1, \ldots, s_n$. For each script s_i, there is an event e_{s_i} which corresponds to the execution of s_i. By abuse of notation, we write s_i for e_{s_i}.

We say that e *posts* e' if $post(e, e')$ appears in the event execution of e. We say that e *transitively posts* e' if there is a sequence $e = e_1, \ldots, e_k = e'$, $k \geq 1$, such that for all $1 \leq i < k$, e_i posts e_{i+1}; i.e., we take the reflexive-transitive closure.

Suppose script s transitively posts event e. We call e a *near event* if, for all scripts s', s hb s' implies e hb s'. Otherwise, we call e a *far event*. We say that a script s is *DOM-accessing* iff there is a near event e such that e reads from or writes to the DOM.

Now, consider two events e_i and e_j such that $i < j$. We say that e_i *must come before* e_j iff both e_i and e_j access the same object (including variables, DOM nodes, object fields and other mutable state) and at least one of the accesses is a write. For two scripts s_i and s_j, $i < j$, we say that s_i must come before s_j iff there is a near events $e_{i'}$ of s_i and an event $e_{j'}$ such that $s_j \, \mathrm{hb} \, e_{j'}$ and $e_{i'}$ must come before $e_{j'}$. The dependency order $s_i \preceq s_j$ is then defined as the reflexive-transitive closure of the must-come-before relation.

Theorem 1. *Let p be a page with scripts $s_1, \dots, s_n$ and $D \subseteq \{s_1, \dots, s_n\}$. D is a safe deferral set if the following two conditions hold:*

1. *If $s_i \in D$, then script s_i is not DOM-accessing in any execution.*
2. *If $s_i \in D$ and $s_i \preceq s_j$ in any execution, then $s_j \in D$.*

The proof can be found in the technical report [17]. The gist of the proof is that all scripts whose behavior is reflected in the DOM trace are not deferred and hence executed in the same order (even with regard to the rest of the document). Due to the second condition, each script starts in a state that it could start in during an execution of the original page, so its behavior with regard to DOM changes is reflected in the DOM behavior of the original page.

The distinction between near and far events comes from an empirical observation: when analyzing traces produced by web pages in the wild, script-posted events clearly separate in these two classes. Near events are created by the `dispatchEvent` function, or using the `setTimeout` function with a delay of less than 10 milliseconds. On the other hand, far events are event handlers for longer-term operations (e.g., XMLHttpRequest), animation frame handlers, or created using `setTimeout` with a delay of at least 100 milliseconds. There is a noticeable gap in `setTimeout` handlers, with delays between 10 and 100 milliseconds being noticeably absent.

We make use of this observation by treating a script and its near events as an essentially sequential part of the program, checking the validity of this assumption by ensuring that the near events are not involved in any races. This allows us to formulate a final criterion, which can be checked on a single trace:

Theorem 2. *Let page p and set D be given as above, and consider a single trace executing events $e_1, \dots, e_n$. D is a safe deferral set if the following holds:*

1. *If e is a near event of s and accesses the DOM, $s \notin D$.*
2. *If e is involved in a race or has non-deterministic control flow, $s \, \mathrm{hb} \, e$ and s' happens before s in program order (including $s = s'$), then $s' \notin D$.*
3. *D is $\preceq$-upward closed.*

The proof can be found in [17]. The key idea of this proof is that all scripts in D are "deterministic enough," so the conditions of the previous theorem collapse to checking a unique trace.

3.3   JSDefer: A dynamic analysis for deferrability

The major obstacle in finding a deferrable set of scripts is the handling of actual JavaScript code, which cannot be feasibly analyzed statically. This is because of the dynamic nature of the language and its complex interactions with browsers, including the heavy use of introspection, `eval` and similar constructs, and variations in different browser implementations. In the following, we present a dynamic analysis for finding a safe deferral set that we call *JSDefer*.

Assumption: For reasons of tractability, we assume in this paper that no user interaction occurs before the page is fully loaded. This is because it is well-known that early user interaction is often not properly handled; compare [1]. Hence, we assume that early user interaction either does not occur or is handled as in [1].

With this assumption at hand, as reasoned above, we only need to consider scripts themselves and their near events; we call this the *script initialization code*. This part of the code is run during page loading and, empirically is "almost deterministic": it does not run unbounded loops and, for the most part, only exhibits limited use of non-determinism. We provide experimental evidence for this observation below. We use the second criterion in the previous section above, aggressively marking potentially non-deterministic scripts.

JSDefer use an instrumented browser from the EventRacer project [23] to generate a trace, including a happens-before relation. For now, we use a simple, not entirely sound heuristic to detect non-deterministic behavior: We extended the instrumentation to also include coarse information about scripts getting data from non-deterministic and environment-dependent sources, marking three sources: The random number generator, the current time, and various bits of browser state. In JSDefer, we check if a given script accesses any of these sources of non-determinism. We leave the integration of a proper taint-tracking based non-determinism check (e.g., building on [4]) as future work.

We perform deferrability analysis on the collected trace using Theorem 2. This calculation computes a safe deferrable set. We then rewrite the top-level HTML file of the page to add defer attributes to all scripts in the deferrable set.

4   Evaluation

We evaluated JSDefer on the websites of the Fortune 500 companies [10] as a corpus. To gather deferrability information, we used an instrumented WebKit browser from the EventRacer project [23] to generate event traces. Out of these 500 pages, we could successfully collect 451 pages; 38 websites timed out, 11 websites returned an error and 2 contained invalid HTML.

In the evaluation, we want to answer five main questions:

1. How much and in what way is defer and async already used?
2. Are our assumptions about determinism justified?
3. How many deferrable scripts can we infer?
4. What kind of scripts are deferrable?
5. Does deferring these scripts gain performance?

Async or defer	#pages		Async only: Only standard scripts?	#pages
Neither	32		Only standard scripts and snippets	256
Defer only	0		Other	148
Async only	404			
Both	15			

Table 1. Number of pages in the corpus that use async or defer. The sub-classification of async scripts was done manually, with unclear cases put into "others".

4.1   How are async and defer used so far?

As a first analysis step, we analyzed if pages were using async and defer annotations already, and in which situations this was the case. The numbers are given in Table 1.

The first observation from the numbers is that defer is very rarely used, while there is a significant numbers of users of async. Further analysis shows many of these asynchronous scripts come from advertising, tracking, web analytics, and social media integration. For instance, Google Analytics is included in this way on at least 222 websites[4]. Another common source is standard frameworks that include some of their scripts this way. In these cases, the publishers provide standard HTML snippets to load their scripts, and the standard snippets include an async annotation. On the other hand, 254 pages include some of their own scripts using async. In some pages, explicit dependency handling is used to make scripts capable of asynchronous loading, simulating a defer-style loading process.

4.2   Are our assumptions justified?

The second question is if our assumptions about non-determinism are justified. We answer it in two parts, first considering the use of non-deterministic functions, and then looking at race conditions.

Non-determinism: To perform non-determinism analysis, we used a browser that was instrumented for information flow control. This allowed us to identify scripts that actually use non-deterministic data in a way that may influence other scripts, by leaking non-deterministic data or influencing the control flow. We considered three classes of non-determinism sources:

1. `Math.random`. For most part, this function is used to generate unique identifiers, but we found a significant amount of scripts that actually use this function to simulate stochastic choice.
2. `Date.now` and relatives. These functions are included since their result depends on the environment. We found that usually, these functions are called to generate unique identifiers or time stamps, and to calculate time-outs.

---

[4] Many common scripts are available under numerous aliases, so we performed a best-effort hand count.

Nevertheless, we found examples for which it would not be feasible to automatically detect safety automatically. For instance, we found one page that had a busy-wait loop in the following style:

```
var end = Date.now() + timeout; while (Date.now() < end) {}
```

Automatically detecting that such code can be deferred seems quite difficult.

3. Functions and properties about the current browser state, including window size, window position and document name. While we treat these as a source of non-determinism, it would be better to classify them as environment dependent values; we find that in the samples we analyzed, they are not used in way that would engender non-determinism. Rather, they are used to calculate positions of windows and the like.

As it turns out, many standard libraries make at least some use of non-determinism. For instance, jQuery and Google's analytics and advertising libraries generate unique identifiers this way.

Additionally, many scripts and libraries have non-deterministic control flow. We found 1704 cases of scripts with non-deterministic control flow over all the pages we analyzed. That being said, this list contains a number of duplicates: In total, at least 546 of these scripts were used one more than one page[5]. They form 100 easily-identified groups, the largest of which are Google Analytics (187 instances), jQuery (40 instances) and YouTube (20 instances).

More importantly, we analyzed how many of the scripts we identified as deferrable have non-deterministic control flow. As it turns out, there was no overlap between the two sets: Our simple heuristic of scripts calling a source of non-determinism was sufficient to rule out all non-deterministic scripts.

Race conditions: We additionally analyzed whether non-determinism due to race conditions played a role. In this case, the findings were, in fact, simple: While there are numerous race conditions, they all occur between far events. We did not encounter any race conditions that involved a script or its near events.

One further aspect is that tracing pages does not exercise code in event handlers for user inputs. This may hide additional dependencies and race conditions. As reasoned above, we assume that no user interaction occurs before the page is loaded (in particular, after deferred scripts have run). The reasoning for this was given above; we plan to address this limitation in further work.

4.3   Can we derive deferrability annotations for scripts?

To evaluate the potential of inferring deferrability annotations, we used the analysis described above to classify the scripts on a given page into five broad classes:

– The script is loaded synchronously and can be deferred,

---

[5] We clustered by URL (dropping all but the last two components of the domain name and all query parameters), which misses some duplicates

Table 2. Number and percentage of deferrable scripts. The number of deferrable scripts includes pages with no scripts; for the percentage, we only consider pages with at least one deferrable script.

# deferrable scripts	# pages	% deferrable scripts	# pages
no scripts	11	$< 10\%$	180
0	156	$10 - 20\%$	56
1	86	$20 - 30\%$	37
2	55	$30 - 40\%$	14
3–5	89	$40 - 50\%$	6
6–10	47	$50 - 60\%$	1
more than 10	18	$60 - 70\%$	1

- The script is already loaded with defer or async (no annotation needs to be inferred here);
- The script is an inline script; in this case, deferring would require to make the script external, with questionable performance impact;
- The script is not deferrable since it performs DOM writes;
- The script is not deferrable because it is succeeded by a non-deferrable script in the dependency order.

The general picture is that the number of deferrable scripts highly depends on the page being analyzed. 295 of all pages contain deferrable scripts, and 209 of all pages permit deferring multiple scripts. Moreover, on 18 of the pages considered, at least 11 scripts can be deferred. Among these top pages, most have between 11 and 15 deferrable scripts (4 with 11, 2 with 12, 4 with 13, 5 with 15), while the top three pages have 16, 17 and 38 deferrable scripts on them; see the left column of Tab. 2. We also analyzed what percentage of scripts are deferrable on a given page; discarding the pages that had no deferrable scripts on them, we get the picture in the right column of Tab. 2.

Further analysis shows that some pages have been hand-optimized quite heavily, so that everything that could conceivably be deferred is already loaded with defer or async. Conversely, some pages have many scripts that can be deferred.

Many scripts are marked as non-deferrable because of dependencies. In many cases, these dependencies are hard ordering constraints: For instance, jQuery is almost never deferrable since later non-deferrable scripts will use the functionality it provides. That being said, we observe some spurious dependencies between scripts; this indicates room for improvement of the analysis. As an example, consider the jQuery library again. Among other things, it has a function for adding event handlers to events. Each of these event handlers is assigned a unique identifier by jQuery. For this, it uses a global variable guid that is incremented each time an event handler is added; clients treat the ID as an opaque handle. Nevertheless, if multiple scripts attach event handlers in this way, there is a an ordering constraint between them due to the reads and writes to guid, event though the scripts may commute with each other.

Looking at the pages with a high number of deferrable scripts, we find that there are two broad classes that cover many deferrable scripts: "Class definitions", which create or extend an existing JavaScript object with additional attributes (this would correspond to class definitions in languages such as Java), and "poor man's deferred scripts", which install an event handler for one of the events triggered at page load time (load, DOMContentLoaded and jQuery variants thereof) and only then execute their code.

4.4   Does deferring actually gain performance?

Since we found a significant number of scripts that can actually be deferred, we also measure how performance and behavior is affected by adding defer annotations. We used a proxy-based setup to present versions of each web page with and without the additional defer annotations from deferrability analysis to Web-PageTest [27]. We then measured the time-to-render (i.e., the time from starting the page load to the first drawing command of the page) for each version of each page, We choose time-to-render as the relevant metric because the content delivery industry uses it as the best indicator of the user's perception of page speed. This belief is supported by studies, e.g. [11].

Since our setup did not allow us to interpose on SSL connections, we had to drop pages that force an upgrade to SSL. In total, out of the 500 pages considered, 209 force an SSL upgrade. Taking the intersection of the sets of pages that have deferrable scripts and don't force an SSL upgrade, we were left with 169 pages.

We took between 38 and 50 measurements for each case, with a median of 40. The measurements were taken for each page that had at least one deferrable script and could successfully be rewritten.

The first observation to make is that the load time distribution tends to be highly non-normal and multi-modal. This can be seen in a few samples of load time distribution, as shown in Fig. 1. These violin plots visualize an approximation of the probability distribution of the loading time for each case.

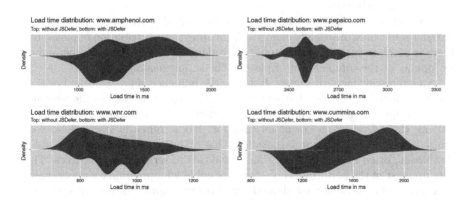

Fig. 1. Violin plots of load time distributions for some pages, before and after applying JSDefer. The graphs show a smoothed representation of the sample distribution.

For this reason, we quantify the changes in performance by considering the *median change in time-to-render* for each page, meaning we calculate the median of all the pairwise differences in time-to-render between the modified and the unmodified version of the page. This statistic is used as a proxy for the likely change in loading time by applying JSDefer. In the following, we abbreviate the median change in time-to-render as MCTTR. We additionally use the Mann-Whitney U test to ensure that we only consider those cases where MCTTR gives us statistically significant results.

Out of the 169 considered pages, 66 had a statistically significant MCTTR.

The actual median changes are shown in Fig. 2, together with confidence intervals. The data is also given in Table 3. This table also contains the median TTR of the original page. Several things are of note here:

1. As promised in the introduction, the median improvement in TTR is 198.5ms in the examples provided, while their median load time is 3097ms.
2. Most of the pages that pass the significance test have positive MCTTR, meaning that applying JSDefer provides benefits to time-to-render: For 59 pages, JSDefer had a positive effect, versus 7 pages where it had a negative effect. (85 versus 14 including SSL pages).
3. 49 of the pages in our sample have an estimated MCTTR of at least 100ms=0.1s. This difference corresponds to clearly perceptible differences in time-to-render. Even when taking the lower bound of the 95% confidence interval, 32 of the pages still have this property.
4. For 7 pages, we get a negative MCTTR, corresponding to worse loading time. This indicates that JSDefer should not be applied blindly.

We tried to analyze the root causes for the worsening of load times. For this, we used Chrome Developer Tools to generate a time-line of the page load, as well as a waterfall diagram of resource loading times. The results were mostly inconclusive; we could observe that the request for loading some scripts on two of these pages was delayed, and conjecture that we are hitting edge cases in the browser's I/O scheduler.

Another observation that can be made by analyzing the violin plots is that JSDefer sometimes drastically changes the loading time distribution of pages, but there is no clear pattern. The interested reader may want to see for themselves by looking at the complete set of plots in the supplementary material.

An interesting factor in the analysis was the influence of *pre-loading*: For each resource (including scripts) that is encountered on a page, as soon as the reference to the script is read (which may well be quite some time before "officially" parsing the reference), a download task for that resource is started[6], so that many download tasks occur in parallel. This manifests itself in many parallel downloads, often reducing latency for downloads of scripts and resources. This eats up most of the performance we could possibly win; preliminary experiments with pre-loading switched off showed much bigger improvements. Nevertheless, even in the presence of such pre-loading, we were able to gain performance.

---

[6] Glossing over the issue of connection limits

Table 3. MCTTR values for pages with significant MCTTR, sorted by ascending MCTTR. All times are given in milliseconds.

Page	MCTTR	MCTTR 95% confidence interval	Median TTR of original page
www.williams.com	-452.0	[-698.0,-201.0]	2300.0
www.visteon.com	-401.0	[-899.0,-99.0]	6996.0
www.mattel.com	-401.0	[-900.0,-1.0]	3995.0
www.statestreet.com	-299.0	[-400.0,-100.0]	2596.0
www.fnf.com	-201.6	[-500.0,-1.0]	3896.0
www.cbscorporation.com	-99.0	[-100.0,0.0]	1296.0
www.wnr.com	-98.0	[-100.0,0.0]	895.0
www.lansingtradegroup.com	98.6	[1.0,118.0]	2597.0
www.kiewit.com	99.0	[0.0,101.0]	1096.0
www.emcorgroup.com	99.0	[0.0,201.0]	1696.0
www.dovercorporation.com	99.0	[0.0,100.0]	1896.0
www.domtar.com	99.0	[1.0,100.0]	1896.0
www.eogresources.com	99.0	[0.0,100.0]	1896.0
www.johnsoncontrols.com	99.0	[0.0,101.0]	3296.0
www.altria.com	99.0	[0.0,101.0]	499.0
www.jmsmucker.com	99.0	[0.0,199.0]	996.0
www.itw.com	99.0	[1.0,100.0]	1295.0
www.walgreensbootsalliance.com	100.0	[1.0,101.0]	1096.0
www.bostonscientific.com	100.0	[1.0,101.0]	1297.0
www.apachecorp.com	100.0	[0.0,199.0]	1396.0
www.lifepointhealth.net	100.0	[99.0,100.0]	1396.0
www.marathonoil.com	100.0	[99.0,101.0]	1097.0
www.cstbrands.com	100.0	[99.0,199.0]	1897.0
www.mohawkind.com	101.0	[100.0,200.0]	1496.0
www.delekus.com	101.0	[98.0,200.0]	1795.0
www.stanleyblackanddecker.com	103.0	[100.0,199.0]	1196.0
www.fanniemae.com	112.3	[1.0,296.0]	2999.0
www.citigroup.com	114.0	[99.0,201.0]	1296.0
www.microsoft.com	130.0	[14.0,206.0]	1455.0
www.pultegroupinc.com	139.0	[93.0,219.0]	1120.0
www.mosaicco.com	196.0	[100.0,200.0]	1496.0
www.tysonfoods.com	198.0	[100.0,280.0]	1796.0
www.iheartmedia.com	198.0	[1.0,300.0]	1696.0
www.rrdonnelley.com	199.0	[104.0,201.0]	2097.0
www.raytheon.com	199.0	[0.0,401.0]	1697.0
www.navistar.com	199.6	[53.0,318.0]	2740.0
www.genesishcc.com	200.0	[1.0,399.0]	4497.0
www.chs.net	200.0	[100.0,298.0]	1796.0
www.newellbrands.com	200.0	[100.0,299.0]	1197.0
www.navient.com	200.0	[0.0,304.0]	2597.0
www.ncr.com	200.0	[96.0,300.0]	2096.0
www.sempra.com	200.0	[100.0,300.0]	1696.0
www.univar.com	200.0	[101.0,300.0]	1496.0
www.avoncompany.com	200.0	[100.0,300.0]	1596.0
www.pricelinegroup.com	200.0	[199.0,201.0]	1596.0
www.pacificlife.com	201.0	[100.0,399.0]	3296.0
www.weyerhaeuser.com	242.2	[200.0,300.0]	2497.0
www.techdata.com	298.0	[100.0,303.0]	2296.0
www.tenneco.com	299.0	[200.0,300.0]	1896.0
www.dana.com	299.0	[200.0,300.0]	1496.0
www.cablevision.com	299.0	[298.0,300.0]	2196.0
www.amphenol.com	300.0	[200.0,400.0]	1496.0
www.calpine.com	300.0	[201.0,302.0]	2098.0
www.nov.com	300.0	[103.0,498.0]	3396.0
www.harman.com	303.0	[300.0,400.0]	2195.0
www.burlingtonstores.com	395.0	[200.0,501.0]	4179.0
www.centene.com	398.0	[308.0,412.0]	2306.0
www.cummins.com	398.9	[299.0,496.0]	1695.0
www.markelcorp.com	500.0	[498.0,501.0]	1596.0
www.spectraenergy.com	501.0	[499.0,600.0]	2395.0
www.spiritaero.com	598.0	[499.0,601.0]	1797.0
www.wholefoodsmarket.com	611.7	[412.0,790.0]	2138.0
www.deanfoods.com	700.0	[401.0,3900.0]	3796.0
www.mutualofomaha.com	702.0	[700.0,800.0]	2396.0
www.lkqcorp.com	800.0	[700.0,900.0]	3301.0
www.ppg.com	891.4	[514.0,1299.0]	5096.0

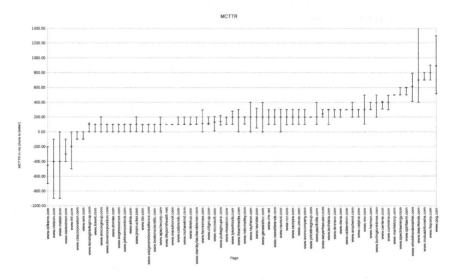

Fig. 2. MCTTR values for pages with significant MCTTR; Visualization of Table 3.

We also performed some timing analysis of page downloads to understand how performance is gained or lost, and found that the most important factor is, indeed, the time spent waiting for scripts to become available. The time saved by executing scripts later was only a minor factor.

Finally, to judge the impact of the improvements we achieved, we discussed the results with our industrial collaborator. Instead of considering the MCTTR, they analyzed the violin plots directly, and they indicated that they consider the improvement that JSDefer can achieve to be significant.

4.5   Threats to validity

There are some threats to validity due to the set-up of the experiments.

1. External validity, questions 2–5: Websites often provide different versions of their website for different browsers, or have browser-dependent behavior.

   In practice, one would address this by providing different versions of the website as well. An efficient way of doing this is part of further work.
2. Internal validity, question 5: We could not completely control for network delays in the testing set-up.
3. Internal validity, question 2: Due to the set-up of the analysis, we could not ensure that the pages did not change between analysis steps. Thus, in the non-determinism matching step, we may have missed cases. We did cross-check on a few samples, but could not do so exhaustively.

5   Related work

Accelerating web page loading: One key ingredient of website performance is front-end performance: How long does it take to load and display the page, and how responsive is it? One factor is script loading time [26]. Google's guidelines [12] recommend using `async` and `defer` to speed up page loading.

The question of asynchronous JavaScript loading and improving page loading times in general has lead to various patents, e.g., [19,18,9]; they describe specific techniques for "do-it-yourself" asynchronous script loading. Only one of them describes a technique for selecting scripts to load asynchronously, which boils down to loading *all* scripts this way.

Apart from asynchronous loading, another technique to improve script loading times is to make the scripts themselves smaller. Besides compression (including compiler techniques to optimize the code for size, e.g. [13]), one may "page out" functions from scripts by replacing function bodies with stubs that, if called, download the function implementation from the network [20]. Asynchronous loading complements these techniques, as well as the many other techniques to improve load time.

Parallelisation and commutativity: The deferring transform can be seen as a close relative of transformations employed by parallelizing compilers. In particular, we can phrase the question of deferrability in terms of *commutativity*[24,2]: In Rinard et al.'s work, two functions A and B commute if executing A and then B gives the same results that executing B and then A gives. In our setting, a script is deferrable if it does not access the DOM and commutes with all (later) non-deferrable scripts.

The Bernstein Criteria [3] describe that two program blocks A and B are parallelizable if A neither reads nor writes memory cells that B writes, and vice versa. This is used to define the dependency graph that identifies parallelizable parts of a program; our dependency order is constructed in a similar way.

Semantics analysis of JavaScript and web pages: The semantics of JavaScript and HTML are complex and unusual; natural-language descriptions can be found in [7] (JavaScript) and [28] (HTML). There are various formalizations of JavaScript [14,21,5], and formalizations of fragments of browser behavior, considering the event mode [6], information flow control [4] and race detection [22,23].

Additional analysis tools exist for JavaScript, including Jalangi2 [25], which performs a dynamic analysis using source-to-source-translation, and various static analysis like TAJS [15], JSAI [16] and the type inference engine flow [8].

References

1. Adamsen, C.Q., Møller, A., Karim, R., Sridharan, M., Tip, F., Sen, K.: Repairing event race errors by controlling nondeterminism. In: ICSE 2017 (2017)
2. Aleen, F., Clark, N.: Commutativity analysis for software parallelization: letting program transformations see the big picture. In: ASPLOS '09 (2009)
3. Bernstein, A.J.: Analysis of programs for parallel processing. IEEE Trans. Elec. Comp. (5), 757–763 (1966)

4. Bichhawat, A., Rajani, V., Garg, D., Hammer, C.: Information flow control in webkit's javascript bytecode. In: POST 2014 (2014)
5. Bodin, M., Charguéraud, A., Filaretti, D., Gardner, P., Maffeis, S., Naudziuniene, D., Schmitt, A., Smith, G.: A trusted mechanised javasript specification. In: POPL '14 (2014)
6. Bohannon, A., Pierce, B.C.: Featherweight firefox: Formalizing the core of a web browser. In: WebApps'10 (2010)
7. ECMA International: ECMAScript 2015 Language Specification (2015)
8. Facebook, Inc.: flow: a static type checker for JavaScript, https://flowtype.org
9. FAINBERG, L., Ehrlich, O., Shai, G., Gadish, O., DOBO, A., Berger, O.: Systems and methods for acceleration and optimization of web pages access by changing the order of resource loading (Feb 3 2011), https://www.google.com/patents/US20110029899, US Patent App. 12/848,559
10. Fortune 500 (2016), http://beta.fortune.com/fortune500/
11. Gao, Q., Dey, P., Ahammad, P.: Perceived performance of webpages in the wild: Insights from large-scale crowdsourcing of above-the-fold QoE (2017), arXiv:1704.01220
12. Google, Inc.: Remove Render-Blocking JavaScript (Apr 2015), https://developers.google.com/speed/docs/insights/BlockingJS
13. Google, Inc.: Closure tools (2016), https://developers.google.com/closure/
14. Guha, A., Saftoiu, C., Krishnamurthi, S.: The Essence of JavaScript. In: ECOOP 2010. See also http://arxiv.org/abs/1510.00925
15. Jensen, S.H., Møller, A., Thiemann, P.: Type analysis for javascript. In: SAS 09
16. Kashyap, V., Dewey, K., Kuefner, E.A., Wagner, J., Gibbons, K., Sarracino, J., Wiedermann, B., Hardekopf, B.: JSAI: a static analysis platform for javascript. In: FSE-22 (2014)
17. Kloos, J., Majumdar, R., McCabe, F.: Deferrability analysis for JavaScript. Tech. rep., MPI-SWS (2017), see http://www.mpi-sws.org/~jkloos/jsdefer-tr.pdf
18. Kuhn, B., Marifet, K., Wogulis, J.: Asynchronous loading of scripts in web pages (Apr 29 2014), https://www.google.com/patents/US8713424
19. Lipton, E., Roy, B., Calvert, S., Gibbs, M., Kothari, N., Harder, M., Reed, D.: Dynamically loading scripts (Mar 30 2010), https://www.google.com/patents/US7689665, US Patent 7,689,665
20. Livshits, V.B., Kiciman, E.: Doloto: code splitting for network-bound web 2.0 applications. In: FSE '08 (2008)
21. Maffeis, S., Mitchell, J.C., Taly, A.: An operational semantics for javascript. In: APLAS 2008 (2008)
22. Petrov, B., Vechev, M.T., Sridharan, M., Dolby, J.: Race detection for web applications. In: PLDI 2012 (2012)
23. Raychev, V., Vechev, M.T., Sridharan, M.: Effective race detection for event-driven programs. In: OOPSLA 2013 (2013)
24. Rinard, M.C., Diniz, P.C.: Commutativity analysis: A new analysis framework for parallelizing compilers. In: PLDI '96 (1996)
25. Sen, K., Kalasapur, S., Brutch, T.G., Gibbs, S.: Jalangi: a selective record-replay and dynamic analysis framework for javascript. In: ESEC/FSE'13 (2013)
26. Souders, S.: High-performance web sites. Commun. ACM 51(12), 36–41 (Dec 2008)
27. Viscomi, R., Davies, A., Duran, M.: Using WebPageTest: Web Performance Testing for Novices and Power Users. O'Reilly Media, Inc., 1st edn. (2015)
28. WHATWG: HTML – Living Standard (Sep 2016), https://html.spec.whatwg.org/multipage/

A Verifier of Directed Acyclic Graphs for Model Checking with Memory Consistency Models

Tatsuya Abe

STAIR Lab, Chiba Institute of Technology
abe@stair.center

Abstract. This paper introduces VeriDAG, a verification tool for directed acyclic graphs that represent concurrent programs under memory consistency models. VeriDAG has two novel aspects. First, VeriDAG does not handle concurrent programs directly, but operates on directed acyclic graphs whose edges denote dependencies between instructions in the concurrent programs. This provides software model checking under various memory consistency models by replacing the definitions of edge connections, whereas many model checkers are specific to certain memory consistency models. Second, an engine for exploring execution traces is fully implemented in Haskell with manageable exploration strategies. In contrast, similar model checkers use external engines such as SMT solvers and model checkers that ignore relaxed memory consistency models. Thus, VeriDAG provides a research framework on which we can design new memory consistency models and apply exploration strategies for execution traces under memory consistency models. As evidence, this paper compares VeriDAG with an existing model checker, and implements reordering controls, which are heuristic searches for counterexample detection in directed model checking.

Keywords: Memory consistency model, software model checking, instruction dependency, directed acyclic graph, Haskell implementation, reordering control, heuristic search, counterexample detection

1 Introduction

Relaxed memory consistency models (MCMs) allow instructions and their effects on computer architectures to be *reordered*. Because such reordering often promotes parallel processing on modern multi/many-core architectures, and improves computing performance, relaxed MCMs have been adopted by modern computer architectures and programming languages. However, reordering is a burden for programmers because it relaxes the behavior of programs and complicates programming on relaxed MCMs. Therefore, programming on relaxed MCMs requires supporting procedures such as program verification.

Software model checking is a promising program verification method. Although most conventional model checkers ignore relaxed MCMs, some model checkers with MCMs have recently been developed [32, 2, 5], and conventional model checkers also started to support MCMs [35, 1, 31].

O. Strichman and R. Tzoref-Brill (Eds.): HVC 2017, LNCS 10629, pp. 51–66, 2017.
https://doi.org/10.1007/978-3-319-70389-3_4

To the best of our knowledge, most of these model checkers use external tools such as SMT solvers and conventional model checkers that ignore MCMs, and rely on their engines for exploring execution traces of programs. One reason for this is that it is very hard to develop model checkers from scratch. Another reason is that existing tools such as SMT solvers perform well, and exploiting them by using reduction techniques is reasonable.

Nevertheless, this paper introduces VeriDAG, a new model checker with MCMs that is fully implemented in Haskell along with an exploration engine. VeriDAG is developed towards a research framework on which we can propose new MCMs and apply exploration strategies for execution traces under these MCMs. VeriDAG is available at https://bitbucket.org/abet/veridag/.

VeriDAG is a testbed on which we can design new MCMs that do not currently exist. We cannot use most existing model checkers with arbitrary MCMs because they are specific to certain MCMs. VeriDAG translates C programs or LLVM IRs into directed acyclic graphs called *program graphs* [4]. Nodes in a program graph denote instructions or the effects of instructions, and edges in a program graph denote dependencies between nodes. VeriDAG takes the dependencies of a program graph as its inputs. Thus, VeriDAG provides a framework that allows MCM designers to construct new MCMs.

VeriDAG performs well, and is comparable with a existing model checker with MCMs. The Glasgow Haskell compiler (GHC) has been energetically developed, and generates executable codes that are comparable with conventional compilers for imperative programming languages. Also, model checkers with MCMs that use external tools contain overheads to reduce behavior under MCMs to behavior under sequential consistency. The challenge in the development of VeriDAG is to achieve the performance of existing model checkers.

Exploration strategies for execution traces in VeriDAG are manageable. It does not use external tools such as SMT solvers, and its exploration strategies are free from any external limitation. In this paper, we implement reordering controls [6], which are heuristic searches for counterexample detection in directed model checking, by using the flexibility of its exploration strategies.

The remainder of this paper is organized as follows. In Sect. 2, we explain MCMs and program graphs that contain the behavior of programs under MCMs. In Sect. 3, we present the design of VeriDAG, a model checker for program graphs. In Sect. 4, we explain the implementation of the approaches in VeriDAG. In Sect. 5, we present a comparison with an existing model checker with MCMs. In Sect. 6, we implement reordering control to show the flexibility of the exploration strategies in VeriDAG. In Sect. 7, we discuss related work, and in Sect. 8, we conclude the paper by identifying future researches.

2   Program Graphs: Programs with MCMs

In this section, we explain *program graphs* introduced in [4], which are representations of concurrent programs with MCMs, to motivate a development of a model checker based on the new notion of program graphs.

Relaxed MCMs allow instructions and their effects to be reordered. For example, consider the program $(r_0 = y; r_1 = x) \parallel (x = 1; y = 1)$ where ; and $\parallel$ are sequential and parallel compositions, respectively. The variables r_0 and r_1 are thread-local variables, and the variables x and y are shared. The assignments $r_0 = y$ and $r_1 = x$ load the values of y and x from a shared memory, and the assignments $x = 1$ and $y = 1$ store an immediate value 1 to the shared memory. All variables are initialized to 0. Under sequential consistency (SC) [19], which prohibits all reorderings, we can immediately determine that the property $r_0 = 1 \supset r_1 = 1$ holds, by examining all cases of the interleaving of instructions.

The same assertion holds under total store ordering (TSO) [8], which only allows load instructions to overtake store instructions, because the program order of $x = 1$ and $y = 1$ is preserved in its execution. On the other hand, under partial store ordering (PSO) [8], which allows store instructions to overtake other store instructions, the assertion does not hold because $y = 1$ is invoked in the first thread before $x = 1$ is invoked in the second thread. Moreover, under relaxed memory ordering (RMO) [8], which allows reordering of load and store instructions, the assertion does not hold regardless of execution order of $x = 1$ and $y = 1$ in the second thread, because the first thread may not necessarily invoke $r_0 = y$ and $r_1 = x$ in the program order. Thus, properties of programs are sensitive to the MCMs under which the programs run. However, it is tedious to construct a verification theory for each MCM.

We have previously proposed a notion of program graphs in [4], which are data structures containing programs and MCMs. By handling program graphs rather than directly handling programs, we do not have to construct a verification theory for each MCM.

Our intermediate language consists of declarations of shared variables $x, \ldots$ and basic blocks. A basic block is a sequence of instructions with a label L, and its last instruction is a jump or return instruction. Distinct basic blocks have distinct labels. Instructions are defined as follows.

$$i ::= \text{Alloca}\, r \mid r = \text{Move}\, t \mid r = \text{Load}^A\, x \mid x = \text{Store}^A\, t \mid \text{Fence}^A$$
$$\mid \text{XCHG}\, x\, r \mid r = \text{CAS}\, x\, t\, t \mid r = \text{Call}\, f\, t \mid r = \text{Fork}\, f\, t \mid \text{Join}\, r$$
$$\mid \text{Branch}\, \varphi?L : L \mid \text{NDChoice}\, L : L \mid \text{Return}\, t \mid \text{Assert}\, \Phi$$
$$t ::= v \mid r \mid t = t \mid t < t \mid t + t \mid t - t \mid \cdots \; .$$

Term t denotes an expression. Here, r denotes a thread-local variable, v denotes an immediate value such as a rational number, f denotes a function symbol, and $t_0 = t_1, t_0 < t_1, t_0 + t_1, t_0 - t_1, \ldots$ denote arithmetic expressions in a standard manner. We note that t contains *no* shared variable. In this section, we do not refer to arrays and pointers in the definition of terms, *for simplicity*, although our model checker VeriDAG, which is introduced in Sect. 3, supports them, and the programs used in the experiments that are conducted in Sect. 5 actually contain arrays and pointers. As explained in Sect. 3, VeriDAG uses LLVM IRs. Representations of arrays and pointers in VeriDAG are similar to those in LLVM.

The memory operations **Load**, **Store**, and **Fence** have a set of attributes A that are used to control reordering of instructions. We next explain attributes so that we can refer to them when we explain reordering of instructions. A formula φ is a first-order formula consisting only of thread-local variables. A formula Φ can contain both thread-local and shared variables.

The instructions have the following meanings. The instruction $\mathtt{Alloca}\, r$ denotes the allocation of r. The instruction $r = \mathtt{Move}\, t$ denotes the assignment of an evaluation of a term t to r, which does not affect the other threads. The instruction $r = \mathtt{Load}^A\, x$ denotes loading x from its own memory and assigning the value to r. The instruction $x = \mathtt{Store}^A\, t$ denotes storing an evaluation of t to x in its own memory. The instruction $\mathtt{Fence}^A$ denotes a memory fence, which guarantees the preceding memory operations. In fact, $\mathtt{Fence}$ instructions themselves do not access shared variables and are used as separators for the effects of $\mathtt{Load}/\mathtt{Store}$ instructions. The attributes A have no effect, and are only used to control the reordering of instructions. The instruction $\mathtt{XCHG}\, x\, r$ is an atomic instruction that denotes exchanging the values of x and r. The instruction $r_0 = \mathtt{CAS}\, x\, t_0\, t_1$ is also an atomic instruction that denotes *compare-and-swap*. That is, if the value of x is equal to the evaluation of t_0, then the evaluation of t_1 and 1 (denoting success) are stored as x and r_0, respectively. Otherwise, x is unchanged and 0 (denoting failure) is stored as r_0. The instruction $r = \mathtt{Call}\, f\, t$ denotes a call of the function f with the argument t, and the returned value is stored as r. The instruction $r = \mathtt{Fork}\, f\, t$ denotes a fork of a thread f with the argument t, with a thread identifier stored as r. The instruction $\mathtt{Join}\, r$ denotes a join between a thread and its identifier in r. The instruction $\mathtt{Branch}\, \varphi?L_0 : L_1$ is a conditional jump where the program counter indicates L_0 if φ holds and L_1 otherwise. Note that φ contains no shared values; to jump to L_0 or L_1 depending on a shared variable x, it is necessary to perform $r = \mathtt{Load}^A\, x$ first. The instruction $\mathtt{NDChoice}\, L_0 : L_1$ denotes a non-deterministic jump to L_0 or L_1. The instruction $\mathtt{Return}\, t$ returns a value of t. The instruction $\mathtt{Assert}\, \Phi$ is an assertion with no effect, and is used for program verification.

The formal definition of reordering of instructions in our intermediate language is given indirectly through the *effects* of instructions. By distinguishing instructions from their effects, we observe that reordering instructions can be represented naturally. Our definition is operational against the axiomatic definitions seen in [34, 33].

We define two kinds of *operations* on instructions $\mathtt{Iss}^j\, i$ and $\mathtt{Eff}^j_K\, i$. For an instruction i, the issue operation $\mathtt{Iss}^j\, i$ is defined and denotes an intra-thread effect of the instruction. The superscript j denotes the j-th operation of instruction i. An instruction may be executed multiple times because our language contains jump instructions $\mathtt{Branch}$ and $\mathtt{NDChoice}$. To take reordering into account under MCMs, operations have to be distinguished from each other. An execution trace is defined as a sequence of operations.

For the $\mathtt{Store}$ instructions that operate on shared variables, additional operations are defined. The effect operation $\mathtt{Eff}^j_K\, i$ denotes an inter-thread effect of i. To identify multiple effects for an instruction, an effect has a set of identifiers K. For a store instruction i, the effect $\mathtt{Eff}^j_K\, i$ denotes storing to the shared memory that can be observed by threads K but not another. For example, consider an execution trace $\text{Iss}^0 i_0; \text{Iss}^0 i_{1,1}; \text{Eff}^0_{\{0,1,2\}} i_0; \text{Iss}^0 i_{1,2}$ where i_0 is $x = \text{Store}^\varnothing 1$, and $i_{1,k}$ is $r = \text{Load}^\varnothing x$ on thread k. While r is equal to 0 on thread 1 since $\text{Iss}^0 i_{1,1}$ is performed before $\text{Eff}^0_{\{0,1,2\}} i_0$, r is equal to 1 on thread 2 since $\text{Iss}^0 i_{1,2}$ is performed after $\text{Eff}^0_{\{0,1,2\}} i_0$. A small-step operational semantics was formally defined in [4], although notation is slight changed.

We next formally define the reordering of instructions. In an execution trace of a program, issue operations follow the program order. However, this is not the case for effect operations. For example, assume that a program consisting of two threads contains $i_0; i_1$ on one thread. Each instruction has one effect. The execution trace $\text{Iss}^0 i_0; \text{Iss}^0 i_1; \text{Eff}^0_{\{0,1\}} i_1; \text{Eff}^0_{\{0,1\}} i_0$ is admissible under an MCM, which allows the effects of issued instructions to be reordered. The effects of the last execution trace are reordered, whereas the order between issues is preserved. Thus, distinguishing the effects from the issuing of instructions enables a representation of the reordering of instructions.

Some instructions have attributes that are user-defined. Attributes have no effects themselves, and are used as landmarks when operations are reordered. For example, the attributes **acquire** and **release** are used for reordering under so-called *acquire-release* consistency. The effects of the instruction **Store** with the attribute **release** cannot overtake those of preceding instructions, and cannot be overtaken by those of other **Store** instructions even under an MCM that allows such reorderings. The instruction **Load** with the attribute **acquire** is similar. The instruction **Fence** with an attribute such as L->L or L->S forces the orders Load/Load and Load/Store, that is, it works as a separator of Load/Load and Load/Store, respectively.

Nodes in program graphs correspond to instructions or their effects, that is, operations in this paper. To be precise, nodes have identifiers so that we distinguish distinct nodes with the same operation. Such identifiers are carefully designed to not disturb *partial order reduction* (e.g., see [17]), which is explained in Sect. 4. However, in this paper, we omit an explanation of identifiers of nodes, for simplicity. The effects of instructions are separated from the instruction themselves. This can represent a delay of the effects of a store instruction because of the existence of an execution trace that the store instruction invokes on a thread, whereas its effects may not be reflected in the other threads.

The edges of a program graph denote dependencies between operations. A key point about program graphs is that the connectivity of edges depends on MCMs. For example, the nodes denoting the effects of $x = 1$ and $y = 1$ are connected under SC and TSO, while they are not connected under PSO and RMO. For example, the following left and right program graphs correspond wit the program introduced at the beginning in this section under TSO and PSO, respectively,

$$
\begin{array}{ccc}
\text{Iss}^0 i_0 & \text{Iss}^0 i_2 \to \text{Eff}^0_{\{0,1\}} i_2 \\
\downarrow & \downarrow \qquad\qquad \downarrow \\
\text{Iss}^0 i_1 & \text{Iss}^0 i_3 \to \text{Eff}^0_{\{0,1\}} i_3
\end{array}
\qquad
\begin{array}{ccc}
\text{Iss}^0 i_0 & \text{Iss}^0 i_2 \to \text{Eff}^0_{\{0,1\}} i_2 \\
\downarrow & \downarrow \\
\text{Iss}^0 i_1 & \text{Iss}^0 i_3 \to \text{Eff}^0_{\{0,1\}} i_3
\end{array}
$$

where $i_0 \equiv r_0 = \text{Load}\, y$, $i_1 \equiv r_1 = \text{Load}\, x$, $i_2 \equiv x = \text{Store}^\varnothing 1$, and $i_3 \equiv y = \text{Store}^\varnothing 1$.

The roots of program graphs are nodes that have in-degree zero. Roots denote executable operations. Reordering is represented by multiple roots, which can be reordered because they have no dependencies.

Various dependencies can be represented by edges of program graphs. For example, the acquire-release consistency, which is used by C++11, can be represented as discussed in [4]. The author would like to note that the definition of the acquire-release consistency in [4] has slight typographical errors, which can be easily fixed.

Although program graphs have been formally defined in [4], this definition is extended and modified in this paper. First, function calls and thread creations have not been formally defined in [4]. Next, all branch and loop statements are unfolded in [4] for convenience in constructing concurrent program logic that agrees with program semantics with MCMs. In developing a model checker in this paper, branch and loop statements are unfolded the first time that conditional statements are evaluated. Finally, store instructions are extended to have multiple effects that are identified by multiple threads. This represents the so-called *non-multi-copy atomicity* [28] which the IBM POWER adopts, that is, one thread may observe a memory update while another thread may not observe the memory update. This extension enables to distinguish the IBM POWER MCM from SPARC RMO which assumes multi-copy-atomicity.

3   Design

Our model checker VeriDAG consists of the following three parts: **(Parse)** translates models written by users into LLVM IRs, **(Generate)** generates program graphs from the LLVM IRs in accordance with an input MCM, and **(Explore)** performs model checking of program graphs.

One modeling language used in VeriDAG is C. Users model algorithms, protocols, and so on in C using POSIX threads. The other modeling language is LLVM IR. The front-end of VeriDAG translates C programs into LLVM IRs.

VeriDAG generates program graphs from a basic block consisting of LLVM IRs. The nodes of program graphs are generated from the IRs themselves. LLVM is designed for a framework of compiler constructions, and LLVM contains redundant IRs for model checking with MCMs. To reduce the total number of nodes, VeriDAG is designed to take optimizations that compound LLVM IRs to generate nodes of program graphs.

VeriDAG connects nodes in accordance with MCMs. The edges which denote dependencies based on MCMs as explained in Sect. 2, are defined as a Haskell function. For example, TSO, which allows load instructions to overtake store instructions, is defined as follows:

```
tso x@(Eff _ (Store _ _ _)) y@(Eff _ (Load _ _ _)) = data_depend x y
tso x@(Eff _ (Store _ _ _)) y@(Eff _ ((Store _ _ _)) = prohibited
tso ...
```

The first line says that the succeeding `Load` may overtake `Store` in accordance with an intrinsic function `data_depend` in VeriDAG, which denotes whether there is data dependency between the two instructions of the arguments. Even under TSO, load instructions cannot always overtake store instructions. For example, if the load and store instructions read from and write to the same location, then the load instruction should be prohibited from overtaking the store instruction. In this sense, the `data_depend` function is used to define TSO. On the other hand, reordering of store instructions is always prohibited as seen in the second line.

The following is a part of a function corresponding to PSO.

```
pso x@(Eff _ (Store _ _ _)) y@(Eff _ (Load _ _ _)) = data_depend x y
pso x@(Eff _ (Store _ _ _)) y@(Eff _ (Store _ _ _)) = data_depend x y
pso ...
```

It differs from the `tso` function by allowing reordering of store instructions.

The main function of VeriDAG is processing program graphs and conducting *stateful* model checking. *Stateless* model checking for TSO, PSO, and the POWER memory model was proposed in [1, 3]. Although stateless model checking often has better performance than stateful model checking, implementations of intelligent explorations of execution traces in stateless model checking tend to be complicated, which motivated the development of VeriDAG as a stateful model checker.

A local state is defined as a triple of stack, heap, and buffer, or a thread-local state, a global state such as a shared memory, and a thread-local store buffer. Each thread has one local state. The reader may wonder why each thread has one global state that is usually shared by all threads. This is a key point for model checking with MCMs. The multiple global states formulation allows global states observed by multiple threads to not immediately coincide.

VeriDAG chooses *arbitrarily* one root of a program graphs, and executes the operation attached to the root. The roots which were not chosen (and the program graph) are remembered to be used when the exploration backtracks. The execution of an operation updates a global state. This update is performed in a standard manner. For example, the execution of a store instruction updates a store buffer. The effect of a store instruction on a thread removes the *oldest* buffered value from the buffer, and updates the heap on the thread. The execution of a load instruction first tries to see the *latest* value in the buffer. If such a value exists, the local stack is updated by the value. Otherwise, the local stack is updated by the value on the heap.

The chosen root is removed from the program graph. All the nodes to which there is an edge directed from the root are checked for whether there are any other edges directed to them. Such a node that has no other edge directed to it *may* be a root of the updated program graph. Because a program graph is a directed acyclic graph, the updated program graph has roots unless it is empty. If the updated program graph has no root, the exploration backtracks.

When the nodes attached to the POSIX thread join function `pthread_join` are removed, the variables for joins are examined to check whether the threads can be joined.

Criteria for which nodes are new roots of an updated program graph can be *changed* by giving a Haskell function as a *hook* of the function of VeriDAG that chooses a root. For example, a hook which denotes a criterion that *load instruction nodes are preferably chosen* is defined as follows:

```
hook = f [] []
  where f ld ow (nd@(Node _ (Eff _ (Load _ _ _))):nds) = f (nd:ld) ow nds
        f ld ow (nd:nds) = f ld (nd:ow) nds
        f ld ow [] = (reverse ld)++(reverse ow)
```

The function `hook` takes a list of nodes as an argument. Load instructions are stacked on `ld`, and the others are stacked on `ow`. Finally, `hook` returns a sorted list which load instructions are preferably at the front. Thus exploration strategies of VeriDAG are manageable.

When function calls including the POSIX thread creation `pthread_create` and branch instructions corresponding to `call` and `br` in LLVM IRs are removed, program graphs are enlarged.

Thus, for one program and one MCM, **(Parse)** is done once, and **(Generate)** and **(Explore)** are repeated until the program graph is empty. The **(Generate)**-**(Explore)** loop corresponds with a recursive function `dfs` introduced in Sect. 4.

Model checking of VeriDAG is unbounded. VeriDAG can be bounded by restricting the number of nodes related to the effects of store instructions. This corresponds to restricting the sizes of buffers.

A property to be verified is given an assertion as a formula in a program to be verified. For example, an assertion that the values of the variable r_0 is equal to 1 is as follows.

```
#pragma VeriDAG assert(variable(r0)==1)
```

An assertion that the values of the variable x on the shared memory which thread 0 observes is equal to 1 is as follows.

```
#pragma VeriDAG assert(memory(x,0)==1)
```

Proposition variables consist of variables on states and constants. A state may refer to a state at an `assert` pragma or a state at a `checkpoint` pragma, and can be inserted anywhere in a model. For example, a checkpoint pragma which stores a value 1 in some state as `chk_r0` for use in a later assertion can be written as follows.

```
#pragma VeriDAG checkpoint(chk_r0)
r0=1;
```

4   Implementation

Models written in the C programming language are translated into LLVM IRs via Clang. Because LLVM IRs are slightly redundant in model checking with MCMs as explained in Sect. 3, the **(Parse)** part of VeriDAG generates its own intermediate representations for optimization from LLVM IRs to reduce the number of operations that are attached to nodes in program graphs, although the current version of VeriDAG does not support the whole LLVM IRs. VeriDAG can handle LLVM IRs at any optimization stage of Clang, although it cannot handle assemblies specific to computer architectures. This is straight-forward and needs no further explanation,

VeriDAG moves to a **(Generate)** part after the **(Parse)** part and whenever nodes which consist of r=Call$f\,t$, r=Fork$f\,t$, Branchφ?L:L, and NDChoice$L$:L are processed. VeriDAG updates a program graph by considering the dependency between instructions which the MCM specifies, and the basic block (written in our intermediate languages) which has the function f or label L designated by the instruction.

At an **(Explore)** part, VeriDAG uses a *depth-first search* to explore execution traces. A function dfs of VeriDAG collects roots of program graphs (by using a function getRoots), which should be chosen, and executed and removed as follows:

```
dfs ((pg,gst):rests) ... =
  dfs (concatMap ⟨updatePg pg,updateGst gst⟩ (getRoots pg):rests) ...
```

where pg and gst denote a program graph and a global state, respectively. The function concatMap is defined in neither Prelude nor Data.List, and defined by using Data.IntMap [21] for improving performance. The function $\langle f, g \rangle$ denotes the function which returns the pair $(f\mathbf{x}, g\mathbf{x})$ for any x. Functions updatePg and updateGst update the program graph and global states, respectively.

VeriDAG is carefully implemented by standard techniques to address the state explosion in model checking. VeriDAG uses the so-called *memoization* technique to remember program graphs and states that are visited. To be concrete, the dfs function is extended to be with memoization as follows:

```
dfs ((pg,gst):rests) memos ... =
  dfs (filterMemos memos (concatMap ...):rests) ...
```

where the function filterMemos is also defined by using Data.IntMap. The careful implementation avoids repeating expensive exploration histories. This promotes the so-called partial order reduction, in which states and program graphs are memoized regardless of histories of execution traces.

We finally remark about the so-called *fairness* of the scheduler in model checking with MCMs. Consider a program (while(x==0){y=1}) ‖ x=1 . In conventional model checking, which ignores relaxed MCMs, memoization avoids an infinite execution trace consisting of instructions from the first thread because the state is not changed. However, in model checking with relaxed MCMs, the buffer on the first thread is changed each time y=1 is invoked. In this sense, it is difficult to support fairness in model checking with MCMs. In this paper, we have implemented parameterization of buffer sizes by limiting the numbers of effect nodes for store instructions in the generation of program graphs. Under the buffer size limitation, the program finishes in a finite step. In Sect. 6, we conduct experiments for programs that contain loop statements with the buffer size limitation.

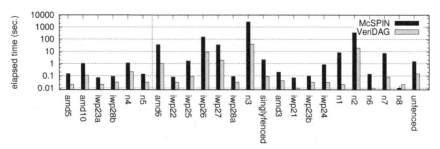

Fig. 1. McSPIN vs. VeriDAG with RMO

5   Performance Evaluation

In this section, we compare VeriDAG with McSPIN, a model checker with MCMs [5]. Although some model checkers with MCMs are being developed, most of them cannot take *user-defined* memory models as inputs, and do not provide functions that allow MCM designers to draw new memory models. Although the tool herd [9] can take a user-defined MCM as an input, it is difficult to compare the herd with VeriDAG fairly since the herd cannot take models written in the C programming language. The herd also adopts its own format of input MCMs. Nidhugg [1] partially supports relaxed MCMs such as the POWER MCM (similar to RMO). However, Nidhugg does not completely support atomic primitives such as compare-and-swap under the POWER MCM as seen in [23].

McSPIN can take user-defined memory models as inputs, and performs model checking with the memory models. McSPIN uses the SPIN model checker [17] as an engine for exploring execution traces. Because SPIN provides model checking with sequential consistency of code written in the modeling language PROMELA only, McSPIN takes a memory model and a program written in C as inputs, and generates a PROMELA code that contains all the relaxed behaviors under the memory model.

For the experimental environment, the CPU was an Intel Xeon E5-2620 2.10GHz, and the memory was a DDR4-2400 128GB. McSPIN used SPIN version 6.4.6, and GCC version 6.3.0. VeriDAG was compiled by GHC 8.0.2, and used Clang 5.0.0.

In the experiment, we use the x86 litmus test originally developed to distinguish x86-TSO from x86-CC [24]. This has 24 programs, and each program has one assertion. Under RMO, 6 assertions hold, and 18 assertions are violated. Under PSO, 14 assertions hold, and 10 assertions are violated. In this experiment, model checking is terminated by an exhaustive search of execution traces or detection of a counterexample.

Figure 1 shows a comparison between McSPIN and VeriDAG under RMO. The y-axis denotes elapsed time for model checking. The assertions in the 6 programs (amd5, amd10, iwp23b, iwp28a, n4, n5) to the left of the vertical line hold. The assertions in the remaining 18 programs are violated. VeriDAG was better

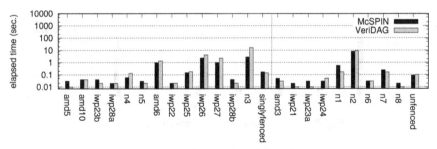

Fig. 2. McSPIN vs. VeriDAG with PSO

than McSPIN in all cases except **n8**. The exceptional case is an assertion that is violated under RMO, and SPIN found a counterexample in its exploration.

VeriDAG occupied at most 325 MB of memory while McSPIN occupied at most 66 GB of memory. Because McSPIN generates PROMELA code containing descriptions to control behaviors with MCMs, McSPIN uses a large amount of memory for its exploration engine SPIN.

Figure 2 shows a comparison between McSPIN and VeriDAG under PSO. VeriDAG was competitive with McSPIN. We think that *stage* optimization [7] improves model checking under PSO on McSPIN. Although stage optimization affects model checking under arbitrary memory models, it significantly improves performance under stricter memory models such as TSO and PSO because reordering of load instructions is prohibited. Further details of stage optimization are beyond the scope of this paper. Similarly, model checkers specific to TSO and PSO often have better performance because simple implementation of store buffers that work with sequential consistency is sufficient to simulate behaviors under TSO and PSO. Such optimization has not been applied to the current version of VeriDAG.

Nevertheless, we claim that the development of VeriDAG is significant for the following two reasons. First, VeriDAG has not yet been sufficiently optimized. We can apply some optimizations specific to stricter memory models such as TSO and PSO to VeriDAG, potentially improving VeriDAG so that it is competitive with McSPIN under stricter memory models as in the experimental results with RMO. Second, weak memory models such as RMO are becoming more important than strict memory models such as TSO and PSO because modern multi/many-core architectures use relaxed MCMs to spread parallel processing.

6   Reordering Control

In this section, we introduce an implementation of *reordering control* [6] in VeriDAG to show the flexibility of exploration strategies using VeriDAG.

Reordering control is one of the practical uses of directed model checking [15], and is a promising method for detecting counterexamples more quickly. In directed model checking, the exploration of execution traces are guided by the *cost*

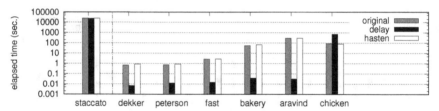

Fig. 3. Effectiveness of the reordering controls

of reaching the next state. The directed model checker HSF-SPIN [14] offers a wide variety of exploration strategies. However, in conventional model checking which ignores MCMs, there are not many practical uses of directed model checking as described in the manual for HSF-SPIN [13].

Reordering control focuses on instructions that are reordered or not under MCMs. Reordering control prevents some instructions from being reordered, and may lead to counterexamples more quickly. Consider the program $(x = 1; r_0 = y) \parallel (y = 1; r_1 = x)$. The assertion $r_0 = 1 \vee r_1 = 1$ for this program is violated by the execution trace $\mathtt{Iss}^0 \, i_0; \mathtt{Iss}^0 \, i_1; \mathtt{Iss}^0 \, i_2; \mathtt{Iss}^0 \, i_3; \mathtt{Eff}^0_{\{0,1\}} \, i_0; \mathtt{Eff}^0_{\{0,1\}} \, i_2$ where $i_0 \equiv x = \mathtt{Store}^\varnothing \, 1, i_1 \equiv r_0 = \mathtt{Load}^\varnothing \, y, i_2 \equiv y = \mathtt{Store}^\varnothing \, 1$, and $i_3 \equiv r_1 = \mathtt{Load}^\varnothing \, x$, and each load and store instruction has one effect under multi-copy-atomicity, which has *two* reorderings of $x = 1; r_0 = y$ and $y = 1; r_1 = x$. Moreover, the assertion is violated by the trace $\mathtt{Iss}^0 \, i_0; \mathtt{Iss}^0 \, i_1; \mathtt{Iss}^0 \, i_2; \mathtt{Eff}^0_{\{0,1\}} \, i_2; \mathtt{Iss}^0 \, i_3; \mathtt{Eff}^0_{\{0,1\}} \, i_0$ which has only *one* reordering of $x = 1; r_0 = y$.

The exploration strategy of VeriDAG can be changed easily by choosing the roots of program graphs as explained in Sect. 3. In this paper, we introduce two reordering controls, *delay* and *hasten*, to delay and hasten the effects of `Store` by choosing the latest and earliest instances possible, respectively. Definitions are straight-forward as follows:

```
hasten = f [] []
  where f st ow (nd@(Node _ (Eff _ (Store _ _ _))):nds) = f (nd:st) ow nds
        f st ow (nd:nds) = f st (nd:ow) nds
        f st ow [] = (reverse st)++(reverse ow)
```

```
delay = f [] []
  where f st ow (nd@(Node _ (Eff _ (Store _ _ _))):nds) = f (nd:st) ow nds
        f st ow (nd:nds) = f st (nd:ow) nds
        f st ow [] = (reverse ow)++(reverse st)
```

We conduct experiments to show the effectiveness of reordering control.

The programs for the experiments consist of two sets. The first includes popular mutual exclusion algorithms, such as Dekker's algorithm [12], Lamport's bakery algorithm [18], Peterson's algorithm [25], Lamport's fast algorithm [20], and Aravind's algorithm [10]. These programs run correctly under SC; however, they should not run correctly under TSO because they were not designed for relaxed MCMs.

The second includes concurrent copying protocols used in concurrent copying garbage collection algorithms, such as Chicken [26] and Staccato [22], which are larger than the standard mutual exclusion algorithms described above. Although these algorithms are based on a common idea, they are expected to behave differently because Chicken appears to be designed for Intel architectures such as x86 which uses TSO, and Staccato appears to be designed for POWER architectures which use more relaxed MCMs. In the experiments, we used the programs that were modeled in [7].

The experimental environment was the same as that in Sect. 5. Also, model checking is terminated by an exhaustive search of execution traces or detection of a counterexample as for the experiments in Sect. 5. All the experiments in this section are conducted under RMO.

Figure 3 shows the effectiveness of the delay and hasten reordering controls. In all the experiments using the mutual exclusion algorithms, model checking with the delay reordering control detected counterexamples more quickly. However, in the experiment using Chicken, model checking with the hasten reordering control detected a counterexample more quickly. Thus the delay reordering control does not always have the best performance.

The exploration strategies for the original implementation and using the hasten reordering control had similar performances. This is because the original strategy implemented on VeriDAG is similar to the hasten reordering control.

In the experiment using Staccato, the reordering controls gave no improvement. This is because Staccato was designed for the POWER MCM and runs correctly under RMO. That is, Staccato had no counterexample under RMO, while the other algorithms did have counterexamples under RMO.

7 Related Work

There do exist some model checkers that use MCMs. To the best of our knowledge, most of these are specific to certain MCMs, and most of them use external engines such as SMT solvers and model checkers that ignore relaxed MCMs [35, 31, 32, 2, 5].

The tool herd [9] also aims at model checking with various MCMs by one tool. However, there exist two differences from VeriDAG. First, the herd does not support C-style models, and accepts text files in a language which the developers themselves call *adhoc* [9]. Second, configuration files for MCMs are written in its own format whose extension is .cat, differently from that VeriDAG adopts Haskell functions that denote dependencies between operations to specify MCMs. It is significant to clarify differences between the expressive powers is significant. Investigating flexibility of exploration strategies in [9] is also significant.

Model checkers specific to certain MCMs have advantages in performance. CSeq [16], which was developed to support TSO and PSO, has great performance [31]. Weak2SC also supports TSO and PSO [32]. Both Weak2SC and McSPIN use SPIN as back-end engines. However, Weak2SC also has better performance than McSPIN since program counters can denote computational configurations under TSO and PSO, while program graphs denote those under more relaxed MCMs on VeriDAG. Program graphs is similar to that of *sb-graphs* proposed in [32], which are graph representations of programs with MCMs. However, *sb-graphs* cannot handle RMO because they do not support reordering of load instructions. We only compared VeriDAG with McSPIN, so VeriDAG should have a poorer performance than Weak2SC. We do not expect the best performance for model checking with MCMs from VeriDAG, but retain the high flexibility of allowing various user-defined memory models as a research framework.

McSPIN also has the flexibility of allowing various user-defined memory models as inputs. However, because McSPIN, which uses SPIN as a back-end engine, has the limitation that changing exploration strategies is difficult, we cannot necessarily apply new exploration strategies to McSPIN with ease. VeriDAG has no such limitation because it has been fully developed from scratch.

Weak2SC and VeriDAG use the same preprocessing via Clang, and both generate graph representations of programs with MCMs. However, sb-graphs, which are graph representations in Weak2SC, cannot represent programs with RMO differently from VeriDAG as explained in Sect. 2. Weak2SC also generates PROMELA codes, and has to use SPIN to explore execution traces, while VeriDAG has its own exploration engine.

DIVINE [30, 29] also uses Clang, and supports model checking with TSO and the LLVM memory model through the LLVM-to-LLVM program transformation with store buffers. However, the method seems to lack flexibility of supporting various MCMs since it is necessary to implement one kind of store buffers at each MCM. Actually, DIVINE does not support more relaxed MCMs that allow reordering of load instructions such as RMO.

LTSmin [11], which was developed to support MCMs [35], uses a notion of *cost* introduced by Reffel et al. [27], and conducts model checking under TSO, PSO, and LMO (a restriction of RMO) simultaneously. However, it is not clear how to input user-defined MCMs and define their costs. Moreover, LTSmin suggests a reason to not support RMO, and clarifies a problem about reordering of load instructions in [35]. However, LTSmin may be restricted by its use of several external solvers. VeriDAG can take user-defined memory models as Haskell functions, which denote dependencies between instructions, and generate program graphs, thus avoiding the problem. VeriDAG does not use external solvers in exploring execution traces.

HSF-SPIN [14] is an extension of SPIN, and provides various heuristic searches for directed model checking [15]. However, it has not been used for the heuristic searches in this paper for model checking with relaxed MCMs.

8   Conclusion and Future Work

This paper provides VeriDAG, a model checker for program graphs corresponding to concurrent programs with MCMs. VeriDAG has good flexibility and allows for easy implementation of reordering control. VeriDAG is expected to be a useful research framework for model checking with MCMs.

There remain several areas of interest for future research. This paper provides no experiment to compare VeriDAG with tools which are developed by other research groups. It is significant since such experiment shows a trade-off of the flexibility of VeriDAG. VeriDAG cannot currently take temporal logic formulas such as linear time temporal logic (LTL) formulas which correspond to Büchi automata. We would like to support assertion consisting of LTL formulas by implementing a special program graph corresponding to the so-called *never claim* of the SPIN model checker [17], and enhancing the acceptance cycle detection which is compatible with the memoization of VeriDAG. In the experiments in Sect. 6, we showed that reordering controls affect the performance of counterexample detection, and presented some comparisons between various reordering controls. A more detailed investigation of this issue is left.

Acknowledgments. The author thanks Johan Tibell and Kazuhiko Yamamoto, who gave advices on the use of GHC and its modules to improve the performance of VeriDAG. The author also thanks the anonymous reviewers for several comments to improve the paper. This work was supported by JSPS KAKENHI Grant Number 16K21335.

References

1. Abdulla, P.A., Aronis, S., Atig, M.F., Jonsson, B., Leonardsson, C., Sagonas, K.F.: Stateless model checking for TSO and PSO. In: Proc. of TACAS. Volume 9035 of LNCS. (2015) 353–367
2. Abdulla, P.A., Atig, M.F., Bouajjani, A., Ngo, T.P.: Context-bounded analysis for POWER. In: Proc. of TACAS. Volume 10206. (2017) 56–74
3. Abdulla, P.A., Atig, M.F., Jonsson, B., Leonardsson, C.: Stateless model checking for POWER. In: Proc. of CAV. Volume 9780 of LNCS. (2016) 134–156
4. Abe, T., Maeda, T.: Concurrent program logic for relaxed memory consistency models with dependencies across loop iterations. Journal of Information Processing **25** (2017) 244–255
5. Abe, T., Maeda, T.: A general model checking framework for various memory consistency models. International Journal on Software Tools for Technology Transfer **19**(5) (2017) https://bitbucket.org/abet/mcspin/.
6. Abe, T., Ugawa, T., Maeda, T.: Reordering control approaches to state explosion in model checking with memory consistency models. In: Proc. of VSTTE. (2017)
7. Abe, T., Ugawa, T., Maeda, T., Matsumoto, K.: Reducing state explosion for software model checking with relaxed memory consistency models. In: Proc. of SETTA. Volume 9984 of LNCS. (2016) 118–135
8. Adve, S.V., Gharachorloo, K.: Shared memory consistency models: a tutorial. Computer **29**(12) (1996) 66–76
9. Alglave, J., Maranget, L., Tautschnig, M.: Herding cats: Modelling, simulation, testing, and data mining for weak memory. ACM Transactions on Programming Languages and Systems **36**(2) (2014) http://diy.inria.fr/herd/.
10. Aravind, A.A.: Yet another simple solution for the concurrent programming control problem. IEEE Transactions on Parallel and Distributed Systems **22**(6) (2011) 1056–1063

11. Blom, S., van de Pol, J., Weber, M.: LTSmin: Distributed and symbolic reachability. In: Proc. of CAV. Volume 6174 of LNCS. (2010) 354–359
12. Dijkstra, E.W.: Cooperating sequential processes. In: Programming Languages: NATO Advanced Study Institute. Academic Press (1968) 43–112
13. Edelkamp, S., Lafuente, A.L.: HSF-SPIN User Manual. (2006)
14. Edelkamp, S., Lafuente, A.L., Leue, S.: Directed explicit model checking with HSF–SPIN. In: Proc. of SPIN. Volume 2057. (2001) 57–79
15. Edelkamp, S., Schuppan, V., Bosnacki, D., Wijs, A., Fehnker, A., Aljazzar, H.: Survey on directed model checking. In: Proc. of MoChArt. Volume 5348 of LNCS. (2008) 65–89
16. Fischer, B., Inverso, O., Parlato, G.: CSeq: A concurrency pre-processor for sequential C verification tools. In: Proc. of ASE. (2013) 710–713
17. Holzmann, G.J.: The SPIN Model Checker. Addison-Wesley (2003)
18. Lamport, L.: A new solution of Dijkstra's concurrent programming problem. Comm. ACM **17**(8) (1974) 453–455
19. Lamport, L.: How to make a multiprocessor computer that correctly executes multiprocess programs. IEEE Transactions on Computers (9) (1979) 690–691
20. Lamport, L.: A fast mutual exclusion algorithm. ACM Transactions on Computer Systems **5**(1) (1987) 1–11
21. Leijen, D., Palamarchuk, A.: The IntMap module. `https://hackage.haskell.org/package/containers-0.5.10.2/docs/Data-IntMap.html`.
22. McCloskey, B., Bacon, D.F., Cheng, P., Grove, D.: Staccato: A parallel and concurrent real-time compacting garbage collector for multiprocessors. Research Report RC24504, IBM (2008)
23. Nidhugg: Nidhugg Manual, Version 0.2. (2016) `https://github.com/nidhugg`.
24. Owens, S., Sarkar, S., Sewell, P.: A better x86 memory model: x86-TSO. Technical Report UCAM-CL-TR-745, Computer Laboratory, University of Cambridge (2009)
25. Peterson, G.L.: Myths about the mutual exclusion problem. Information Processing Letters **12**(3) (1981) 115–116
26. Pizlo, F., Petrank, E., Steensgaard, B.: A study of concurrent real-time garbage collectors. In: Proc. of PLDI. (2008) 33–44
27. Reffel, F., Edelkamp, S.: Error detection with directed symbolic model checking. In: Proc. of FM. Volume 1708 of LNCS. (1999) 195–211
28. Sarkar, S., Sewell, P., Alglave, J., Maranget, L., Williams, D.: Understanding POWER multiprocessors. In: Proc. of PLDI. (2011) 175–186
29. Still, V.: LLVM transformations for model checking. Master's thesis, Masaryk University (2016)
30. Still, V., Rockai, P., Barnat, J.: Weak memory models as LLVM-to-LLVM transformations. In: Proc. of MEMICS. Volume 9548 of LNCS. (2015) 144–155
31. Tomasco, E., Truc Nguyen Lam, O.I., Fischer, B., Torre, S.L., Parlato, G.: Lazy sequentialization for TSO and PSO via shared memory abstractions. In: Proc. of FMCAD. (2016) 193–200
32. Travkin, O., Wehrheim, H.: Verification of concurrent programs on weak memory models. In: Proc. of ICTAC. Volume 9965 of LNCS. (2016) 3–24
33. Turon, A., Vafeiadis, V., Dreyer, D.: GPS: Navigating weak memory with ghosts, protocols, and separation. In: Proc. of OOPSLA. (2014) 691–707
34. Vafeiadis, V., Narayan, C.: Relaxed separation logic: A program logic for C11 concurrency. In: Proc. of OOPSLA. (2013) 867–884
35. van der Berg, F.: Model checking LLVM IR using LTSmin: Using relaxed memory model semantics. Master's thesis, University of Twente (2013)

Trace-based Analysis of Memory Corruption Malware Attacks

Zhixing Xu[1], Aarti Gupta[2], and Sharad Malik[1]

[1] Department of Electrical Engineering, Princeton University
[2] Department of Computer Science, Princeton University

Abstract. Understanding malware behavior is critical for cybersecurity. This is still largely done through expert manual analysis of the malware code/binary. In this work, we introduce a fully automated method for malware analysis that utilizes memory traces of program execution. Given both benign and malicious execution traces of a program, the method identifies memory segments specific to the malware attack, and then uses them to localize the attack in the source code. We evaluated our method on the RIPE benchmark for memory corruption malware attacks and demonstrated its ability to: (i) perform diagnosis by identifying the program location of both code corruption (e.g. buffer overflow location) and attack execution (e.g. control flow to payload), (ii) recognize the characteristics of different attacks.

1 Introduction

Malicious software, referred to as *malware*, continues to grow in sophistication. IDC and the National University of Singapore estimate that enterprises spent $127 billion in 2014 dealing with malware security issues [7]. Therefore, analysis/detection of malware is a priority research area.

Program analysis is an important first step for malware detection. This involves analyzing potential malware samples and vulnerable target programs either statically or dynamically. Static analysis for malware performs source code scan which matches the code pattern with known malware "signatures" in order to find program sections that cause malicious behavior or security problems [21, 13]. It is susceptible to obfuscation [3] and fails to take into consideration the actual program paths during execution.

Dynamic analysis for malware detection has been proposed to address these issues [16, 19, 9]. It examines program execution by generating test input and monitoring its execution behavior. Malicious execution is detected if part of the program execution behavior conforms with malware "signatures" or is considered abnormal. Since the execution traces keep knowledge of program state at each step during program execution, the malicious/vulnerable code sections and the corresponding conditions of the security vulnerability can be located and recognized in the source code. To reduce the overhead of generating proper test inputs, some dynamic analysis tools have successfully used concolic execution, albeit for small and less complicated programs [18, 25].

This work was supported in part by SONIC (one of the six SRC STARnet centers, sponsored by MARCO and DARPA) and NSF Grant 1525936. Any opinions, findings, and conclusions presented here are those of the authors and do not necessarily reflect those of SONIC or NSF.

O. Strichman and R. Tzoref-Brill (Eds.): HVC 2017, LNCS 10629, pp. 67–82, 2017.
https://doi.org/10.1007/978-3-319-70389-3_5

Both static and dynamic program analysis/malware detection approaches mentioned above require databases of syntactic "signatures" for malware behavior. These databases are usually derived from malware samples with expert human input. This is expensive and the databases may not be complete as malware behavior may sometimes be too complicated for human analysis. What is missing is automation for determining the "signatures" for malware attacks. In contrast to these program analysis approaches requiring human input, statistical techniques based on machine learning have been used to find patterns corresponding to malicious program behavior [22, 8]. Examples of feature sets in machine learning for malware detection are network metadata [22] and system call sequences [8]. These feature sets are used to train a machine learning classifier to classify whether an unknown program run is malicious or not. Recent work on malware detection with machine learning has started using feature sets at the hardware level such as Hardware Performance Counters (HPC) [6], instruction mixes [14] and memory access patterns [26].

Although the models learned through statistical methods are effective in classifying malware attacks, they do not help much in diagnosis. It is hard to translate the "signature" machine learning model obtained to program semantics such as regular expressions of program constructs. This is especially true when the feature sets used in machine learning are at a low level of the computer system, (e.g., hardware level). Thus, they are unable to diagnose program vulnerability at the software source level as done by dynamic analysis approaches. This source-level information is often important for patching vulnerabilities and preventing attacks.

Dynamic analysis is a white-box approach in that it uses knowledge of program source code for diagnosis. However, human inputs for determining the malware "signature" are required. In contrast, statistical malware detection is a black-box approach since it only uses low-level program features without knowledge of the program source code. It achieves automation but does not aid diagnosis.

This paper proposes a diagnosis method for understanding malware attacks. It aims for the automation benefits of statistical methods, with the diagnosis capabilities provided by the dynamic analysis approaches. It does so through a novel *trace-based analysis approach that identifies different malware attacks and program vulnerabilities without expert human input.* Inspired by the effectiveness of using low-level features for malware detection, this approach utilizes virtual memory access traces which require minimum source code knowledge, unlike traditional traces with program states used in dynamic analysis. Using memory access traces from normal program runs and program runs for different attacks, it automatically identifies the memory accesses that are specific to attacks, and relates them to the program source using a code localization method based on the memory traces.

A key insight underlying this approach is that *malware attacks have to modify the control-flow and/or key data structures in normal system execution to achieve their malicious purpose.* This modification is reflected in just the address trace, without the need for associated program state. Events represented in the memory accesses are then related to the program source with little extra effort.

A major challenge for the analysis is the sheer volume of memory accesses in each trace. We address this by first identifying maximal address *segments* which are exclusively accessed by malicious runs. We then find a subset of these segments that *cover* all malicious traces. This cover provides a set of addresses in each malicious trace that distinguish it from all benign traces. These distinguishing addresses are then connected back to the source code to localize the malicious activity. This includes finding the vulnerability (e.g., buffer overflow location) as well as the actual attack that exploits this vulnerability (e.g., control flow redirection). Experiments on a large benchmark of memory corruption attacks (RIPE benchmark [24]) show the efficacy of this approach.

We make the following contributions in this paper:

– We introduce a technique for malware analysis that uses address traces without associated program state.
– We develop a novel algorithm to identify a minimum set of memory segments that distinguish all malicious runs from benign runs. These segments are then used for identifying the vulnerability and attack in the code.
– We have experimentally evaluated this method on a comprehensive benchmark for memory corruption attacks (RIPE benchmark) and demonstrated its effectiveness in identifying locations for program code vulnerability and attack, as well as recognizing the characteristics of different attacks.

We propose our approach as a general methodology for malware attack analysis. While our evaluation in this paper has focused on memory corruption attacks, we believe it is applicable to other types of malware attacks.

2   Malware Attacks and Program Memory Traces

We now give a brief description of common malware attack techniques and how they affect program memory traces.

2.1   Memory Corruption Attacks

Code infection at the user level primarily occurs through memory corruption vulnerabilities: buffer overflow, heap overflow, format string vulnerability, etc. Buffer overflow (BOF) is possibly the most common vulnerability exploited. The attacker overflows a program buffer's boundary and overwrites adjacent memory locations. A carefully constructed buffer input can contain malicious payload and change the program's control flow to this payload. Vanilla buffer overflow attacks that transfer control to locations outside the existing code base are easy to catch using program memory traces since it always redirects control flow to anomalous locations. Sophisticated code reuse techniques transfer control to locations in the existing code base and are more challenging.

Modern computer systems have prevention techniques against these attacks. Data Execution Prevention (DEP) does not allow data in certain memory sectors (e.g., the stack) to be executed. Address Space Layout Randomization (ASLR) shifts the code and data segments by adding a randomized offset to their initial addresses. However, current memory exploit attacks are capable of successfully bypassing these preventions [15]. Even when the address space is fully randomized, it is possible to calculate the base address and offset at runtime [10], or even with brute-force methods [20].

Consider return-oriented programming (ROP) attacks as an example. This attack executes a sequence of assembly code snippets called gadgets. Gadgets are carefully chosen from an existing code base, and are chained to implement the malicious objective. It naturally bypasses DEP, and ASLR using the techniques mentioned above. However, when examining the memory access traces, these code sections are executed in an anomalous way, thereby leaving some evidence of the attack. For example, how and where control flow transfers to gadgets will be different from normal execution.

2.2 RIPE Benchmark

RIPE [24] is a testbed that generates a synthetic benchmark which contains a total of 850 different memory corruption attacks in various forms including modern attacks such as return-to-libc attacks, return-oriented programming, etc. The attacks in RIPE are a good representation of non-synthetic memory corruption attacks in the wild. The benchmark is built to cover five dimensions:

1. Location: 4 types of locations of buffers in memory – Stack, Heap, BSS, and Data segment
2. Target code pointer: 16 target code pointers to redirect to the attack code; e.g., return address, base pointer, longjmp buffer, function pointer, etc.
3. Overflow technique: direct, indirect overflow techniques
4. Code reuse techniques for attack: ROP attack (as mentioned in §2.1), return-to-libc attack (where the attacker uses existing code from libc-function to perform attack).
5. Function exploited: 10 functions being exploited (memory unsafe functions that got attacked using BOF); e.g., memcpy(), strcpy()

A user can specifically choose the attack type in each dimension. The complete set of useful combinations across the dimensions yields the 850 different attacks. We also build a "benign" version of RIPE where the vulnerabilities are patched. Each type of attack is implemented on both the "benign" and the original version of RIPE program and the memory traces for both executions are collected. The memory traces include the instruction address of every memory operation (data access/control flow) and its target address. They also record the basic block address and the function name that each such instruction appears in.

3   Automated Trace Analysis: Challenges and Solutions

The primary challenge of memory trace analysis is the large number of memory accesses in each program run. The memory trace for one program run contains millions to billions of memory accesses. Therefore, we first create a "summary" of the trace. This summary should serve two main purposes: it should reduce analysis overhead, and it should extract *relevant* distinctions of malicious runs in comparison to benign runs.

We implement this summary by: (i) first creating address *segments* that are exclusive to malicious executions, and then (ii) selecting the most important segments among them for further analysis. A memory segment is a range of contiguous memory addresses. Using important memory segments instead of individual addresses greatly reduces the number of candidates for diagnosis, i.e., candidate locations in the source code that need to be examined to localize the malware attack. This reduction from potentially billions to a few tens is a key contribution of our approach.

Another challenge is dynamically allocated data structures in memory traces. Programs often have data structures that are assigned to memory only at runtime (e.g., data structures in heap), making the memory region for these data structures vary across different runs even for the same program. The solution we use is to: (i) associate a dynamic data structure with the basic block(s) in which it is accessed, (ii) run the code with the same input multiple times to track the complete data structure across different runs, and (iii) "normalize" the addresses across the different runs. In our current implementation, this normalization is done only for the attacked data structures that our approach identifies during diagnosis. We expect that normalization for *all* dynamic data structures would benefit our analysis more. This will be discussed further in §4 and §5.

3.1 Memory segment construction

We now describe how the memory segments are constructed by coalescing memory accesses in traces. Suppose we have B benign and M malicious program traces. Each trace is an ordered set of memory addresses (with associated information as described earlier), i.e., $\{a_1, a_2, a_3, \ldots a_k\}$. Let array A contain all the addresses that appear in any of the traces. It is sorted by address value. Each address is labeled as "malicious" if it appears only in malicious traces and not in any benign trace. It is labeled as "benign" if it appears in any "benign" trace. For an element a in array A, let $a.addr$ denote its memory address and $a.label$ denote its label. For addresses labeled as "malicious", we also record the indices of the traces that this address appears in. Let $a.index$ denote the set of indices of the traces that contain this address.

Algorithm 1 Memory segment construction

```
// Array A of all memory accesses, sorted
// Set MS of malicious segments, initially empty
// Sets MST_i of malicious segments in traces, initially empty
for each memory access a in A do
    if a.label == malicious then
        MS.add(a2ms(a.addr, A))
        for i in a.index do
            MST_i.add(a2ms(a.addr, A))
        end for
    end if
end for
```

Algorithm 1 shows how malicious memory segments are constructed by coalescing addresses. We use a function $a2ms(addr, A)$ to get the maximal address range $(alow, ahigh)$ that includes the malicious memory access $addr$, but does not include any benign memory access. Specifically, given a malicious memory address $addr$ and the sorted array A, it returns an open interval $(alow, ahigh)$ where:

- *alow* is the largest memory address labeled as benign that is smaller than *addr*, and
- *ahigh* is the smallest memory address labeled as benign that is greater than *addr*.

This function can be viewed as *mapping* a given malicious address *addr* to a *malicious segment*, i.e., a contiguous range of addresses that contains no address labeled benign.

The set MS denotes the entire set of malicious segments for all traces, and each set $MST_i, i = 1, 2, ..., M$ contains the malicious segments accessed in malicious trace i. The boundaries of these malicious segments are the nearest memory addresses that were accessed in some benign trace. This boundary choice gives the most separation from existing benign accesses to malicious accesses. It can also lead to large malicious segments. Large segments may combine together the malicious accesses that are specific to different attacks, making it harder to distinguish between them. One can easily use additional criteria to direct the boundary choice, including criteria related to program semantics. For example, one may want the size of malicious memory segments be within value n, which may capture the typical size of memory structures in the program. If some segment has size larger than n, it would be divided into smaller segments.

In our implementation, we keep two sorted arrays of memory addresses, one for control flow memory accesses (call, branch, etc.), and the other for data accesses. As a result, the malicious memory segments that we construct are also specific to one of these two types of accesses, and segments of different types can overlap with each other. Distinguishing control flow and data accesses gives these segments an extra layer of information that we utilize later for diagnosis. We now show how these segments help narrow the search for the malicious code programs.

3.2   Covering memory segments

Each trace i ($i = 1, 2, ..., M$) is now associated with a set of malicious segments MST_i. However, these sets are still quite large. Analyzing all of them for each trace to diagnose the malware attack is not practical. Instead, what we take advantage of is that multiple malicious traces will likely have the same vulnerability that is exploited (e.g., same buffer) and the same attack (e.g., same malicious code executed). What is useful in this context is "small explanations" that are sufficient to diagnose the attacks in all the traces. Thus, in terms of these memory segments, it translates to identifying a set of memory segments that between them include an address from each of the malicious traces. In other words, this set of segments "covers" all traces. Such a cover set further helps narrow the search for malicious code in programs.

Determining this cover of malicious segments can be framed as a set covering problem. Assume the size of set MS is N (this set MS includes the memory segments from both control flow and data accesses). We construct an $M * N$ matrix $C = \|c_{ij}\|$. The rows of the matrix C represent the malicious traces, and the columns represent the malicious memory segments. The entries of the matrix represent whether a memory segment contains an address in the corresponding trace:

$$c_{ij} = 1 \quad \text{iff} \quad j^{th} \text{ malicious segment} \in MST_i$$

The following integer linear programming (ILP) problem can be formed to find the smallest subset of MS to cover all the traces. Binary variable x_j, $1 \leq j \leq N$ indicates if column j is in the cover or not.

$$\text{Minimize} \quad \sum_{j=1}^{N} x_j$$

$$\text{Subject to} \quad \sum_{j=1}^{N} c_{ij} x_j \geq 1 \quad i = 1, ..., M$$

$$x_j = 0 \text{ or } 1$$

The solution can be represented by set X_1 where

$$j \in X_1 \quad \text{iff} \quad x_j = 1$$

Set X_1 contains the indices of the smallest covering of malicious segments in MS for all traces. Potentially, the covering problem could be solved directly using memory addresses instead of memory segments. However, as ILP is NP-hard, the reduction in number of columns that is obtained through segmentation is critical in making the instance sizes manageable in practice.

The memory segments in the cover are the most commonly accessed across all malicious traces and are likely to provide the most common explanation across the different attacks. We call this result the first level solution. If we are seeking a finer distinction between different attacks, these segments may not be the most informative. For example, RIPE has some parts of code/memory accesses that are used to set up the attacks, which are therefore common to most malicious traces and the associated attacks. They themselves do not provide information on how different attacks are constructed. To further identify the distinguishing characteristics of these different attacks, there is value in going beyond this first level solution to find the next largest cover of C. This can be done by dropping the first level solution which is normally done by dropping any one segment in the solution set, using $\sum_j x_j < |X_1|, x_j \in X_1$. The new solution set is different, but many segments in the original solution set may still appear in the new set. In our analysis, we are looking for totally new segments to get new information of the attacks, so we prefer to drop all segments of the first level solution by adding

$$x_j = 0, \quad \text{for} \quad j \in X_1$$

to the original ILP. Let X_2 be the solution of this new ILP. We refer to this as the second level solution. This set of memory segments has more detail of the differences between memory accesses from different attack traces, because the common parts of the different attacks are filtered out when we blocked the first level solution. The practical value of this is seen in §5.

4   Trace-based Analysis Framework

Figure 1 shows the overall framework of our approach. The memory segment construction and selection described in §3 use information only from memory traces to narrow the locations in memory where malicious behavior occurs. We now use these to perform diagnosis to locate in the program: (i) where the attack happens, i.e., where control flow jumps to execute the malicious code, and more importantly (ii) the security vulnerability. This is done through back annotation to the source program.

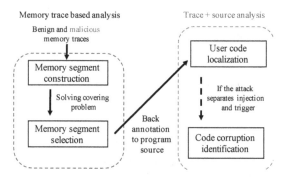

Fig. 1: Overall framework

We illustrate this part of our approach step by step with a real example. Recall from §2, every execution trace from RIPE is an attack built from some combination of 5 different dimensions. Here we take one particular attack as an example. This example attack targets the stack buffer location and overwrites the stack function pointer with direct overflow technique by exploiting the security vulnerability of the strncat() function using the return-to-libc code reuse technique.

4.1 User code localization

Step 1: User machine code localization Since the memory addresses in the malicious segment never appear in benign program runs, the access to this memory segment normally happens in a basic block *outside* the original program's code segment. (Note that attacks using ROP technique may have the memory segment inside the original program code, and will be discussed separately). In this step, an automated trace-back is implemented to determine the *last basic block* inside the original program code, before the occurrence of the malicious memory access. This is easy to do because our trace records the information about the basic blocks, so we know which of them belong to the original code. This basic block corresponds to the last code in the original program that is executed before the control flow jumps to malicious locations.

In our example attack, the malicious memory segment accessed is (0x80487a6, 0x80487c0). This was obtained from the covering. We first locate the memory access *ma* in this segment in the trace. We then do an automated backward search in the memory trace, to determine the last basic block executed in original program code before the occurrence of access *ma*. Table 1 shows a snippet of the memory trace which shows this basic block. Note that the memory address shown here is for sake of completeness. The address itself is not important, but it allows us to track the attack characteristics in terms of malicious memory accesses. The left-most column denotes whether the access is the start of a basic block ('BBL' if it is). The column "Access type" tells us whether the access is a read or write, "Code addr" shows the address of the instruction and "R/W location" shows the target data location of this memory access.

Step 2: User source code localization After identifying the last basic block executed in the trace, we can locate it in the original program based on its address (0x0804a253

Table 1: Machine code localization

	Access type	Code addr	R/W location
BBL	R	0x0804a253	0xbfb6a10c
MEM	W	0x0804a259	0xbfb530e4
MEM	W	0x0804a261	0xbfb530e0
MEM	W	0x0804a268	0xbfb530dc

here, as shown above). The corresponding line for this basic block in source code is line 1066. We see that a function pointer stack_func_ptr is getting called by the program with some argument provided by the benchmark. The address of this function pointer can be inferred by using the method for determining dynamically assigned addresses described in §3.

```
1065    case FUNC_PTR_STACK_VAR:
1066      ((int (*)(char *,int)) (*stack_func_ptr))
    ("/tmp/rip-eval/f_xxxx" 700);
1067      break;
```

From this information, we can see that this pointer is now directed to execute the malicious payload. However, the pointer itself got overwritten somewhere before this line. Note that this example shows a function pointer as the target. In general, the control flow to payload may happen by targeting other kinds of code pointers, e.g., by changing contents of longjump buffer, or by overwriting function return address on stack. Whichever way the code pointer gets attacked, what interests us most is where the overwriting occurs, since it helps us to locate the actual vulnerability in the code.

For ROP attacks, since the malicious payload is typically a chain of gadgets, the malicious segment is usually *inside* the original program. In this case, the segment already gives us information about the control flow redirection. The return addresses on stack of the gadgets are target pointers of the attack. We can use the location where they got overwritten to locate the vulnerability. Doing a trace-back in the memory trace can help identify the gadgets and the starting point of control flow redirection.

4.2 Code corruption identification

In our example, the attack trigger (call of the function pointer) and the injection (where memory corruption happens and the pointer gets overwritten) happen in different locations. Therefore, after the user code localization, we need to analyze further in order to find out where the injection happens.

Step 1: Machine code corruption identification Using the information obtained from the last step (function pointer stack_func_ptr and its address 0xbf99f83c), we analyze the memory trace again and search for the location where this pointer got overwritten outside the program's original code. Table 2 shows a snippet of the basic block where this pointer is overwritten, i.e. the code corruption location.

Now, we again use an automated trace-back to determine the last basic block accessed inside the original program, before this code corruption access. The resulting basic block is shown in Table 3. We then use its address (0xb61f74d0) to go back to the program source to identify the code corruption location in the original program. Here, the basic block address 0xb61f74d0 corresponds to libc.so.6:strncat, which also identifies the function getting attacked. Again, it is not the the address itself that is important but its tracking with the basic block and the function in the source code.

Table 2: Machine code corruption identification

	Access type	Code addr	R/W location
BBL	R	0xb61f74d0	0x805079c
MEM	W	0xb61f74d5	0x0bf99f83c

Step 2: Source code corruption identification This step is similar to the corresponding step in user code localization. The basic block we found led us to the code where the buffer overflow happens. Line 914 corresponds to the basic block in Table 3. We find that the function strncat is what the malware used for the buffer overflow attack. At this point, we have determined the location of the vulnerability in the original code. This completes our diagnoses for this example.

Table 3: Source code corruption identification

	Access type	Code addr	R/W location
BBL	R	0x08049e33	0xbf99f900
MEM	R	0x08049e36	0xbf98bb30
MEM	W	0x08049e3c	0xbf988818
MEM	R	0x08049e40	0xbf99f908

```
913 case STRNCAT:
914   strncat(buffer, input_buffer, input_size);
915   break;
```

A natural question to ask here is why the memory segment identified in the covering led us first to where the attack triggers, but not to where the attack is injected. The buffer overflow write operation should also correspond to a malicious memory segment, since it is accessed only in malicious code. The reason is that we are using a small cover of the malicious memory segments. Since the buffers in the program are allocated dynamically, they have different memory addresses in each memory trace. Thus, these segments are not likely to be part of a small cover. They may be discovered after many levels of solutions are blocked. However, this is likely to be computationally very expensive. In comparison, the small cover helps us quickly get to the attack trigger, which is common across a large number of traces as it is an instruction address and not the address of a dynamic data structure. This reinforces one of the main benefits of our trace-based approach – we gain by automatically extracting common relevant information from multiple traces.

As mentioned in §3, it is possible to analyze *all* the different dynamic addresses in different traces that may represent the same data structure. However, this may require additional knowledge of the source program, e.g., the basic block addresses where the data structures are used. In our method, we perform such analysis only for the data structures that are attacked, for which the accessing basic block addresses can be automatically inferred from traces. With additional effort, we can perform a normalization for *all* dynamic addresses. With full normalization, we believe it is possible that a small cover will directly help identify the vulnerability.

5   Evaluation

5.1   Experimental Setup

In our evaluation, the RIPE benchmark was executed on a QEMU virtual machine with Ubuntu 6.06 system and Linux kernel version 2.6.15. The host machine uses 2.53GHz Intel Xeon X3440 processor with 16GB memory. Among the 850 RIPE attacks, 752 were successful on our target system. The memory traces are collected with ASLR turned off. (For ASLR turned on, the randomized memory addresses in our traces can be "de-randomized" the same way that attackers circumvent ASLR as mentioned in 2.1)

For trace collection, we developed a "pintool" using a binary instrumentation tool Pin [12] to collect the memory access trace during the execution of the target program. The "pintool" is designed to record the address of each memory operation and its target address. It also provides information about the basic block and the function name that each instruction appears in. It took on average 2.43 sec. to execute the attacked program without Pin instrumentation, and 3.45 sec. with Pin instrumentation on our QEMU virtual machine. [1]

We used the Matlab ILP solver `intlinprog` on a 2GHz Intel Core i7 with 8GB memory machine to solve the covering problem. The ILP runs took 3.14 sec. on average.

5.2   Memory segment construction and selection

We used our approach on the 752 "pairs" of benign and malicious traces. Algorithm 1 constructed a total of 118,819 malicious memory segments. The construction of these segments took 401.54 sec. on average, on the host machine mentioned in §5.1

In contrast, the total number of memory addresses labeled malicious is 1,192,954, which is about 10 times the size of segments. This reduction is critical in generating ILP instances that can be solved in practice. Most of the segments are specific to only a few traces, due to execution-specific memory accesses. Nonetheless, the actual number of memory segments needed to cover all malicious traces can still be very small. In fact, after running the covering algorithm on these segments, we obtained a cover that contains only 4 memory segments that cover all 752 malicious traces. This is a significant reduction in the original number of malicious memory segments. The "level 1" part of Table 4 shows the 4 memory segments selected.

Some explanations of the identified segments are also shown in the table (column "Explanation of the segment"). Some segments are very large, and the explanation is for a small part. We can relate these memory segments with their attack types. For example, the return-to-libc attacks all access the malicious memory segment of the procedure linkage table. Similarly return oriented programming attacks all access memory segments corresponding to their gadgets. This is because with our instrumentation of RIPE benchmark, the gadgets are not accessed in the benign traces, but this is not always the case for general ROP attacks. We argue that our approach can catch other characteristics of ROP attacks. For example, after normalization of dynamic data structure addresses (as described earlier), we argue that low-level covers will include malicious segments where a buffer is overwritten.

Table 4: Minimum set covers for malicious memory segments

COVERING LEVEL	INDEX	TYPE	EXPLANATION OF THE SEGMENT [1]	TYPICAL ATTACK TYPES	# OF TRACES
level 1	1	control	lib/ld-linux.so.2.text	attacks at stack location without code reuse	182
	2	control	memory region near .txt including read only segments	attacks at .bbs, heap and .data location	415
	3	control	.plt (procedure linkage table)	return to libc	150
	4	control	unaccessed gadget in the program	rop attack	10
level 2	1	data	.bss (block started by symbol)	bss pointer attack	154
	2	data	libc.so.6:_libc_free	heap pointer attack	136
	3	data	.data	data pointer attack	154
			....		

As discussed in §3, the second level solution obtained by blocking every element of the first level solution can give us more detailed information of different attack types. The "level 2" part of Table 4 shows some example memory segments selected from the 61 segments in the second level solution. We see these segments can also be related to their respective attack type. We see that some attack classification that was coarse at level 1 is finer at level 2. The three level 2 segments shown in Table 4 cover attacks to three different types of locations (.bss, .data, heap, respectively) and lead to characteristics of these attacks. Note that these attacks could not be distinguished from each other using level 1 segments. This result shows us that at the second level the segments are more fine-grained in terms of covering specific types of attack. We also noticed that level 1 segments are all accesses of control flow. However, level 2 memory segments have more data accesses. Among the 61 level 2 segments, 44 are for data accesses and 17 of are for control flow accesses. This is because control flow locations are normally the most distinguishing traits for malicious attacks. We can discover the distinguishing data accesses in different attacks only after the control flow locations are blocked.

5.3 Source code identification

After construction and selection of the malicious memory segments, we do the back annotation to identify the user code that contains the jump location to the malicious payload. Some traces may have multiple malicious segments in the covering set. We found that they all go back to the same source code section.

Table 5 shows some results for user code localization and for corruption identification. Each row shows the source code identification result for one attack, and we have

---

[1] The code of pin-tools, RIPE benchmark, memory traces and detailed segments explanation can be found at https://bitbucket.org/zhixing-xu/hvc17.

shown 6 among the total 752 rows (attacks) as examples here. The combined column "Dimension of attack" shows the type of the attack. The remaining columns show the information that we generated by our analysis. Specifically, the columns under "Attack execution identification" show information about the source code from which control flows to the malicious payload. Similarly, the columns under "Memory corruption identification" show information about where the memory corruption happens.

As an example, consider the first attack in the table. The attacker targets a buffer located in the .bss region, and overwrites a function pointer in .bss with direct overflow technique, by exploiting the security vulnerability of the fscanf() function, without using any code reuse attack technique. Using our approach, we identified the address of the last basic block in the program before malicious payload execution as 0x0804a3e2, and the corresponding source code at line 1112, where the function pointer located in the .bss region got called. The actual buffer overflow happens at source code line 925, where function fscanf got called and has the basic block address of 0x08049ef3. Thus, here our approach successfully located the code fragment where the attack is executed, and where the buffer overflow happens. Overall, for all 752 traces, we were able to successfully locate such information.

Table 5: Results of Trace Analysis and Diagnosis

DIMENSIONS OF ATTACK					ATTACK EXECUTION IDENTIFICATION	MEMORY CORRUPTION & IDENTIFICATION
LOCATION	OVERFLOW TECH	TARGET POINTER	CODE REUSE TECHNIQUE	ATTACK FUNCTION	ATTACK EXECUTION CODE LINE & CONTENT	BOF CODE LINE & CONTENT
bss	direct	structfuncptrbss	none	fscanf	1112: bss function pointer called	925: fscanf
stack	direct	ret	none	strncpy	1140: return from wrapper function	898: strncpy
bss	direct	longjmpbss	returntolibc	snprintf	1099: jump with longjmp buffer	908: snprintf
data	indirect	funcptrdata	none	homebrew	1080: data func pointer called	939: homebrew
stack	direct	ret	rop	fscanf	1140: return from wrapper function	925: fscanf

In summary, we evaluated our approach on RIPE benchmark with a total of 752 different memory corruption attacks. By analyzing the level 1 and 2 malicious segments, we show the value of memory segment construction and selection in reducing diagnosis overhead and extracting *relevant* distinction from benign runs. We then successfully utilize these segments for back annotation to the program source code, which demonstrates the approach's capability to identify both the attack payload execution location and code corruption point.

6 Extensions to Unlabeled Traces

We now consider the potential application of our framework to handle unlabeled traces, where we would like to first identify and diagnose potentially malicious traces. In this setting, we already have existing traces labeled as benign and malicious, and we need to classify a new unlabeled trace. Here we can leverage our framework as follows. We start by assuming that the new trace is malicious and run our segmentation and covering method by including this trace. This provides us with a set of segments from the cover labeled as malicious and containing addresses from this trace. These segments can then be back-annotated to the source code, and help us narrow our analysis to these sections of the code.

Consider the case where the segments contain an address that has already been analyzed for previous traces. Here, the vulnerability has already been identified and classified for that address. This can be reused and repeated analysis is not needed. Now consider the case where cover segments contain addresses that have not been seen in previous malicious runs. Here the analysis may find a new vulnerability, or declare the trace to be benign. The key value of the framework is the elimination of addresses from benign runs, and the covering algorithm for the malicious traces to narrow the set of candidates for diagnosis. This extension has not been implemented and will be the subject of future work.

7   Related Work

Work most closely related is in two categories: (i) dynamic malware analysis/detection, and (ii) statistical approaches for malware detection. None of them provide the combination of automation and diagnosis provided by our approach.

7.1   Dynamic malware analysis/detection

Dynamic malware analysis/detection observes the behavior of the system as it executes [16, 9, 4]. As the name suggests, dynamic *behavior-based detection* attempts to detect deviations from normal behavior of a program as it operates. The advantage of dynamic detection is that it is resilient to malware variants [13] which static analysis fails to handle. For example, semantic-aware signature checking is implemented to improve detection of malware polymorphic and metamorphic variants [4]. Instead of checking the runtime behavior of provided tests, some tools perform concrete and symbolic execution of a program simultaneously to explore additional execution paths besides the current one [18, 25]. Despite the approach taken, these analysis/detection methods always need some form of human input.

Control flow integrity (CFI) approaches [1, 23, 5] have been widely explored as a form of dynamic malware detection. They check program execution so that its execution always follows the program's known Control-Flow Graph (CFG). Any deviation from the CFG is recognized as an attack. However, the deviation does not provide any information on attack diagnosis which will need further human input.

Earlier efforts on automatic malware diagnosis aimed at signature generation for network worm attacks [19, 11]. While these techniques don't rely on base knowledge of the memory unsafe conditions, they rely on the assumption that the attack would always trigger an exception or a crash due to common memory corruption defense techniques (e.g., ASLR). This exception/crash then points to the responsible instructions. However, as common defense techniques can be compromised by modern attacks, this assumption may not hold. Our method does not rely on this assumption and generates the attacked memory location automatically through memory trace based analysis.

7.2 Statistical malware detection

Demme *et al.* [6] collect hardware performance counter statistics for programs and malware under execution. They show that machine learning tools can effectively classify malware using these statistics. Ozsoy *et al.* build on this evidence to develop a lightweight online hardware-supported malware detector MAP using feature sets including hardware performance counters and instruction mix [14]. Xu *et al.* explore a framework using virtual memory access patterns as feature set for online malware detection in a per-application based scenario [26].

A number of earlier works explore sub-semantic features for malware detection. Bilar *et al.* [2] examine the frequency of opcode use in malware. Runwal *et al.* [17] study opcode sequence similarity graphs. None of the trained models in these approaches have been utilized for providing diagnosis about the malware behavior and for localizing the vulnerability.

8 Conclusions

In this paper, we presented a fully automated approach for analyzing malware attacks based on program memory trace analysis. We narrow down potentially billions of addresses to a selected few for diagnosis to identify the code vulnerability. We do this by first coalescing memory accesses specific to the malicious traces into memory segments. We then select a minimum subset from these segments that covers all malicious traces, to further help narrow the search for vulnerable code. These remaining segments are then used in back-annotation from memory traces to actual program source to identify the code vulnerabilities. This judicious combination of segmentation and covering is key in obtaining the final results.

We evaluated our method on the RIPE benchmark which includes common memory corruption malware attacks and demonstrated its ability to identify the program location of both code corruption and attack execution. We also successfully identified the characteristics of different attacks. A key value of the proposed approach is using automation in profiling malware behavior using mainly low-level trace data. This provides a promising direction for automated malware analysis with potential application even beyond the memory corruption attacks that are the focus here.

References

1. ABADI, M., BUDIU, M., ERLINGSSON, U., AND LIGATTI, J. Control-flow integrity. In *Proceedings of the 12th ACM conference on Computer and communications security.*
2. BILAR, D. Opcodes as predictor for malware. *International Journal of Electronic Security and Digital Forensics* (2007), 156–168.
3. CHRISTODORESCU, M., AND JHA, S. Static analysis of executables to detect malicious patterns. Tech. rep., DTIC Document, 2006.
4. CHRISTODORESCU, M., JHA, S., SESHIA, S. A., SONG, D., AND BRYANT, R. E. Semantics-aware malware detection. In *Security and Privacy, 2005 IEEE Symposium on.*
5. DAVI, L., HANREICH, M., PAUL, D., SADEGHI, A.-R., KOEBERL, P., SULLIVAN, D., ARIAS, O., AND JIN, Y. Hafix: Hardware-assisted flow integrity extension. In *Proceedings of the 52nd Annual Design Automation Conference* (2015), ACM, p. 74.

6. DEMME, J., MAYCOCK, M., SCHMITZ, J., TANG, A., WAKSMAN, A., SETHUMADHAVAN, S., AND STOLFO, S. On the feasibility of online malware detection with performance counters. *SIGARCH Comput. Archit. News 41*, 3 (June 2013), 559–570.

7. F. GANTZ, J., FLOREAN, A., LEE, R., LIM, V., SIKDAR, B., LAKSHMI, S. K. S., MADHAVAN, L., AND NAGAPPAN, M. The link between pirated software and cybersecurity breaches. https://news.microsoft.com/download/presskits/dcu/docs/idc_031814.pdf.

8. HOFMEYR, S. A., FORREST, S., AND SOMAYAJI, A. Intrusion detection using sequences of system calls. *Journal of Computer Security 6*, 3 (Aug. 1998), 151–180.

9. JACOB, G., DEBAR, H., AND FILIOL, E. Behavioral detection of malware: from a survey towards an established taxonomy. *Journal in computer Virology 4*, 3 (2008), 251–266.

10. LI, H. Understanding and exploiting flash actionscript vulnerabilities, 2011.

11. LIANG, Z., AND SEKAR, R. Fast and automated generation of attack signatures: A basis for building self-protecting servers. In *Proceedings of the 12th ACM conference on Computer and communications security* (2005), ACM, pp. 213–222.

12. LUK, C.-K., COHN, R., MUTH, R., PATIL, H., KLAUSER, A., LOWNEY, G., WALLACE, S., REDDI, V. J., AND H, K. Pin: building customized program analysis tools with dynamic instrumentation. In *ACM Conference on Programming Language Design and Implementation* (2005).

13. MOSER, A., KRUEGEL, C., AND KIRDA, E. Limits of static analysis for malware detection. In *Computer security applications conference, 2007. ACSAC 2007. Twenty-third annual.*

14. OZSOY, M., DONOVICK, C., GORELIK, I., ABU-GHAZALEH, N., AND PONOMAREV, D. Malware-aware processors: A framework for efficient online malware detection. In *High Performance Computer Architecture (HPCA), 2015 IEEE 21st International Symposium on.*

15. PAPPAS, V., POLYCHRONAKIS, M., AND KEROMYTIS, A. D. Transparent rop exploit mitigation using indirect branch tracing. In *USENIX Security* (2013), vol. 30, p. 38.

16. RINGENBURG, M. F., AND GROSSMAN, D. Preventing format-string attacks via automatic and efficient dynamic checking. In *Proceedings of the 12th ACM conference on Computer and communications security* (2005), ACM, pp. 354–363.

17. RUNWAL, N., LOW, R. M., AND STAMP, M. Opcode graph similarity and metamorphic detection. *Journal in Computer Virology 8* (2012), 37–52.

18. SEN, K., MARINOV, D., AND AGHA, G. Cute: a concolic unit testing engine for c. In *ACM SIGSOFT Software Engineering Notes* (2005), vol. 30, ACM, pp. 263–272.

19. SEZER, E. C., NING, P., KIL, C., AND XU, J. Memsherlock: an automated debugger for unknown memory corruption vulnerabilities. In *Proceedings of the 14th ACM conference on Computer and communications security* (2007), ACM, pp. 562–572.

20. SHACHAM, H., PAGE, M., PFAFF, B., GOH, E.-J., MODADUGU, N., AND BONEH, D. On the effectiveness of address-space randomization. In *Proceedings of the 11th ACM conference on Computer and communications security* (2004), ACM, pp. 298–307.

21. VIEGA, J., BLOCH, J.-T., KOHNO, Y., AND MCGRAW, G. Its4: A static vulnerability scanner for c and c++ code. In *Computer Security Applications, 2000.*

22. WANG, K., AND STOLFO, S. J. Anomalous payload-based network intrusion detection. In *Recent Advances in Intrusion Detection* (2004), Springer, pp. 203–222.

23. WANG, Z., AND JIANG, X. Hypersafe: A lightweight approach to provide lifetime hypervisor control-flow integrity. In *Security and Privacy (SP), 2010 IEEE Symposium on.*

24. WILANDER, J., NIKIFORAKIS, N., YOUNAN, Y., KAMKAR, M., AND JOOSEN, W. Ripe: runtime intrusion prevention evaluator. In *27th Computer Security Applications Conference* (2011).

25. XU, R.-G., GODEFROID, P., AND MAJUMDAR, R. Testing for buffer overflows with length abstraction. In *Proceedings of the 2008 international symposium on Software testing and analysis* (2008), ACM, pp. 27–38.

26. XU, Z., RAY, S., SUBRAMANYAN, P., AND MALIK, S. Malware detection using machine learning based analysis of virtual memory access patterns. In *Proceedings of the 2017 Design, Automation & Test in Europe Conference & Exhibition* (2017).

Trace-Based Run-Time Analysis of Message-Passing Go Programs

Martin Sulzmann and Kai Stadtmüller

Faculty of Computer Science and Business Information Systems
Karlsruhe University of Applied Sciences
Moltkestrasse 30, 76133 Karlsruhe, Germany
martin.sulzmann@hs-karlsruhe.de
kai.stadtmueller@live.de

Abstract. We consider the task of analyzing message-passing programs by observing their run-time behavior. We introduce a purely library-based instrumentation method to trace communication events during execution. A model of the dependencies among events can be constructed to identify potential bugs. Compared to the vector clock method, our approach is much simpler and has in general a significant lower run-time overhead. A further advantage is that we also trace events that could not commit. Thus, we can infer more alternative communications. This provides the user with additional information to identify potential bugs. We have fully implemented our approach in the Go programming language and provide a number of examples to substantiate our claims.

1 Introduction

We consider run-time analysis of programs that employ message-passing. Specifically, we consider the Go programming language [4] which integrates message-passing in the style of Communicating Sequential Processes (CSP) [6] into a C style language. We assume the program is instrumented to trace communication events that took place during program execution. Our objective is to analyze program traces to assist the user in identifying potential concurrency bugs.

Motivating Example In Listing 1.1 we find a Go program implementing a system of newsreaders. The `main` function creates two synchronous channels, one for each news agency. Go supports (a limited form of) type inference and therefore no type annotations are required. Next, we create one thread per news agency via the keyword `go`. Each news agency transmits news over its own channel. In Go, we write `ch <- "REUTERS"` to send value `"REUTERS"` via channel `ch`. We write `<-ch` to receive a value via channel `ch`. As we assume synchronous channels, both operations block and only unblock once a sender finds a matching receiver. We find two newsreader instances. Each newsreader creates two helper threads that wait for news to arrive and transfer any news that has arrived to a common channel. The intention is that the newsreader wishes to receive *any* news whether it be from Reuters or Bloomberg. However, there is a subtle bug (to be explained shortly).

© Springer International Publishing AG 2017
O. Strichman and R. Tzoref-Brill (Eds.): HVC 2017, LNCS 10629, pp. 83–98, 2017.
https://doi.org/10.1007/978-3-319-70389-3_6

```
func reuters(ch chan string) { ch <- "REUTERS" } // r!
func bloomberg(ch chan string) { ch <- "BLOOMBERG" } // b!

func newsReader(rCh chan string, bCh chan string) {
  ch := make(chan string)
  go func() { ch <- (<-rCh) }()          // r?; ch!
  go func() { ch <- (<-bCh) }()          // b?; ch!
  x := <-ch                              // ch?
}

func main() {
  reutersCh := make(chan string)
  bloombergCh := make(chan string)
  go reuters(reutersCh)
  go bloomberg(bloombergCh)
  go newsReader(reutersCh, bloombergCh) // N1
  newsReader(reutersCh, bloombergCh)    // N2
}
```

Listing 1.1. Message passing in Go

Trace-Based Run-Time Verification We only consider finite program runs and therefore each of the news agencies supplies only a finite number of news (exactly one in our case) and then terminates. During program execution, we trace communication events, e.g. send and receive, that took place. Due to concurrency, a bug may not manifest itself because a certain 'bad' schedule is rarely taken in practice.

Here is a possible trace resulting from a 'good' program run.

`r!; N1.r?; N1.ch!; N1.ch?; b!; N2.b?; N2.ch!; N2.ch?`

We write `r!` to denote that a send event via the Reuters channel took place. As there are two instances of the **newsReader** function, we write `N1.r?` to denote that a receive event via the local channel took place in case of the first **newsReader** call. From the trace we can conclude that the Reuters news was consumed by the first newsreader and the Bloomberg news by the second newsreader.

Here is a trace resulting from a bad program run.

`r!; b!; N1.r?; N1.b?; N1.ch!; N1.ch?; DEADLOCK`

The helper thread of the first newsreader receives the Reuters *and* the Bloomberg news. However, only one of these messages will actually be read (consumed). This is the bug! Hence, the second newsreader gets stuck and we encounter a deadlock. The issue is that such a bad program run may rarely show up. So, the question is how can we assist the user based on the trace information resulting from a good program run? How can we infer that alternative schedules and communications may exist?

Event Order via Vector Clock Method A well-established approach is to derive a partial order among events. This is usually achieved via a vector of (logical) clocks. The vector clock method was independently developed by Fidge [1] and Mattern [8]. For the above good program run, we obtain the following partial order among events.

```
r! < N1.r?          b! < N2.b?
N1.r? < N1.ch!      N2.b? < N2.ch!   (1)
N1.ch! < N1.ch?     N2.ch! < N2.ch?  (2)
```

For example, (1) arises because N2.ch! happens (sequentially) after N2.b? For synchronous send/receive, we assume that receive happens after send. See (2). Based on the partial order, we can conclude that alternative schedules are possible. For example, b! could take place before r!. However, it is not clear how to infer alternative communications. Recall that the issue is that one of the newsreaders may consume both news messages. Our proposed method is able to clearly identify this issue and has the advantage to require a much simpler instrumentation We discuss these points shortly. First, we take a closer look at the details of instrumentation for the vector clock method.

Vector clocks are a refinement of Lamport's time stamps [7]. Each thread maintains a vector of (logical) clocks of all participating partner threads. For each communication step, we advance and synchronize clocks. In pseudo code, the vector clock instrumentation for event sndR.

```
vc[reutersThread]++
ch <- ("REUTERS", vc, vcCh)
vc' := max(vc, <-vcCh)
```

We assume that vc holds the vector clock. The clock of the Reuters thread is incremented. Besides the original value, we transmit the sender's vector clock and a helper channel vcCh. For convenience, we use tuple notation. The sender's vector clock is updated by building the maximum among all entries of its own vector clock and the vector clock of the receiving party. The same vector clock update is carried out on the receiver side.

Our Method We propose a much simpler instrumentation and tracing method to obtain a partial order among events. Instead of a vector clock, each thread traces the events that might happen and have happened. We refer to them as pre and post events. In pseudo code, our instrumentation for sndR looks like follows.

```
pre(hash(ch), "!")
ch <- ("REUTERS", threadId)
post(hash(ch), "!")
```

The bang symbol ('!') indicates a send operation. Function **hash** builds a hash index of channel names. The sender transmits its thread id number to the receiver. This is the only intra-thread overhead. No extra communication link is necessary.

Here are the traces for individual threads resulting from the above good program run.

```
R:              pre(r!); post(r!)
N1_helper1:     pre(r?); post(R#r?); pre(ch1!); post(ch1!)
N1_helper2:     pre(b?)
N1:             pre(ch1?); post(N1_helper1#ch1?)
B:              pre(b!); post(b!)
N2_helper1:     pre(r?)
N2_helper2:     pre(b?); post(B#b?); pre(ch2!); post(ch2!)
N2:             pre(ch2?); post(N2_helper2#ch2?)
```

We write `pre(r!)` to indicate that a send via the Reuters channel might happen. We write `post(R#r?)` to indicate that a receive has happened via thread `R`. The partial order among events is obtained by a simple post-processing phase where we linearly scan through traces. For example, within a trace there is a strict order and therefore

```
N2_helper2:     pre(b?); post(B#b?); pre(ch2!); post(ch2!)
```

implies `N2.b? < N2.ch!`. Across threads we check for matching pre/post events. Hence,

```
R:              pre(r!); post(r!)
N1_helper1:     pre(r?); post(R#r?); ...
```

implies `r! < N1.r?`. So, we obtain the same (partial order) information as the vector clock approach but with less overhead.

The reduction in terms of tracing overhead compared to the vector clock method is rather drastic assuming a library-based tracing scheme with no access to the Go run-time system. For each communication event we must exchange vector clocks, i.e. n additional (time stamp) values need to be transmitted where n is the number of threads. Besides extra data to be transmitted, we also require an extra communication link because the sender requires the receivers vector clock. In contrast, our method incurs a constant tracing overhead. Each sender transmits in addition its thread id. No extra communication link is necessary. This results in *much* less run-time overhead as we will see later.

The vector clock tracing method can be improved assuming we extend the Go run-time system. For example, by maintaining a per-thread vector clock and having the run-time system carrying out the exchange of vector clocks for each send/receive communication. There is still the $O(n)$ space overhead. Our method does not require any extension of the Go run-time system to be efficient and therefore is also applicable to other languages that offer similar features as found in Go.

A further advantage of our method is that we also trace (via pre) events that could not commit (post is missing). Thus, we can easily infer alternative communications. For example, for `R: pre(r!); ...` there is the alternative match `N2_helper1: pre(r?)`. Hence, instead of `r! < N1.r?` also `r! < N2.r?` is possible. This indicates that one newsreader may consume both news message. The vector clock method, only traces events that could commit, post events in our notation. Hence, the above alternative communication could not be derived.

Contributions Compared to earlier works based on the vector clock method, we propose a much more light-weight and more informative instrumentation and tracing scheme. Specifically, we make the following contributions:

- We give a precise account of our run-time tracing method (Section 3) for message-passing as found in the Go programming language (Section 2) where for space reasons we only formalize the case of synchronous channels and selective communications.
- A simple analysis of the resulting traces allows us to detect alternative schedules and communications (Section 4). For efficiency reasons, we employ a directed dependency graph to represent happens-before relations (Section 4.1).
- We show that vector clocks can be easily recovered based on our tracing method (Section 5). We also discuss the pros and cons of both methods for analysis purposes.
- Our tracing method can be implemented efficiently as a library. We have fully implemented the approach supporting all Go language features dealing with message-passing such as buffered channels, select with default or timeout and closing of channels (Section 6).
- We provide experimental results measuring the often significantly lower overhead of our method compared to the vector clock method assuming based methods are implemented as libraries (Section 6.2).

The online version of this paper contains an appendix with further details.[1]

2 Message-Passing Go

Syntax For brevity, we consider a much simplified fragment of the Go programming language. We only cover straight-line code, i.e. omitting procedures, if-then-else etc. This is not an onerous restriction as we only consider finite program runs. Hence, any (finite) program run can be represented as a program consisting of straight-line code only.

Definition 1 (Program Syntax).

$x, y, \ldots$		*Variables, Channel Names*
$i, j, \ldots$		*Integers*
b	$::= x \mid i \mid \mathsf{hash}(x) \mid \mathsf{head}(b) \mid \mathsf{last}(b) \mid bs \mid \mathsf{tid}$	*Expressions*
bs	$::= [] \mid b : bs$	
e, f	$::= x \leftarrow b \mid y :=\leftarrow x$	*Transmit/Receive*
c	$::= y := b \mid y := \mathsf{makeChan} \mid \mathsf{go}\ p \mid \mathsf{select}\ [e_i \Rightarrow p_i]_{i \in I}$	*Commands*
p, q, r	$::= [] \mid c : p$	*Program*

For our purposes, values are integers or lists (slices in Go terminology). For lists we follow Haskell style notation and write $b : bs$ to refer to a list with head element b and tail bs. We can access the head and last element in a list via

---

[1] https://arxiv.org/abs/1709.01588

primitives head and last. We often write $[b_1, \ldots, b_n]$ as a shorthand $b_1 : \cdots : []$. Primitive tid yields the thread id number of the current thread. We assume that the main thread always has thread id number 1 and new thread id numbers are generated in increasing order. Primitive hash() yields a unique hash index for each variable name. Both primitives show up in our instrumentation.

A program is a sequence of commands where commands are stored in a list. Primitive makeChan creates a new synchronous channel. Primitive go creates a new go routine (thread). For send and receive over a channel we follow Go notation. We assume that a receive is always tied to an assignment. For assignment we use symbol := to avoid confusion with the mathematical equality symbol =. In Go, symbol := declares a new variable with some initial value. We also use := to overwrite the value of existing variables. As a message passing command we only support selective communication via select. Thus, we can fix the bug in our newsreader example.

```
func newsReaderFixed(rCh chan string, bCh chan string) {
  ch := make(chan string)
  select {
    case x := <-rCh:
    case x := <-bCh:
  }
}
```

The select statement guarantees that at most one news message will be consumed and blocks if no news are available. In our simplified language, we assume that the $x \leftarrow b$ command is a shorthand for select $[x \leftarrow b \Rightarrow []]$. For space reasons, we omit buffered channels, select paired with a default/timeout case and closing of channels. All three features are fully supported by our implementation.

Trace-Based Semantics The semantics of programs is defined via a small-step operational semantics. The semantics keeps track of the trace of channel-based communications that took place. This allows us to relate the traces obtained by our instrumentation with the actual run-time traces.

We support multi-threading via a reduction relation

$$(S, [i_1 \sharp p_1, \ldots, i_n \sharp p_n]) \xrightarrow{T} (S', [j_1 \sharp q_1, \ldots, j_n \sharp q_n]).$$

We write $i \sharp p$ to denote a program p that runs in its own thread with thread id i. We use lists to store the set of program threads. The state of program variables, before and after execution, is recorded in S and S'. We assume that threads share the same state. Program trace T records the sequence of communications that took place during execution. We write $x!$ to denote a send operation on channel x and $x?$ to denote a receiver operation on channel x. The semantics of expressions is defined in terms a big-step semantics. We employ a reduction relation $(i, S) \vdash b \Downarrow v$ where S is the current state, b the expression and v the result of evaluating b. The formal details follow.

Definition 2 (State).

$$
\begin{aligned}
v &::= x \mid i \mid [\,] \mid vs & \textit{Values} \\
vs &::= [\,] \mid v : vs \\
s &::= v \mid Chan & \textit{Storables} \\
S &::= (\,) \mid (x \mapsto s) \mid S \lhd S \;\textit{State}
\end{aligned}
$$

A state S is either empty, a mapping, or an override of two states. Each state maps variables to storables. A storable is either a plain value or a channel. Variable names may appear as values. In an actual implementation, we would identify the variable name by a unique hash index. We assume that mappings in the right operand of the map override operator $\lhd$ take precedence. They overwrite any mappings in the left operand. That is, $(x \mapsto v_1) \lhd (x \mapsto v_2) = (x \mapsto v_2)$.

Definition 3 (Expression Semantics $(i, S) \vdash b \Downarrow v$).

$$
\frac{S(x) = v}{(i, S) \vdash x \Downarrow v}
\qquad
(i, S) \vdash j \Downarrow j
\qquad
(i, S) \vdash [\,] \Downarrow [\,]
\qquad
\frac{(i, S) \vdash b \Downarrow v \;\; (i, S) \vdash bs \Downarrow vs}{(i, S) \vdash b : bs \Downarrow v : vs}
$$

$$
\frac{(i, S) \vdash b \Downarrow v : vs}{(i, S) \vdash \mathsf{head}(b) \Downarrow v}
\qquad
\frac{(i, S) \vdash b \Downarrow [v_1, \ldots, v_n]}{(i, S) \vdash \mathsf{last}(b) \Downarrow v_n}
\qquad
(i, S) \vdash \mathsf{tid} \Downarrow i
\qquad
(i, S) \vdash \mathsf{hash}(x) \Downarrow x
$$

Definition 4 (Program Execution $(S, P) \overset{T}{\Rightarrow} (S', Q)$).

$$
\begin{aligned}
&i \sharp p & &\textit{Single program thread} \\
P, Q &::= [\,] \mid i \sharp p : P & &\textit{Program threads} \\
t &:= i \sharp x! \mid i \leftarrow j \sharp x? & &\textit{Send and receive event} \\
T &::= [\,] \mid t : T & &\textit{Trace}
\end{aligned}
$$

We write $(S, P) \Rightarrow (S', Q)$ as a shorthand for $(S, P) \overset{[\,]}{\Rightarrow} (S', Q)$.

Definition 5 (Single Step).

$$
\textit{(Terminate)} \; (S, i \sharp [\,] : P) \Rightarrow (S, P)
$$

$$
\textit{(Assign)} \; \frac{(i, S) \vdash b \Downarrow v \quad S' = S \lhd (y \mapsto v)}{(S, i \sharp (y := b : p) : P) \Rightarrow (S', i \sharp p : P)}
$$

$$
\textit{(MakeChan)} \; \frac{S' = S \lhd (y \mapsto Chan)}{(S, i \sharp (y := \mathsf{makeChan} : p) : P) \Rightarrow (S', i \sharp p : P)}
$$

Definition 6 (Multi-Threading and Synchronous Message-Passing).

$$(Go) \frac{i \notin \{i_1, \ldots, i_n\}}{(S, i_1 \natural (go \ p : p_1) : P) \Rightarrow (S, i \natural p : i_1 \natural p_1 : P)}$$

$$(Sync) \frac{\exists l \in J, m \in K . e_l = x \leftarrow b \quad f_m = y :=\leftarrow x \quad S(x) = Chan \quad (i_1, S) \vdash b \Downarrow v \quad S' = S \lhd (y \mapsto v)}{(S, i_1 \natural (select \ [e_j \Rightarrow q_j]_{j \in J} : p_1) : i_2 \natural (select \ [f_k \Rightarrow r_k]_{k \in K} : p_2) : P)}$$

$$\xrightarrow{[i_1 \natural x!, i_2 \leftarrow i_1 \natural x?]}$$

$$(S', i_1 \natural (q_l \ {+\!\!+} \ p_1) : i_2 \natural (r_m \ {+\!\!+} \ p_2) : P)$$

Definition 7 (Scheduling).

$$(Schedule) \frac{\pi \ permutation \ on \ \{1, \ldots, n\}}{(S, [i_1 \natural p_1, \ldots, i_n \natural p_n]) \Rightarrow (S, [\pi(i_1) \natural p_{\pi(1)}, \ldots, \pi(i_n) \natural p_{\pi(n)}])}$$

$$(Closure) \frac{(S, P) \xrightarrow{T} (S', P') \quad (S', P') \xrightarrow{T'} (S'', P'')}{(S, P) \xrightarrow{T \ {+\!\!+} \ T'} (S'', P'')}$$

3   Instrumentation and Run-Time Tracing

For each message passing primitive (send/receive) we log two events. In case of send, (1) a *pre* event to indicate the message is about to be sent, and (2) a *post* event to indicate the message has been sent. The treatment is analogous for receive. In our instrumentation, we write $x!$ to denote a single send event and $x?$ to denote a single receive event. These notations are shorthands and can be expressed in terms of the language described so far. We use $\equiv$ to define short-forms and their encodings. We define $x! \equiv [\text{hash}(x), 1]$ and $x? \equiv [\text{hash}(x), 0]$. That is, send is represented by the number 1 and receive by the number 0.

As we support non-deterministic selection, we employ a list of pre events to indicate that one of several events may be chosen For example, $pre([x!, y?])$ indicates that there is the choice among sending over channel x and receiving over channel y. This is again a shorthand notation where we assume $pre([b_1, \ldots, b_n]) \equiv [0, b_1, \ldots, b_n]$.

A post event is always singleton as at most one of the possible communications is chosen. As we also trace communication partners, we assume that the sending party transmits its identity, the thread id, to the receiving party. We write $post(i \natural x?)$ to denote reception via channel x where the sender has thread id i. In case of a post send event, we simply write $post(x!)$. The above are yet again shorthands where $i \natural x? \equiv [\text{hash}(x), 0, i]$ and $post(b) \equiv [1, b]$.

Pre and post events are written in a fresh thread local variable, denoted by x_{tid} where *tid* refers to the thread's id number. At the start of the thread the variable is initialized by $x_{tid} := []$. Instrumentation ensures that pre and post events are appropriately logged. As we keep track of communication partners, we must also inject and project messages with additional information (the sender's thread id).

We consider instrumentation of select $[x \leftarrow 1 \Rightarrow [], y :=\leftarrow x \Rightarrow [z \leftarrow y]]$. We assume the above program text is part of a thread with id number 1. We non-deterministically choose between a send an receive operation. In case of receive, the received value is further transmitted. Instrumentation yields the following.

$$
\begin{aligned}
&[x_1 := x_1 \;\text{++}\; pre([x!, x?]), \\
&\quad \text{select } [x \leftarrow [\text{tid}, 1] \Rightarrow [x_1 := x_1 \;\text{++}\; post(x!)], \\
&\qquad\quad y' :=\leftarrow x \Rightarrow [x_1 := x_1 \;\text{++}\; post(\text{head}(y')\sharp x?), y := \text{last}(y'), \\
&\qquad\qquad\qquad z \leftarrow [\text{tid}, y]]]
\end{aligned}
$$

We first store the pre events, either a read or send via channel x. The send is instrumented by additionally transmitting the senders thread id. The post event for this case simply logs that a send took place. Instrumentation of receive is slightly more involved. As senders supply their thread id, we introduce a fresh variable y'. Via $\text{head}(y')$ we extract the senders thread id to properly record the communication partner in the post event. The actual value transmitted is accessed via $\text{last}(y')$.

Definition 8 (Instrumentation of Programs). *We write $instr(p) = q$ to denote the instrumentation of program p where q is the result of instrumentation. Function $instr(\cdot)$ is defined by structural induction on a program. We assume a similar instrumentation function for commands.*

$$
\begin{aligned}
instr([]) &= [] \\
instr(c : p) &= instr(c) : instr(p) \\[6pt]
instr(y := b) &= [y := b] \\
instr(y := \text{makeChan}) &= [y := \text{makeChan}] \\
instr(\text{go } p) &= [\text{go } ([x_{tid} := []\; \text{++}\; instr(p)])] \\
instr(\text{select } [e_i \Rightarrow p_i]_{i \in \{1,\dots,n\}}) &= [x_{tid} := x_{tid} \;\text{++}\; [pre([retr(e_1), \dots, retr(e_n)])]], \\
&\quad\quad \text{select } [instr(e_i \Rightarrow p_i)]_{i \in \{1,\dots,n\}}] \\
instr(x \leftarrow b \Rightarrow p) &= x \leftarrow [\text{tid}, b] \Rightarrow (x_{tid} := x_{tid} \;\text{++}\; [post(x!)]) \;\text{++}\; instr(p) \\
instr(y :=\leftarrow x \Rightarrow p) &= y' :=\leftarrow x \Rightarrow [x_{tid} := x_{tid} \;\text{++}\; [post(\text{head}(y')\sharp x?)], \\
&\quad\quad y := \text{last}(y')] \;\text{++}\; instr(p)
\end{aligned}
$$

$$
retr(x \leftarrow b) = x! \qquad retr(y =\leftarrow x) = x?
$$

Run-time tracing proceeds as follows. We simply run the instrumented program and extract the local traces connected to variables x_{tid}. We assume that thread id numbers are created during program execution and can be enumerated by $1 \dots n$ for some $n > 0$ where thread id number 1 belongs to the main thread.

Definition 9 (Run-Time Tracing). *Let p and q be programs such that $instr(p) = q$. We consider a specific instrumented program run where $((), [1\sharp[x_1 := []] ++ q]) \stackrel{T}{\Rightarrow} (S, 1\sharp[] : P)$ for some S, T and P. Then, we refer to T as p's* actual run-time trace. *We refer to the list $[1\sharp S(x_1), \ldots, n\sharp S(x_n)]$ as the* local traces *obtained via the instrumentation of p.*

Command $x_1 := []$ is added to the instrumented program to initialize the trace of the main thread. Recall that main has thread id number 1. This extra step is necessary because our instrumentation only initializes local traces of threads generated via **go**. The final configuration $(S, 1\sharp[] : P)$ indicates that the main thread has run to full completion. This is a realistic assumption as we assume that programs exhibit no obvious bug during execution. There might still be some pending threads, in case P differs from the empty list.

4   Trace Analysis

We assume that the program has been instrumented and after some program run we obtain a list of local traces. We show that the actual run-time trace can be recovered and we are able to point out alternative behaviors that could have taken place. Alternative behaviors are either due alternative schedules or different choices among communication partners.

We consider the list of local traces $[1\sharp S(x_1), \ldots, n\sharp S(x_n)]$. Their shape can be characterized as follows.

Definition 10 (Local Traces).

$$
\begin{aligned}
U, V &::= [] \mid i\sharp L : U \\
L &::= [] \mid pre(as) : M \\
as &::= [] \mid x! : as \mid x? : as \\
M &::= [] \mid post(x!) : L \mid post(i\sharp x?) : L
\end{aligned}
$$

We refer to $U = [1\sharp L_1, \ldots, n\sharp L_n]$ as a residual list of local traces if for each L_i either $L_i = []$ or $L_i = [pre(\ldots)]$.

To recover the communications that took place we check for matching pre and post events recorded in the list of local traces. For this purpose, we introduce a relation $U \stackrel{T}{\Rightarrow} V$ to denote that 'replaying' of U leads to V where communications T took place. Valid replays are defined via the following rules.

Definition 11 (Replay $U \overset{T}{\Rightarrow} V$).

$$(Sync) \quad \frac{\begin{array}{c} L_1 = pre([\ldots, x!, \ldots]) : post(x!) : L_1' \\ L_2 = pre([\ldots, x?, \ldots]) : post(i_1 \sharp x?) : L_2' \end{array}}{i_1 \sharp L_1 : i_2 \sharp L_2 : U \xrightarrow{[i_1 \sharp x!, i_2 \leftarrow i_1 \sharp x?]} i_1 \sharp L_1' : i_2 \sharp L_2' : U}$$

$$(Schedule) \quad \frac{\pi \ permutation \ on \ \{1, \ldots, n\}}{[i_1 \sharp L_1, \ldots, i_n \sharp L_n] \overset{[]}{\Rightarrow} [i_{\pi(1)} \sharp L_{\pi(1)}, \ldots, i_{\pi(n)} \sharp L_{\pi(n)}]}$$

$$(Closure) \quad \frac{U \overset{T}{\Rightarrow} U' \quad U' \overset{T'}{\Rightarrow} U''}{U \xrightarrow{T \ + \! + \ T'} U''}$$

Rule (Sync) checks for matching communication partners. In each trace, we must find complementary pre events and the post events must match as well. Recall that in the instrumentation the sender transmits its thread id to the receiver. Rule (Schedule) shuffles the local traces as rule (Sync) only considers the two leading local traces. Via rule (Closure) we perform repeated replay steps.

We can state that the actual run-time trace can be obtained via the replay relation $U \overset{T}{\Rightarrow} V$ but further run-time traces are possible. This is due to alternative schedules.

Proposition 1 (Replay Yields Run-Time Traces). *Let p be a program and q its instrumentation where for a specific program run we observe the actual behavior T and the list $[1 \sharp L_1, \ldots, n \sharp L_n]$ of local traces. Let $\mathcal{T} = \{T' \mid [1 \sharp L_1, \ldots, n \sharp L_n] \overset{T'}{\Rightarrow} 1 \sharp [] : U \ for \ some \ residual \ U\}$. Then, we find that $T \in \mathcal{T}$ and for each $T' \in \mathcal{T}$ we have that $((), p) \overset{T'}{\Rightarrow} (S, 1 \sharp [] : P)$ for some S and P.*

Definition 12 (Alternative Schedules). *We say $[1 \sharp L_1, \ldots, n \sharp L_n]$ contains alternative schedules iff the cardinality of the set $\{T' \mid [1 \sharp L_1, \ldots, n \sharp L_n] \overset{T'}{\Rightarrow} 1 \sharp [] : U \ for \ some \ residual \ U\}$ is greater than one.*

We can also check if even further run-time traces might have been possible by testing for alternative communications.

Definition 13 (Alternative Communications). *We say $[1 \sharp L_1, \ldots, n \sharp L_n]$ contains alternative matches iff for some i, j, x, L, L' we have that (1) $L_i = pre([\ldots, x!, \ldots]) : L$, (2) $L_j = pre([\ldots, x?, \ldots]) : L'$, and (3) if $L = post(x!) : L''$ for some L'' then $L' \neq post(j \sharp x?) : L'''$ for any L'''.*

We say $U = [1 \sharp L_1, \ldots, n \sharp L_n]$ contains alternative communications iff U contains alternative matches or there exists T and V such that $U \overset{T}{\Rightarrow} V$ and V contains alternative matches.

The alternative match condition states that a sender could synchronize with a receiver (see (1) and (2)) but this synchronization did not take place (see (3)). For an alternative match to result in an alternative communication, the match must be along a possible run-time trace.

$$[x := \mathsf{makeChan}, y := \mathsf{makeChan},$$
$$\mathsf{go}\ [z := (\leftarrow y)_6], \mathsf{go}\ [(y \leftarrow 1)_4, (x \leftarrow 1)_5], \mathsf{go}\ [(x \leftarrow 1)_3],$$
$$x := (\leftarrow x)_1, x := (\leftarrow x)_2]$$

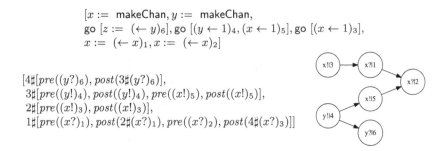

$[4\sharp[pre((y?)_6), post(3\sharp(y?)_6)],$
$3\sharp[pre((y!)_4), post((y!)_4), pre((x!)_5), post((x!)_5)],$
$2\sharp[pre((x!)_3), post((x!)_3)],$
$1\sharp[pre((x?)_1), post(2\sharp(x?)_1), pre((x?)_2), post(4\sharp(x?)_3)]]$

Fig. 1: Dependency Graph among Events

4.1   Dependency Graph for Efficient Trace Analysis

Instead of replaying traces to check for alternative schedules and communications, we build a dependency graph where the graph captures the partial order among events. It is much more efficient to carry out the analysis on the graph than replaying traces. Figure 1 shows a simple example.

We find a program that makes use of two channels and four threads. For reference, send/receive events are annotated (as subscript) with unique numbers. We omit the details of instrumentation and assume that for a specific program run we find the list of given traces on the left. Pre events consist of singleton lists as there is no select. Hence, we write $pre((y?)_6)$ as a shorthand for $pre([(y?)_6])$. Replay of the trace shows that the following locations synchronize with each other: $(4, 6)$, $(3, 1)$ and $(5, 2)$. This information as well as the order among events can be captured by a dependency graph. Nodes are obtained by a linear scan through the list of traces. To derive edges, we require another scan for each element in a trace as we need to find pre/post pairs belonging to matching synchronizations. This results overall in $O(m * m)$ for the construction of the graph where m is the number of elements found in each trace. To avoid special treatment of dangling pre events (with not subsequent post event), we assume that some dummy post events are added to the trace.

Definition 14 (Construction of Dependency Graph). *Each node corresponds to a send or a receive operation in the program text. Edges are constructed by observing events recorded in the list of traces. We draw a (directed) edge among nodes if either*

- *the pre and post events of one node precede the pre and post events of another node in the trace, or*
- *the pre and post events belonging to both nodes can be synchronized. See rule (Sync) in Definition 11. We assume that the edge starts from the node with the send operation.*

Applied to our example, this results in the graph on the right. See Figure 1. For example, $x!|3$ denotes a send communication over channel x at program location 3. As send precedes receive we find an edge from $x!|3$ to $x?|1$. In general, there may be several initial nodes. By construction, each node has at most one outgoing edge but may have multiple incoming edges.

The trace analysis can be carried out directly on the dependency graph. To check if one event happens-before another event we seek for a path from one event to the other. This can be done via a depth-first search and takes time $O(v + e)$ where v is the number of nodes and e the number of edges. Two events are concurrent if neither happens-before the other. To check for alternative communications, we check for matching nodes that are concurrent to each other. By matching we mean that one of the nodes is a send and the other is a receive over the same channel. For our example, we find that $x!|5$ and $x?|1$ represents an alternative communication as both nodes are matching and concurrent to each other.

To derive (all) alternative schedules, we perform a backward traversal of the graph. Backward in the sense that we traverse the graph by moving from children to parent node. We start with some final node (no outgoing edge). Each node visited is marked. We proceed to the parent if all children are marked. Thus, we guarantee that the happens-before relation is respected. For our example, suppose we visit first $y?6$. We cannot visit its parent $y!4$ until we have visited $x?2$ and $x!5$. Via a (backward) breadth-first search we can 'accumulate' all schedules.

5   Comparison to Vector Clock Method

Via a simple adaptation of the Replay Definition 11 we can attach vector clocks to each send and receive event. Hence, our tracing method strictly subsumes the vector clock method as we are also able to trace events that could not commit.

Definition 15 (Vector Clock).

$$cs ::= [] \mid n : cs$$

For convenience, we represent a vector clock as a list of clocks where the first position belongs to thread 1 etc. We write $cs[i]$ to retrieve the i-th component in cs. We write $\mathsf{inc}(i, cs)$ to denote the vector clock obtained from cs where all elements are the same but at index i the element is incremented by one. We write $\mathsf{max}(cs_1, cs_2)$ to denote the vector clock where we per-index take the greater element. We write i^{cs} to denote thread i with vector clock cs. We write $i \sharp x!^{cs}$ to denote a send over channel x in thread i with vector clock cs. We write $i \leftarrow j \sharp x?^{cs}$ to denote a receive over channel x in thread i from thread j with vector clock cs.

Definition 16 (From Trace Replay to Vector Clocks).

$$(Sync) \quad \frac{\begin{array}{c} L_1 = pre([\ldots, x!, \ldots]) : post(x!) : L_1' \\ L_2 = pre([\ldots, x?, \ldots]) : post(i_1 \sharp x?) : L_2' \\ cs = \mathsf{max}(\mathsf{inc}(i_1, cs_1), \mathsf{inc}(i_2, cs_2)) \end{array}}{i_1^{cs_1} \sharp L_1 : i_2^{cs_2} \sharp L_2 : U \xrightarrow{[i_1 \sharp x!^{cs}, i_2 \leftarrow i_1 \sharp x?^{cs}]} i_1^{cs} \sharp L_1' : i_2^{cs} \sharp L_2' : U}$$

Like the construction of the dependency graph, the (re)construction of vector clocks takes time $O(m * m)$ where m is the number of elements found in each trace.

To check for an alternative communication, the vector clock method seeks for matching events. This incurs the same (quadratic in the size of the trace) cost as for our method. However, the check that these two events are concurrent to each other can be performed more efficiently via vector clocks. Comparison of vector clocks takes time $O(n)$ where n is the number of threads. Recall that our graph-based method requires time $O(v + e)$ where v is the number of nodes and e the number of edges. The number n is smaller than $v + e$.

However, our dependency graph representation is more efficient in case of exploring alternative schedules. In case of the vector clock method, we need to continuously compare vector clocks whereas we only require a (backward) traversal of the graph. We believe that the dependency graph has further advantages in case of user interaction and visualization as it is more intuitive to navigate through the graph. This is something we intend to investigate in future work.

6   Implementation

We have fully integrated the approach laid out in the earlier sections into the Go programming language and have built a prototype tool. We give an overview of our implementation which can be found here [5]. A detailed treatment of all of Go's message-passing features can be found in the extended version of this paper.

6.1   Library-Based Instrumentation and Tracing

We use a pre-processor to carry out the instrumentation as described in Section 3. In our implementation, each thread maintains an entry in a lock-free hashmap where each entry represents a thread (trace). The hashmap is written to file either at the end of the program or when a deadlock occurs. We currently do not deal with the case that the program crashes as we focus on the detection of potential bugs in programs that do not show any abnormal behavior.

6.2   Measurement of Run-Time Overhead Library-Based Tracing

We measure the run-time overhead of our method against the vector clock method. Both methods are implemented as libraries assuming no access to the Go run-time system. For experimentation we use three programs where each program exercises some of the factors that have an impact on tracing. For example, dynamic versus static number of threads and channels. Low versus high amount of communication among threads.

The **Add-Pipe (AP)** example uses n threads where the first $n - 1$ threads receive on an input channel, add one to the received value and then send the new value on their output channel to the next thread. The first thread sends the initial value and receives the result from the last thread.

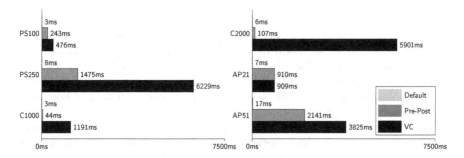

Fig. 2: Performance overhead using Pre/Post vs Vector clocks(VC) in ms.

In the **Primesieve (PS)** example, the communication among threads is similar to the **Add-Pipe** example. The difference is that threads and channels are dynamically generated to calculate the first n prime numbers. For each found prime number a 'filter' thread is created. Each thread has an input channel to receive new possible prime numbers v and an output channel to report each number for which $v \mod prime \neq 0$ where $prime$ is the prime number associated with this filter thread. The filter threads are run in a chain where the first thread stores the prime number 2.

The **Collector (C)** example creates n threads that produce a number which is then sent to the main thread for collection. This example has much fewer communications compared to the other examples but uses a high number of threads.

Figure 2 summarizes our results. Results are carried out on some commodity hardware (Intel i7-6600U with 12 GB RAM, a SSD and Go 1.8.3 running on Windows 10 was used for the tests). Our results show that a library-based implementation of the vector clock method does not scale well for examples with a dynamic number of threads and/or a high amount communication among threads. See examples **Primesieve** and **Add-Pipe**. None of the vector clock optimizations [3] apply here because of the dynamic number of threads and channels. Our method performs much better. This is no surprise as we require less (tracing) data and no extra communication links. We believe that the overhead can still be further reduced as access to the thread id in Go is currently rather cumbersome and expensive.

7 Conclusion

One of the challenges of run-time verification in the concurrent setting is to establish a partial order among recorded events. Thus, we can identify potential bugs due to bad schedules that are possible but did not take place in some specific program run. Vector clocks are the predominant method to achieve this task. For example, see work by Vo [11] in the MPI setting and work by Tasharofi [10] in the actor setting. There are several works that employ vector clocks in the shared memory setting For example, see Pozniansky's and Schuster's work [9] on data race detection. Some follow-up work by Flanagan and Freund [2] employs some optimizations to reduce the tracing overhead by recording only a single clock instead of the entire vector. We leave to future work to investigate whether such optimizations are applicable in the message-passing setting and how they compare to existing optimizations such as [3].

We have introduced a novel tracing method that has much less overhead compared to the vector clock method. Our method can deal with all of Go's message-passing language features and can be implemented efficiently as a library. We have built a prototype that can automatically identify alternative schedules and communications. In future work we plan to conduct some case studies and integrate heuristics for specific scenarios, e.g. reporting a send operation on a closed channel etc.

Acknowledgments

We thank some HVC'17 reviewers for their constructive feedback on an earlier version of this paper.

References

1. C. J. Fidge. Timestamps in message-passing systems that preserve the partial ordering. 10(1):56–66, 1987.
2. C. Flanagan and S. N. Freund. Fasttrack: Efficient and precise dynamic race detection. In *Proc. of PLDI '09*, pages 121–133. ACM, 2009.
3. V. K. Garg, C. Skawratananond, and N. Mittal. Timestamping messages and events in a distributed system using synchronous communication. *Distributed Computing*, 19(5-6):387–402, 2007.
4. The Go programming language. https://golang.org/.
5. Trace-based run-time analysis of message-passing Go programs. https://github.com/KaiSta/gopherlyzer-GoScout.
6. C. A. R. Hoare. Communicating sequential processes. *Commun. ACM*, 21(8):666–677, Aug. 1978.
7. L. Lamport. Time, clocks, and the ordering of events in a distributed system. *Communications of the ACM*, 21(7):558–565, 1978.
8. F. Mattern. Virtual time and global states of distributed systems. In *Parallel and Distributed Algorithms*, pages 215–226. North-Holland, 1989.
9. E. Pozniansky and A. Schuster. Multirace: efficient on-the-fly data race detection in multithreaded C++ programs. *Concurrency and Computation: Practice and Experience*, 19(3):327–340, 2007.
10. S. Tasharofi. *Efficient testing of actor programs with non-deterministic behaviors.* PhD thesis, University of Illinois at Urbana-Champaign, 2013.
11. A. Vo. *Scalable Formal Dynamic Verification of Mpi Programs Through Distributed Causality Tracking.* PhD thesis, University of Utah, 2011. AAI3454168.

Software Verification: Testing vs. Model Checking
A Comparative Evaluation of the State of the Art

Dirk Beyer and Thomas Lemberger

LMU Munich, Germany

Abstract. In practice, software testing has been the established method for finding bugs in programs for a long time. But in the last 15 years, software model checking has received a lot of attention, and many successful tools for software model checking exist today. We believe it is time for a careful comparative evaluation of automatic software testing against automatic software model checking. We chose six existing tools for automatic test-case generation, namely AFL-FUZZ, CPATIGER, CREST-PPC, FSHELL, KLEE, and PRTEST, and four tools for software model checking, namely CBMC, CPA-SEQ, ESBMC-INCR, and ESBMC-KIND, for the task of finding specification violations in a large benchmark suite consisting of 5 693 C programs. In order to perform such an evaluation, we have implemented a framework for test-based falsification (TBF) that executes and validates test cases produced by test-case generation tools in order to find errors in programs. The conclusion of our experiments is that software model checkers can (i) find a substantially larger number of bugs (ii) in less time, and (iii) require less adjustment to the input programs.

1 Introduction

Software testing has been the standard technique for identifying software bugs for decades. The exhaustive and sound alternative, software model checking, is believed to be immature for practice. Some often-named disadvantages are the need for experts in formal verification, extreme resource consumption, and maturity issues when it comes to handling large software systems.

But are these concerns still true today? We claim that the answer is No, and show with experiments on a large benchmark of C programs that software model checkers even find more bugs than testers. We found it is time for a comparative evaluation of testing tools against model-checking tools, motivated by the success of software model checkers as demonstrated in the annual International Competition on Software Verification (SV-COMP) [4], and by the move of development groups of large software systems towards formal verification, such as Facebook [1], Microsoft [2,44], and Linux [38].

Our contribution is a thorough experimental comparison of software testers against software model checkers. We performed our experimental study on 5 693 programs from a widely-used and state-of-the-art benchmarking set.[2] To represent the state of the art in terms of tools, we use AFL-FUZZ, CPATIGER,

---

[1] http://fbinfer.com/   [2] https://github.com/sosy-lab/sv-benchmarks

© Springer International Publishing AG 2017
O. Strichman and R. Tzoref-Brill (Eds.): HVC 2017, LNCS 10629, pp. 99–114, 2017.
https://doi.org/10.1007/978-3-319-70389-3_7

CREST-PPC, FSHELL, KLEE, and PRTEST as software testers, and CBMC, CPA-SEQ, ESBMC-INCR, and ESBMC-KIND as software model checkers.[3] The goal in our study is to evaluate the ability to reliably find specification violations in software. While the technique of model checking was originally developed as a proof technique for showing formal correctness, rather than for efficiently finding bugs, this study evaluates all tools exclusively against the goal of finding bugs.

To make the test generators comparable, we developed a unifying framework for test-based falsification (TBF) that interfaces between input programs, test generators, and test cases. For each tester, the infrastructure needs to (a) prepare the input program source code to match the input format that the tester expects and can consume, (b) run the tester to generate test cases, (c) extract test vectors from the tester's proprietary format for the produced test cases, and (d) execute the tests using a test harness to validate whether the generated test cases cover the bug in the program under test (i.e., whether at least one test case exposes the bug). If a bug is found, the framework outputs a witnessing test case in two different, human- and machine-readable formats: (1) a compilable test harness that can be used to directly provoke the bug in the program through execution and (2) a violation witness in a common exchange format for witnesses [7], which can be given to a witness validator to check the specification violation formally or by execution. This allows us to use input programs, produce executable tests, and check program behavior independently from a specific tester's quirks and requirements. We make the following contributions:

- Our framework, TBF, makes AFL-FUZZ, CPATIGER, CREST-PPC, FSHELL, KLEE, and PRTEST applicable to a large benchmark set of C programs, without any manual pre-processing. It is easily possible to integrate new tools. TBF is available online and completely open-source.[4]

- TBF provides two different, human-readable output formats for test cases generated by AFL-FUZZ, CPATIGER, CREST-PPC, FSHELL, KLEE, and PRTEST, and can validate whether a test case describes a specification violation for a program under test. Previously, there was no way to automatically generate test cases with any of the existing tools that are (i) executable and (ii) available in an exchangeable format. This helps in understanding test cases and supports debugging.

- We perform the first comparison regarding bug finding of test-case generation tools and software model checkers at a large scale. The experiments give the interesting insight that software model checkers can identify more program bugs than the existing test-case generators, using less time. All our experimental data and results are available on a supplementary web page.[5]

---

[3] The choice of using C programs is justified by the fact that C is still the most-used language for safety-critical software. Thus, one can assume that this is reflected in the research community and that the best test-generation and model checking technology is implemented in tools for C. The choice of the particular repository is justified by the fact that this is the largest and most diverse open benchmark suite (cf. SV-COMP [4]).

[4] https://github.com/sosy-lab/tbf   [5] https://www.sosy-lab.org/research/test-study/

Related Work. A large-scale comparative evaluation of the bug-finding capabilities of software testers and software model checkers is missing in the literature and this work is a first contribution towards filling this gap. In the area of software model checking, SV-COMP serves as a yearly comparative evaluation of a large set of model checkers for C programs and the competition report provides an overview over tools and techniques [4]. A general survey over techniques for software model checking is available [37]. In the area of software testing, there is work comparing test-case generators [28]. Surveys provide an overview of different test techniques [1] and a detailed web site is available that provides an overview over tools and techniques [6].

2   Background: Technology and Tools

In this paper, we consider only fully automatic techniques for testing and model checking of whole programs. This means that (i) a verification task consists of a program (with function `main` as entry) and a specification (reduced to reachability of function `__VERIFIER_error` by instrumentation), (ii) the comparison excludes all approaches for partial verification, such as unit testing and procedure summarization, and (iii) the comparison excludes all approaches that require interaction as often needed for deductive verification.

2.1   Software Testing

Given a software system and a specification of that system, testing executes the system with different input values and observes whether the intended behavior is exhibited (i.e., the specification holds). A *test vector* $\langle \eta_1, \cdots, \eta_n \rangle$ is a sequence of n input values η_1 to η_n. A *test case* is described by a test vector, where the i-th input of the test case is given by the i-th value η_i of the test vector. A *test suite* is a set of test cases. A *test harness* is a software that supports the automatic execution of a test case for the program under test, i.e., it feeds the values from the test vector one by one as input to the program. *Test-case generation* produces a set of test vectors that fulfills a specific coverage criterion. Program-branch coverage is an example of a well-established coverage criterion.

There are three major approaches to software test-case generation: symbolic or concolic execution [18, 19, 29, 39, 45, 46], random fuzz testing [30, 36], and model checking [5, 10, 35]. In this work, we use one tester based on symbolic execution (KLEE), one based on concolic execution (CREST-PPC), one based on random generation (PRTEST), one based on random fuzzing (AFL-FUZZ), and two based on model-checking (CPATIGER and FSHELL), which we describe in the following in alphabetic order. Table 1 gives an overview over testers and model checkers. **AFL-FUZZ** [17] is a coverage-based greybox fuzzer. Given a set of start inputs, it performs different mutations (e.g., bit flips, simple arithmetics) on the existing inputs, executes these newly created inputs, and checks which parts of the program are explored. Depending on these, it decides which inputs to keep, and which to use for further mutations. *Output:* AFL-FUZZ outputs each generated

---

[6] Provided by Z. Micskei: `http://mit.bme.hu/~micskeiz/pages/code_based_test_generation.html`

Table 1: Overview of test generators and model checkers used in the comparison

Tool	Ref.	Version	Technique
AFL-fuzz	[17]	2.46b	Greybox fuzzing
Crest-ppc	[39]	f542298d	Concolic execution, search-based
CPATiger	[10]	r24658	Model checking-based testing, based on CPAchecker
FShell	[35]	1.7	Model checking-based testing, based on Cbmc
Klee	[19]	c08cb14c	Symbolic execution, search-based
PRtest		0.1	Random testing
Cbmc	[40]	sv-comp17	Bounded model checking
CPA-Seq	[25]	sv-comp17	Explicit-state, predicate abstraction, k-Induction
Esbmc-incr	[43]	sv-comp17	Bounded model checking, incremental loop bound
Esbmc-kInd	[27]	sv-comp17	Bounded model checking, k-Induction

test case in its own file. The file's binary representation is read 'as is' as input, so generated test cases do not have a specific format.

CPATiger [10] uses model checking, more specifically, predicate abstraction [12], for test case generation. Is is based on the software-verification tool CPAchecker [11] and uses the FShell query language (FQL) [35] for specification of coverage criteria. If CPATiger finds a feasible program path to a coverage criterion with predicate abstraction, it computes test inputs from the corresponding predicates used along that path. It is designed to create test vectors for complicated coverage criteria. *Output:* CPATiger outputs generated test cases in a single text file, providing the test input as test vectors in decimal notation together with additional information.

Crest [18] uses concolic execution for test-case generation. It is search-based, i.e., it chooses test inputs that reach yet uncovered parts of the program furthest from the already explored paths. Crest-ppc [39] improves on the concolic execution used in Crest by modifying the input generation method to query the constraint solver more often, but using only a small set of constraints for each query. We performed experiments to ensure that Crest-ppc outperforms Crest. The results are available on our supplementary web page. *Output:* Crest-ppc outputs each generated test case in a text file, listing the sequence of used input values in decimal notation.

FShell [35] is another model-checking-based test-case generator. It uses CBMC (described in Sect. 2.2) for state-space exploration and also uses FQL for specification of coverage criteria. *Output:* FShell outputs generated test cases in a single text file, listing input values of tests together with additional information. Input values of tests are represented in decimal notation.

Klee [19] uses symbolic execution for test-case generation. After each step in a program, Klee chooses which of the existing program paths to continue on next, based on different heuristics, including a search-based one and one preventing inefficient unrolling of loops. Since Klee uses symbolic execution, it can explore the full state space of a program and can be used for software verification, not just test-case generation. As we are interested in exploring the capabilities of testing, we only consider the test cases produced by KLEE. *Output:* KLEE outputs each generated test case in a binary format that can be read with KLEE. The input values of tests are represented by their bit width and bit representation. **PRTEST** is a simple tool for plain random testing. The tool is delivered together with TBF and serves as base line in our experiments. *Output:* PRTEST outputs each generated test case in a text file, listing the sequence of used input values in hexadecimal notation.

2.2   Software Model Checking

Software model checking tries to prove a program correct or find a property violation in a program, by exploring the full state space and checking whether any of the feasible program states violate the specification. A lot of different techniques exist to do this. Since the number of concrete states of a program can be, in general, infinite, a common principle is *abstraction*. A good abstraction is, on the one hand, as coarse as possible —to keep the state space that must be explored small— and, on the other hand, precise enough to eliminate false alarms.

Tools for software model checking combine many different techniques, for example, counterexample-guided abstraction refinement (CEGAR) [21], predicate abstraction [31], bounded model checking (BMC) [16, 22], lazy abstraction [9, 34], k-induction [8, 27], and interpolation [23, 42]. A listing of the widely-used techniques, and which tools implement which technique, is given in the SV-COMP'17 report [4] in Table 4. In this work, we use a general-purpose bounded model checker (CBMC), a sequential combination of approaches (CPA-SEQ), a bounded model checker with incrementally increasing bounds (ESBMC-INCR), and a k-induction based model checker (ESBMC-KIND).

CBMC [22, 40] uses bit-precise BMC with MiniSat [26] as SAT-solver backend. BMC performs model checking with limited loop unrolling, i.e., loops are only unrolled up to a given bound. If no property violation can be found in the explored state space under this restriction, the program is assumed to be safe in general.

CPA-SEQ [25] is based on CPACHECKER that combines explicit-state model checking [13], k-induction [8], and predicate analysis with adjustable-block abstraction [12] sequentially. CPA-SEQ uses the bit-precise SMT solver MATHSAT5 [20].

ESBMC-INCR [43] is a fork of CBMC with an improved memory model. It uses an iterative scheme to increase its loop bounds, i.e., if no error is found in a program analysis using a certain loop bound, then the bound is increased. If no error is found after a set number of iterations, the program is assumed to be safe.

ESBMC-KIND [27] uses automatic k-induction to compute loop invariants in the context-bounded model checking of ESBMC. It performs the three phases of k-induction in parallel, which often yields a performance advantage.

2.3   Validation of Results

It is well-understood that when testers and model checkers produce test cases and error paths, respectively, sometimes the results contain false alarms. In order to avoid investing time on false results, test cases can be validated by reproducing a real crash [24, 41] and error paths can be evaluated by witness validation [7, 15]. A *violation witness* is an automaton that describes a set of paths through the

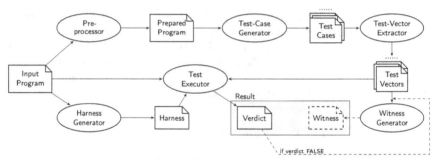

Fig. 1: Workflow of TBF

program that contain a specification violation. Each state transition contains a *source-code guard* that specifies the program-code locations at which the transition is allowed, and a *state-space guard* that constrains the set of possible program states after the transition. We considered four existing witness validators.

CPAchecker [7] uses predicate analysis with adjustable-block abstraction combined with explicit-state model checking for witness validation.

CPA-witness2test[7] creates a compilable test harness from a violation witness and checks whether the specification violation is reached through execution.

FShell-witness2test[8] also performs execution-based witness validation, but does not rely on any verification tool.

Ultimate Automizer [32] uses an automata-centric approach [33] to model checking for witness validation.

In this work, we evaluate the results from testers with TBF by considering for each test case, one by one, whether compiled with a test harness and the program, the execution violates the specification, and we evaluate the results of model checkers by validating the violation witness using four different witness validators. This way, we count bug reports only if they can be reproduced.

3   Framework for Test-Based Falsification

We designed a framework for test-based falsification (TBF) that makes it possible to uniformly use test-case generation tools. Figure 1 shows the architecture of this approach. Given an input program, TBF first pre-processes the program into the format that the test-case generator requires ('prepared program'). This includes, e.g., adding function definitions for assigning new symbolic values and compiling the program in a certain way expected by the generator. The prepared program is then given to the test-case generator, which stores its output in its own, proprietary format ('test cases'). These test cases are given to a test-vector extractor to extract the test vectors and store them in an exchangeable, uniform format ('test vectors'). The harness generator produces a test harness for the input program, which is compiled and linked together with the input program and executed by the test executor. If the execution reports a specification violation, the verdict is FALSE. In all other cases, the verdict

---

[7] https://github.com/sosy-lab/cpachecker

[8] https://github.com/tautschnig/cprover-sv-comp/tree/test-gen/witness2test

```
int nondet_int();
short nondet_short();
void __VERIFIER_error();

int main() {
  int x = nondet_int();
  int y = x;

  if (nondet_short()) {
    x++;
  } else {
    y++;
  }

  if (x > y) {
    __VERIFIER_error();
  }
}
```

Fig. 2: An example C program

```
int nondet_int(){
    int __sym;
    CREST_int(__sym);
    return __sym;
}
```

Fig. 3: A function definition prepared for CREST-PPC

```
void __VERIFIER_error() {
  fprintf(stderr, "__TBF_error_found.\n");
  exit(1);
}

int nondet_int() {
  unsigned int inp_size = 3000;
  char * inp_var = malloc(inp_size);
  fgets(inp_var, inp_size, stdin);
  return *((int *) parse_inp(inp_var));
}

short nondet_short() {
  unsigned int inp_size = 3000;
  char * inp_var = malloc(inp_size);
  fgets(inp_var, inp_size, stdin);
  return *((short *) parse_inp(inp_var));
}
```

Fig. 4: Excerpt of a test harness; test vectors are passed by standard input (`fgets`, `parse_inp`)

is UNKNOWN. If the verdict of a program is FALSE, TBF produces a self-contained, compilable test harness and a violation witness to the user.

Input Program. TBF is designed to evaluate test-case generation tools and supports the specification encoding that is used by SV-COMP. In this work, all programs are C programs and have the same specification: "Function `__VERIFIER_error` is never called."

Pre-processor. TBF has to adjust the input programs for the respective test-case generator that is used. Each test-case generator uses certain techniques to mark input values. We assume that, except for special functions that are defined by the rules for the repository[9], all undefined functions in the program are free of side effects and return non-deterministic values of their corresponding return type. For each undefined function, we append a definition to the program under test to inject a new input value whenever the specific function is called. The meaning of the special functions defined by the repository rules are also represented in the code. Figure 2 shows a program with undefined functions `nondet_int` and `nondet_short`. As an example, Fig. 3 shows the definition of `nondet_int` that tells CREST-PPC to use a new (symbolic) input value. We display the full code of pre-processed example programs for all considered tools on our supplementary web page. After pre-processing, we compile the program as expected by the test-case generator, if necessary.

Test-Vector Extractor. Each tool produces test cases as output as described in Sect. 2.1. For normalization, TBF extracts test vectors from the generated test cases in an exchangeable format. We do not wait until the test generator is finished, but extract a test vector whenever a new test case is written, in parallel.

---

[9] https://sv-comp.sosy-lab.org/2017/rules.php

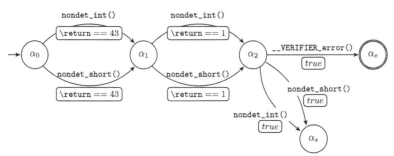

Fig. 5: Violation witness for test vector $\langle 43, 1 \rangle$ and two non-deterministic methods

Harness Generator and Test Executor. We provide an effective and efficient way of checking whether a generated test vector represents a property violation: We create a test harness for the program under test that can feed an input value into the program for each call to a non-deterministic function. For performance reasons, it gets these input values from standard input. For each test vector extracted from the produced test cases, we execute the pre-compiled test harness with the vector as input and check whether a property violation occurs during execution. An example harness is shown in Fig. 4.

Witness Generation. A test vector $\langle \eta_1, \cdots, \eta_n \rangle$ can be represented by a violation witness that contains one initial state α_0, one accepting state α_e, one sink sate α_s, and, for each value η_i of the test vector, a state α_i with, for each non-deterministic function occurring in the program, a transition from α_{i-1} to α_i with the call to the corresponding function as source-code guard and η_i as return value for the corresponding function as state-space guard, i.e.: the transition can only be taken if the corresponding function is called, and, if the transition is taken, it is assumed that the return value of the corresponding function is η_i. From α_n, there is one transition to α_e for each occurring call to __VERIFIER_error, and one transition to α_s for each non-deterministic function in the program. Each such transition has the corresponding function call as source-code guard and no state-space guard. The transitions to sink state α_s make sure that no path is considered that may need an additional input value. While such a path may exist in the program, it can not be the path described by the test vector. Fig. 5 shows an example of such a witness. Each transition between states is labeled with the source-code guard (no box) and the state-space guard (boxed). The value '*true*' means that no state-space guard exists for that transition.

When validating the displayed violation witness, a validator explores the state-space until it encounters a call to nondet_int or nondet_short. Then, it is told to assume that the encountered function returns the concrete value 43, described by the special identifier \return. When it encounters one of the two functions for the second time, it is told to assume that the corresponding function returns the concrete value 1. After this, if it encounters a call to __VERIFIER_error, it confirms the violation witness. If it encounters a call to one of the two non-deterministic functions for the third time, it enters the sink state α_s, since our witnessed counterexample only contains two calls to non-deterministic functions.

4   Experimental Evaluation

We compare automatic test generators against automatic software model checkers regarding bug finding abilities in a large-scale experimental evaluation.

4.1   Experiment Setup

Programs under Test. To get a representative set of programs under test, we used all 5 693 verification tasks of the SV-BENCHMARKS set[10] in revision 879e141f[11] whose specification is that function `__VERIFIER_error` is not called. Of the 5 693 programs, 1 490 programs contain a known bug (at most one bug per program), i.e., there is a path through the program that ends in a call to `__VERIFIER_error`, and 4 203 programs are correct. The benchmark set is partitioned into categories. A description of the kinds of programs in the categories of an earlier version of the repository can be found in the literature (cf. [3], Sect. 4). For each category (e.g., 'Arrays'), the defining set of contained programs (`.set` file [12]), and a short characterization and the bit architecture of the contained programs (`.cfg` file [13]) can be found in the repository itself.

Availability. More details about the programs under test, generated test cases, generated witnesses, and other experimental data are available on the supplementary web page.[14]

Tools. We used the test generators and model checkers in the versions specified in Table 1. TBF[15] is implemented in Python `3.5.2` and available as open-source; we use TBF in version `0.1`. For CREST-PPC, we use a modified revision that supports long data types. For readability, we add superscripts T and M to the tool names for better visual identification of the testers and model checkers, respectively. We selected six testing tools that (i) support the language C, (ii) are freely available, (iii) cover a spectrum of different technologies, (iv) are available for 64-bit GNU/Linux, and (v) generate test cases for branch coverage or similar: AFL-FUZZ, CPATIGER, CREST-PPC, FSHELL, KLEE, and PRTEST. For the model checkers, we use the four most successful model checkers in category 'Falsification' of SV-COMP'17[16], i.e., CBMC, CPA-SEQ, ESBMC-INCR, and ESBMC-KIND. To validate the results of violation witnesses, we use CPACHECKER and ULTIMATE AUTOMIZER in the revision from SV-COMP'17, CPA-WITNESS2TEST in revision r24473 of the CPACHECKER repository, and FSHELL-WITNESS2TEST in revision 2a76669f from branch `test-gen` in the CPROVER repository[17].

Computing Resources. We performed all experiments on machines with an Intel Xeon E3-1230 v5 CPU, with 8 processing units each, a frequency of 3.4 GHz, 33 GB of memory, and a Ubuntu 16.04 operating system with kernel Linux 4.4.

---

[10] https://sv-comp.sosy-lab.org/2017/benchmarks.php

[11] https://github.com/sosy-lab/sv-benchmarks/tree/879e141f

[12] https://github.com/sosy-lab/sv-benchmarks/blob/879e141f/c/ReachSafety-Arrays.set

[13] https://github.com/sosy-lab/sv-benchmarks/blob/879e141f/c/ReachSafety-Arrays.cfg

[14] https://www.sosy-lab.org/research/test-study/   [15] https://github.com/sosy-lab/tbf

[16] https://sv-comp.sosy-lab.org/2017/results/

[17] https://github.com/tautschnig/cprover-sv-comp

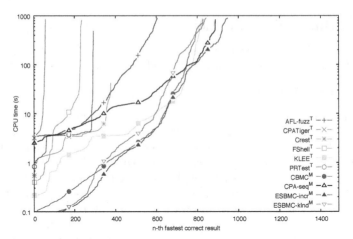

Fig. 6: Quantile plots for the different tools for finding bugs in programs

We limited each benchmark run to 2 processing units, 15 GB of memory, and 15 min of CPU time. All CPU times are reported with two significant digits.

4.2   Experimental Results

Now we report the results of our experimental study. For each of the 1 490 programs that contain a known bug, we applied all testers and model checkers in order to find the bug. For the testers, a bug is found if one of the generated test cases executes the undesired function call. For the model checkers, a bug is found if the tools returns answer FALSE together with a violation witness.

Qualitative Overview. We illustrate the overall picture using the quantile plot in Fig. 6. For each data point (x, y) on a graph, the quantile plot shows that x bugs can be correctly identified using at most y seconds of CPU time. The x-position of the right-most data point for a tool indicates the total number of bugs the tool was able to identify. In summary, each model checker finds more bugs than the best tester, while the best tester (KLEE^T) closely follows the weakest model checker (CBMC^M).

The area below the graph is proportional to the overall consumed CPU time for successfully solved problems. The visualization makes it easy to see, e.g., by looking at the 400 fastest solved problems, that most testers time out while most model checkers use only a fraction of their available CPU time. In summary, the ratio of returned results by invested resources is much better for the model checkers.

Quantitative Overview. Next, we look at the numerical details as shown in Table 2. The columns are partitioned into four parts: the table lists (i) the category/row label together with the number of programs (maximal number of found bugs), (ii) the number of found bugs for the six testers, (iii) the number of found bugs for the four model checkers, and (iv) the union of the results for testers, model checkers, and overall. In the two parts for the testers and model checkers, we highlight the best result in bold (if equal, the fastest result is highlighted). The rows are partitioned into three parts: the table shows first

Table 2: Results for testers and model checkers on programs with a bug

	No. Programs	AFL-FUZZ^T	CPATIGER^T	CREST-PPC^T	F-SHELL^T	KLEE^T	P-RTEST^T	CBMC^M	CPA-SEQ^M	ESBMC-INCR^M	ESBMC-KIND^M	Union Testers	Union MC	Union All
Arrays	81	**26**	0	20	4	22	25	**6**	3	6	4	31	13	33
BitVectors	24	**11**	5	7	5	11	10	12	12	12	**12**	14	17	19
ControlFlow	42	15	0	11	3	**20**	3	**41**	23	36	35	21	42	42
ECA	413	234	0	51	0	**260**	0	143	**257**	221	169	286	42	338
Floats	31	**11**	2	2	4	2	11	**31**	29	17	13	13	31	31
Heap	66	46	22	16	13	**48**	32	**64**	31	62	58	48	66	66
Loops	46	**45**	27	29	5	40	33	**42**	36	42	38	41	38	43
ProductLines	265	169	1	204	156	**255**	144	263	**265**	265	263	265	265	265
Recursive	45	44	0	35	22	**45**	31	**42**	41	40	40	45	43	45
Sequentialized	170	4	0	1	24	**123**	3	**135**	122	135	134	123	141	147
LDV	307	0	0	0	0	0	0	51	70	**113**	78	0	147	147
Total Found	1 490	605	57	376	236	**826**	292	830	889	**949**	844	887	1 092	1 176
Compilable	1 115	605	57	376	236	**826**	292	779	819	**830**	761	887	930	1 014
Wit. Confirmed	1 490							761	**857**	705	634	887	979	1 068
Median CPU Time (s)		11	4.5	**3.4**	6.2	3.6	3.6	**1.4**	15	1.9	2.3			
Average CPU Time (s)		82	38	**4.1**	27	33	6.7	**46**	51	61	69			

the results for each of the 11 categories of the programs under test, second the results for all categories together, and third the CPU times required.

The row 'Total Found' shows that the best tester (KLEE^T) is able to find 826 bugs, while all model checkers find more, with the best model checker (ESBMC-INCR^M) finding 15 % more bugs (949) than the best tester. An interesting observation is that the different tools have different strengths and weaknesses: column 'Union Testers' shows that applying all testers together increases the amount of solved tasks considerably. This is made possible using our unifying framework TBF, which abstracts from the differences in input and output of the various tools and lets us use all testers in a common work flow. The same holds for the model checkers: the combination of all approaches significantly increases the number of solved problems (column 'Union MC'). The combination of testers and model checkers (column 'Union All') in a bug-finding workflow can further improve the results significantly, i.e., there are program bugs that one technique can find but not the other, and vice versa.

While it is usually considered an advantage that model checkers can be applied to incomplete programs that are not yet fully defined (as expected by static-analysis tools), testers obviously cannot be applied to such programs (as they are dynamic-analysis tools). This issue applies in particular to the category 'LDV' of device drivers, which contain non-deterministic models of the operating-system environment. This kind of programs is important because it is successfully used to find bugs in systems code [18] [47], but in order to provide a comparison without the influence of this issue, we also report the results restricted to those programs that are compilable (row 'Compilable').

---

[18] http://linuxtesting.org/results/ldv

For the testers, TBF validates whether a test case is generated that identifies the bug as found. This test case can later be used to reproduce the error path using execution, and a debugger helps to comprehend the bug. For the model checkers, the reported violation witness identifies the bug as found. This witness can later be used to reproduce the error path using witness validation, and an error-path visualizer helps to comprehend the bug. Since the model checkers usually do not generate a test case, we cannot perform the same validation as for the testers, i.e., execute the program with the test case and check if it crashes. However, all four model checkers that we use support exchangeable violation witnesses [7], and we can use existing witness validators to confirm the witnesses. We report the results in row 'Wit. Confirmed', which counts only those error reports that were confirmed by at least one witness validator. While this technique is not always able to confirm correct witnesses (cf. [4], Table 8), the big picture does not change. The test generators do not need this additional confirmation step, because TBF takes care of this already. There are two interesting insights: (1) Software model checkers should in addition produce test data, either contained in the violation witness or as separate test vector. This makes it easier to reproduce a found bug using program execution and explore the bug with debugging. (2) Test generators should in addition produce a violation witness. This makes it easier to reproduce a found bug using witness validation and explore the bug with error-path visualization [6].

Consideration of False Alarms. So far we have discussed only the programs that contain bugs. In order to evaluate how many false alarms the tools produce, we have also considered the 4 203 programs without known bug. All testers report only 3 bugs on those programs. We manually investigated the cause and found out that we have to blame the benchmark set for these, not the testers.[19] Each of the four model checkers solves at least one of these three tasks with verdict TRUE, implying an imprecise handling of floating-point arithmetics. The model checkers also produce a very low number of false alarms, the largest number being 6 false alarms reported by ESBMC-INCR[M].

4.3   Validity

Validity of Framework for Test-Based Falsification. The results of the testers depend on a correctly working test-execution framework. In order to increase the confidence in our own framework TBF, we compare the results obtained with TBF against the results obtained with a proprietary test-execution mechanism that KLEE provides: KLEE-REPLAY[20]. Figure 7 shows the CPU time in seconds required by KLEE[T] using TBF (x-axis) and KLEE-REPLAY (y-axis) for each verification task that could be solved by either one of them. It shows that KLEE[T] (and thus, TBF) is very similar to KLEE's native solution. Over all verification

---

[19] There are three specific programs in the *ReachSafety-Floats* category of SV-COMP that are only safe if compiled with 64-bit rounding mode for floats or for a 64-bit machine model. The category states the programs should be executed in a 32-bit machine model, which seems incorrect.

[20] http://klee.github.io/tutorials/testing-function/#replaying-a-test-case

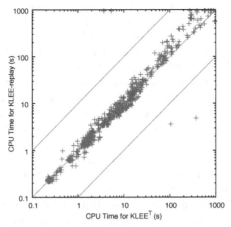

Fig. 7: CPU time required by KLEE^T and KLEE-REPLAY to solve tasks

tasks, KLEE^T is able to find bugs in 826 tasks, while KLEE-REPLAY is able to find bugs in 821 tasks. There are 15 tasks that KLEE-REPLAY can not solve, while KLEE^T can, and 10 tasks that KLEE-REPLAY can solve, while KLEE^T can not.

For KLEE^T, one unsolved task is due to missing support of a corner case for the conversion of KLEE's internal representation of numbers to a test vector. The remaining difference is due to an improper machine model: for KLEE-REPLAY, we only had 64-bit libraries available, while most tasks of SV-COMP are intended to be analyzed using a 32-bit architecture. This only results in a single false result, but interprets some of the inputs generated for 32-bit programs differently, thus reaching different parts of the program in a few cases. This also explains the few outliers in Fig. 7. The two implementations both need a median of 0.43 s of CPU time to find a bug in a task. This shows that our implementation is similarly effective and efficient to KLEE's own, tailored test-execution mechanism.

Other Threats to Internal Validity. We used the state-of-the-art benchmarking tool BENCHEXEC [14] to run every execution in an isolated container with dedicated resources, making our results as reliable as possible. Our experimental results for the considered model checkers are very close to the results of SV-COMP'17[21], indicating their accuracy. Our framework TBF is a prototype and may contain bugs that degrade the real performance of test-based falsification. Probably more tasks could be solved if more time was invested in improving this approach, but we tried to keep our approach as simple as possible to influence the results as less as possible.

Threats to External Validity. There are several threats to external validity. All tools that we evaluated are aimed at analyzing C programs. It might be the case that testing research is focused on other languages, such as C++ or Java. Other languages may contain other quirks than C that make certain approaches to test-case generation and model checking more or less successful. In addition,

---

[21] https://sv-comp.sosy-lab.org/2017/results/

there may be tools using more effective testing or model-checking techniques that were developed for other languages and thus are not included here.

The selection of testers could be biased by the authors' background, but we reflected the state-of-the-art (see discussion of selection) and related work in our choice. While we tried to represent the current landscape of test-case generators by using tools that use fundamentally different approaches, there might be other approaches that may perform better or that may be able to solve different tasks. We used most of the recent, publicly available test-case generators aimed at sequential C programs. We did not include model-based or combinatorial test-case generators in our evaluation.

For representing the current state-of-the-art in model checking, we only used four tools to limit the scope of this work. The selection of model checkers is based on competition results: we simply used the four best tools in SV-COMP'17. There are many other model-checking tools available. Since we performed our experiments on a subset of the SV-COMP benchmark set and used a similar execution environment, our results can be compared online with all verifiers that participated in the competition. The software model checkers might be tuned towards the benchmark set, because all of the software model checkers participated in SV-COMP, while of the testers, only FSHELL participated in SV-COMP before.

While we tried to achieve high external validity by using the largest and most diverse open benchmark set, there is a high chance that the benchmark set does not appropriately represent the real landscape of existing programs with and without bugs. Since the benchmark set is used by the SV-COMP community, it might be biased towards software model checkers, and thus, must stay a mere approximation.

5   Conclusion

Our comparison of software testers with software model checkers has shown that the considered model checkers are competitive for finding bugs on the used benchmark set. We developed a testing framework that supports the easy comparison of different test-case generators with each other, and with model checkers. Through this, we were able to perform experiments that clearly showed that model checking is mature enough to be used in practice, and even outperforms the bug-finding capabilities of state-of-the-art testing tools. It is able to cover more bugs in programs than testers and also finds those bugs faster. With this study, we do not pledge to eradicate testing, whose importance and usability can not be stressed enough. But we laid ground to show that model checking should be considered for practical applications. Perhaps the most important insight of our evaluation is that is does not make much sense to distinguish between testing and model checking if the purpose is finding bugs, but to leverage the strengths of different techniques to construct even better tools by combination.

References

1. S. Anand, E. K. Burke, T. Y. Chen, J. A. Clark, M. B. Cohen, W. Grieskamp, M. Harman, M. J. Harrold, and P. McMinn. An orchestrated survey of methodologies for automated software test-case generation. *Journal of Systems and Software*, 86(8):1978–2001, 2013.

2. T. Ball and S. K. Rajamani. The SLAM project: Debugging system software via static analysis. In *Proc. POPL*, pages 1–3. ACM, 2002.

3. D. Beyer. Competition on software verification (SV-COMP). In *Proc. TACAS*, LNCS 7214, pages 504–524. Springer, 2012.

4. D. Beyer. Software verification with validation of results (Report on SV-COMP 2017). In *Proc. TACAS*, LNCS 10206, pages 331–349. Springer, 2017.

5. D. Beyer, A. J. Chlipala, T. A. Henzinger, R. Jhala, and R. Majumdar. Generating tests from counterexamples. In *Proc. ICSE*, pages 326–335. IEEE, 2004.

6. D. Beyer and M. Dangl. Verification-aided debugging: An interactive web-service for exploring error witnesses. In *Proc. CAV*, LNCS 9780. Springer, 2016.

7. D. Beyer, M. Dangl, D. Dietsch, M. Heizmann, and A. Stahlbauer. Witness validation and stepwise testification across software verifiers. In *Proc. FSE*, pages 721–733. ACM, 2015.

8. D. Beyer, M. Dangl, and P. Wendler. Boosting k-induction with continuously-refined invariants. In *Proc. CAV*, LNCS 9206, pages 622–640. Springer, 2015.

9. D. Beyer, T. A. Henzinger, R. Jhala, and R. Majumdar. The software model checker BLAST. *Int. J. Softw. Tools Technol. Transfer*, 9(5-6):505–525, 2007.

10. D. Beyer, A. Holzer, M. Tautschnig, and H. Veith. Information reuse for multi-goal reachability analyses. In *Proc. ESOP*, LNCS 7792, pages 472–491. Springer, 2013.

11. D. Beyer and M. E. Keremoglu. CPACHECKER: A tool for configurable software verification. In *Proc. CAV*, LNCS 6806, pages 184–190. Springer, 2011.

12. D. Beyer, M. E. Keremoglu, and P. Wendler. Predicate abstraction with adjustable-block encoding. In *Proc. FMCAD*, pages 189–197. FMCAD, 2010.

13. D. Beyer and S. Löwe. Explicit-state software model checking based on CEGAR and interpolation. In *Proc. FASE*, LNCS 7793, pages 146–162. Springer, 2013.

14. D. Beyer, S. Löwe, and P. Wendler. Reliable benchmarking: Requirements and solutions. *Int. J. Softw. Tools Technol. Transfer*, 2017.

15. D. Beyer and P. Wendler. Reuse of verification results: Conditional model checking, precision reuse, and verification witnesses. In *Proc. SPIN*, LNCS. Springer, 2013.

16. A. Biere, A. Cimatti, E. M. Clarke, and Y. Zhu. Symbolic model checking without BDDs. In *Proc. TACAS*, LNCS 1579, pages 193–207. Springer, 1999.

17. M. Böhme, V. Pham, and A. Roychoudhury. Coverage-based greybox fuzzing as Markov chain. In *Proc. SIGSAC*, pages 1032–1043. ACM, 2016.

18. J. Burnim and K. Sen. Heuristics for scalable dynamic test generation. In *Proc. ASE*, pages 443–446. IEEE, 2008.

19. C. Cadar, D. Dunbar, and D. R. Engler. KLEE: Unassisted and automatic generation of high-coverage tests for complex systems programs. In *Proc. OSDI*, pages 209–224. USENIX Association, 2008.

20. A. Cimatti, A. Griggio, B. J. Schaafsma, and R. Sebastiani. The MathSAT5 SMT solver. In *Proc. TACAS*, LNCS 7795, pages 93–107. Springer, 2013.

21. E. M. Clarke, O. Grumberg, S. Jha, Y. Lu, and H. Veith. Counterexample-guided abstraction refinement for symbolic model checking. *J. ACM*, 50(5):752–794, 2003.

22. E. M. Clarke, D. Kröning, and F. Lerda. A tool for checking ANSI-C programs. In *Proc. TACAS*, LNCS 2988, pages 168–176. Springer, 2004.

23. W. Craig. Linear reasoning. A new form of the Herbrand-Gentzen theorem. *J. Symb. Log.*, 22(3):250–268, 1957.

24. C. Csallner and Y. Smaragdakis. Check 'n' crash: Combining static checking and testing. In *Proc. ICSE*, pages 422–431. ACM, 2005.

25. M. Dangl, S. Löwe, and P. Wendler. CPACHECKER with support for recursive programs and floating-point arithmetic. In *Proc. TACAS*, LNCS. Springer, 2015.
26. N. Eén and N. Sörensson. An extensible SAT solver. In *Proc. SAT*, LNCS 2919, pages 502–518. Springer, 2003.
27. M. Y. R. Gadelha, H. I. Ismail, and L. C. Cordeiro. Handling loops in bounded model checking of C programs via k-induction. *STTT*, 19(1):97–114, 2017.
28. S. J. Galler and B. K. Aichernig. Survey on test data generation tools. *STTT*, 16(6):727–751, 2014.
29. P. Godefroid, N. Klarlund, and K. Sen. DART: Directed automated random testing. In *Proc. PLDI*, pages 213–223. ACM, 2005.
30. P. Godefroid, M. Y. Levin, and D. A. Molnar. Automated whitebox fuzz testing. In *Proc. NDSS*. The Internet Society, 2008.
31. S. Graf and H. Saïdi. Construction of abstract state graphs with PVS. In *Proc. CAV*, LNCS 1254, pages 72–83. Springer, 1997.
32. M. Heizmann, D. Dietsch, J. Leike, B. Musa, and A. Podelski. ULTIMATE AUTOMIZER with array interpolation. In *Proc. TACAS*, LNCS 9035, pages 455–457. Springer, 2015.
33. M. Heizmann, J. Hoenicke, and A. Podelski. Software model checking for people who love automata. In *Proc. CAV*, LNCS 8044, pages 36–52. Springer, 2013.
34. T. A. Henzinger, R. Jhala, R. Majumdar, and G. Sutre. Lazy abstraction. In *Proc. POPL*, pages 58–70. ACM, 2002.
35. A. Holzer, C. Schallhart, M. Tautschnig, and H. Veith. How did you specify your test suite? In *Proc. ASE*, pages 407–416. ACM, 2010.
36. K. Jayaraman, D. Harvison, V. Ganesh, and A. Kiezun. jFuzz: A concolic whitebox fuzzer for Java. In *Proc. NFM*, pages 121–125, 2009.
37. R. Jhala and R. Majumdar. Software model checking. *ACM Computing Surveys*, 41(4), 2009.
38. A. V. Khoroshilov, V. Mutilin, A. K. Petrenko, and V. Zakharov. Establishing Linux driver verification process. In *Proc. Ershov Memorial Conference*, LNCS 5947, pages 165–176. Springer, 2009.
39. Y. Köroglu and A. Sen. Design of a modified concolic testing algorithm with smaller constraints. In *Proc. ISSTA*, pages 3–14. ACM, 2016.
40. D. Kröning and M. Tautschnig. CBMC: C bounded model checker (competition contribution). In *Proc. TACAS*, LNCS 8413, pages 389–391. Springer, 2014.
41. K. Li, C. Reichenbach, C. Csallner, and Y. Smaragdakis. Residual investigation: Predictive and precise bug detection. In *Proc. ISSTA*, pages 298–308. ACM, 2012.
42. K. L. McMillan. Interpolation and SAT-based model checking. In *Proc. CAV*, LNCS 2725, pages 1–13. Springer, 2003.
43. J. Morse, M. Ramalho, L. Cordeiro, D. Nicole, and B. Fischer. ESBMC 1.22 (competition contribution). In *Proc. TACAS*, LNCS 8413. Springer, 2014.
44. Z. Pavlinovic, A. Lal, and R. Sharma. Inferring annotations for device drivers from verification histories. In *Proc. ASE*, pages 450–460. ACM, 2016.
45. K. Sen, D. Marinov, and G. Agha. CUTE: A concolic unit testing engine for C. In *Proc. ESEC/FSE*, pages 263–272. ACM, 2005.
46. H. Seo and S. Kim. How we get there: A context-guided search strategy in concolic testing. In *Proc. FSE*, pages 413–424. ACM, 2014.
47. I. S. Zakharov, M. U. Mandrykin, V. S. Mutilin, E. Novikov, A. K. Petrenko, and A. V. Khoroshilov. Configurable toolset for static verification of operating systems kernel modules. *Programming and Computer Software*, 41(1):49–64, 2015.

A Supervisory Control Algorithm Based on Property-Directed Reachability

Koen Claessen[1], Jonatan Kilhamn[1], Laura Kovács[13], and Bengt Lennartson[2]

[1] Department of Computer Science and Engineering,
[2] Department of Electrical Engineering,
Chalmers University of Technology
[3] Faculty of Informatics, Vienna University of Technology
{koen, jonkil, laura.kovacs, bengt.lennartson}@chalmers.se

Abstract. We present an algorithm for synthesising a controller (supervisor) for a discrete event system (DES) based on the property-directed reachability (PDR) model checking algorithm. The discrete event systems framework is useful in both software, automation and manufacturing, as problems from those domains can be modelled as discrete supervisory control problems. As a formal framework, DES is also similar to domains for which the field of formal methods for computer science has developed techniques and tools. In this paper, we attempt to marry the two by adapting PDR to the problem of controller synthesis. The resulting algorithm takes as input a transition system with forbidden states and uncontrollable transitions, and synthesises a safe and minimally-restrictive controller, correct-by-design. We also present an implementation along with experimental results, showing that the algorithm has potential as a part of the solution to the greater effort of formal supervisory controller synthesis and verification.

Keywords: Supervisory control ·Discrete-event systems ·Property-directed reachability ·Synthesis ·Verification ·Symbolic transition system

1 Introduction

Supervisory control theory deals with the problems of finding and verifying controllers to given systems. One particular problem is that of controller synthesis: given a system and some desired properties—safety, liveness, controllability—automatically change the system so that it fulfills the properties. There are several approaches to this problem, including ones based on binary decision diagrams (BDD) [14, 6], predicates [11] and the formal safety checker IC3 [18].

In this work we revisit the application of IC3 to supervisory control theory. Namely, we present an algorithm for synthesising a controller (supervisor) for a discrete event system (DES), based on property-directed reachability [4] (PDR, a.k.a. the method underlying IC3 [2]). Given a system with a safety property and uncontrollable transitions, the synthesised controller is provably *safe*, *controllable* and *minimally restrictive* [16].

1.1 An illustrative example

Let us explain our contributions by starting with an example. Figure 1 shows the transition system of a finite state machine extended with integer variables x and y. The

© Springer International Publishing AG 2017
O. Strichman and R. Tzoref-Brill (Eds.): HVC 2017, LNCS 10629, pp. 115–130, 2017.
https://doi.org/10.1007/978-3-319-70389-3_8

formulas on the edges denote guards (transition cannot happen unless formula is true) and updates (after transition, x takes the value specified for x' in the formula). This represents a simple but typical problem from the domain of control theory, and is taken from [17].

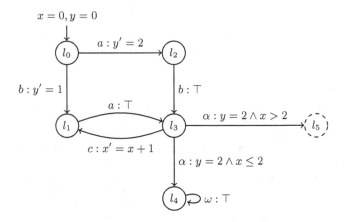

Fig. 1. The transition system of the example.

In a controller synthesis problem, a system such as this is the input. The end result is a restriction of the original system, i.e. one whose reachable state space is a subset of that of the original one. In this extended finite state machine (denoted as EFSM) representation, this is written as new and stronger guard formulas on some of the transitions.

Our example has two more features: the location l_5, a dashed circle in the figure, is *forbidden*, while the event α is *uncontrollable*. The latter feature means that the synthesised controller must not restrict any transition marked with the event α.

To solve this problem, we introduce an algorithm based on PDR [4] used in a software model checker (Section 3). Intuitively, what our algorithm does is to incrementally build an inductive invariant which in turn implies the safety of the system. This invariant is constructed by ruling out paths leading into the bad state, either by proving these bad states unreachable from the initial states, or by making them unreachable via strengthening the guards.

In our example, the bad state l_5 is found to have a preimage under the transition relation $\mathbf{T}$ in $l_3 \wedge y = 2 \wedge x > 2$. The transition from l_3 to l_5 is uncontrollable, so in order to guarantee safety, we must treat this prior state as unsafe too. The transitions leading into l_3 are augmented with new guards, so that the system may only visit l_3 if the variables make a subsequent transition to l_5 impossible. By applying our work, we refined Figure 1 with the necessary transition guards and a proof that the new system is safe. We show the refined system obtained by our approach in Figure 2.

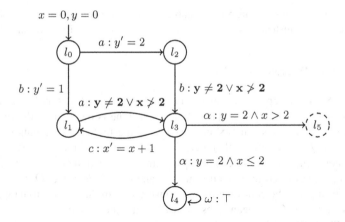

$x = 0, y = 0$

Fig. 2. The transition system from the example, with guards updated to reflect the controlled system.

1.2 Our Contributions

1. In this paper we present a novel algorithm based on PDR for controller synthesis (Section 3) and prove correctness and termination of our approach (Section 4). To the best of our knowledge, PDR has not yet been applied to supervisory control systems in this fashion. We prove that our algorithm terminates (given finite variable domains) and that the synthesised controller is safe, minimally-restrictive, and respects the controllability constraints of the system. Our algorithm encodes system variables in the SAT domain; we however believe that our work can be extended by using satisfiability modulo theory (SMT) reasoning instead of SAT.

2. We implemented our algorithm in the model checker Tip [5]. We evaluated our implementation on a number of control theory problems and give practical evidence of the benefits of our work (see Section 6).

2 Background

We use standard terminology and notation from first-order logic (FOL) and restrict formulas mainly to quantifier-free formulas. We reserve $\mathbf{P}, \mathbf{R}, \mathbf{T}, \mathbf{I}$ to denote formulas describing, respectively, safety properties, "frames" approximating reachable sets, transition relations and initial properties of control systems; all other formulas will be denoted with ϕ, ψ, possibly with indices. We write variables as x, y and sets of variables as X, Y. A *literal* is an atom or its negation, a *clause* a disjunction of literals, and a *cube* a conjunction of literals. We use $\mathcal{R}$ to denote a set of clauses, intended to be read as the conjunction of those clauses. When a formula ranges over variables in two or more variable sets, we take $\phi(X, Y)$ to mean $\phi(X \cup Y)$.

For every variable x in the control system, we assume the existence of a unique variable x' representing the *next-state value* of x. Similarly, the set X' is the set $\{x' | x \in$

X}. As we may sometimes drop the variable set from a formula if it is clear from the context, i.e. write ϕ instead of $\phi(X)$, we take ϕ' to mean $\phi(X')$ in a similar fashion.

2.1 Modelling Discrete Event Systems

A given DES can be represented in several different ways. The simple, basic model is the finite state machine (FSM) [10]. A state machine is denoted by the tuple $G = \langle Q, \Sigma, \delta, Q^i \rangle$, where Q is a finite set of states, Σ the finite set of events (alphabet), $\delta \subseteq Q \times \Sigma \times Q$ the transition relation, and $Q^i \subseteq Q$ the set of initial states.

In this notation, a *controller* can be represented as a function $C : Q \to 2^\Sigma$ denoting which events are enabled in a given state. For any $\sigma \in \Sigma$ and $q \in Q$, the statement $\sigma \in C(q)$ means that the controller allows transitions with the event σ to happen when in q; conversely, $\sigma \notin C(q)$ means those transitions are prohibited.

Extended Finite State Machine. The state machine representation is general and monolithic. In order to more intuitively describe real supervisory control problems, other formalisms are also used. Firstly, we have the extended finite state machine (EFSM), which is an FSM extended with FOL formulas over variables. In effect, we split the states into *locations* and *variables*, and represent the system by the tuple $A = \langle X, L, \Sigma, \Delta, l^i, \Theta \rangle$. Here, X is a set of variables, L a set of locations, Σ the alphabet, Δ the set of transitions, $l^i \in L$ the initial location and $\Theta(X)$ a formula describing the initial values of the variables.

A transition in Δ is now a tuple $\langle l, a, m \rangle$ where l, m are the entry and exit locations, respectively, while the action $a = (\sigma, \phi)$ consists of the event $\sigma \in \Sigma$ and $\phi(X, X')$. The interpretation of this is that the system can make the transition from l to m if the formula $\phi(X, X')$ holds. Since the formula can include next-state variables—ϕ may contain arbitrary linear expressions over both X and X'—the transition can specify updated variable values for the new state.

We have now defined almost all of the notation used in the example in Figure 1. In the figure, we write $\sigma : \phi$ to denote the action (σ, ϕ). Furthermore, the figure is simplified greatly by omitting next-state assignments on the form $x' = x$, i.e. x keeping its current value. If a variable does not appear in primed form in a transition formula, that formula is implied to have such an assignment.

Symbolic Representation. Moving from FSM to EFSM can be seen as "splitting" the state space into two spaces: the locations and the variables. A given feature of an FSM can be represented as either one (although we note that one purpose for using variables is to easier extend the model to cover an infinite state space). Using this insight we can move to the "other extreme" of the *symbolic transition system* (STS): a representation with only variables and no locations.

The system is here represented by the tuple $S_A = \langle \hat{X}, \mathbf{T}(\hat{X}, \hat{X}'), \mathbf{I}(\hat{X}) \rangle$ where $\hat{X}$ is the set of variables extended by two new variables x_L and x_Σ with domains L and Σ, respectively. With some abuse of notation, we use event and variable names to denote formulas over those variables, such as l_n for the literal $x_L = l_n$ and $\neg\sigma$ for the literal $x_\Sigma \neq \sigma$. The initial formula $\mathbf{I}$ and transition formula $\mathbf{T}$ are constructed from the corresponding EFSM representation as $\mathbf{I}(\hat{X}) = (x_L = l^i) \wedge \Theta(X)$ and $\mathbf{T}(\hat{X}, \hat{X}') = \bigvee_{\langle l, (\sigma, \phi), m \rangle \in \Delta} (l \wedge \sigma \wedge \phi(X, X') \wedge m')$.

In this paper, we will switch freely between the EFSM and STS representations of the same system, depending on which is the best fit for the situation. Additionally, we will at times refer to $\hat{X}$ as only X, as long as the meaning is clear from context. In either representation, we will use *state* to refer to a single assignment of location and variables, and *path* for a sequence of states $s_0, s_1, ..., s_k$.

2.2 Supervisory Control

The general problem of supervisory control theory is this: to take a transition system, such as the ones we have described so far, and modify it so that it fulfils some property which the unmodified system does not. There are several terms in this informal description that require further explanation.

The properties that we are interested in are generally *safety*, *non-blocking*, and/or *liveness*, which can be seen as a stronger form of non-blocking. Controlling for a safety property means that in the controlled system, there should be no sequence of events which enables transitions leading from an initial state to a forbidden state.

Non-blocking and liveness are defined relative to a set of marked state. The former means that at least one such state is reachable from every state which is reachable from the initial states. The latter, liveness, implies non-blocking, as it is the guarantee that the system not only *can* reach but *will* return to a marked state infinitely often. In this work we have reduced the scope of the problem by considering only safety.

Furthermore, we talk about the property of *controllability*. This is the notion that some events in a DES are uncontrollable, which puts a restriction on any proposed controller: in order to be valid, the transitions involving uncontrollable events must not be restricted. Formally, in an (E)FSM it is enough to split the alphabet into the uncontrollable $\Sigma_u \subseteq \Sigma$ and the controllable $\Sigma_c = \Sigma \setminus \Sigma_u$. In an STS, this is expressed by the transition relation taking the form $\mathbf{T} = \mathbf{T}_u \vee \mathbf{T}_c$, where $\mathbf{T}_c$ and $\mathbf{T}_u$ include literals $x_L = \sigma$ for, respectively, only controllable and only uncontrollable events σ.

Finally there is the question of what form this "controlled system" takes, since a controller function $C : Q \to 2^{\Sigma}$ can be impractical. A common method is that of designating a separate state machine as the supervisor, and taking the controlled system to be the *synchronous composition* of the original system and the supervisor [8]. In short, this means running them both in parallel, but only allowing a transition with a shared event σ to occur simultaneously in both sub-systems.

However, the formidable theory of synchronised automata is not necessary for the present work. Instead, we take the view that the controlled system is the original system, either in the EFSM or STS formulation, with some additions.

In the EFSM case, the controlled system has the exact same locations and transitions, but additional guards and updates may be added. In other words, the controlled system augments each controllable transition by replacing the original transition formula ϕ with the new formula $\phi^s = \phi \wedge \phi^{\text{new}}$. The uncontrollable transitions are left unchanged. In the STS case, the new transition function is $\mathbf{T}^S = \mathbf{T}_u \vee \mathbf{T}_c^S$ where $\mathbf{T}_c^S = \mathbf{T}_c \wedge \mathbf{T}_c^{\text{new}}$. This way, all uncontrollable transitions are guaranteed to be unmodified in the controlled system.

Finally, a controlled system, regardless of which properties the controller is set out to guarantee, is often desired to be *minimally restrictive* (eqiv. maximally permissive).

The restrictiveness of a controlled system is defined as follows: out of two controlled versions S_1 and S_2 of the same original system S, S_1 is more restrictive than S_2 if there is at least one state, reachable under the original transition function $\mathbf{T}$, which is reachable under $\mathbf{T}^{S_2}$ but unreachable under $\mathbf{T}^{S_1}$. A controlled system is minimally restrictive if no other (viable) controlled system exists which is less restrictive. The word "viable" in brackets shows that one can talk about the minimally restrictive *safe* controller, the minimally restrictive *non-blocking* controller and so on; for each combination of properties, the minimally restrictive controller for those properties is different.

3   PDRC: Property-Driven Reachability-Based Control

Property-driven reachability (PDR) [4] is a name for the method underlying IC3 [2], used to verify safety properties in transition systems. In this paper we present Property-Driven Reachability-based Control (PDRC), which extends PDR from verifying safety to synthesising a controller which makes the system safe. In order to explain PDRC, we first review the main ingredients of PDR.

PDR works by successively *blocking* states that are shown to lead to unsafe states in certain number of steps. Blocking a state at step k here means performing SAT-queries to show that the state is unreachable from the relevant *frame* $\mathbf{R}_k$. A frame $\mathbf{R}_k$ is a predicate over-approximating the set of states reachable from the initial states $\mathbf{I}$ in k steps.

When a state is blocked—i.e. shown to be unreachable—the relevant frame is updated by excluding that state from the reachable-set approximation. If a state cannot be blocked at $\mathbf{R}_k$, the algorithm finds its preimage s and proceeds to block s at $\mathbf{R}_{k-1}$. If a state that needs to be blocked intersects with the initial states, the safety property of the system has been proven false. Conversely, if two adjacent frames $\mathbf{R}_i, \mathbf{R}_{i+1}$ are identical after an iteration, we have reached a fixed-point and a proof of the property P in one of them entails a proof of P for the whole system.

With PDRC, we focus on the step where PDR has found a bad cube s (representing unsafe states) in frame $\mathbf{R}_k$, and proceeds to check whether it is reachable from the previous frame $\mathbf{R}_{k-1}$. If it is not, this particular cube was a false alarm: it was in the over-approximation of k-reachable states, but after performing this check we can sharpen that approximation to exclude s. If s was reachable, PDR proceeds to find its preimage t which is in $\mathbf{R}_{k-1}$. Note that t is also a bad cube, since there is a path from t to an unsafe state. However, in a supervisory control setting, there is no reason not to immediately control the system by restricting all controllable transitions from t to s. This observation is the basis of our PDRC algorithm.

3.1   Formal Description of PDRC

As PDRC is very similar to PDR, this description and the pseudocode procedures draw heavily from [4].

Our PDRC algorithm is given in Algorithm 1. As input, we take a transition system that can be represented by a transition function $\mathbf{T}(X, X') = \mathbf{T}_c \vee \mathbf{T}_u$, i.e. one where each possible transition is either controllable or uncontrollable; and a safety property

---

Algorithm 1: Blocking and propagation for one iteration of N.

```
   // finding and blocking bad states
1  while SAT[R_N ∧ ¬P] do
2  │    extract a bad state m from the SAT model;
3  │    generalise m to a cube s;
4  │    recursively block s as per block(s, N);
   │    // at this point R and/or T have been updated to rule
   │       out m
5  end
   // propagation of proven clauses
6  add new empty frame R_{N+1};
7  for k ∈ [1, N] and c ∈ R_k do
8  │    if R_k ⊨ c' then
9  │    │    add c to R_{k+1};
10 │    end
11 end
```

$P(X)$. The variables in X are boolean, in order to allow the use of a SAT solver – although see Section 3.2 describing an extension from SAT to SMT.

Throughout the run of the algorithm, we keep a *trace*: a series of frames $R_i, 0 \leq i \leq N$. Each $R_i(X)$ is a predicate that over-approximates the set of states reachable from I in i steps or less. $R_0 = I$, where I is a formula encoding the initial states.

Each frame $R_i, i > 0$ can be represented by a set of clauses $\mathcal{R}_i = \{c_{ij}\}_j$, such that $\bigwedge_j c_{ij}(X) = R_i(X)$. An empty frame $\mathcal{R}_j = \{\}$ is considered to encode $\top$, i.e. the most over-approximating set possible.

We maintain the following invariants:

1. $R_i \rightarrow R_{i+1}$
2. $R_i \rightarrow P$, except for $i = N$
3. R_{i+1} is an over-approximation of the image of R_i under T

Starting with $N = 1$ and $\mathcal{R}_1 = \{\}$, we proceed to do the first iteration of the blocking and propagation steps, as shown in Algorithm 1.

The "blocking step" consists of the while-loop (lines 1–5) of Algorithm 1, and coming out of that loop we know that $R_N \rightarrow P$. The propagation step follows (lines 6–11), and here we consider for each clause in some frame of the trace whether it also holds in the next frame.

Afterwards, we check for a fix-point in R_i; i.e. two syntactically equal adjacent frames $R_i = R_{i+1}$. Unless such a pair is found, we increment N by 1 and repeat the procedure.

The most important step inside the **while** loop is the call to block (line 4). This routine is shown in Algorithm 2. Here, we take care of the bad states in a straightforward way. First, we consider its preimage under the controllable transition function T_c (line 2). The preimage cube t can be found by taking a model of the satisfiable query $R_{k-1} \wedge \neg s \wedge T_c \wedge s'$ and dropping the primed variables. Each such cube encodes

---

Algorithm 2: The blocking routine, which updates the supervisor.

Data: A cube s and a frame index k
```
// first consider the controllable transitions:
```
1 **while** $SAT[\mathbf{R}_{k-1} \wedge \neg s \wedge \mathbf{T}_c \wedge s']$ **do**
2 $\quad\mid\quad$ extract and generalise a bad cube t in the preimage of $\mathbf{T}_c$;
3 $\quad\mid\quad$ update $\mathbf{T}_c := \mathbf{T}_c \wedge \neg t$;
4 **end**
```
// then consider the uncontrollable transitions:
```
5 **while** $SAT[\mathbf{R}_{k-1} \wedge \neg s \wedge \mathbf{T}_u \wedge s']$ **do**
6 $\quad\mid\quad$ **if** $k=1$ **then**
7 $\quad\mid\quad\quad\mid\quad$ throw error: **system uncontrollable**;
8 $\quad\mid\quad$ **end**
9 $\quad\mid\quad$ extract and generalise a bad cube t in the preimage of $\mathbf{T}_u$;
10 $\quad\mid\quad$ call $\texttt{block}\,(t, k-1)$;
11 **end**
12 add $\neg s$ to $\mathbf{R}_i, i \leq k$;

---

states from which a bad state is reachable in one step. Thus, we update the supervisor to disallow transitions from those bad states (line 3). This accounts for the first while-loop in Algorithm 2.

The second while-loop (lines 5–11)is very similar, but considers the uncontrollable transitions, encoded by $\mathbf{T}_u$, instead. If a preimage cube is found here, we cannot rule it out by updating the supervisor. That preimage instead becomes a bad state on its own, to be controlled in the previous frame $k-1$.

Example 1. **Example, revisited.** Recall the example in Figure 1. Since it uses integer variables it seems to require an SMT-based version of PDRC. This particular example is so simple, however, that "bit-blasting" the problem into SAT by treating the proposition $x < i$ as a separate boolean variable for each value of i in the domain of x will yield the same solution.

PDRC requires 3 iterations to completely supervise the system. In the first, the clause $\neg l_5$ is added to the first frame $\mathcal{R}_1$, after proving that it is not in the initial states. In the second, $\neg l_5$ is found again but this time the uncontrollable transition from l_3 is followed backwards, and the clause $\neg \alpha \vee \neg l_3 \vee y \neq 2 \vee x \not> 2$ is also added to $\mathcal{R}_1$, which allows us to add $\neg l_5$ to $\mathcal{R}_2$. Finally, in the third, the trace of preimages lead to the controllable transitions $l_1 \rightarrow l_3$ and $l_2 \rightarrow l_3$, and we add new guards to both (technically, we add new constraints to the transition function).

The updated system is the one shown in Figure 2. The third iteration also proves the system safe, as we have $\mathbf{R}_1 = \mathbf{R}_2$. These frames then hold the invariant, $(\neg \alpha \vee \neg l_3 \vee y \neq 2 \vee x \not> 2) \wedge \neg l_5$, which implies $\mathbf{P}$ and is inductive under the updated $\mathbf{T}$.

3.2 Extension to SMT

Our PDRC algorithm in Algorithm 1 uses SAT queries, and is straightforward to use with a regular SAT solver on systems with a propositional transition function. However, like in [3, 9] it is possible to extend it to other theories, such as Linear Integer Arithmetic, using an SMT solver. The SAT query in Algorithm 1 provides no diffuculty, but some extra thought is required for the ones in the blocking procedure, which follow this pattern:

> **while** $SAT[\mathbf{R}_i \wedge \neg s \wedge \mathbf{T} \wedge s']$ **do**
> extract and generalise a bad cube t in the preimage of $\mathbf{T}$;

If one only replaces the SAT solver by an SMT solver capable of handling the theory in question, one can extract a satisfying assignment of theory literals. However, each of these might contain both primed and unprimed variables, such as the next-state assignment $x' = x + 1$.

These lines effectively ask the solver to generalise a state m—an assignment of theory literals satisfying some formula $\mathbf{F}$—into a more general cube t, ideally choosing the t that covers the maximal amount of discrete states, while still guaranteeing $t \to \mathbf{F}$. In the SAT case, this is achieved by dropping literals of t that do not affect the validity of $\mathbf{F}(t)$. An alternate method based on ternary simulation, that is useful when the query is for a preimage of a transition function $\mathbf{T}$, is given in [4]. For the SMT case, however, the extent of generalisation depends on the theory and the solver.

In the worst case of a solver that cannot generalise at all, the algorithm is consigned to blocking a single state m in each iteration. This means that the state space simplification gained from using a symbolic transition function in the first place is lost, since the reachability analysis checks states one by one. In conclusion, PDRC could be implemented for systems with boolean variables using a SAT-solver with no further issues, while an SMT version would require carefully selecting the right solver for the domain. We leave this problem as an interesting task for future work.

4   Properties of PDRC

In this section we prove the soundness and termination of our PDRC algorithm.

4.1   Termination

Theorem 1. *For systems with state variables whose domains are finite, the PDRC algorithm always terminates.*

The termination of regular PDR is proven in [4]. In the case of an unsafe system—which for us corresponds to an uncontrollable system—the counterexample proving this must be finite in length, and thus found in finite time. In the case of a safe system, the proof is based on the following observations: that each proof-obligation (call to `block`) must block at least one state in at least one frame; that there are a finite number of frames for each iteration (value of N); that there are a finite number of states of the system; and that each $\mathbf{R}_{i+1}$ must either block at least one more state than $\mathbf{R}_i$, or they are equal.

All these observations remain true for PDRC, substituting "uncontrollable" for "unsafe". This means that the proof of termination from [4] can be used for PDRC with minimal modification.

4.2 Correctness

We claim that the algorithm described above synthesises a minimally restrictive safe controller for the original system.

Theorem 2. *If there exists any safe controller for the system, the controller synthesised by the PDRC algorithm is safe.*

Proof. We prove Theorem 2 by contradiction. Assume there is an unsafe state s, i.e. we have $\neg \mathbf{P}(s)$, that is reachable from an **I**-state in k steps. We must then have $k \geq N$, since invariant (2) states that $\mathbf{R}_i \rightarrow \mathbf{P}, i < N$. Let M be the index of the discovered fix point $\mathbf{R}_M = \mathbf{R}_{M+1}$.

Invariant (1) (from Section 3.1) states that $\mathbf{R}_i \rightarrow \mathbf{R}_{i+1}$, and this applies for all values $0 \leq i \leq M$. Repeated application of this means that any state in any $\mathbf{R}_i, i < M$ is also contained in $\mathbf{R}_M$.

Invariant (3) states that $\mathbf{R}_{i+1}$ is an over-approximation of the image of $\mathbf{R}_i$. This means that any state reachable from $\mathbf{R}_M$ should be in $\mathbf{R}_{M+1}$. Since $\mathbf{R}_M = \mathbf{R}_{M+1}$, such a state is also in $\mathbf{R}_M$ itself. Repeated application of this allows us to extend the trace all the way to $\mathbf{R}_k = \mathbf{R}_{k-1} = \cdots = \mathbf{R}_M$.

Now, for the bad state s, regardless of the number of steps k needed to reach it, we know that s is contained in $\mathbf{R}_k$ and therefore in $\mathbf{R}_M$. Yet when the algorithm terminated it had at one point found $\mathbf{R}_M \wedge \neg \mathbf{P}$ to be UNSAT. The state s, which is both in $\mathbf{R}_M$ and $\neg \mathbf{P}$, would constitute a satisfying assignment to this query. This contradiction proves that s cannot exist. $\qquad \square$

Theorem 3. *A controller synthesised by the PDRC algorithm is minimally restrictive.*

Proof. We prove Theorem 3 also by contradiction. Assume there is a safe path $\pi = s_0, s_1, \ldots, s_k$ through the original system (with transition function $\mathbf{T}$), which is not possible using the controlled transition function $\mathbf{T}^{\text{PDRC}}$; yet there exists another safe, controllable supervisor represented by $\mathbf{T}^S$ where π is possible. By deriving a contradiction, we will prove that no such $\mathbf{T}^S$ can exist.

Consider the first step of π that is not allowed by $\mathbf{T}^{\text{PDRC}}$; in other words, a pair (s_i, s_{i+1}) where we have $\neg \mathbf{T}^{\text{PDRC}}(s_i, s_{i+1})$ while we do have both $\mathbf{T}^S(s_i, s_{i+1})$ and $\mathbf{T}(s_i, s_{i+1})$. The only way that $\mathbf{T}^{\text{PDRC}}$ is more restrictive than $\mathbf{T}$ is due to strengthenings on the form $\mathbf{T}_c^{\text{PDRC}} = \mathbf{T}_c \wedge \neg m$, for some cube m. This means that s_i must be in some cube m that PDRC supervised in this fashion.

This happened inside a call `block (m, j)`. Since π is safe, this call cannot have been made because m itself encoded unsafe states. Instead, there must have been a previous call `block (n, j + 1)`, where m is a minterm of the preimage of n under $\mathbf{T}_u$. This cube n is either itself a bad cube, or it can be traced to a bad cube by following the trace of `block` calls. Since each step in this `block` chain only uses $\mathbf{T}_u$, we can find a series of uncontrollable transitions, starting in some $\tilde{s}_{i+1} \in n$, leading to some cube p which is a generalisation of a satisfying assignment to the query $\mathbf{R}_N \wedge \neg \mathbf{P}$.

This proves that $\mathbf{T}^S$, whose $\mathbf{T}_c^S$ does not restrict transitions from s_i, allows for the system to enter a state $\tilde{s}_{i+1}$, from which there is an uncontrollable path to an unsafe state. This contradicts the assumption that $\mathbf{T}^S$ was safe, proving that the combination of π and $\mathbf{T}^S$ cannot exist. This proves that the controller encoded by $\mathbf{T}^{\text{PDRC}}$ is minimally restrictive. $\qquad \square$

5   Implementation

We have implemented a prototype of PDRC in the model checker Tip (Temporal Inductive Prover [5]). The input format supported by Tip is AIGER [1], where the transition
system is represented as a circuit, which is not a very intuitive way to view an EFSM or
STS. For this reason, our prototype also includes Haskell modules for creating a transition system in a control-theory-friendly representation, converting it to AIGER, and
using the output from the Tip-PDRC to reflect the new, controlled system synthesised by
PDRC. Finally, it also includes a parser from the .wmod format used by WATERS and
Supremica [13], into our Haskell representation. Altogether, our implementation consists of about 150 lines of code added or changed in the Tip source, and about 1600 lines
of Haskell code. Our tools, together with the benchmarks we used, is available through
github.com/JonatanKilhamn/supermini and github.com/JonatanKilhamn/tipcheck.

When converting transition systems into circuits, certain choices have to be made.
Our encoding allows for synchronised automata with *one-hot-encoded* locations (e.g.
location l_3 out of 5 is represented by the bits $[0, 0, 1, 0, 0]$) and *unary-encoded* integer
variables (e.g. a variable ranging from 0 to 5 currently having the value 3 is represented
by $[1, 1, 1, 0, 0]$). Each of these encoding has a corresponding invariant: with one-hot,
exactly one bit must be set to 1; with unary, each bit implies the previous one. However,
these invariants need not be explicitly enforced by the transition relation (i.e. as guards
on every transition), rather, it is enough that they are preserved by all variable updates.

It should be noted that although the PDRC on a theoretical level works equally
well on STS as EFSM, our implementation does assume the EFSM division between
locations and variables for the input system. However, our implementation retains the
generality of PDRC in how the state space is explored—the algorithm described in
Section 3 is run on the circuit representation, where the only difference between the
location variable x_L and any other variable is the choice of encoding.

6   Experiments

For an empirical evaluation, we ran PDRC on several standard benchmark problems:
the extended dining philosophers (EDP) [15], the cat and mouse tower (CMT) [15] and
the parallell manufacturing example (PME) [12]. The runtimes of these experiments
are shown in Table 1 below. The benchmarks were performed on a computer with a 2.7
GHz Intel Core i5 processor and 8GB of available memory.

6.1   Problems

For the dining philosophers, $EDP(n, k)$ denotes the problem of synthesising a safe
controller for n philosophers and k intermediary states that each philosopher must go
through between taking their left fork and taking their right one. The transition system
is written so that all philosophers respect when their neighbours are holding the forks,
except for the even-numbered ones who will try to take the fork to their left even if it is
held, which leads (uncontrollably) to a forbidden state.

For the cat and mouse problem, $CMT(n, k)$ similarly denotes the problem with n floors of the tower, k cats and k mice. Again, the transition system already prohibits cats and mice from entering the same room (forbidden state) except by a few specified uncontrollable pathways.

Finally, the parallel manufacturing example (PME) represents an automated factory, with an industrial robot and several shared resources. It differs from the other in that its scale comes mainly from the number of different synchronised automata. In return, it does not have a natural parameter that can be set to higher values to increase the complexity further.

6.2 Results

We compare PDRC to Symbolic Supervisory Control using BDD (SC-BDD) [14, 6], which is implemented within Supremica. We wanted to include the Incremental, Inductive Supervisory Control (IISC) algorithm [18], which also uses PDR but in another way. However, the IISC implementation from [18] is no longer maintained. Despite this failed replication, we include figures for IISC taken directly from [18]—with all the caveats that apply when comparing runtimes obtained from different machines. Table 1 shows runtimes, where the problems are denoted as above and "×" indicates time-out (5 min). The parameters for EDP and CMT were chosen to show a wide range from small to large problems, while still mostly choosing values for which [18] reports runtimes for IISC. We see that while SC-BDD might have the advantage on certain small problems, PDRC quickly outpaces it as the problems grow larger.

Table 1. Performance of PDRC (our contribution), SC-BDD and IISC on standard benchmark problems. Note that the IISC implementation was not reproducible by us; the numbers here are lifted from [18]. "×" indicates timeout (5 min), and "–" means this particular problem was not included in [18].

Model	PDRC	IISC[18]	SC-BDD
CMT(1,5)	0.09	0.13	0.007
CMT(3,3)	1.3	0.43	1.12
CMT(5,5)	8.3	0.73	×
CMT(7,7)	30.02	0.98	×
EDP(5,10)	0.03	0.98	0.031
EDP(10,10)	0.15	–	0.10
EDP(5,50)	0.03	0.12	0.26
EDP(5,200)	0.06	0.12	×
EDP(5,10e3)	0.19	0.12	×
PME	0.72	2.3	8.1

7 Discussion

In this section, we relate briefly how BDD-SC [14, 6] and IISC [18] work, in order to compare and contrast to PDRC.

7.1 BDD-SC

BDD-SC works by modelling an FSM as a *binary decision diagram* (BDD). The algorithm generates a BDD, representing the safe states, by searching backwards from the forbidden states. However, the size of this BDD grows with the domain of the integer variables. The reason is that the size of the BDD is quite sensitive to the number of binary variables, but also the ordering of the variables in the BDD. Even when more recent techniques on partitioning of the problem are used [6], the size of the BDD blows up, and we see in Table 1 that BDD-SC very quickly goes from good performance to time-out.

7.2 IISC

It is natural to compare PDRC to IISC [18], since the latter is also inspired by PDR (albeit under the name IC3). In theory, PDRC has some advantages.

The first advantage is one of representation. IISC is built on the EFSM's separation between locations and variables, as described in 2.1. PDRC, on the other hand, handles the more general STS representation. Specifically, IISC explicitly unrolls the entire sub-state-space spanned by the locations. This sub-space can itself suffer a space explosion when synchronising a large number of automata.

To once again revisit our example (Figure 1): IISC would unroll the graph, starting in l_0, into an *abstract reachability tree*. Each node in such a tree can cover any combination of variable values, but only one location. Thus, IISC effectively does a forwards search for bad locations, and the full power of PDR (IC3) is only brought to bear on the assignment of variables along a particular error trace. Thus, a bad representation choice w.r.t. which parts of the system are encoded as locations versus as variables can hurt IISC, while PDRC is not so vulnerable.

PDRC, in contrast, leverages PDR's combination of forwards and backwards search: exploring the state space backwards from the bad states in order to construct an inductive invariant which holds in the initial states. One disadvantage of the backwards search is that PDRC might add redundant safeguards. For example, the safeguard on the transition from l_1 to l_3 in Figure 2 is technically redundant, as there is no way to reach l_2 with the restricted variable values from the initial states. As shown in [18], IISC does not add this particular guard. However, since both methods are proven to yield minimally-restrictive supervisors, any extra guards added by PDRC are guaranteed not to affect the behaviour of the final system.

The gain, on the other hand, is that one does not need to unroll the whole path from the initial state to the forbidden state in order to supervise it. Consider: each such error path must have a "point of no return"—the last controllable transition. When synthesising for safety, this transition must never be left enabled (our proof of Theorem 3 hinges upon this). In order to find this point, PDRC traverses only the path between the point of no return and the forbidden state, whereas IISC traverses the whole path. In a sense, PDRC does not care about how one might end up close to forbidden state, but only where to put up the fence.

In practice, our results have IISC outperforming PDRC on both PDE and CMT. We believe the main reason is that unlike IISC which uses IC3 extended to SMT [3], our implementation of PDRC works in SAT. This means that while both algorithms are theoretically equipped to abstract away large swathes of the state space, IISC does it much easier on integer variables than PDRC, which needs to e.g. represent each possible value of a variable as a separate gate.

The one point where PDRC succeeds also in practice is on the PME problem. Here, most of the system's complexity comes from the number of different locations across the synchronised automata, rather than from large variable domains. In order to further explore this difference in problem type, we would have liked to evaluate PDRC and IISC on more problems with more synchronised automata, such as EDP(10,10). Sadly, this was impossible since the IISC implementation is no longer maintained.

8   Conclusions and Future Work

We have presented PDRC, an algorithm for controller synthesis of discrete event systems with uncontrollable transitions, based on property-driven reachability. The algorithm is proven to terminate on all solvable problem instances, and its synthesised controllers are proven to be safe and minimally restrictive. We have also implemented a prototype in the SAT-based model checker Tip. Our experiments show that even this SAT-based implementation outperforms a comparable BDD-based approach, but not the more recent IISC. However, since the implementation of IISC we compare against uses an SMT solver, not to mention that it is not maintained anymore, we must declare the algorithm-level comparison inconclusive.

The clearest direction for future research would be to implement PDRC using an SMT solver, to see if this indeed does realise further potential of the algorithm like we believe. Both [3] and [9] provide good insights for this task. However, another interesting direction is to use both PDRC and IISC as a starting point to tackling the larger problem: safe *and nonblocking* controller synthesis. Expanding the problem domain like this cannot be done by a trivial change to PDRC, but hopefully the insights from this work can contribute to a new algorithm. Another technique to draw from is that of IICTL [7]. As discussed in Section 2.2, by restricting our problem to only safety, we remove ourselves from real-world applications. For this reason, we do not present PDRC as a contender for any sort of throne, but as a stepping stone towards the real goal: formal, symbolic synthesis and verification of discrete supervisory control.

References

[1]   Armin Biere. *AIGER*. 2014. URL: http://fmv.jku.at/aiger/ (visited on 07/24/2017).

[2]   Aaron R. Bradley. "SAT-Based Model Checking without Unrolling". In: *Verification, Model Checking, and Abstract Interpretation: 12th International Conference, VMCAI 2011, Austin, TX, USA, January 23-25, 2011. Proceedings*. Ed. by Ranjit Jhala and David Schmidt. Berlin, Heidelberg: Springer Berlin Heidelberg, 2011, pp. 70–87. ISBN: 978-3-642-18275-4. DOI: 10.1007/978-3-642-18275-4_7.

[3]   Alessandro Cimatti and Alberto Griggio. "Software Model Checking via IC3". In: *Computer Aided Verification: 24th International Conference, CAV 2012, Berkeley, CA, USA, July 7-13, 2012 Proceedings*. Ed. by P. Madhusudan and Sanjit A. Seshia. Berlin, Heidelberg: Springer Berlin Heidelberg, 2012, pp. 277–293. ISBN: 978-3-642-31424-7. DOI: 10.1007/978-3-642-31424-7_23.

[4]   Niklas Eén, Alan Mishchenko, and Robert Brayton. "Efficient Implementation of Property Directed Reachability". In: *Proceedings of the International Conference on Formal Methods in Computer-Aided Design*. FMCAD '11. Austin, Texas: FMCAD Inc, 2011, pp. 125–134. ISBN: 978-0-9835678-1-3. URL: http://dl.acm.org/citation.cfm?id=2157654.2157675.

[5]   Niklas Eén and Niklas Sörensson. "Temporal Induction by Incremental SAT Solving". In: *Electronic Notes in Theoretical Computer Science* 89.4 (2003), pp. 543–560. ISSN: 1571-0661. DOI: http://dx.doi.org/10.1016/S1571-0661(05)82542-3.

[6]   Z. Fei et al. "A symbolic approach to large-scale discrete event systems modeled as finite automata with variables". In: *2012 IEEE International Conference on Automation Science and Engineering (CASE)*. Aug. 2012, pp. 502–507. DOI: 10.1109/CoASE.2012.6386479.

[7]   Zyad Hassan, Aaron R. Bradley, and Fabio Somenzi. "Incremental, Inductive CTL Model Checking". In: *Proceedings of the 24th International Conference on Computer Aided Verification*. CAV'12. Springer-Verlag, 2012, pp. 532–547.

[8]   C. A. R. Hoare. *Communicating Sequential Processes*. Upper Saddle River, NJ, USA: Prentice-Hall, Inc., 1985. ISBN: 0-13-153271-5.

[9]   Kryštof Hoder and Nikolaj Bjørner. "Generalized Property Directed Reachability". In: *Proceedings of the 15th International Conference on Theory and Applications of Satisfiability Testing*. SAT'12. Trento, Italy: Springer-Verlag, 2012, pp. 157–171. ISBN: 978-3-642-31611-1. DOI: 10.1007/978-3-642-31612-8_13.

[10] John E. Hopcroft, Rajeev Motwani, and Jeffrey D. Ullman. *Introduction to Automata Theory, Languages, and Computation (3rd Edition)*. Boston, MA, USA: Addison-Wesley Longman Publishing Co., Inc., 2006. ISBN: 0321462254.

[11] R. Kumar, V. Garg, and S. I. Marcus. "Predicates and predicate transformers for supervisory control of discrete event dynamical systems". In: *IEEE Transactions on Automatic Control* 38.2 (Feb. 1993), pp. 232–247. ISSN: 0018-9286. DOI: 10.1109/9.250512.

16   REFERENCES

[12] R. J. Leduc, M. Lawford, and W. M. Wonham. "Hierarchical interface-based supervisory control-part II: parallel case". In: *IEEE Transactions on Automatic Control* 50.9 (Sept. 2005), pp. 1336–1348. ISSN: 0018-9286. DOI: 10.1109/TAC.2005.854612.

[13] Robi Malik. *Waters/Supremica IDE*. 2014. URL: http://www.cs.waikato.ac.nz/~robi/download_waters/ (visited on 07/24/2017).

[14] S. Miremadi, B. Lennartson, and K. Akesson. "A BDD-Based Approach for Modeling Plant and Supervisor by Extended Finite Automata". In: *IEEE Transactions on Control Systems Technology* 20.6 (Nov. 2012), pp. 1421–1435. ISSN: 1063-6536. DOI: 10.1109/TCST.2011.2167150.

[15] Sajed Miremadi, Knut Akesson, et al. "Solving two supervisory control benchmark problems using Supremica". In: *2008 9th International Workshop on Discrete Event Systems*. May 2008, pp. 131–136. DOI: 10.1109/WODES.2008.4605934.

[16] P.J. Ramadge and W.M. Wonham. "The control of discrete event systems". In: *Proceedings of the IEEE, Special Issue on Discrete Event Dynamic Systems* 77.1 (1989), pp. 81–98. ISSN: 0018-9219.

[17] Mohammad Reza Shoaei. *Incremental and Hierarchical Deadlock-Free Control of Discrete Event Systems with Variables: A Symbolic and Inductive Approach*. PhD thesis, Series 3827. Chalmers University of Technology, Dept. of Signals and Systems, Automation, 2015, pp. 44–45. ISBN: 978-91-7597-146-9.

[18] Mohammad Reza Shoaei, Laura Kovács, and Bengt Lennartson. "Supervisory Control of Discrete-Event Systems via IC3". In: *Hardware and Software: Verification and Testing: 10th International Haifa Verification Conference, HVC 2014, Haifa, Israel, November 18-20, 2014. Proceedings*. Ed. by Eran Yahav. Springer International Publishing, 2014, pp. 252–266.

SMT-based Synthesis of Safe and Robust PID Controllers for Stochastic Hybrid Systems

Fedor Shmarov[1], Nicola Paoletti[2], Ezio Bartocci[3], Shan Lin[4], Scott A. Smolka[2], and Paolo Zuliani[1]

[1] School of Computing, Newcastle University, UK
{f.shmarov,paolo.zuliani}@ncl.ac.uk
[2] Department of Computer Science, Stony Brook University, NY, USA
{nicola.paoletti,sas}@cs.stonybrook.edu
[3] Faculty of Informatics, TU Wien, Austria
ezio.bartocci@tuwien.ac.at
[4] Department of Electrical and Computer Engineering, Stony Brook University, NY, USA
shan.x.lin@stonybrook.edu

Abstract. We present a new method for the automated synthesis of safe and robust Proportional-Integral-Derivative (PID) controllers for stochastic hybrid systems. Despite their widespread use in industry, no automated method currently exists for deriving a PID controller (or any other type of controller, for that matter) with safety and performance guarantees for such a general class of systems. In particular, we consider hybrid systems with nonlinear dynamics (Lipschitz-continuous ordinary differential equations) and random parameters, and we synthesize PID controllers such that the resulting closed-loop systems satisfy safety and performance constraints given as probabilistic bounded reachability properties. Our technique leverages SMT solvers over the reals and nonlinear differential equations to provide formal guarantees that the synthesized controllers satisfy such properties. These controllers are also robust by design since they minimize the probability of reaching an unsafe state in the presence of random disturbances. We apply our approach to the problem of insulin regulation for type 1 diabetes, synthesizing controllers with robust responses to large random meal disturbances, thereby enabling them to maintain blood glucose levels within healthy, safe ranges.

1 Introduction

Proportional-Integrative-Derivative (PID) controllers are among the most widely deployed and well-established feedback-control techniques. Application areas are diverse and include industrial control systems, flight controllers, robotic manipulators, and medical devices. The PID controller synthesis problem entails finding the values of its control parameters (proportional, integral and derivative gains) that are optimal in terms of providing stable feedback control to the target system (the plant) with desired response behavior. Despite the limited number of parameters, this problem is far from trivial, due to the presence of multiple (and often conflicting) performance criteria that a controller is required to meet (*e.g.*, normal transient response, stability).

© Springer International Publishing AG 2017
O. Strichman and R. Tzoref-Brill (Eds.): HVC 2017, LNCS 10629, pp. 131–146, 2017.
https://doi.org/10.1007/978-3-319-70389-3_9

Developing PID controllers for *cyber-physical systems* is even more challenging because their dynamics are typically hybrid, nonlinear, and stochastic in nature. Moreover, it is imperative that the closed-loop controller-plus-plant system is safe (*i.e.*, does not reach a bad state) and robust (*i.e.*, exhibits desired behavior under a given range of disturbances). To the best of our knowledge, however, the current techniques for synthesizing PID controllers (see *e.g.*, [34,9,13]) simply ignore these issues and do not provide any formal guarantees about the resulting closed-loop system.

In this paper, we present a new framework for the automated synthesis of PID controllers for *stochastic hybrid systems* such that the resulting closed-loop system *provably* satisfies a given (probabilistic) safety property in a robust way with respect to random disturbances. Specifically, we formulate and tackle two different, yet complementary, problems: *controller synthesis, i.e.*, find a PID controller that minimizes the probability of violating the property, thus ensuring robustness against random perturbations; and *maximum disturbance synthesis, i.e.*, find, for a given controller, the largest disturbance that the resulting control system can sustain without violating the property. To the best of our knowledge, we are the first to present a solution to these problems (see also the related work in Section 6) with formal guarantees.

It is well known that safety verification is an inherently difficult problem for nonlinear hybrid systems — it is in general undecidable, hence it must be solved using approximation methods. Our technique builds on the frameworks of delta-satisfiability [16] and probabilistic delta-reachability [32] to reason formally about nonlinear and stochastic dynamics. This enables us to circumvent undecidability issues by returning solutions with numerical guarantees up to an arbitrary user-defined precision.

We express safety and performance constraints as probabilistic bounded reachability properties, and encode the synthesis problems as SMT formulae over ordinary differential equations. This theory adequately captures, besides the reachability properties, the hybrid nonlinear dynamics that we need to reproduce, and leverages appropriate SMT solvers [17,31] that can solve the delta-satisfiability problem for such formulae.

We demonstrate the utility of our approach on an artificial pancreas case study, *i.e.* the closed-loop insulin regulation for type 1 diabetes. In particular, we synthesize controllers that can provide robust responses to large random meal disturbances, while keeping the blood glucose level within healthy, safe ranges.

To summarize, in this paper, we make the following main contributions:

- We provide a solution to the *PID controller synthesis* and *maximum disturbance synthesis* problems using an SMT-based framework that supports hybrid plants with *nonlinear ODEs* and *random parameters*.
- We encode in the framework safety and performance requirements, and state the corresponding formal guarantees for the *automatically synthesized* PID controllers.
- We demonstrate the practical utility of our approach by synthesizing provably safe and robust controllers for an artificial pancreas model.

2   Background

Hybrid systems extend finite-state automata by introducing continuous state spaces and continuous-time dynamics [2]. They are especially useful when modeling systems that combine discrete and continuous behavior such as cyber-physical systems, including biomedical devices (*e.g.*, infusion pumps and pacemakers). In particular, continuous dynamics is usually expressed via (solutions of) ordinary differential equations (ODEs). To capture a wider and more realistic family of systems, in this work we consider hybrid systems whose behavior depends on both *random* and *nondeterministic* parameters, dubbed *stochastic parametric hybrid systems (SPHS)* [32]. In particular, our synthesis approach models both the target system and its controller as a single SPHS. It is thus important to adopt a formalism that allows random *and* nondeterministic parameters: the former are used to model system disturbances and plant uncertainties, while the latter are used to constrain the search space for the controller synthesis.

Definition 1. (SPHS)*[32] A Stochastic Parametric Hybrid System is a tuple* $H =< Q, \Upsilon, X, P, Y, R, \text{jump}, \text{goal} >$, *where*

- $Q = \{q_0, \cdots, q_m\}$ *is the set of modes (discrete states) of the system;*
- $\Upsilon \subseteq \{(q, q') : q, q' \in Q\}$ *is the set of possible mode transitions (discrete dynamics);*
- $X = [u_1, v_1] \times \cdots \times [u_n, v_n] \times [0, T] \subset \mathbb{R}^{n+1}$ *is the continuous system state space;*
- $P = [a_1, b_1] \times \cdots \times [a_k, b_k] \subset \mathbb{R}^k$ *is the parameter space of the system, which is represented as* $P = P_R \times P_N$, *where* P_R *is domain of random parameters and* P_N *is the domain of nondeterministic parameters (and either domain may be empty);*
- $Y = \{\mathbf{y}_q(\mathbf{p}) : q \in Q, \mathbf{p} \in X \times P\}$ *is the continuous dynamics where* $\mathbf{y}_q : X \times P \to X$;
- $R = \{\mathbf{g}_{(q,q')}(\mathbf{p}) : (q, q') \in \Upsilon, \mathbf{p} \in X \times P\}$ *is the set of 'reset' functions* $\mathbf{g}_{(q,q')} : X \times P \to X \times P$ *defining the continuous state at time* $t = 0$ *in mode* q' *after taking the transition from mode* q.

and predicates (or relations)

- $\text{jump}_{(q,q')}(\mathbf{p})$ *is true iff the discrete transition* $(q, q') \in \Upsilon$ *may occur upon reaching state* $(\mathbf{p}, q) \in X \times P \times Q$,
- $\text{goal}_q(\mathbf{p})$ *is true iff* $\mathbf{p} \in X \times P$ *is a goal state for mode* q.

The goal predicate is the same for all modes and is used to define the safety requirements for the controller synthesis (see (4.6) in Section 4). We assume that the SPHS has an initial state $(\mathbf{x_0}, q_0) \in X \times Q$. The continuous dynamics Y is given as an initial-value problem with Lipschitz-continuous ODEs over a bounded time domain $[0, T]$, which have a unique solution for any given initial condition $\mathbf{p} \in X \times P$ (by the Picard-Lindelöf theorem). System parameters are treated as variables with zero derivative, and thus are part of the initial conditions. Finally, parameters may be random discrete/continuous (capturing system disturbances and uncertainties) with an associated probability measure, and/or nondeterministic (*i.e.* the parameters to synthesize), in which case only their bounded domain is known.

Probabilistic Delta-Reachability: For our purposes we need to consider *probabilistic bounded* reachability: what is the *probability that a SPHS* (which models system *and* controller) *reaches a goal state in a* **finite** *number of discrete transitions?* Reasoning about reachability in nonlinear hybrid systems entails deciding first-order formulae over the reals. It is well known that such formulae are undecidable when they include, *e.g.*, trigonometric functions. A relaxed notion of satisfiability (δ-satisfiability [16]) can be utilized to overcome this hurdle, and SMT solvers such as dReal [17] and iSAT-ODE [10] can "δ-decide" a wide variety of real functions, including transcendental functions and solutions of nonlinear ODEs. (Essentially, those tools implement solving procedures that are sound and complete up to a given arbitrary precision.)

A probabilistic extension of bounded reachability in SPHSs was presented in [32], which basically boils down to measuring the *goal set*, *i.e.* the set of parameter points for which the system satisfies the reachability property. Recall that the set of goal states for a SPHS is described by its goal predicate. When nondeterministic parameters are present, the system may exhibit a range of reachability probabilities, depending on the value of the nondeterministic parameters. That is, the reachability probability is given by a function $\mathbf{Pr}(v) = \int_{G(v)} d\mathbb{P}$, defined for any $v \in P_N$, where $G(v)$ is the goal set and $\mathbb{P}$ is the probability measure of the random parameters. The ProbReach tool utilizes the notion of δ-satisfiability when computing the goal set, thereby computing *probabilistic δ-reachability* [31]. In particular, ProbReach computes probability *enclosures* for the range of function $\mathbf{Pr}$ over parameter sets $\mathcal{N} \subseteq P_N$, *i.e.*, intervals $[a, b]$ such that

$$\forall v \in \mathcal{N} \quad \mathbf{Pr}(v) \in [a, b] \tag{2.1}$$

where $0 \leqslant a \leqslant b \leqslant 1$ (but $a = b$ can only be achieved in very special cases, of course). To solve our synthesis problems we leverage ProbReach's formal approach and statistical approach for the computation of probability enclosures.

Formal Approach: ProbReach guarantees that the returned enclosures satisfy (2.1) *formally* and *numerically* [31]. In particular, any enclosure either has a desired width $\varepsilon \in \mathbb{Q}^+$, or the size of the corresponding parameter box $\mathcal{N} \subseteq P_N$ is smaller than a given lower limit. The computational complexity of this approach increases exponentially with the number of parameters, so it might not be feasible for large systems.

Statistical Approach: It trades computational complexity with correctness guarantees [32], by solving approximately the problem of finding a value v^* for the nondeterministic parameters that minimizes (maximizes) the reachability probability $\mathbf{Pr}$:

$$v^* \in \underset{v \in P_N}{\arg\min} \, \mathbf{Pr}(v) \qquad \left(v^* \in \underset{v \in P_N}{\arg\max} \, \mathbf{Pr}(v) \right). \tag{2.2}$$

ProbReach returns an estimate $\hat{v}$ for v^* and a probability enclosure $[a, b]$ that are *statistically* and *numerically* guaranteed to satisfy:

$$\text{Prob}(\mathbf{Pr}(\hat{v}) \in [a, b]) \geqslant c \tag{2.3}$$

where $0 < c < 1$ is an arbitrary confidence parameter. In general, the size of the enclosure $[a, b]$ cannot be arbitrarily chosen due to undecidability reasons, although it may be possible to get tighter enclosures by increasing the numerical precision of δ-reachability. Also, the statistical approach utilizes a Monte Carlo (Cross Entropy) method, so it cannot guarantee that $\hat{v}$ is a global optimum, *i.e.*, that satisfies (2.2).

PID control: A PID control law is the sum of three kinds of control actions, *Proportional, Integral and Derivative actions*, each of which depends on the *error value, e, i.e.* the difference between a target trajectory, or *setpoint sp*, and the measured output of the system y. At time t, the resulting control law $u(t)$ and error $e(t)$ are given by:

$$u(t) = \underbrace{K_p e(t)}_{P} + \underbrace{K_i \int_0^t e(\tau)\,d\tau}_{I} + \underbrace{K_d \dot{e}(t)}_{D}, \qquad e(t) = sp(t) - y(t) \qquad (2.4)$$

where constants K_p, K_i and K_d are called *gains* and fully characterize the PID controller.

The above control law assumes a continuous time domain, which is quite common in the design stage of a PID controller. Alternatively, PID control can be studied over discrete time, where the integral term is replaced by a sum and the derivative by a finite difference. However, the analysis of discrete-time PID controllers is impractical for non-trivial time bounds because they induce a discrete transition for each time step, and thus, they directly affect the unrolling/reachability depth required for the bounded reachability analysis, which is at the core of our synthesis method.

3   PID Control of Hybrid Plants

We formally characterize the system given by the feedback loop between a plant SPHS H and a PID controller, so called *closed-loop system* (see Figure 1). We would like to stress that we support plants specified as hybrid systems, given that a variety of systems naturally exhibit hybrid dynamics (regard-

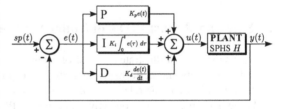

Fig. 1. PID control loop

less of the controller). For instance, in the artificial pancreas case study of Section 5, discrete modes are used to describe different meals, while the glucose metabolism is captured by a set of ODEs.

We assume that the controller is an additive input and can manipulate only one of the state variables of H, x_u, and that for each mode q of H, there is a measurement function h_q that provides the output of the system at q. To enable synthesis, we further assume that the PID controller gains $\mathbf{k} = (K_p, K_i, K_d)$ are (unknown) nondeterministic parameters with domain K. To stress this dependency, below we use the notation $u(\mathbf{k}, t)$ to denote the PID control law of Equation 2.4.

Definition 2 (PID-SPHS control system). *Let $H = \langle Q,\, \Upsilon,\, X,\, P,\, Y,\, R,\, \text{jump}, \text{goal} \rangle$ be a plant SPHS, and let u be a PID controller (2.4) with gain parameters $\mathbf{k} \in K \subset \mathbb{R}^3$. For $q \in Q$, let $h_q : X \to \mathbb{R}$ be the corresponding measurement function. Let x_u be the manipulated state variable, $i_u \in \{1,\dots,n\}$ be the corresponding index in the state vector, and $sp : [0,t] \to \mathbb{R}$ be the desired setpoint. The PID-SPHS control system with plant H is the SPHS $H \parallel u = \langle Q, \Upsilon, X, P \times K, Y', R', \text{jump}, \text{goal} \rangle$, where*

– $Y' = \{y'_q(\mathbf{p}, \mathbf{k}, t) : q \in Q, \mathbf{p} \in X \times P, \mathbf{k} \in K, t \in [0,1]\}$, *where the continuous dynamics of each state variable with index $i = 1, \ldots, n$ is given by*

$$y'_{q,i}(\mathbf{p}, \mathbf{k}, t) = \begin{cases} y_{q,i}(\mathbf{p}, t) + u(\mathbf{k}, t) & \text{if } i = i_u \\ y_{q,i}(\mathbf{p}, t) & \text{otherwise} \end{cases}$$

where $y_{q,i}$ is the corresponding continuous dynamics in the plant SPHS H, and $u(\mathbf{k}, t)$ is the PID law described in (2.4), with error

$$e(t) = sp(t) - h_q(y'_q(\mathbf{p}, \mathbf{k}, t)); \text{ and}$$

– $R' = \{g'_{(q,q')}(\mathbf{p}, \mathbf{k}, t) : (q, q') \in \Upsilon, \mathbf{p} \in X \times P, \mathbf{k} \in K, t \in [0, T]\}$, *where $g'_{(q,q')}(\mathbf{p}, \mathbf{k}, t) = g_{(q,q')}(\mathbf{p}, t)$, i.e. the reset $g'_{(q,q')}$ is not affected by the controller parameters $\mathbf{k}$ and is equal to the corresponding reset of the plant H, $g_{(q,q')}$.*

In other words, the PID-SPHS control system is obtained by applying the same PID controller to the continuous dynamics of each discrete mode of the hybrid plant, meaning that the PID-SPHS composition produces the same number of modes of the plant SPHS. We remark that external disturbances as well as plant uncertainties can be encoded through appropriate random variables in the plant SPHS.

4   Safe and Robust PID Controller Synthesis

In this section we first illustrate the class of synthesis properties of interest, able to capture relevant safety and performance objectives. Second, we formulate the PID control synthesis problem and the related problem of maximum disturbance synthesis.

We remark that our main objective is designing PID controllers with formal **safety guarantees**, *i.e.* a given set of bad states should never be reached by the system, or reached with very small probability. Similarly, we aim to synthesize controllers able to guarantee, by design, prescribed performance levels. For instance, the designer might need to keep the settling time within strict bounds, or avoid large overshoot.

To this purpose, we consider two well-established performance measures, the fundamental index (FI) and the weighted fundamental index (FI_w) [24,25][5], defined by:

$$FI(t) = \int_0^t (e(\tau))^2 \, d\tau \qquad FI_w(t) = \int_0^t \tau^2 \cdot (e(\tau))^2 \, d\tau. \tag{4.5}$$

FI and FI_w quantify the cumulative error between output and set-point, thus providing a measure of how much the system deviates from the desired behavior. Crucially, they also indirectly capture key transient response measures such as steady-state error, *i.e.* the value of $e(t)$ when $t \to \infty$, or maximum overshoot, *i.e.* the highest deviation from the setpoint[6]. In fact, small FI values typically indicate good transient response (*e.g.* small

---

[5] FI and FI_w are also also known as "integral of square error" and "integral of square time weighted square error", respectively.

[6] In PID theory, transient response measures are often evaluated after applying a step function to the set-point. However, we do not restrict ourselves to this scenario.

overshoot or short rise-time), while FI_w weighs errors with the corresponding time, in this way stressing steady state errors.

We now formulate the main reachability property for the synthesis of safe and robust controllers, which is expressed by predicate goal. The property captures the set of bad states that the controller should avoid (predicate bad) as well as performance constraints through upper bounds $FI^{\mathrm{max}}, FI_w^{\mathrm{max}} \in \mathbb{R}^+$ on the allowed values of FI and FI_w, respectively, and is given by:

$$\text{goal} = \text{bad} \vee (FI > FI^{\mathrm{max}}) \vee (FI_w > FI_w^{\mathrm{max}}). \tag{4.6}$$

In the case that the designer is not interested in constraining FI or FI_w, we allow FI^{max} and FI_w^{max} to be set $+\infty$.

We now introduce the PID controller synthesis problem that aims at synthesizing the control parameters yielding the minimal probability of reaching the goal (*i.e.* the undesired states). Importantly, this corresponds to minimizing the effects on the plant of random disturbances, that is, to *maximizing the robustness* of the resulting system.

We remark that the unrolling depth and the goal predicate are implicit in the reachability probability function **Pr** (see Section 2).

Problem 1 (PID controller synthesis). Given a PID-SPHS control system $H \parallel u$ with unknown control parameters $\mathbf{k} \in K$, find the parameters $\mathbf{k}^*$ that minimize the probability of reaching the goal:

$$\mathbf{k}^* \in \arg\min_{\mathbf{k} \in K} \mathbf{Pr}(\mathbf{k}).$$

For the duality between safety and reachability, Problem 1 is equivalent to synthesizing controllers that maximize the probability that ¬goal always holds. If $H \parallel u$ has no random parameters (but only nondeterministic parameters), then Problem 1 is equivalent to synthesizing, if it exists, a controller that makes goal unsatisfiable.

As previously explained, the control parameters $\mathbf{k}$ that we aim to synthesize must be defined as nondeterministic parameters in the SPHS $H \parallel u$. Crucially, we can employ both the formal and the statistical approach alike to solve this problem.

In general, it is not possible to know the exact minimizing parameter because of the inherent undecidability. However, using the formal approach one could select the synthesized controller parameter $\mathbf{k}^*$ *as the midpoint of the parameter box whose enclosure has the least midpoint*. Through the following proposition, we show that this solution can be made arbitrarily precise when all of the returned enclosures have length $\leq \varepsilon$, the user-defined parameter that determines the desired length of the enclosure as explained in Section 2 (however, this cannot be always guaranteed).

Proposition 1. *Suppose that the returned enclosures by the formal approach have all length $\leq \varepsilon$. Let P^* be the actual minimal probability, and let $\mathbf{k}^*$ be the solution of the formal approach for Problem 1. Then, it holds that*

$$\mathbf{Pr}(\mathbf{k}^*) < P^* + \frac{3}{2}\varepsilon.$$

Proof. See Appendix A in [30].

On the other hand, the statistical algorithm returns an over-approximation $\hat{P}$ of the minimum probability, c-confidence interval $[\hat{P}]$ such that $\hat{P} \in [\hat{P}]$, and synthesized parameters $\mathbf{k}^*$ whose reachability probability is included in $[\hat{P}]$ with probability at least c, as per Equations 2.2 and 2.3.

Below, we define the maximum disturbance synthesis problem, aimed at finding, given a concrete controller, the maximum disturbance value that the resulting control system can support without violating a given property. This problem is complementary to the PID synthesis problem, since it allows the designer to formally evaluate the robustness of a known controller, possibly synthesized in a previous step. Specifically, we assume that the disturbance is represented by a vector of nondeterministic parameters $\mathbf{d}$ in the plant SPHS, and that $\mathbf{d}$ ranges over some bounded domain D.

Problem 2 (Maximum disturbance synthesis). Given a PID-SPHS control system $H \parallel u$ with *known* control parameters $\mathbf{k}^* \in K$ and *unknown* disturbance $\mathbf{d} \in D$, and a probability threshold p, find the highest disturbance $\mathbf{d}^*$ for which the probability of reaching the goal does not exceed p, *i.e.* such that:

$$\mathbf{d}^* = \max\{\mathbf{d} \in D \mid \mathbf{Pr}(\mathbf{d}) \leq p\}.$$

For the duality between safety and reachability, the probability of reaching goal is below p if and only if the probability that $\neg$goal always holds is above $1 - p$. If $H \parallel u$ has no random parameters (but only nondeterministic parameters), then Problem 2 reduces to finding the largest disturbance for which the PID-SPHS system either reaches or does not reach the goal.

Note that the maximum disturbance synthesis problem is fundamentally different from the controller synthesis problem, because the kind of parameters that we seek to synthesize represent external factors that cannot be controlled. That is why we are interested in knowing the maximum (worst-case) value they can attain such that the requirements are met with given probability constraints. In particular, we restrict to upper-bound constraints because we want to limit the probability of reaching a given goal (undesired) state, even though lower bound constraints can be equally supported by the synthesis method.

Problem 2 is solved through the formal approach, which allows identifying the parameters boxes whose probability enclosures are guaranteed to be below the threshold p, *i.e.*, they are intervals of the form $[P_{\min}, P_{\max}]$ with $P_{\max} \leq p$. Then, the synthesized parameter $\mathbf{d}^*$ is selected as the highest value among all such parameter boxes.

It follows that the returned $\mathbf{d}^*$ is guaranteed to meet the probability constraint $(\mathbf{Pr}(\mathbf{d}^*) \leq p)$, but, due to the iterative refinement, $\mathbf{d}^*$ under-estimates the actual maximum disturbance. In this sense, $\mathbf{d}^*$ is a safe under-approximation. The reason is that there might exist some "spurious" parameter boxes $[\mathbf{d}]$ (not returned by the algorithm), *i.e.* such that p lies within the corresponding probability enclosure $[P]$ and $[\mathbf{d}]$ contains a disturbance value $\mathbf{d}'$ that is higher than the synthesized $\mathbf{d}^*$ and that, at the same time, meets the constraint $\mathbf{Pr}(\mathbf{d}') \leq p$.

The statistical approach cannot be applied in this case, because it relies on the Cross Entropy method, which is designed for estimation and optimization purposes and is not suitable for decision problems. Note indeed that the probability bound $\leq p$ induces a Boolean (and not quantitative) property.

5   Case Study: Artificial Pancreas

We evaluate our method on the closed-loop control of insulin treatment for Type 1 diabetes (T1D), also known as the *artificial pancreas (AP)* [20]. Together with model predictive control, PID is the main control technique for the AP [33,22], and is found as well in commercial devices [23].

The main requirement for the AP is to keep blood glucose (BG) levels within tight, healthy ranges, typically between 70-180 mg/dL, in order to avoid *hyperglycemia* (BG above the healthy range) and *hypoglycemia* (BG below the healthy range). While some temporary, postprandial hyperglycemia is typically admissible, hypoglycemia leads to severe health consequences, and thus, it should be avoided as much as possible. This is a crucial safety requirement, which we will incorporate in our synthesis properties.

The AP consists of a continuous glucose monitor that provides glucose measurements to a control algorithm regulating the amount of insulin injected by the insulin pump. The pump administers both *basal insulin*, a low and continuous dose that covers insulin needs outside meals, and *bolus insulin*, a single high dose for covering meals.

Meals represent indeed the major disturbance in insulin control, which is why state-of-the-art commercial systems[7] can only regulate basal insulin and still require explicit meal announcements by the patient for bolus insulin. To this purpose, robust control methods have been investigated [28,35,27], since they are able to minimize the impact of input disturbances (in our case, meals) on the plant (the patient). Thus, they have the potential to provide full closed-loop control of bolus insulin without manual dosing by the patient, which is inherently error-prone and hence, dangerous. Our method for the synthesis of safe and robust controllers is therefore particularly meaningful in this case.

5.1   Plant Model

To model the continuous system's dynamics (*e.g.*, glucose and insulin concentrations), we consider the well-established nonlinear model of Hovorka *et al.* [21].

At time t, the input to the system is the infusion rate of bolus insulin, $u(t)$, which is computed by the PID controller. The system output $y(t)$ is given by state variable $Q_1(t)$ (mmol), describing the amount of BG in the accessible compartment, *i.e.* where measurements are taken, for instance using finger-stick blood samples. For simplicity, we did not include a model of the continuous glucose monitor (see *e.g.* [36]) that instead measures glucose in the tissue fluid, but we assume continuous access to blood sugar values. The state-space representation of the system is as follows:

$$\dot{\mathbf{x}}(t) = \mathbf{F}\left(\mathbf{x}(t), u(t), D_G\right), \qquad y(t) = Q_1(t) \tag{5.7}$$

where $\mathbf{x}$ is the 8-dimensional state vector that evolves according to the nonlinear ODE system $\mathbf{F}$ (see Appendix B in [30] for the full set of equations and parameters). The model assumes a single meal starting at time 0 and consisting of an amount D_G of ingested carbohydrates. Therefore, parameter D_G represents our input disturbance.

---

[7] MINIMED   670G   by   Medtronic   https://www.medtronicdiabetes.com/products/minimed-670g-insulin-pump-system

Instead of the BG mass $Q_1(t)$, in the discussion of the results we will mainly evaluate the BG concentration $G(t) = Q_1(t)/V_G$, where V_G is the BG distribution volume.

The error function of the PID controller is defined as $e(t) = sp - Q_1(t)$ with the constant set point sp corresponding to a BG concentration of 110 mg/dL. Multiple meals can be modeled through a stochastic parametric hybrid system with one mode for each meal. In particular, we consider a one-day scenario consisting of three random meals (breakfast, lunch and dinner), resulting in the SPHS of Figure 2.

Fig. 2. Stochastic parametric hybrid system modelling a scenario of 3 meals over 24 hours. Above each edge, we report the corresponding jump conditions, below, the resets.

The model features five random, normally-distributed parameters: the amount of carbohydrates of each meal, $D_{G_1} \sim \mathcal{N}(40, 10)$, $D_{G_2} \sim \mathcal{N}(90, 10)$ and $D_{G_3} \sim \mathcal{N}(60, 10)$, and the waiting times between meals, $T_1 \sim \mathcal{N}(300, 10)$ and $T_2 \sim \mathcal{N}(300, 10)$.

A meal containing D_{G_1} grams of carbohydrates is consumed at time 0. When the time in the first mode reaches T_1 minutes the system makes a transition to the next mode *Meal* 2 where the value of the variable D_G is set to D_{G_2} and the time is reset to 0. Similarly, the system transitions from mode *Meal* 2 to *Meal* 3, resetting variables D_G and t to D_{G_3} and 0, respectively. All remaining variables are not reset at discrete transitions.

Basal insulin and initial state: The total insulin infusion rate is given by $u(t) + u_b$ where $u(t)$ is the dose computed by the PID controller, and u_b is the basal insulin. As typically done, the value of u_b is chosen in order to guarantee a steady-state BG value of $Q_1 = sp$, and the steady state thus obtained is used as the initial state of the system.

We denote with C_0 the basal controller that switches off the PID controller and applies only u_b (*i.e.*, K_p, K_i and K_d are equal to 0).

5.2   Experiments

We apply the formal and statistical techniques of ProbReach to synthesize the controller parameters K_p, K_d and K_i (Problem 1) and the maximum safe disturbance D_G (Problem 2), considering the probabilistic reachability property of Section 4. All experiments in this section were conducted on a 32-core (Intel Xeon 2.90GHz) Ubuntu 16.04 machine, and the obtained results for the synthesized controllers are summarized in Table 1. We also validate and assess performance of the controllers over multiple random instantiations of the meals, which is reported in Figure 3.

PID controller synthesis Typical healthy glucose levels vary between 4 and 10 mmol/L. Since avoiding hypoglycemia ($G(t) < 4$ mmol/L) is the main safety requirement of the artificial pancreas, while (temporary) hyperglycemia can be tolerated and is inescapable after meals, we will consider a BG range of $[4, 16]$ for our safety properties. In this way we protect against both hypoglycemia and very severe levels of hyperglycemia.

Given that the basal insulin level is insufficient to cover meal disturbances, the basal controller C_0 prevents hypoglycemia but causes severe hyperglycemia when a large meal is consumed ($D_G > 80$) or when the BG level is not low enough by the time the next meal is consumed (see Figure 3).

We used the statistical engine of ProbReach to synthesize several controllers (see Table 1), over domains $K_d \in [-10^{-1}, 0]$, $K_i \in [-10^{-5}, 0]$ and $K_p \in [-10^{-3}, 0]$, which minimize the probability of reaching a bad state at any time instant in the modes *Meal 1*, *Meal 2* and *Meal 3* (reachability depth of 0, 1 or 2, respectively).

The set of unsafe glucose ranges is captured by predicate bad = $G(t) \notin [4, 16]$. Controller C_1 was synthesized considering only safety requirements, corresponding to the reachability specification goal = bad (see Equation 4.6). On the other hand, controllers C_2, C_3 and C_4 were obtained taking into account also performance constraints, by using the default specification (4.6): goal = bad $\vee (FI > FI^{max}) \vee (FI_w > FI_w^{max})$. Thresholds FI^{max} and FI_w^{max} have been set to gradually stricter values, respectively to 3.5×10^6 and 70×10^9 for C_2, 3×10^6 and 50×10^9 for C_3, and 2.7×10^6 and 30×10^9 for C_4.

#	K_d ($\times 10^2$)	K_i ($\times 10^7$)	K_p ($\times 10^4$)	CPU_{syn}	P	CPU_P	$D_{G_1}^{max}$	CPU_{max}
C_0	0	0	0	0	[0.97322,1]	176	69.4	2,327
C_1	-6.02	-3.53	-6.17	92,999	[0.19645,0.24645]	4,937	88.07	3,682
C_2	-5.73	-3.00	-6.39	156,635	[0.31307,0.36307]	64,254	87.62	3,664
C_3	-6.002	-1.17	-6.76	98,647	[0.65141,0.70141]	59,215	88.23	3,881
C_4	-6.24	-7.55	-5.42	123,726	[0.97149,1]	11,336	88.24	3,867

Table 1. Results of PID controller synthesis, where: # – name of the synthesized controller, K_d, K_i and K_p – synthesized values of the gain constants characterizing the corresponding controller (Problem 1), CPU_{syn} – CPU time in seconds for synthesizing the controller parameters, P – 99%-confidence interval for the reachability probability, CPU_P – CPU time in seconds for computing P for synthesized controller, $D_{G_1}^{max}$ – synthesized maximum meal disturbance for which the system never reaches the unsafe state, CPU_{max} – CPU time in seconds for obtaining $D_{G_1}^{max}$.

Due to the high computational complexity of the artificial pancreas model, the controller synthesis was performed in two steps. First, the values of K_p, K_i and K_d were synthesized using a coarse precision (*i.e.*, desired width for confidence intervals P) for computing the probability estimates during the nondeterministic parameter search. Second, the confidence intervals for the obtained controllers were computed with a higher precision. The values of CPU_{syn} and CPU_P in Table 1 represent CPU times used for solving these two steps. The high computation times are due to the fact that the solvers incorporated by ProbReach solve ODEs in a guaranteed manner which is, for general Lipschitz-continuous ODEs, a PSPACE-complete problem, and thus, it is the main bottleneck of the implemented algorithms.

Besides C_0 that unsurprisingly yields the highest probability of safety violation (highest P for the reachability probability), results in Table 1 evidence that controllers

$C_1, \ldots, C_4$ fail to maintain the safe state with increasingly higher probability. As we shall see in more detail later, this behaviour is mostly due to the performance constraints that become harder and harder to satisfy.

Maximum disturbance synthesis We solve Problem 2 for each of the obtained controllers in Table 1. We consider a domain of $[0, 120]$ for the maximum meal disturbance, and apply the formal approach of ProbReach for synthesizing the maximum size $D_{G_1}^{max}$ of the first meal, such that, given any disturbance $D_{G_1} \in [0, D_{G_1}^{max}]$, the system does not reach the unsafe state within 12 hours. Note that this corresponds to setting the probability threshold p of Problem 2 to 0. Since we are interested in just one meal, we consider a reachability depth of 0 (path length of 1) for the bounded reachability property.

The results in Table 1 indicate that applying a PID controller increases the size of the allowed meal from approximately 69g of the basal controller to about 88g, and at the same time, the difference between the synthesized controllers is negligibly small.

Although introducing a controller does not increase the maximum disturbance dramatically with respect to the basal case, a PID control decreases the BG level sufficiently enough so that a subsequent meal of similar size can be consumed without the risk of experiencing severe hyperglycemia. In contrast, C_0 does not bring the glucose level low enough before the following meal.

Note that, being normally distributed with mean 90 g, the second random meal exceeds such obtained maximum disturbances, which explains why the synthesized controllers fail with some probability to avoid unsafe states.

Performance and safety evaluation In this experiment, we evaluate safety and performance of the controllers by simulating 1,000 instantiations of the random meals. Such obtained glucose profiles and statistics are reported in Figure 3. No hypoglycemia episode ($G < 4$) was registered.

Plots evidence that all four synthesized controllers ($C_1, \ldots, C_4$) perform dramatically better than the basal controller C_0, which stays, on the average, 23.59% of the time in severe hyperglycemia (see index t_{bad}). In particular, all the traces simulated for C_0 violate the safe BG constraints $G \in [4, 16]$ (100% value of $\%_{\text{bad}}$).

On the other hand, controllers $C_1, \ldots, C_4$ violate safe BG constraints for 17-22% of their traces, but this happens only for a very short while (no more than 0.45% of the time) after the second (the largest) meal. This comes with no surprise since we already formally proven that the second meal exceeds the allowed maximum meal disturbance.

C_0 has the worst performance in terms of FI and FI_w, with mean FI and FI_w values (indices $\overline{FI}$ and $\overline{FI_w}$, resp.) significantly larger than those of $C_1, \ldots, C_4$. Among the synthesized controllers, C_3 has the best steady-state behavior (as visible in Figure 3, plot d), keeping the glucose level very close to the set point towards the end of the simulation. C_3 yields indeed the best mean FI_w value (index $\overline{FI_w}$), while the worse steady-state behavior is observed for C_4. On the other hand, mean FI values are very similar, meaning that $C_1, \ldots, C_4$ maintain the BG levels equally far from the set point on the average.

One would expect C_4 to have the best performance in terms of FI_w, since it was synthesized with the stricter FI_w constraint ($FI_w^{max} = 30 \times 10^9$). This constraint is, however, too strong to be satisfied, as demonstrated by the 100% value of index $\%_{FI_w > FI_w^{\max}}$ (see Figure 3), implying all traces fail to satisfy $FI_w \leq FI_w^{\max}$. In general, we observe that strengthening the performance constraints leads to higher chances of violating them (see the last three indices of Figure 3). We conclude that performance constraints (and their violation) largely contribute to the reachability probabilities computed by ProbReach (see Table 1) for C_2, C_3 and C_4, whose traces violate FI or FI_w constraints for 28%, 67%, and 100% of the times, respectively.

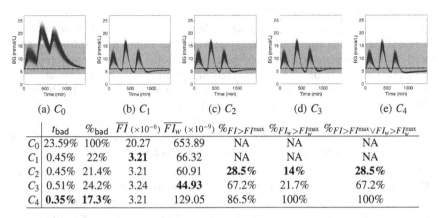

(a) C_0 (b) C_1 (c) C_2 (d) C_3 (e) C_4

	t_{bad}	$\%_{\text{bad}}$	$\overline{FI}$ ($\times 10^{-6}$)	$\overline{FI_w}$ ($\times 10^{-9}$)	$\%_{FI > FI^{\max}}$	$\%_{FI_w > FI_w^{\max}}$	$\%_{FI > FI^{\max} \vee FI_w > FI_w^{\max}}$
C_0	23.59%	100%	20.27	653.89	NA	NA	NA
C_1	0.45%	22%	**3.21**	66.32	NA	NA	NA
C_2	0.45%	21.4%	3.21	60.91	**28.5%**	**14%**	**28.5%**
C_3	0.51%	24.2%	3.24	**44.93**	67.2%	21.7%	67.2%
C_4	**0.35%**	**17.3%**	3.21	129.05	86.5%	100%	100%

Fig. 3. BG profiles simulated for 1,000 random meals (shaded blue lines). Grey areas indicate healthy BG ranges ($G \in [4, 16]$). Dashed black lines indicate the ideal setpoint. t_{bad}: mean proportion of time where $G \notin [4, 16]$ (all traces yielded $G > 4$, *i.e.* no hypoglycemia). $\%_{\text{bad}}$: proportion of traces violating $G \in [4, 16]$. $\overline{FI}$ and $\overline{FI_w}$: mean FI and FI_w, resp. $\%_{FI > FI^{\max}}$, $\%_{FI_w > FI_w^{\max}}$ and $\%_{FI > FI^{\max} \vee FI_w > FI_w^{\max}}$: proportion of traces violating, resp., either and both performance constraints. The best value for each index is highlighted in bold.

6   Related Work

A number of approaches have been proposed for the PID control of nonlinear and stochastic systems. Among these, nonlinear PID control [34] defines the controller gains as nonlinear functions of the system state, even though performance guarantees have been established only for subclasses of nonlinear systems. Adaptive PID (APID) control [13] supports nonlinear plants with partly unknown dynamics, but no requirements can be guaranteed by design since the unknown dynamics is estimated via sampling the plant output. In contrast, we can synthesize controllers with guaranteed performance for a large class of nonlinear systems (Lipschitz-continuous) while retaining the complete system dynamics. This allows for a fully model-based approach to controller synthesis, which is key in safety-critical applications, where, on the contrary, the model-free online tuning of APID is potentially dangerous.

PID control for Markov jump systems, *i.e.* where the plant is a linear system with stochastic coefficients, is solved as a convex optimization problem in [18,19], while in [9], robust PID control for stochastic systems is reduced to a constrained nonlinear optimization problem. Compared to these approaches, we support models where stochasticity is restricted to random (both discrete and continuous) parameters, with nondeterministic (*i.e.*, arbitrary) parameters and much richer nonlinear dynamics. Another key strength of our method with respect to the above techniques is that design specifications are given in terms of probabilistic reachability properties. These provide rigor and superior expressiveness and can encode common performance indices for PID controllers [25], as shown in Section 4.

Other related work includes the Simplex architecture [29] where, whenever the plant is at risk of entering an unsafe state, the system switches from a high-performance advanced controller to a pre-certified (safe) baseline controller (with worse performance), leading to a potential trade-off between safety and performance. In our approach, performance and safety are instead equal cohorts in the synthesis process. Unlike Simplex, in the *Control Barrier Function* (CBF) approach [3], there is no baseline controller to fall back on: a CBF minimally perturbs a (possibly erroneous) control input to the plant so the plant remains in the safe region. As far as we know, neither Simplex nor CBFs have been designed with a stochastic plant model in mind.

The controller synthesis problem under safety constraints (bounded STL properties in this case) is also considered in [12]. The main differences between this approach and ours is that they focus on Model Predictive rather than PID control, and their system model does not support stochastic parameters. There are a number of formal approaches (*e.g.*, [1]) to control synthesis that consider the sample-and-hold schema typical of discrete-time controllers, but they do not yield PID controllers and cannot handle stochastic hybrid systems. Verification of hybrid control systems with non-deterministic disturbances is considered in [26] and solved through a combination of explicit model checking and simulation. However, unlike our method, it does not support controller synthesis and arbitrary probability distributions for the disturbances.

There has been a sizable amount of work on tools for formal analysis of probabilistic reachability, although they all have limitations that make them unsuitable for our approach. SiSAT [15] uses an SMT approach for probabilistic hybrid systems with discrete nondeterminism, while continuous nondeterminism is handled via Monte Carlo techniques only [11]; UPPAAL [7] uses statistical model checking to analyze nonlinear stochastic hybrid automata; ProHVer [37] computes upper bounds for maximal reachability probabilities, but continuous random parameters are analyzed via discrete over-approximations [14]; U-Check [5] enables parameter synthesis and statistical model checking of stochastic hybrid systems [4]). However, this approach is based on Gaussian process emulation and optimisation, and provides only statistical guarantees and requires certain smoothness conditions on the satisfaction probability function.

Other approaches to solving SMT problems over nonlinear real arithmetic include the complete (over polynomials), yet computationally expensive, cylindrical algebraic decomposition method implemented in solvers like Z3 [8], as well as a recent method [6] based on the incremental linearization of nonlinear functions. However, none of these support ODEs and transcendental functions.

7   Conclusions and Future Work

The design of PID controllers for complex, safety-critical cyber-physical systems is challenging due to the hybrid, stochastic, and nonlinear dynamics they exhibit. Motivated by the need for high-assurance design techniques in this context, in this paper we presented a new method for the automated synthesis of PID controllers for stochastic hybrid systems from probabilistic reachability specifications. In particular, our approach can provide rigorous guarantees of safety and robustness for the resulting closed-loop system, while ensuring prescribed performance levels for the controller. We demonstrated the effectiveness of our approach on an artificial pancreas case study, for which safety and robustness guarantees are paramount.

As future work, we plan to study more advanced variants of the PID design such as nonlinear PID controllers, as well as investigate how common PID tuning heuristics can be integrated in our automated approach to speed up the search for suitable controllers.

Acknowledgements: Research supported in part by EPSRC (UK) grant EP/N031962/1, FWF (Austria) S 11405-N23 (RiSE/SHiNE), AFOSR Grant FA9550-14-1-0261 and NSF Grants IIS-1447549, CNS-1446832, CNS-1445770, CNS-1445770, CNS-1553273, CNS-1536086, CNS 1463722, and IIS-1460370.

References

1. V. Alimguzhin, F. Mari, I. Melatti, I. Salvo, and E. Tronci. Linearising discrete time hybrid systems. *IEEE Transactions on Automatic Control*, PP(99):1–1, 2017.
2. R. Alur, C. Courcoubetis, T. A. Henzinger, and P.-H. Ho. Hybrid automata: An algorithmic approach to the specification and verification of hybrid systems. In *Hybrid Systems*, volume 736 of *LNCS*, pages 209–229, 1992.
3. A. D. Ames and J. Holley. Quadratic program based nonlinear embedded control of series elastic actuators. In *CDC*, pages 6291–6298. IEEE, 2014.
4. E. Bartocci, L. Bortolussi, L. Nenzi, and G. Sanguinetti. System design of stochastic models using robustness of temporal properties. *Theor. Comput. Sci.*, 587:3–25, 2015.
5. L. Bortolussi, D. Milios, and G. Sanguinetti. U-check: Model checking and parameter synthesis under uncertainty. In *QEST*, volume 9259 of *LNCS*, pages 89–104, 2015.
6. A. Cimatti, A. Griggio, A. Irfan, M. Roveri, and R. Sebastiani. Invariant checking of NRA transition systems via incremental reduction to LRA with EUF. In *TACAS*, volume 10205 of *LNCS*, pages 58–75, 2017.
7. A. David, K. Larsen, A. Legay, M. Mikučionis, and D. B. Poulsen. UPPAAL SMC tutorial. *International Journal on Software Tools for Technology Transfer*, 17(4):397–415, 2015.
8. L. De Moura and N. Bjørner. Z3: An efficient SMT solver. In *TACAS*, volume 4963 of *LNCS*, pages 337–340, 2008.
9. P. L. T. Duong and M. Lee. Robust PID controller design for processes with stochastic parametric uncertainties. *Journal of Process Control*, 22(9):1559–1566, 2012.
10. A. Eggers, M. Fränzle, and C. Herde. SAT modulo ODE: A direct SAT approach to hybrid systems. In *ATVA*, pages 171–185, 2008.
11. C. Ellen, S. Gerwinn, and M. Fränzle. Statistical model checking for stochastic hybrid systems involving nondeterminism over continuous domains. *International Journal on Software Tools for Technology Transfer*, 17(4):485–504, 2015.
12. S. S. Farahani, V. Raman, and R. M. Murray. Robust model predictive control for signal temporal logic synthesis. In *ADHS*, 2015.

13. M. Fliess and C. Join. Model-free control. *International Journal of Control*, 86(12):2228–2252, 2013.
14. M. Fränzle, E. M. Hahn, H. Hermanns, N. Wolovick, and L. Zhang. Measurability and safety verification for stochastic hybrid systems. In *HSCC*, pages 43–52, 2011.
15. M. Fränzle, T. Teige, and A. Eggers. Engineering constraint solvers for automatic analysis of probabilistic hybrid automata. *J. Log. Algebr. Program.*, 79(7):436–466, 2010.
16. S. Gao, J. Avigad, and E. M. Clarke. Delta-decidability over the reals. In *LICS*, pages 305–314, 2012.
17. S. Gao, S. Kong, and E. M. Clarke. dReal: An SMT solver for nonlinear theories over the reals. In *CADE-24*, volume 7898 of *LNCS*, pages 208–214, 2013.
18. L. Guo and H. Wang. PID controller design for output PDFs of stochastic systems using linear matrix inequalities. *IEEE T. Sys, Man, and Cyb., Part B (Cyb.)*, 35(1):65–71, 2005.
19. S. He and F. Liu. Robust stabilization of stochastic markovian jumping systems via proportional-integral control. *Signal Processing*, 91(11):2478–2486, 2011.
20. R. Hovorka. Closed-loop insulin delivery: from bench to clinical practice. *Nature Reviews Endocrinology*, 7(7):385–395, 2011.
21. R. Hovorka et al. Nonlinear model predictive control of glucose concentration in subjects with type 1 diabetes. *Physiological Measurement*, 25(4):905, 2004.
22. L. M. Huyett et al. Design and evaluation of a robust PID controller for a fully implantable artificial pancreas. *Industrial & Engineering Chemistry Research*, 54(42):10311–10321, 2015.
23. S. S. Kanderian Jr and G. M. Steil. Apparatus and method for controlling insulin infusion with state variable feedback, July 15 2014. US Patent 8,777,924.
24. W. S. Levine. *The control handbook*. CRC Press, 1996.
25. Y. Li, K. H. Ang, G. C. Chong, W. Feng, K. C. Tan, and H. Kashiwagi. CAutoCSD-evolutionary search and optimisation enabled computer automated control system design. *International Journal of Automation and Computing*, 1(1):76–88, 2004.
26. T. Mancini, F. Mari, A. Massini, I. Melatti, F. Merli, and E. Tronci. System level formal verification via model checking driven simulation. In *CAV*, volume 8044 of *LNCS*, pages 296–312, 2013.
27. N. Paoletti, K. S. Liu, S. A. Smolka, and S. Lin. Data-driven robust control for type 1 diabetes under meal and exercise uncertainties. In *CMSB, accepted*, 2017.
28. R. S. Parker, F. J. Doyle, J. H. Ward, and N. A. Peppas. Robust H_∞ glucose control in diabetes using a physiological model. *AIChE Journal*, 46(12):2537–2549, 2000.
29. L. Sha. Using simplicity to control complexity. *IEEE Software*, 18(4):20–28, 2001.
30. F. Shmarov, N. Paoletti, E. Bartocci, S. Lin, S. A. Smolka, and P. Zuliani. Automated synthesis of safe and robust PID controllers for stochastic hybrid systems. *arXiv:1707.05229*, 2017.
31. F. Shmarov and P. Zuliani. ProbReach: Verified probabilistic δ-reachability for stochastic hybrid systems. In *HSCC*, pages 134–139. ACM, 2015.
32. F. Shmarov and P. Zuliani. Probabilistic hybrid systems verification via SMT and Monte Carlo techniques. In *HVC*, volume 10028 of *LNCS*, pages 152–168, 2016.
33. G. M. Steil et al. The effect of insulin feedback on closed loop glucose control. *The Journal of Clinical Endocrinology & Metabolism*, 96(5):1402–1408, 2011.
34. Y. Su, D. Sun, and B. Duan. Design of an enhanced nonlinear PID controller. *Mechatronics*, 15(8):1005–1024, 2005.
35. P. Szalay, G. Eigner, and L. A. Kovács. Linear matrix inequality-based robust controller design for type-1 diabetes model. *IFAC Proceedings Volumes*, 47(3):9247–9252, 2014.
36. M. E. Wilinska et al. Simulation environment to evaluate closed-loop insulin delivery systems in type 1 diabetes. *Journal of diabetes science and technology*, 4(1):132–144, 2010.
37. L. Zhang, Z. She, S. Ratschan, H. Hermanns, and E. M. Hahn. Safety verification for probabilistic hybrid systems. In *CAV*, volume 6174 of *LNCS*, pages 196–211, 2010.

A Symbolic Approach to Safety LTL Synthesis

Shufang Zhu[1], Lucas M. Tabajara[2], Jianwen Li[2]*, Geguang Pu[1]**, and Moshe Y. Vardi[2]

[1] East China Normal University, Shanghai, China
[2] Rice University, Texas, USA

Abstract. Temporal synthesis is the automated design of a system that interacts with an environment, using the declarative specification of the system's behavior. A popular language for providing such a specification is Linear Temporal Logic, or LTL. LTL synthesis in the general case has remained, however, a hard problem to solve in practice. Because of this, many works have focused on developing synthesis procedures for specific fragments of LTL, with an easier synthesis problem. In this work, we focus on Safety LTL, defined here to be the Until-free fragment of LTL in Negation Normal Form (NNF), and shown to express a fragment of safe LTL formulas. The intrinsic motivation for this fragment is the observation that in many cases it is not enough to say that something "good" will eventually happen, we need to say by when it will happen. We show here that Safety LTL synthesis is significantly simpler algorithmically than LTL synthesis. We exploit this simplicity in two ways, first by describing an explicit approach based on a reduction to Horn-SAT, which can be solved in linear time in the size of the game graph, and then through an efficient symbolic construction, allowing a BDD-based symbolic approach which significantly outperforms extant LTL-synthesis tools.

1 Introduction

Research on synthesis is the culmination of the ideal of declarative programming. By describing a system in terms of what it should do, rather than how it should be done, we are able to simplify the design process while also avoiding human mistakes. In the framework defined by synthesis, we describe a specification of a system's behavior in a formal language, and the synthesis procedure automatically designs a system satisfying this specification [30]. Reactive synthesis [24] is one of the most popular variants of this problem, in which we wish to synthesize a system that interacts continuously with an environment. Such systems include, for example, operating systems and controllers for mechanical devices. To specify the behavior of such systems, we need a specification language that can reason about changes over time. A popular such language is Linear Temporal Logic, or LTL [23].

Despite extensive research, however, synthesis from LTL formulas remains a difficult problem. The classical approach is based on translating the formula to a deterministic parity automaton and reducing the synthesis problem to solving a parity game [24]. This translation, however, is not only theoretically hard, given its doubly-exponential

---

* Corresponding author
** Corresponding author

O. Strichman and R. Tzoref-Brill (Eds.): HVC 2017, LNCS 10629, pp. 147–162, 2017.
https://doi.org/10.1007/978-3-319-70389-3_10

upper bound, but also inefficient in practice due to the lack of practical algorithms for determinization [15]. Furthermore, despite the recent quasi-polynomial algorithm [7] for parity games, it is still not known if they can be solved efficiently. A promising approach to mitigating this problem consists of developing synthesis techniques for certain fragments of LTL that cover interesting classes of specifications but for which the synthesis problem is easier. Possibly the most notable example is that of Generalized Reactivity(1) formulas, or GR(1) [3], a fragment for which the synthesis problem can be solved in cubic time with respect to the game graph.

Here we focus on the Safety LTL fragment, which we define to be the fragment of LTL composed of Until-free formulas in Negation Normal Form (NNF). Such formulas express *safety properties*, meaning that every violating trace has a finite bad prefix that falsifies the formula [19]. The intrinsic motivation for this fragment is the observation that in many cases it is not enough to say that something "good" will eventually happen, we need to say by *when* it will happen [21]. For this strict subset of LTL, the synthesis problem can be reduced to a *safety game*, which is far easier to solve. In fact, for such a game the solution can be computed in linear time with respect to the game graph [1]. Some novel techniques for safety game solving have been developed in the context of the Annual Synthesis Competition (SyntComp) [3], but there the input consists of an AIGER model, while in this paper we are concerned with synthesis from Safety LTL formulas. See further discussion in the Concluding Remarks.

Our first contribution is a new solution to safety games by reducing to Horn satisfiability (Horn-SAT). There have been past works using SAT in the context of bounded synthesis [2], but our approach is novel in using a reduction to Horn-SAT, which can be solved in linear time [11]. Because, however, the Horn formula is proportional to the size of the state graph, in which the number of transitions is exponential in the number of input/output variables and the number of states can be in the worst case doubly exponential in the size of the Safety LTL formula, this approach becomes infeasible for larger instances. To avoid this problem, we pursue an alternative approach that uses a symbolic representation of the game graph via Binary Decision Diagrams (BDDs) [5].

Symbolic solutions to safety games have played an important part in LTL synthesis tools following the idea of *Safraless synthesis* [20], which avoids the high cost of determinization and the parity acceptance condition of classical LTL synthesis by instead employing a translation to universal co-Büchi automata. Unbeast [14], a symbolic BDD-based tool for bounded synthesis, decomposes the LTL specification into safety and non-safety parts, using an incremental bound to allow the non-safety part to also be encoded as a safety game. Another tool, Acacia+ [4], takes a bounded synthesis approach that allows the synthesis problem to be reduced to a safety game, then explores the structure of the resulting game to implement a symbolic antichain-based algorithm.

In the above approaches the safety game is constructed from a co-Büchi automaton of the LTL specification. Our insight in this paper is that, since every bad trace of a formula in the Safety LTL fragment has a finite prefix, we can construct from the negation of such a formula a deterministic finite automaton that accepts exactly the language corresponding to bad prefixes. This DFA can be seen as the dual of a *safety automaton* defining a safety game over the same state space. Using a DFA as the basis for our safety

---

[3] http://www.syntcomp.org/

game allows us to leverage tools and techniques developed for symbolic construction, determinization and minimization of finite automata.

Our symbolic synthesis framework is inspired by a recent approach [29] for synthesis of LTL over finite traces. This problem can be seen as the dual of Safety LTL synthesis, and as such we can inter-reduce the realizability problem between the two by negating the result. Nevertheless, the strategy generation is irreducible since the two problems are solving the game for different players. Therefore, we modify the algorithm to produce a strategy for the safety game instead. The procedure consists of two phases. First we construct symbolically a safety automaton from the Safety LTL formula instead of direct construction. For that we present a translation from the negation of Safety LTL to first-order logic over finite traces, which allows us to symbolically construct the dual DFA of the safety automaton. Second, we solve the safety game by computing the set of winning states through a backwards symbolic fixpoint computation, and then applying a boolean-synthesis procedure [16] to symbolically construct a strategy.

In summary, our contribution in this paper is to introduce a fragment of LTL called Safety LTL and present two approaches for the synthesis problem for this fragment, an explicit one based on a reduction to Horn-SAT and a symbolic one exploiting techniques for symbolic DFA construction. Since Safety LTL is a fragment of general LTL, existing LTL synthesis tools can likewise be used to solve the Safety LTL synthesis problem. To demonstrate the benefits of developing specialized synthesis techniques, we perform an experimental comparison with Unbeast and Acacia+, both tools for general LTL synthesis. Our results show that the explicit approach is able to outperform these tools when the formula is small, while the symbolic approach has the best performance overall.

2 Preliminaries

2.1 Safety/Co-safety LTL

Linear Temporal Logic (LTL), first introduced in [23], extends propositional logic by introducing temporal operators. Given a set $\mathcal{P}$ of propositions, the syntax of LTL formulas is defined as $\phi ::= \top \mid \bot \mid p \mid \neg\phi \mid \phi_1 \wedge \phi_2 \mid X\phi \mid \phi_1 U \phi_2$.

$\top$ and $\bot$ represent *true* and *false* respectively. $p \in \mathcal{P}$ is an *atom*, and we define a literal l to be an atom or the negation of an atom. X (Next) and U (Until) are temporal operators. We also introduce the dual operator of U, namely R (Release), defined as $\phi_1 R \phi_2 \equiv \neg(\neg\phi_1 U \neg\phi_2)$. Additionally, we define the abbreviations $F\phi \equiv \top U \phi$ and $G\phi \equiv \bot R \phi$. Standard boolean abbreviations, such as $\vee$ (or) and $\rightarrow$ (implies) are also used. An LTL formula ϕ is *Until-free/Release-free* iff it does not contain the Until/Release operator. Moreover, we say ϕ is in Negation Normal Form (NNF), iff all negation operators in ϕ are pushed only in front of atoms.

A *trace* $\rho = \rho_0\rho_1 \ldots$ is a sequence of propositional interpretations (sets), in which $\rho_m \in 2^{\mathcal{P}}$ ($m \geq 0$) is the m-th interpretation of ρ, and $|\rho|$ represents the length of ρ. Intuitively, ρ_m is interpreted as the set of propositions which are *true* at instant m. Trace ρ is an *infinite* trace if $|\rho| = \infty$, which is formally denoted as $\rho \in (2^{\mathcal{P}})^{\omega}$. Otherwise ρ is a *finite* trace, denoted as $\rho \in (2^{\mathcal{P}})^*$. LTL formulas are interpreted over infinite traces. Given an infinite trace ρ and an LTL formula ϕ, we inductively define when ϕ is *true* in ρ at step i ($i \geq 0$), written $\rho, i \models \phi$, as follows:

- $\rho, i \models \top$ and $\rho, i \not\models \bot$;
- $\rho, i \models p$ iff $p \in \rho_i$;
- $\rho, i \models \neg\phi$ iff $\rho, i \not\models \phi$;
- $\rho, i \models \phi_1 \wedge \phi_2$, iff $\rho, i \models \phi_1$ and $\rho, i \models \phi_2$;
- $\rho, i \models X\phi$, iff $\rho, i + 1 \models \phi$;
- $\rho, i \models \phi_1 U \phi_2$, iff there exists $j \geq i$ such that $\rho, j \models \phi_2$, and for all $i \leq k < j$, we have $\rho, k \models \phi_1$.

An LTL formula ϕ is *true* in ρ, denoted by $\rho \models \phi$, if and only if $\rho, 0 \models \phi$.

Informally speaking, a *safe* LTL formula rejects traces whose "badness" follows from a finite prefix. Dually, a *co-safe* LTL formula accepts traces whose "goodness" follows from a finite prefix. Thus, ϕ is a safe formula iff $\neg\phi$ is a co-safe formula. To define the *safe/co-safe* formulas, we need to introduce the concept of *bad/good prefix*.

Definition 1 (Bad/Good Prefix [19]). *Consider a language L of infinite words over $\mathcal{P}$. A finite word x over $\mathcal{P}$ is a bad/good prefix for L if and only if for all infinite words y over $\mathcal{P}$, the concatenation $x \cdot y$ of x and y isn't/is in L.*

Safe/co-safe LTL formulas are defined as follows.

Definition 2 (safe/co-safe [19]). *An LTL formula ϕ is safe/co-safe iff every word that violates/satisfies ϕ has a bad/good prefix.*

We use $pref(\phi)$ to denote the set of bad prefixes for safe formula ϕ, equivalently, we denote by $co\text{-}pref(\neg\phi)$, the set of good prefixes for $\neg\phi$, which is co-safe. Indeed, $pref(\phi) = co\text{-}pref(\neg\phi)$ [19].

Theorem 1. *An LTL formula ϕ is safe iff $\neg\phi$ is co-safe, and each bad prefix for safe formula ϕ is a good prefix for $\neg\phi$.*

Checking if a given LTL formula is safe/co-safe is PSPACE-complete [19]. We now introduce a fragment of LTL where safety/co-safety is a syntactical feature.

Theorem 2 ([26]). *If an LTL formula ϕ in NNF is Until-free/Release-free, then ϕ is safe/co-safe.*

Motivated by this theorem, we define now the syntactic fragment of *Safety/Co-Safety* LTL.

Definition 3. *Safety/Co-Safety LTL formulas are in NNF and Until-free/Release-free, respectively.*

Remark: To the best of our knowledge, it is an open question whether every safe LTL formula is equivalent to some Safety LTL formula. We conjecture that this is the case.

2.2   Boolean Synthesis

In this paper, we utilize the *boolean synthesis* technique proposed in [16].

Definition 4 (Boolean Synthesis [16]). *Given two disjoint atom sets* $\mathcal{I}, \mathcal{O}$ *of input and output variables, respectively, and a boolean formula* ξ *over* $\mathcal{I} \cup \mathcal{O}$, *the boolean-synthesis problem is to construct a function* $\gamma : 2^{\mathcal{I}} \to 2^{\mathcal{O}}$ *such that, for all* $I \in 2^{\mathcal{I}}$, *if there exists* $O \in 2^{\mathcal{O}}$ *such that* $I \cup O \models \xi$, *then* $I \cup \gamma(I) \models \xi$. *We call* γ *the implementation function.*

We treat boolean synthesis as a black box, applying it to the key operation of Safety LTL synthesis proposed in this paper. For more details on algorithms and techniques for boolean synthesis we refer to [16].

3   Safety LTL Synthesis

In this section we give the definition of Safety LTL synthesis. We then show how this problem can be modeled as a *safety game* played over a kind of deterministic automaton, called a *safety automaton*. In the following sections we describe approaches to construct this automaton from a Safety LTL formula and solve the game that it specifies.

Definition 5 (Safety LTL Synthesis). *Let* ϕ *be an* LTL *formula over an alphabet* $\mathcal{P}$ *and* $\mathcal{X}, \mathcal{Y}$ *be two disjoint atom sets such that* $\mathcal{X} \cup \mathcal{Y} = \mathcal{P}$. $\mathcal{X}$ *is the set of* input (environment) *variables and* $\mathcal{Y}$ *is the set of* output (controller) *variables.* ϕ *is realizable with respect to* $\langle \mathcal{X}, \mathcal{Y} \rangle$ *if there exists a strategy* $g : (2^{\mathcal{X}})^* \to 2^{\mathcal{Y}}$, *such that for an arbitrary infinite sequence* $X_0, X_1, \ldots \in (2^{\mathcal{X}})^\omega$, ϕ *is true in the infinite trace* $\rho = (X_0 \cup g(X_0)), (X_1 \cup g(X_0, X_1)), (X_2 \cup g(X_0, X_1, X_2)) \ldots$. *The* synthesis *procedure is to compute such a strategy if* ϕ *is realizable.*

There are two versions of the Safety LTL synthesis, depending on the first player. Here we consider that the environment moves first, but the version where the controller moves first can be obtained by a small modification.

The Safety LTL synthesis is a subset of LTL synthesis by restricting the property to be a Safety LTL formula. Therefore, we can use general LTL-synthesis methods to solve the Safety LTL synthesis problem. Classical approaches to LTL synthesis problems involve two steps: 1) Convert the LTL formula to a deterministic automaton; 2) Reduce LTL synthesis to an infinite game over the automaton. We now present the automata corresponding to the class of Safety LTL formulas.

Definition 6 (Deterministic Safety Automata). *A deterministic safety automaton (DSA) is a tuple* $A^s = (2^{\mathcal{P}}, S, s_0, \delta)$, *where* $2^{\mathcal{P}}$ *is the alphabet,* S *is a finite set of states with* s_0 *as the initial state, and* $\delta : S \times 2^{\mathcal{P}} \to S$ *is a partial transition function. Given an infinite trace* $\rho \in (2^{\mathcal{P}})^\omega$, *a run* r *of* ρ *on* A^s *is a sequence of states* $s_0, s_1, s_2, \ldots$ *such that* $s_{i+1} = \delta(s_i, \rho_i)$. ρ *is accepted by* A^s *if* A^s *has an infinite run* r *of* ρ.

Note that in the definition, δ is a partial function, meaning that given $s \in S$ and $a \in 2^{\mathcal{P}}$, $\delta(s, a)$ can either return a state $s' \in S$ or be undefined. Thus, an infinite run of ρ on A^s may not exist due to the possibility of $\delta(s_i, \rho_i)$ being undefined for some (s_i, ρ_i). A DSA is essentially a deterministic Büchi automaton (DBA) [6] with a partial transition function and a set of accepting states $F = S$.

Deterministic safety games are games between two players, the environment and the controller, played over a DSA. We have two disjoint sets of variables $\mathcal{X}$ and $\mathcal{Y}$. $\mathcal{X}$ contains uncontrollable variables, which are under the control of the environment. $\mathcal{Y}$ contains controllable variables, which are under the control of the controller. A *round* consists of both the controller and the environment setting the value of the variables they control. A *play* of the game is a word $\rho \in (2^{\mathcal{X} \cup \mathcal{Y}})^\omega$ that describes how the environment and the controller set values to the variables during each round. A *run* of the game is the corresponding sequence of states through the play. The *specification* of the game is given by a deterministic safety automaton $A^s = (2^{\mathcal{X} \cup \mathcal{Y}}, S, s_0, \delta)$.

A *winning* play for the controller is an infinite sequence accepted by A^s. A *strategy* for the controller is a function $f : (2^{\mathcal{X}})^* \to 2^{\mathcal{Y}}$ such that given a history of the setting of the environmental variables, f determines how the controller set the controllable variables in $\mathcal{Y}$. A strategy is a *winning strategy* if starting from the initial state s_0, for every possible sequence of assignments of the variables in $\mathcal{X}$, it leads to an infinite run. Checking the existence of such a *winning strategy* counts for the *realizability* problem.

Safety games can be seen as duals of reachability games, where reachability games are won by reaching a set of winning states, while safety games are won by avoiding a set of losing states. Safety games however cannot be reduced to reachability games. The realizability problem of safety game can indeed be reduced to that of reachability game since the two are dual and the underlying game is determined, but this does not work for strategy generation. Safety game does not generate a winning strategy for the environment if it is unrealizable. It is known that reachability games can be solved in linear time in the size of the game graph [1]. One of the ways to do this is by a reduction to Horn Satisfiability, which can be solved in linear time [11]. In the next section we present such a reduction.

4   Explicit Approach to Safety Synthesis

We now show how to solve safety games by reducing to Horn satisfiability (Horn-SAT), a variant of SAT where every clause has at most one positive literal. Horn-SAT is known to be solvable in linear time using constraint propagation, cf. [11]. Modern SAT solvers use specialized data structures for performing very fast constraint propagation [22].

From a DSA $A^s = (2^{\mathcal{X} \cup \mathcal{Y}}, S, s_0, \delta)$ defining a safety game, we construct a Horn formula f such that the game is winning for the system if and only if f is satisfiable. Then, from a satisfying assignment of f we can extract a winning strategy. We now describe the construction of the Horn formula. There are three kinds of Boolean variables in f: (1) state variables: p_s for each state $s \in S$; (2) state-input variables: $p_{(s,X)}$ for each state $s \in S$ and $X \in 2^{\mathcal{X}}$; (3) state-input-output variables: $p_{(s,X,Y)}$ for each state $s \in S$, $X \in 2^{\mathcal{X}}$, and $Y \in 2^{\mathcal{Y}}$.

We first construct a non-Horn boolean formula f', then we show how to obtain a Horn formula f from f'. The intuition of the construction is that first, s_0 must be a winning state. Then, for every winning state, for all inputs there should exist an output such that the corresponding successor is a winning state.

Let n represent the number of possible output assignments: $2^{\mathcal{Y}} = \{Y_1, \ldots, Y_n\}$, $n = 2^{|\mathcal{Y}|}$. f' is a conjunction of p_{s_0} with the following constraints for each state $s \in S$: (1) $p_s \rightarrow p_{(s,X)}$, for each $X \in 2^{\mathcal{X}}$; (2) $p_{(s,X)} \rightarrow \left(p_{(s,X,Y_1)} \vee p_{(s,X,Y_2)} \vee \ldots \vee p_{(s,X,Y_n)}\right)$, for each $X \in 2^{\mathcal{X}}$; (3) $p_{(s,X,Y)} \rightarrow p_{\delta(s,X,Y)}$, for each $X \in 2^{\mathcal{X}}, Y \in 2^{\mathcal{Y}}$, if $\delta(s, X, Y)$ is well defined ; and (4) $\neg p_{(s,X,Y)}$, for each $X \in 2^{\mathcal{X}}, Y \in 2^{\mathcal{Y}}$, if $\delta(s, X, Y)$ is undefined.

Theorem 3. *The formula f' is satisfiable with assignment α' iff the safety game over A^s is realizable and α' encodes a winning strategy.*

Proof. If f' is satisfiable with assignment α', there is a set $C \subseteq S$ of states, where for each state $s \in C$, it is the case that p_s is true in α'. Then, by clauses of type (1), given a state $s \in C$, for all inputs $X \in 2^{\mathcal{X}}$, it is the case that $p_{(s,X)}$ is also true in α'. Furthermore, by clause of type (2), there must be some output $Y \in 2^{\mathcal{Y}}$ such that $p_{(s,X,Y)}$ is true in α'. Since $p_{(s,X,Y)}$ is true, there cannot be a clause $\neg p_{(s,X,Y)}$ of type (4), and therefore it is the case that $\delta(s, X, Y)$ is well defined and, by clause of type (3), $p_{\delta(s,X,Y)}$ is also true in α'. This means that we have a wining strategy such that all states in C, including s_0, are winning. In response to input $X \in 2^{\mathcal{X}}$, the system outputs $Y \in 2^{\mathcal{Y}}$ such that $p_{(s,X,Y)}$ is true in α', and this ensures that the successor state $\delta(s, X, Y)$ is also in C.

If the safety game over A^s is realizable, then there is a winning strategy $g : S \times 2^{\mathcal{X}} \rightarrow 2^{\mathcal{Y}}$ and a set $C \subseteq S$, containing s_0, of winning states such that for each state $s \in C$ and input $X \in 2^{\mathcal{X}}$, the output $Y = g(s, X)$ is such that $\delta(s, X, Y) \in C$. Then the truth assignment α' that makes p_s true iff $s \in C$, and makes $p_{(s,X)}$ and $p_{(s,X,g(s,X))}$ true for all $s \in C$ and $X \in 2^{\mathcal{X}}$ is a satisfying assignment of f.   □

We now transform the formula f' to an equi-satisfiable formula f that is a Horn formula (in which every clause contains at most one positive literal). We replace each variable p_s, $p_{(s,X)}$, and $p_{(s,X,Y)}$ in f' by its negative literal $\neg p_s$, $\neg p_{(s,X)}$, and $\neg p_{(s,X,Y)}$, respectively. We can then rewrite each constraint $(\neg p_s \rightarrow \neg p_{(s,X)})$ as $(p_{(s,X)} \rightarrow p_s)$. Similarly, we can rewrite $(\neg p_{(s,X)} \rightarrow (\neg p_{(s,X,Y_1)} \vee \ldots \vee \neg p_{(s,X,Y_n)}))$ as the equivalent constraint $((p_{(s,X,Y_1)} \wedge \ldots \wedge p_{(s,X,Y_n)}) \rightarrow p_{(s,X)})$. f is equivalent to f' with the polarity of the literals flipped, therefore we have that f is equi-satisfiable to f'. Given a satisfying assignment α for f, we obtain a satisfying assignment α' for f' by, for every variable p, assigning p to be true in α' iff p is assigned false in α.

Since f is a Horn formula, we can obtain a winning strategy in linear time. Note, however, that f is constructed from an explicit representation of the DSA A^s, as a state graph with one transition per assignment of the input and output variables. The challenge for this approach is the blow-up in the size of the state graph with respect to the input temporal formula. To address this challenge we need to be able to express the state graph more succinctly.

Therefore, we present an alternative approach for solving safety games using a symbolic representation of the state graph. Although the algorithm is no longer linear, not having to use an explicit representation of the game makes up for that fact. In order to construct this symbolic representation efficiently, we exploit the fact that safety games are dual to reachability games played over a DFA, allowing us to use techniques for symbolic construction of DFAs. This construction is described in the next section.

5   Symbolic Approach to Safety Synthesis

In order to perform Safety-LTL synthesis symbolically, the first step is to construct a symbolic representation of the DSA from the Safety-LTL formula. The following section explains how we can achieve this. The key insight that we use is that a symbolic representation of the DSA can be derived from the symbolic representation of the DFA encoding the set of bad prefixes of the Safety-LTL formula, allowing us to exploit techniques for symbolic DFA construction. After this, we describe how we can, from this representation, symbolically compute the set of winning states of the safety game, and then extract from them a winning strategy using boolean synthesis.

5.1   From Safety LTL to Deterministic Safety Automata

In this section, we propose a conversion from Safety LTL to DSA. The standard approach to constructing deterministic automata for LTL formulas is to first convert an LTL formula to a nondeterministic Büchi automaton using tools such as SPOT [12], LTL2BA [17], and then apply a determinization construction, e.g., Safra's construction [25]. The conversion from LTL to deterministic automata, however, is intractable in practice, not only because of the doubly-exponential complexity, but also the non-trivial construction of both Safra [25] and Safraless [20] approaches. Therefore, LTL synthesis is able to benefit from a better automata construction technique. One of the contribution in this paper is proving such a technique which efficiently constructs the corresponding safety automata of Safety LTL formulas. The novelty here is a much simpler conversion, thus yielding a more efficient synthesis procedure.

Since every trace rejected by a DSA A^s can be rejected in a finite number of steps, we can alternatively define the language accepted by A^s by the finite prefixes that it rejects. This allows us to work in the domain of finite words, which can be recognized much more easily, using deterministic finite automata. Therefore, a DSA can be seen as the dual of a DFA over the same state space. Given a DFA $D = (2^P, S_d, s_0, \lambda, F_d)$, the corresponding DSA $A^s = (2^P, S, s_0, \delta)$ can be generated by following steps: 1) $S = S_d \backslash F_d$; 2) For $s \in S, a \in 2^P$, if $\lambda(s, a) = s' \in S$, then $\delta(s, a) = s'$, otherwise $\delta(s, a)$ is undefined.

Theorem 4 ([19]). *Given a Safety* LTL *formula* ϕ*, there is a DFA* A_ϕ *which accepts exactly the finite traces that are bad prefixes for* ϕ*.*

Given a Safety LTL formula ϕ and the corresponding DFA A_ϕ, we can construct the DSA A_ϕ^s. The correctness of such construction is guaranteed by the following theorem.

Theorem 5. *For a Safety* LTL *formula* ϕ*, the DSA* $A_\phi^s = (2^P, S, s_0, \delta)$*, which is dual to* $A_\phi = (2^P, S_d, s_0, \lambda, F_d)$*, accepts exactly the traces that satisfy* ϕ*.*

Proof. For an infinite trace ρ, $\rho \models \phi$ implies that an arbitrary prefix ρ' of ρ is not a bad prefix for ϕ, so ρ' cannot be accepted by A_ϕ. Therefore, starting from the initial state s_0, λ always returns some successor $s' \notin F_d$, so the corresponding transition is also in A_ϕ^s. The run r of ρ on A_ϕ^s is indeed infinite. As a result, $\rho \models \phi$ implies that ρ can be accepted by A_ϕ^s.

On the other hand, an infinite trace ρ being accepted by A_ϕ^s implies that the run r of ρ on A_ϕ^s is infinite. Therefore, starting from the initial state s_0, partial function δ can always return some successor $s' \in S$, for which $s' \notin F_d$. There is a corresponding transition in A_ϕ for each transition in A_ϕ^s, then an arbitrary prefix ρ' of ρ is indeed can not be accepted by A_ϕ, such that ρ' is not a bad prefix. As a result, ρ can be accepted by A_ϕ^s implies that $\rho \models \phi$.   □

Based on Theorem 5, the construction of the DSA relies on the construction of the DFA for the Safety formula ϕ. Therefore, we can leverage the techniques and tools developed for DFA construction. Although it still cannot avoid the doubly-exponential complexity, DFA construction is much simpler than that of ω-automata (e.g. parity [25], or co-Büchi [20]). Consider a Safety LTL formula ϕ. From Theorem 1 and 4, we know that $\neg\phi$, which is co-safe, can be interpreted over finite words. Thus, we can construct the DFA A_ϕ from $\neg\phi$.

DFA construction Summarily, the DFA construction is processed as follows: Given a Safety LTL formula ϕ, we first negate it to obtain a Co-Safety LTL formula $\neg\phi$. Taking the translation described below, which restricts the interpretation of $\neg\phi$ over *finite linear ordered traces*, we can obtain a first-order logic formula $fol()$. The DFA for such $fol()$ is obviously able to accept exactly the set of bad prefixes for ϕ (or say, good prefixes for $\neg\phi$).

Consider an infinite trace $\sigma = \rho_0\rho_1 \cdots \rho_n \top\top \cdots$ that satisfies the Co-Safety LTL formula $\psi = \neg\phi$ in NNF, where the finite prefix $\rho = \rho_0\rho_1 \cdots \rho_n$ of σ is a good prefix for ψ. The corresponding FOL interpretation $\mathcal{I} = (\Delta^I, \cdot^{\mathcal{I}})$ of ρ is defined as follows: $\Delta^I = \{0, 1, 2, \cdots, last\}$, where $last = |\rho| - 1$. For each $p \in \mathcal{P}$, its interpretation $p^{\mathcal{I}} = \{i \mid p \in \rho(i)\}$. Intuitively, $p^{\mathcal{I}}$ is interpreted as the set of positions where p is true in ρ. Then we can generate a corresponding FOL formula that opens in x by a function $fol(\psi, x)$ from the Co-Safety LTL formula and a variable x where $0 \le x \le last$, which is defined as follows:

- $fol(p, x) = p(x)$ and $fol(\neg p, x) = \neg p(x)$
- $fol(\psi_1 \wedge \psi_2, x) = fol(\psi_1, x) \wedge fol(\psi_2, x)$
- $fol(\psi_1 \vee \psi_2, x) = fol(\psi_1, x) \vee fol(\psi_2, x)$
- $fol(X\psi, x) = \exists y.succ(x, y) \wedge fol(\psi, y)$
- $fol(\psi_1 U \psi_2, x) = \exists y.x \le y \le last \wedge fol(\psi_2, y) \wedge \forall z.x \le z < y \rightarrow fol(\psi_1, z)$

In the above, the notation *succ* denotes that y is the successor of x. The following theorem guarantees a finite trace ρ is a good prefix of the Co-Safety LTL formula ψ iff the corresponding interpretation $\mathcal{I}$ of ρ models $fol(\psi, 0)$.

Theorem 6. *Given a Co-Safety LTL formula ψ, a finite trace ρ and the corresponding interpretation $\mathcal{I}$ of ρ, ρ is a good prefix for ψ iff $\mathcal{I} \models fol(\psi, 0)$.*

Proof. We prove the theorem by the induction over the structure of ψ.

- Basically, if $\psi = p$ is an atom, ρ is a good prefix for ψ iff $p \in \rho_0$. By the definition of $\mathcal{I}$, we have that $0 \in p^{\mathcal{I}}$. As a result, ρ is a good prefix for ψ iff $\mathcal{I} \models fol(p, 0)$. Moreover, if $\psi = \neg p$ where p is an atom, ρ is a good prefix for ψ iff $p \notin \rho_0$, and iff $0 \notin p^{\mathcal{I}}$, finally iff $\mathcal{I} \models fol(\neg p, 0)$ holds;
- If $\psi = \psi_1 \wedge \psi_2$, ρ is a good prefix for ψ implies ρ is a good prefix for both ψ_1 and ψ_2. By induction hypothesis, it is true that $\mathcal{I} \models fol(\psi_1, 0)$ and $\mathcal{I} \models fol(\psi_2, 0)$. So $\mathcal{I} \models fol(\psi_1, 0) \wedge fol(\psi_2, 0)$, i.e. $\mathcal{I} \models fol(\psi_1 \wedge \psi_2, 0)$ holds. On the other hand, since $\mathcal{I} \models fol(\psi_1 \wedge \psi_2, 0)$, $\mathcal{I} \models fol(\psi_1, 0)$ and $\mathcal{I} \models fol(\psi_2, 0)$ are true. By induction hypothesis, we have that ρ is a good prefix for both ψ_1 and ψ_2. Thus ρ is a good prefix for $\psi_1 \wedge \psi_2$;
- If $\psi = \psi_1 \vee \psi_2$, the proof here is omitted to save space.
- If $\psi = X\psi_1$, ρ is a good prefix for ψ iff suffix $\rho' = \rho_1\rho_2 \ldots, \rho_{|\rho|-1}$ of ρ is a good prefix for ψ_1. Let $\mathcal{I}'$ be the corresponding interpretation of ρ', thus every atom $p \in \mathcal{P}$ satisfies $i \in p^{\mathcal{I}'}$ iff $(i + 1) \in p^{\mathcal{I}}$. By induction hypothesis, $\mathcal{I}' \models fol(\psi_1, 0)$ holds, thus $\mathcal{I} \models fol(\psi_1, 1)$ is true. Therefore, $\mathcal{I} \models fol(X\psi_1, 0)$ holds.
- If $\psi = \psi_1 U\psi_2$, ρ is a good prefix for ψ iff there exists i $(0 \leq i \leq |\rho| - 1)$ such that suffix $\rho' = \rho_i\rho_{i+1} \ldots, \rho_{|\rho|-1}$ of ρ is a good prefix for ψ_2. And for all j $(0 \leq j < i)$, $\rho'' = \rho_j\rho_{j+1} \ldots, \rho_{i-1}$ is a good prefix for ψ_1. Let $\mathcal{I}'$ and $\mathcal{I}''$ be the corresponding interpretations of ρ' and ρ''. Thus every atom $p \in \mathcal{P}$ satisfies that $k \in p^{\mathcal{I}'}$ iff $(i + k) \in p^{\mathcal{I}}$, $k \in p^{\mathcal{I}''}$ iff $(j + k) \in p^{\mathcal{I}}$. By induction hypothesis, $\mathcal{I}' \models fol(\psi_2, 0)$ and $\mathcal{I}'' \models fol(\psi_1, 0)$ holds. Thus $\mathcal{I} \models \exists i.0 \leq i \leq (|\rho| - 1) \cdot fol(\psi_2, i)$ and $\mathcal{I} \models \forall j.0 \leq j < i \cdot fol(\psi_1, j)$ hold. Therefore, $\mathcal{I} \models fol(\psi_1 U\psi_2, 0)$.

$\square$

MONA [18] is a tool that translates *Weak Second-order Theory of One or Two successors* (WS1S/WS2S) [10] formula to minimal DFA, represented symbolically. WS1S subsumes the *First-Order Logic* (FOL) over finite traces, which allows us to adopt MONA to construct the DFA A_ϕ for Safety formula ϕ. Taking the assumption that the DFA generated by MONA accepts exactly the same traces that satisfy $fol(\neg\phi, 0)$, which corresponds to Co-Safety LTL formula $\neg\phi$, by Theorem 6 we can conclude that the DFA returned by MONA is A_ϕ that accepts exactly the bad prefixes for the Safety LTL formula ϕ.

Theorem 7. *Let ϕ be a Safety LTL formula and A_ϕ be the DFA constructed by MONA taking $fol(\neg\phi, 0)$ as input. Finite trace ρ is a bad prefix for ϕ iff ρ is accepted by A_ϕ.*

Deleting all transitions toward the accepting states in A_ϕ and removing the accepting states of A_ϕ derives the safety automaton A_ϕ^s. To solve the Safety LTL synthesis problem, we reduce the problem to a deterministic safety game over this automaton. We first present the standard formulation and algorithm for solving such a game. Then, since MONA constructs the DFA symbolically, we present a symbolic version of this algorithm.

5.2 Solving Safety Games Symbolically

Computing a *winning strategy* of the safety game over DSA solves the synthesis problem. We base our symbolic approach on the algorithm from [9] for DFA (reachability) games, which are the duals of safety games. In this section, we first describe the general algorithm, which computes the set of winning states as a fixpoint. We then show how to perform this computation symbolically using the symbolic representation of the state graph constructed by MONA. Finally, we describe how we can use boolean synthesis to extract a winning strategy from the symbolic representation of the set of winning states.

Consider a set of states $\mathcal{E}$. The *pre-image* of $\mathcal{E}$ is a set $Pre(\mathcal{E}) = \{s \in S \mid \forall X \in 2^{\mathcal{X}}.\exists Y \in 2^{\mathcal{Y}}.\delta(s, (X, Y)) \in \mathcal{E}\}$. That is, $Pre(\mathcal{E})$ is the set of states from which, regardless of the action of the environment, the controller can force the game into a state in $\mathcal{E}$. If the controller moves first, we swap the order of $\exists Y \in 2^{\mathcal{Y}}$ and $\forall X \in 2^{\mathcal{X}}$ to compute the pre-image.

We define $Win(A^s)$ as the greatest-fixpoint of $Win_i(A^s)$, which denotes the set of states in which the controller can remain within i steps. This means that $Win(A^s)$ is the set of states in which the controller can remain indefinitely, that is, the set of winning states. The safety game is solved by computing the fixpoint as follows:

$$Win_0(A^s) = S \tag{1}$$
$$Win_{i+1}(A^s) = Win_i(A^s) \cap Pre(Win_i(A^s)) \tag{2}$$

That is, we start with the set of all states and at each iteration remove those states from which the controller cannot force the game to remain in the current set.

For realizability checking, if $s_0 \in Win(A^s)$, then the game is realizable, otherwise the game is unrealizable. We also consider an *early-termination* heuristic to speed up the realizability checking: after each computation of $Win_i(A^s)$, if $s_0 \notin Win_i(A^s)$, then return unrealizable. To generate the strategy, we define a deterministic finite transducer $\mathcal{T} = (2^{\mathcal{X}}, 2^{\mathcal{Y}}, Q, s_0, \varrho, \omega)$ based on the set $Win(A^s)$, where: $Q = Win(A^s)$ is the set of winning states; $\varrho : Q \times 2^{\mathcal{X}} \to Q$ is the transition function such that $\varrho(q, X) = \delta(q, X \cup Y)$ and $Y = \omega(q, X)$; $\omega : Q \times 2^{\mathcal{X}} \to 2^{\mathcal{Y}}$ is the output function, where $\omega(q, X) = Y$ such that $\delta(q, X \cup Y) \in Q$. Note that there are many possible choices for the output function ω. The transducer $\mathcal{T}$ defines a winning strategy by restricting ω to return only one possible setting of $\mathcal{Y}$.

Following the construction in Section 5.1, MONA produces a symbolic representation of the DFA A_ϕ which accepts all bad prefixes of the Safety LTL formula ϕ. Therefore, in this section we show how to derive a DSA and solve the corresponding safety game from this representation. Following [29], we define a symbolic DFA as $A = (\mathcal{X}, \mathcal{Y}, \mathcal{Z}, Z_0, \eta, f)$, where: $\mathcal{X}$ is a set of input variables; $\mathcal{Y}$ is a set of output variables; $\mathcal{Z}$ is a set of state variables; $Z_0 \in 2^{\mathcal{Z}}$ is the assignment to the state propositions corresponding to the initial state; $\eta : 2^{\mathcal{X}} \times 2^{\mathcal{Y}} \times 2^{\mathcal{Z}} \to 2^{\mathcal{Z}}$ is a boolean function mapping assignments X, Y and Z of the variables of $\mathcal{X}, \mathcal{Y}$ and $\mathcal{Z}$ to a new assignment Z' of the variables of $\mathcal{Z}$; f is a boolean formula over the propositions in $\mathcal{Z}$, such that f is satisfied by an interpretation Z iff Z corresponds to an accepting state.

Given A, the corresponding safety automaton $A^s = (2^{\mathcal{X} \cup \mathcal{Y}}, S, s_0, \delta)$ that avoids all bad prefixes accepted by A is defined by: $\mathcal{X}$ and $\mathcal{Y}$ are the same as in the definition of A; $S = \{Z \in 2^{\mathcal{Z}} \mid Z \not\models f\}$; $s_0 = Z_0$; $\delta : S \times 2^{\mathcal{X} \cup \mathcal{Y}} \to S$ is the partial function such that $\delta(Z, X \cup Y) = \eta(X, Y, Z)$ if $Z \in S$, and is undefined otherwise.

Lemma 1. *If A_ϕ is a symbolic DFA that accepts exactly the bad prefixes of a Safety LTL formula ϕ, then A_ϕ^s is a deterministic safety automaton for ϕ.*

This correspondence allows us to use the symbolic representation of $\mathcal{A}$ to compute the solution of the safety game defined by A^s. To compute the set of winning states, we represent the set $Win_i(A^s)$ by a boolean formula w_i in terms of the state variables $\mathcal{Z}$, such that an assignment $Z \in 2^{\mathcal{Z}}$ satisfies w_i if and only if the state represented by Z is in $Win_i(A^s)$. We define $w_0 = \neg f$ and $w_{i+1}(Z) = w_i(Z) \wedge \forall X.\exists Y.w_i(\eta(X, Y, Z))$, which correspond respectively to (1) and (2) above. The fixpoint computation terminates once $w_{i+1} \equiv w_i$, at which point we define $w = w_i$, representing $Win(A^s)$. We can then test for realizability by checking if the assignment Z_0 representing the initial state satisfies w.

Theorem 8. *The safety game defined by A^s is realizable if and only if $Z_0 \models w$.*

If $Z_0 \models w$, then we wish to construct a transducer $\mathcal{T} = (2^{\mathcal{X}}, 2^{\mathcal{Y}}, Q, s_0, \varrho, \omega)$ representing a winning strategy. We define $Q = \{Z \in 2^{\mathcal{Z}} \mid Z \models w\}$, $s_0 = Z_0$ and $\varrho(Z, X, Y) = \eta(X, Y, Z)$ if $\eta(X, Y, Z) \in Q$ and undefined otherwise. To construct ω, we can use a boolean-synthesis procedure. Recall that the input to this procedure is a boolean formula φ, a set of input variables I and a set of output variables O. In our case, $\varphi(Z, X, Y) = w(\eta(X, Y, Z))$, $I = \mathcal{Z} \cup \mathcal{X}$ and $O = \mathcal{Y}$. The result of the synthesis is a boolean function $\omega : 2^{\mathcal{Z} \cup \mathcal{X}} \to 2^{\mathcal{Y}}$. Then, from the definition of boolean synthesis it follows that if the output is chosen by ω the game remains in the set of winning states. That is, if $Z \in 2^{\mathcal{Z}}$ satisfies w, then for all $X \in 2^{\mathcal{X}}$, $\eta(Z, X, \omega(Z \cup X))$ also satisfies w.

6   Experimental Evaluation

6.1   Implementation

Explicit Approach The main algorithm for the explicit approach consists of three steps: DSA construction, Horn formula generation and SAT solving for synthesis. We adopted SPOT [12] as the DSA constructor since the output automata should be deterministic. Generating the Horn formula follows the rules described in Section 4. Furthermore, here we used Minisat-2.2 [13] for SAT solving. Decoding the variables that are assigned with the truth in the assignment returned by Minisat-2.2 [13] is able to generate the strategy if the Safety LTL formula is realizable with respect to $\langle inputs, outputs \rangle$.

Symbolic Encoding We implemented the symbolic framework for Safety LTL synthesis in the *SSyft* tool, which is written in C++ and utilizes the BDD library CUDD-3.0.0 [28]. The entire framework consists of two steps: the DSA construction and the safety game over the DSA. In the first step, the dual of the DSA, a DFA is constructed via MONA [18] and represented as a *Shared Multi-terminal BDD* (ShMTBDD) [5, 18]. From this ShMTBDD, we construct a representation of the transition relation η by a sequence $\mathcal{B} = \langle B_0, B_1, \ldots, B_{n-1} \rangle$ of BDDs. Each B_i, when evaluated over an assignment of $\mathcal{X} \cup \mathcal{Y}$, outputs an assignment to a state variable $z_i \in \mathcal{Z}$. The boolean formula f representing the accepting states of the DFA is likewise encoded as a BDD B_f.

To perform the fixpoint computation, we construct a sequence $\langle B_{w_0}, B_{w_1}, \ldots, B_{w_i} \rangle$ of BDDs, where B_{w_i} is the BDD representation of the formula w_i. $B_{w_{i+1}}$ is constructed from B_{w_i} by substituting each state variable z_i with the corresponding BDD B_i, which can be achieved by the *Compose* operation in CUDD. Moreover, CUDD provides the operations *UnivAbstract* and *ExistAbstract* for universal and existential quantifier elimination respectively. The fixpoint computation benefits from the canonicity of BDDs by checking the equivalence of $B_{w_{i+1}}$ and B_{w_i}. To check realizability we use the *Eval* operation. Since in our construction the state variables appear at the top of the BDDs, we use the Input-First boolean-synthesis procedure introduced in [16] to synthesize the winning strategy if the game is realizable.

6.2 Experimental Methodology

To show the efficiency of the methods proposed in this paper, we compare our tool *SSyft* based on the symbolic framework and the explicit approach, named as Horn_SAT, with extant LTL synthesis tools Unbeast [14] and Acacia+ [4]. Both of the LTL synthesis tools can use either SPOT [12] or LTL2BA [17] for the automata construction. From our preliminary evaluation, both Unbeast and Acacia+ perform better when they construct automata using LTL2BA. As a result, LTL2BA is the default LTL-to-automata translator of Unbeast and Acacia+ in our experiments. All tests are ran on a platform whose operating system is 64-bit Ubuntu 16.04, with a 2.4 GHz CPU (Intel Core i7) and 8 GB of memory. The timeout was set to be 60 seconds (s).

Input Formulas Our benchmark formulas are collected from [14], called *LoadBalancer*. Since not all cases are safe, here we propose a class of *Expansion Formulas* for safety-property generation. Consider an LTL formula ϕ in NNF. We use a transformation function $ef(\phi, l)$ that given ϕ and a parameter l, which represents the expansion length, returns a Safety LTL formula. The function $ef()$ works in the following way: (1) For each subformula of the form $\phi_1 U \phi_2$, expand to $\phi_2 \vee (\phi_1 \wedge X(\phi_1 U \phi_2))$ for $l - 1$ times; (2) Substitute the remaining $\phi_1 U \phi_2$ with ϕ_2. Note that Safety formulas are Until-free in NNF, thus for LTL formulas in NNF, it is not necessary to deal with the Release operator. The intuition of the expansion is to bound the satisfied length of $\phi_1 U \phi_2$ by adding the Next(X) operator. The parameter l scales to 5 in our test, for each length there are 79 instances. And 395 cases in total.

Correctness The correctness of our implementation was evaluated by comparing the results from our approaches with those from Acacia+ and Unbeast. For the solved cases, we never encountered an inconsistency.

6.3 Results

We evaluated the performance of *SSyft* and Horn_SAT in terms of the number of solved cases and the running time. Our experiments demonstrate that the symbolic approach we introduced here significantly improves the effectiveness of Safety LTL synthesis. The safety game has two versions, depending on which player (environment or controller) moves first. Both our tool *SSyft* and Acacia+ are able to handle these two kinds of games, while Unbeast supports only games with the environment moving first. As a result, we only consider the comparison on the environment-moving-first game. We aim to compare the results on two aspects: 1) the scalability on the expansion length; 2) the number of solved cases in the given time limit.

Fig. 1 shows the number of solved cases for each expansion length (1-5)[4]. As shown in the figure, *SSyft* solves approximately twice as many cases as the other three tools. The advantage of *SSyft* diminishes as the expansion length grows, because MONA cannot generate the automata for such cases. Neither of Acacia+ and Unbeast can solve these cases even in a small expansion length. Horn_SAT performs similarly as *SSyft* when $l = 1$, which derives smaller DSA. The performance of Horn_SAT decreases sharply as the size of the DSA grows, since formula generation dominates the synthesis time. In total, *SSyft* solves a total of 339 cases, while Acacia+, Unbeast and Horn_SAT solve 182, 132 and 159 cases, respectively.

The scatter plot for the total time comparison is shown in Fig. 2, where + plots the data for *SSyft* against Acacia+, △ plots the data for *SSyft* against Unbeast and ○ is for Horn_SAT. Clearly, *SSyft* outperforms the other three tools. The results shown in Fig. 2 confirm the claim that the symbolic approach is much more efficient than Acacia+ and Unbeast. In some cases, Horn_SAT performs better than *SSyft*, nevertheless in general *SSyft* has a significant advantage. Thus, the evidence here indicates that both the symbolic approach and the explicit method introduced in this paper contribute to the improvement of the overall performance of Safety LTL synthesis.

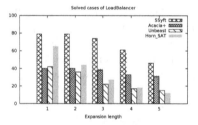

Fig. 1. Comparison of SSyft against Acacia+, Unbeast and the Horn_SAT approach on the number of solved cases as the expansion length grows

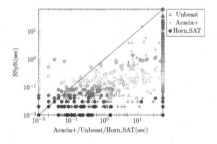

Fig. 2. Comparison of SSyft against Acacia+, Unbeast and the Horn_SAT approach on total solving time

7   Concluding Remarks

We presented here a simple but efficient approach to Safety LTL synthesis based on the observation that a minimal DFA can be constructed for Co-Safety LTL formula. Furthermore, a deterministic safety automaton (DSA) can be generated from the DFA, and a symbolic safety game can be solved over the DSA. A comparison with the reduction to Horn-SAT confirms better scalability of the symbolic approach. Further experiments show that the new approach outperforms existing solutions for general LTL synthesis.

---

[4] We recommend viewing the figures online for better readability.

Both the DSA construction and the symbolic safety game solution contribute to the improvement. It will be interesting to apply our approach to the *safety-first* method [27] for LTL synthesis.

It should be noted, however, that symbolic DSA construction cannot avoid the worst case doubly exponential complexity: it can only make the synthesis simpler and more efficient in practice. Our experiments show that the bottleneck is manifested when the input Safety LTL formula gets larger, and DSA construction becomes unachievable within the reasonable time. A promising solution may be to develop an on-the-fly method to perform the DSA construction and solve the safety game at the same time. We leave this to our future work.

Beyond general LTL-synthesis approaches, another relevant work is on GR(1) synthesis [3]. Although GR(1) synthesis aims to handle a fragment of general LTL as well, it is not comparable to Safety LTL, since GR(1) does not allow arbitrary nesting of the Release (R) and Next (X) operators. For that reason, our experiments do not cover the comparison between our approach and GR(1) synthesis. Another work related is synthesis of the GXW fragment [8]. In this fragment, input formulas are conjuction of certain pattern formulas expressed using the temporal connectives G, X, and W. Because of the limitation to six specific patterns, this fragment is quite less general that the Safety LTL fragment studied here.

Our work is also related to the safety-synthesis track of the Annual Synthesis Competition (SyntComp). While the Safety-LTL-synthesis problem can, in principle, be reduced to safety synthesis, the reduction is quite nontrivial. Safety-synthesis tools from SyntComp take AIGER models[5] as input, while our approach takes Safety LTL formulas as input. A symbolic DSA can be encoded as an AIGER model by adding additional variables to encode intermediate BDD nodes. As we saw, however, the construction of symbolic DSAs is a very demanding part of Safety LTL synthesis, with a worst-case doubly exponential complexity, so the usefulness of such a reduction is questionable.

We have shown here a new symbolic approach to Safety LTL synthesis, in which a more efficient automata-construction technique is utilized. Experiments show that our new approach outperforms existing solutions to general LTL synthesis, as well as a new reduction of safety games to Horn_SAT.

Acknowledgments. Work supported in part by NSF grants CCF-1319459 and IIS-1527668, NSF Expeditions in Computing project "ExCAPE: Expeditions in Computer Augmented Program Engineering", NSFC Projects No. 61572197 and No. 61632005, MOST NKTSP Project 2015BAG19B02, and by the Brazilian agency CNPq through the Ciência Sem Fronteiras program.

References

1. de Alfaro, L., Henzinger, T.A., Kupferman, O.: Concurrent Reachability Games. In: FOCS. pp. 564–575 (1998)
2. Bloem, R., Könighofer, R., Seidl, M.: SAT-based Synthesis Methods for Safety Specs. In: VMCAI. pp. 1–20 (2014)

---

[5] http://fmv.jku.at/aiger/

3. Bloem, R., Jobstmann, B., Piterman, N., Pnueli, A., Sa'ar, Y.: Synthesis of Reactive(1) designs. J. Comput. Syst. Sci. 78(3), 911–938 (2012)
4. Bohy, A., Bruyère, V., Filiot, E., Jin, N., Raskin, J.: Acacia+, a Tool for LTL Synthesis. In: CAV. pp. 652–657 (2012)
5. Bryant, R.E.: Symbolic Boolean Manipulation with Ordered Binary-Decision Diagrams. ACM Comput. Surv. 24(3), 293–318 (1992)
6. Büchi, J.R.: Weak Second-Order Arithmetic and Finite Automata. Z.Math. Logik Grundl. Math. 6, 66–92 (1960)
7. Calude, C.S., Jain, S., Khoussainov, B., Li, W., Stephan, F.: Deciding Parity Games in Quasipolynomial Time. In: STOC. pp. 252–263 (2017)
8. Cheng, C., Hamza, Y., Ruess, H.: Structural Synthesis for GXW Specifications. In: CAV. pp. 95–117 (2016)
9. De Giacomo, G., Vardi, M.Y.: Synthesis for LTL and LDL on Finite Traces. In: IJCAI. pp. 1558–1564 (2015)
10. Doner, J.: Tree Acceptors and Some of Their Applications. J. Comput. Syst. Sci. 4(5), 406–451 (1970)
11. Dowling, W.F., Gallier, J.H.: Linear-Time Algorithms for Testing the Satisfiability of Propositional Horn Formulae. J. Log. Program. 1(3), 267–284 (1984)
12. Duret-Lutz, A., Lewkowicz, A., Fauchille, A., Michaud, T., Renault, E., Xu, L.: Spot 2.0-A Framework for LTL and ω-Automata Manipulation. In: ATVA. pp. 122–129 (2016)
13. Eén, N., Mishchenko, A., Amla, N.: A Single-Instance Incremental SAT Formulation of Proof- and Counterexample-Based Abstraction (2010)
14. Ehlers, R.: Symbolic Bounded Synthesis. In: CAV. pp. 365–379 (2010)
15. Fogarty, S., Kupferman, O., Vardi, M.Y., Wilke, T.: Profile Trees for Büchi Word Automata, with Application to Determinization. In: GandALF. pp. 107–121 (2013)
16. Fried, D., Tabajara, L.M., Vardi, M.Y.: BDD-Based Boolean Functional Synthesis. In: CAV, Part II. pp. 402–421 (2016)
17. Gastin, P., Oddoux, D.: Fast LTL to Büchi Automata Translation. In: CAV. pp. 53–65 (2001)
18. Henriksen, J., Jensen, J., Jørgensen, M., Klarlund, N., Paige, B., Rauhe, T., Sandholm, A.: Mona: Monadic Second-Order Logic in Practice. In: TACAS. pp. 89–110 (1995)
19. Kupferman, O., Vardi, M.Y.: Model Checking of Safety Properties. Formal Methods in System Design 19(3), 291–314 (2001)
20. Kupferman, O., Vardi, M.Y.: Safraless Decision Procedures. In: FOCS. pp. 531–542 (2005)
21. Lamport, L.: What good is temporal logic? In: IFIP Congress. pp. 657–668 (1983)
22. Malik, S., Zhang, L.: Boolean Satisfiability from Theoretical Hardness to Practical Success. Commun. ACM 52(8), 76–82 (2009)
23. Pnueli, A.: The Temporal Logic of Programs. In: FOCS. pp. 46–57 (1977)
24. Pnueli, A., Rosner, R.: On the Synthesis of a Reactive Module. In: POPL. pp. 179–190 (1989)
25. Safra, S.: On the Complexity of omega-Automata. In: FOCS. pp. 319–327 (1988)
26. Sistla, A.P.: Safety, Liveness and Fairness in Temporal Logic. Formal Asp. Comput. 6(5), 495–512 (1994)
27. Sohail, S., Somenzi, F.: Safety First: A Two-Stage Algorithm for LTL Games. In: FMCAD. pp. 77–84 (2009)
28. Somenzi, F.: CUDD: CU Decision Diagram Package 3.0.0. Universiy of Colorado at Boulder (2016)
29. Zhu, S., Tabajara, L.M., Li, J., Pu, G., Vardi, M.Y.: Symbolic LTL$_f$ Synthesis. In: IJCAI. pp. 1362–1369 (2017)
30. Zohar, Z.M., Waldinger, R.: Toward Automatic Program Synthesis. Commun. ACM 14(3), 151–165 (1971)

An Interaction Concept for Program Verification Systems with Explicit Proof Object

Bernhard Beckert, Sarah Grebing, and Mattias Ulbrich

Karlsruhe Institute of Technology
{beckert,sarah.grebing,ulbrich}@kit.edu

Abstract. Deductive program verification is a difficult task: in general, user guidance is required to control the proof search and construction. Providing the right guiding information is challenging for users and usually requires several reiterations. Supporting the user in this process can considerably reduce the effort of program verification.

In this paper, we present an interaction concept for deductive program verification systems that combines point-and-click interaction with the use of a proof scripting language. Our contribution is twofold: Firstly, we present a concept for a flexible and concise proof scripting language tailored to the needs of program verification. Secondly, we explore the correspondences between program debugging and proof debugging and introduce a concept for analysing failed proof attempts which leverages well-established concepts from software debugging. We illustrate our concepts on examples – including small Java programs with non-trivial specifications – using an early prototype implementation of our interaction concepts that is built on top of the program verification system KeY.

1 Introduction

Research in automatic program verification has made a huge progress in recent years. Nevertheless, in the foreseeable future, there will always be programs and properties that are of importance in practice but for which verification systems cannot find correctness proofs automatically without user guidance [1]. Finding the right guiding information that allows a verification system to find a proof is, in general, an iterative process of repeated failed attempts.

Program verification proofs have characteristics considerably different from proofs of mathematical theorems (e.g., properties of algebraic structures). In particular, they consist of many structurally and/or semantically similar cases which are syntactically large, but usually of less intrinsic complexity. The mechanism for providing user guidance should reflect this peculiarity of proofs in the program verification domain and provide appropriate means for interaction.

We present an interaction concept based on using a proof scripting language together with a proof development and debugging approach, tailored to the needs of program verification. Our first contribution is a concept for a concise and flexible proof scripting language which allows the user to formulate proof statements which are applied to a group of syntactically or semantically similar

© Springer International Publishing AG 2017
O. Strichman and R. Tzoref-Brill (Eds.): HVC 2017, LNCS 10629, pp. 163–178, 2017.
https://doi.org/10.1007/978-3-319-70389-3_11

subproblems. The core of the language concept is the possibility to define selection criteria that choose several goals at a time that are then treated uniformly. These selection criteria are resilient to change in the sense that small changes in the proof require small changes in the proof script describing that proof.

Two interaction paradigms have emerged in state-of-the-art interactive verification systems: text-based interaction (proof scripts and source code annotations) and point-and-click interaction. Compared to scripting languages where single proof statements apply to only one goal, and to a textual recording of pure point-and-click interactions, a scripting language with multi-matching allows creating more compact proof scripts.

However, powerful concepts like multi-matching, which allow proof scripts whose structure is different from the proofs they describe, have to be complemented with a suitable method to debug failed proof attempts. Thus, as a second contribution of this paper, we introduce a concept for interactive proof development. The focus of this concept is to aid the user in comprehending failed proof attempts and identifying the next step to successfully continue the proof. Proofs can be constructed using a proof scripting language as well as direct manipulation of the proof object using point-and-click interaction.

We showcase our concept, which is particularly well suited for verification systems with explicit proof objects using a sequent calculus, by applying the concept for the interactive program verifier KeY [2].

The remainder of this paper is structured as follows: In Sections 2 and 3, we discuss the proof characteristics of interactive program verification and related work. Then, we introduce the concepts for a proof scripting language tailored to the peculiarities of proofs in this domain in Section 4; and we present a concept for debugging proofs performed using a scripting language in Section 5, making use of functionalities that are adapted from program debugging. We conclude and discuss future work in Section 6.

2   Interactive Program Verification

Program verification proofs differ from mechanised proofs of mathematical theorems, particularly in the size and complexity of the occurring formulas and in the number of different cases to investigate. Program verification proofs often have a large number of individual subgoals reflecting the control-flow possibilities in the program.

Each subgoal represents the effect of a possible program execution path, and subgoals for similar paths often have a high degree of similarity since they share common path- and postconditions. Such related subgoals may be treated uniformly, using a common proof strategy. During proof construction, the user typically switches between focusing on one particular proof goal and looking at a number of proof branches to decide which ones are semantically similar.

With increasing complexity of programs and specifications, users normally develop proofs in an iterative and explorative manner, as subtleties of the proofs are often only discovered after an attempt fails. These iterations include modifying the specification or the program, as well as adding information to guide the proof search. Until the verification succeeds, (a) failed attempts have to be inspected in order to understand the cause of failure and (b) the next step in the proof process has to be chosen.

Both (a) and (b) are complex tasks. One reason is the inherent difficulty of understanding a mechanised, formal proof for a non-trivial program property. In addition, proofs generated by verification systems are of fine granularity. This makes is difficult for users to understand the *big picture* of a proof – the abstract argumentation for why the program fulfils its specification. To succeed with subtask (b), performing the next proof step, the user has to understand the nature of why the proof failed: Is it a mismatch between specification and program or is the guidance for the proof system insufficient? State-of-the-art tools support the user in both tasks by, e.g., providing counterexamples and means to inspect the (incomplete or failed) proof object. However, performing the proof process is still characterised by trial-and-error phases. We claim that support for *debugging* large proofs is needed, providing means for explicating the correspondence between parts of the proof and parts of the program and its specification, for automating repetitive tasks and applying them to a number of uniform proof goals, and for analysing failed proof attempts.

The interaction has to use a suitable level of granularity. However, most existing verification tools with explicit proof object – i.e., a concrete proof object consisting of atomic rule applications, – only support the most detailed granularity, whereas systems using proof scripts – i.e., the proof object is implicitly known to exist but not actually constructed, – support interaction on a more abstract level and also allow repetition of proof steps (but mostly, repetition can only be applied to single or to all proof goals, but not to matching subsets).

The KeY system. The design of our concept is based on the results of two focus group experiments [3,4] and is targeted towards rule-based program verification systems operating on program logics. Our primary target, in which we exemplarily realize the concept, is the interactive Java verification tool KeY.

The typical workflow of KeY is depicted in Fig. 1: Initially, the user provides a Java program, together with a specification formulated in the Java Modelling Language [5] (step 1a). Proof obligations in KeY are formalised in a program logic called Java DL, and proofs are conducted using a sequent calculus [2]. The result of an automatic proof search (step 2) is (a) the successful verification of the program or (b) either a counterexample or an open proof with goals that remain to be shown. In the latter case, the user may interact directly with KeY (step 3a) by interactively applying calculus rules (e.g., quantifier instantiations or logical cuts). Alternatively, the user may revise the program or specification (step 3b). Often, verifying programs in KeY involves both kinds of interactions, interspersed by automated proof search.

Proofs in KeY are organised in directed, labelled trees whose vertices are called proof nodes. Each node is labelled with a sequent, the root is labelled with the original proof obligation. Inner nodes are additionally labelled with the

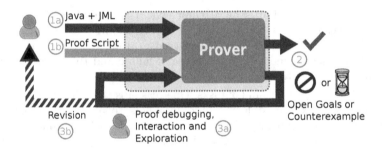

Fig. 1. Interactive Program Verification using scripts

calculus rule that was used to construct the node. When interactively applying rules, KeY allows the user to inspect the whole proof tree with all applied rules. Proof search and guidance is done by using point-and-click interaction, where the user points to a formula and mouseclicks on it to apply a rule. Besides the application of single calculus rules, it is also possible to apply sets of rules in so called *macro* steps, which we also call *prover strategies*. Two important strategies in this paper are auto and symbex. While auto applies all admissible rules, symbex only applies rules performing symbolic execution of the Java program. In this work, we introduce proof scripts (step 1b) to provide an additional way of interacting with the program verification system.

3   Related Work

Many general purpose proof assistants using higher-order logic feature text-based interaction (e.g., Isabelle/HOL [6] and Coq [7]). They mostly use an implicit proof object, where the user can only inspect the goal states but not the intermediate atomic proof states. Proofs are performed either using the system's programming language or by using a language that directly communicates with the system's kernel and builds an abstraction layer on top of the kernel. All such languages have in common that they serve as the only interaction method. Therefore, care has been taken to design proof languages that are both a human-readable input method for proofs and a proof guidance language with which it is possible to control the prover's strategies (also called tactics). Isar [8] is the most prominent state-of-the-art language that serves these purposes. Proof exploration can be done by providing proof commands or by postponing proof tasks using a special keyword.

On top of the proof language the aforementioned systems offer languages that allow to write strategies (e.g., Eisbach [9] for Isabelle or MTac [10] for Coq) to enable users to program their own tactics tailored to the proof problem. *ProofScript* [11] is a proof language inspired by the programming language B-17 and the proof language Isar. It is intended for the use in collaborative proving in *ProofPeer* and is designed to overcome the language stack present in the aforementioned systems, providing one language that fits all purposes. All these languages contain mechanisms for matching terms and formulas to select proof goals for rule application. We refer to [9] for an overview of proof languages.

There also exist approaches to debugging proof tactics and gain more insight. For example, Tinker2 [12] is a graphical tool for inspecting the flow of goals in proof tactics. And Hentschel [13] applies debugging concepts to the verification domain in his symbolic execution debugger built into KeY. This debugger supports the user in case the cause of a failed proof attempt is a mismatch between the program and its specification. However, it does not give significant insights if the proof fails because of insufficient user guidance.

4   Concept for a Proof Scripting Language

It is part of our interaction concept to support the combination of point-and-click with scripting. The control-structures of our proof scripting language can be used to control the application of strategies of the underlying verification system. The basic principles of the language are introduced in the following.

Important Features. The characteristics of proofs for program verification (Sect. 2) lead to the following important elements of our concept for a proof scripting language:

1. integration of domain specific entities like *goal, formula, term* and *rule* as first-class citizens into the language;
2. an expressive proof goal selection mechanism
   - to identify and select individual proof branches,
   - to easily switch between proof branches,
   - to select multiple branches for uniform treatment (*multi-matching*);
   that is resilient to small changes in the proof;
3. a repetition construct which allows repeated application of proof strategies;
4. support for proof exploration within the language.

The objects manipulated during proof construction are called *proof goals*. We assume that each proof goal is unique and identifiable by its contents (e.g., its sequent, when using a sequent calculus).

Applying calculus rules or proof strategies to a proof goal results in the creation of new proof goals that are added to the proof.

Performing proof construction is characterised by explorative phases in which the user tries to determine the best way to approach the remaining proof tasks. One example for this is when the user suspects that a fact is derivable but is not certain. In such cases, the user may try different proof strategies or different lightweight techniques (such as, bounded model-checkers to find counterexamples). These exploration activities have to be considered for the design of a proof scripting language – for example by supporting (hypothetical) queries to the underlying proof system or other reasoning systems without disturbing the current proof state.

4.1   Preliminaries for the Proof Scripting Language

In the following, we introduce a concept for a proof scripting language taking the aforementioned principles into account. We present it using an abstract syntax and demonstrate the language constructs on smaller examples within the KeY system.

The script language supports local variables of types boolean and integer, and of domain-specific types such as goal, formula and term. Expressions can be constructed using arithmetic operators, boolean connectives, subterm selection, and substitution expressions for concrete and schematic terms and formulas. Evaluations of expressions and assignments to variables are defined as usual.

We distinguish between two kinds of states for the evaluation of a proof script: (a) proof states of the verification system characterised by the set of open proof goals and (b) script states, which in addition to a proof state contain the value of state variables that are local for each open proof goal.

There are three cases in which the evaluation of a script terminates: (1) there are no further statements to execute (the end of the script is reached), (2) an error state is reached, or (3) the set of remaining open proof goals is empty.

Running Example. Our example (see Listing 1) uses a Java class Simple with a method transitive(int[] a), which creates a copy of the argument array, sorts it, and copies the result. The goal is to prove (using KeY) that, after the execution of transitive(), the output array is a permutation of the input array. After applying KeY's symbolic execution strategy and a simplification strategy, the user is left with eleven open goals of which four cases correspond to the post states of the two conditional statements (in lines 11 and 12). These cases are similar as they share the same postcondition and differ only a little in their path conditions. For each of these cases, it has to be shown that the output array is a permutation of the input array, i.e., that the permutation property is preserved across the method calls in the body of transitive().

The informal argument for why this holds is that the invoked methods copyArray() and sort() each preserve the permutation property (as specified in lines 17 and 25), and that the method log() does not change the heap (line 30). These methods are called in the body of transitive() on the array a (lines 8–13).

In the following, we first demonstrate script language features on smaller examples but will finally return to our running example at the end of this section and show a full script for the proof.

4.2   Script Language Constructs

The three main building blocks of the scripting language are *mutators*, *control-flow* structures, and *selectors* for proof goals. We describe the general concepts and use the KeY system as a showcase for our examples. The abstract syntax of our language concept is summarised in Fig. 2.

Mutators. Mutators (M in Fig. 2) are the most basic building blocks that when executed change the script state and the proof state by adding nodes to

```
1   public final class Simple {
2     boolean b1, b2;
3
4     /*@ public normal_behavior
5       @ ensures seqPerm(array2seq(\result), \old(array2seq(a)));
6       @ assignable \everything;  */
7     public int[] transitive(int[] a){
8       a = Simple.copyArray(a);
9       sort(a);
10      int[] b = Simple.copyArray(a);
11      if(b1) { b = Simple.copyArray(a); }
12      if(b2) { log(b); }
13      return b;
14    }
15
16    /*@ public normal_behavior
17      @ ensures seqPerm(array2seq(a), \old(array2seq(a)));
18      @ assignable a[*];  */
19    public void sort(int[] a) { /* in-place sorting */ }
20
21    /*@ public normal_behavior
22      @ ensures (∀ int i; 0 <= i < input.length; input[i]==\result[i])
23      @ && \result.length == input.length;
24      @ ensures \fresh(\result);
25      @ ensures seqPerm(array2seq(\result), array2seq(input));
26      @ assignable \nothing;  */
27    public /*@ helper @*/ static int[] copyArray(int[] input) { /* deep-copy */ }
28
29    /*@ public normal_behavior
30      @ assignable \strictly_nothing;  */
31    public void log(int[] a) { /* ... */}
32  }
```

Listing 1. Java program with JML annotations (running example).

the proof tree. Proof commands that correspond to calculus rule applications or strategy applications are called *native* as their implementation is not written in the proof scripting language. Additionally, the language allows calling other scripts as mutators.

The semantics for both mutator types is similar: they change the set of open proof goals of the proof state. However, native proof commands are only applicable to a single goal in our concept. If the goal set of a proof state consists of more than one goal, it is ambiguous to which of these the command should be applied. To avoid confusing results, we define this to result in an error state.

The termination of native proof commands depends on the underlying proof system. Native commands that may run indefinitely long thus allow the specification of a timeout or a maximal number of rules application as arguments.

Example 1. The mutator

$$\texttt{applyEq on=}\overbrace{\texttt{'==> x==y'}}^{\textit{mutation target}} \texttt{with=}\overbrace{\texttt{'y==1 ==>'}}^{\textit{side condition}}$$

in KeY has the semantics that an equality y==1 occurring in the antecedent (the part to the left of ==> in the goal) is to be applied to the formula x==y in the

$M ::= (script\_name \mid native\_command)\ args$

$C ::= C_1; C_2 \mid var := expression \mid \texttt{repeat } \{C\} \mid \texttt{foreach } \{C\} \mid \texttt{theonly } \{C\}$
$\quad\ \mid \texttt{cases } \{\texttt{case } S_1 : \{C_1\} \ \ldots \ \texttt{case } S_n : \{C_n\} \ \} \mid S$

$S ::= expression \mid \texttt{matchSeq } schemaSeq \mid \texttt{closes } \{C\} \mid$
$\quad\ \mid \texttt{matchLabel } regexp \mid \texttt{matchRule } rulename$

Fig. 2. Abstract syntax of the proof scripting language.

succedent (the part right of ==>), replacing x==y with the formula x==1.

$$\overbrace{\texttt{x==1, y==1 ==> x==y}}^{\text{state before applyEq}} \quad\rightsquigarrow\quad \overbrace{\texttt{x==1, y==1 ==> x==1}}^{\text{state after applyEq}}$$

If either of the formulas y==1 and x==y is not present in the goal, this mutator is not applicable.

Control Flow. Besides sequential composition and variable assignment, the language supports control structures (C in Fig. 2) targeting command application to one or more proof goals. To be able to apply proof commands to a single goal node repeatedly, we include a repeat statement. The semantics of the statement is that the command following repeat is applied until it does not modify the state anymore.

Example 2. Consider the following example script for KeY containing a repeat command: repeat { andLeft }. As long as the non-splitting rule andLeft is applicable in a sequent, it is applied. This is a typical situation for the verification tasks in the KeY system where the original proof obligation contains a conjunction of formulas resulting from the method's preconditions.

After applying this script to the sequent A && (B && C) ==> D && E, we get the new sequent A, B, C ==> D && E. The rule andLeft does not have arguments, therefore the underlying verification system needs to find the right formulas to apply the rule to. In case there is more than one formula that the rule can be applied to, an argument indicating the right formula is needed. Note that, by its definition, the rule andLeft is only applied to the conjunctions in the antecedent.

Selectors. As the application of calculus rules can cause a proof goal to split into different cases, it would be ambiguous to apply a proof command after a split. Therefore, one must be able to indicate to which proof goals a proof command is to be applied. Selectors (S in Fig. 2) can be used to select one or more proof goals. Our language concept includes the *cases*-command for this purpose. It is tailored to the needs of proving in the domain of program verification, allowing the formulation of proof goal sets using *matching conditions*. These are expressions evaluated for each proof goal; all goals which satisfy a matching condition S_i are then subject to the corresponding proof command C_i. Thus uniform treatment for several goals can be realised. If a proof goal satisfies more than one matching condition, the first one wins. The application of a cases command results in a script state consisting of the union of all open goals of each case, after the corresponding commands have been executed.

In our language concept, we support three fundamentally different types of matching conditions: *State conditions* consist of an expression over the script variables. Script evaluation selects those proof goals in which the specified expression evaluates to true. *Syntactical conditions* (keyword matchSeq) allow the specification of a logical sequent with schematic placeholders. The condition satisfies those proof goals for which the schematic sequent can be unified with the proof goal's sequent. *Semantic conditions* (notated as closes {C}) involve the deductive capacities of the verification system to decide the selection of proof goals. A proof goal is selected if and only if the evaluation of the proof command C would close this goal.

Syntactic matching is not limited to the goal's sequent (using matchSeq) but can also be applied to rule names (using matchRule) and to labels put on the branches of a rule application (using matchLabel).

In addition to the cases command, foreach {C} and theonly {C} are included for convenience purposes. Both apply command C to each goal in the state and are semantically equivalent to cases { case true: {C} }. Command theonly can be used in situations where the user expects that there is exactly one goal in the proof state. If there is more than one when the command is evaluated, a warning is passed to the user.

Schematic placeholders used for syntactic goal matching have names that start with '?'. When they are instantiated while matching against the sequent of a proof goal, these instantiations can be accessed also in the embedded proof command (e.g., as argument for a calculus rule) to direct the proof using information present on the sequent. If there is more than one possibility for instantiating the schema variables during constraint solving, the first match is used.

Example 3. Consider the following simple example for the use of a matching condition within a cases selector, where the template matches sequents containing an implication in the succedent:

```
case matchSeq '==> ?A -> ?B' : { impRight; andLeft on='?A' }
```

In case of a match, the left side of the implication is assigned to the variable ?A and the right side is assigned to ?B. Then, the proof command is executed. After applying the rule impRight, the rule andLeft is applied to the formula bound to ?A. This example reveals a requirement for the underlying verification system: it needs to check whether the formula bound to ?A is still on the sequent when applying the rule andLeft. If there is more than one occurrence in the sequent, one of them is chosen for rule application. If the formula is not present anymore (because other rules have been applied before) the rule is not applicable, which results in an error state.

Proof Exploration. To support proof exploration in the scripting language, we include the statement "closes { C }". It examines whether applying the proof command C would close the current goal (without actually effecting the current state). Besides its use for exploration, `closes` can be used in the cases statement as matching condition.

Example 4. Assume that a proof command is (only) to be applied to those goals, which can be closed once some formula F is added to the succedent of the goal's sequent (i.e., the formula F is derivable from the sequent). This can be expressed using `closes` as follows: `closes (assume '==> F'; auto)`, where `assume '==> F'` is a proof command adding F to the succedent. Adding arbitrary formulas to the proof obligation during proof construction is unsound. Thus, the `assume` command is only allowed in `closes` statements. The proof command `auto` is then used to try to prove the newly created proof obligation.

Explorations that check whether a certain formula is derivable (as shown in the above example), come in handy, when we want to match a formula, such as x > 0, but on the sequent a stronger formula, such as x > 1, is present. While `case matchSeq 'x > 0'` would miss the goal node, an expression checking for derivability of x > 0 would match the sequent.

Running Example. In Fig. 2, a proof script for proving the correctness of the method `transitive` (see Fig. 1) is shown, which uses the building blocks described above. After symbolic execution and some simplification steps (lines 2–3), the KeY system stops in a state with 11 open goals. The tricky cases are those where the postcondition of the method `transitive` has to be shown to be consequences of the postconditions of the called methods `copyArray`, `sort` and `log`. Corresponding schematic sequent templates (lines 6–10 and 22–25) are then used in a cases statement to select the relevant goal nodes which need user interaction. The cases statements select goal nodes that contain predicates `seqPerm(seq1, seq2)` formalising that sequence seq1 is a permutation of sequence seq2. Rules deriving relations about different heaps using the symmetry and transitivity properties of the permutation predicate are applied (lines 11–18 and 26–31). Each condition matches two goals, the commands close them. To all other goal nodes not selected by the two matching conditions, the proof command `auto` is applied with at most 10000 rule applications (line 34).

Without the script and the matching feature it uses, the rule applications in the two cases statements would have to be applied separately to each of the four open branches. Additionally, the two cases are similar, so the user is able to copy-paste the first case and adjust it to the situation of the second case. Note that the scripting language is especially useful when used together with the point-and-click features of the system, to ease the selection process for applying rules/strategies onto terms. This allows one to make use of the mechanism for suggesting applicable rules of the underlying system.

5   Concept for Debugging Proof Attempts

5.1   Analogy between Programs and Proof Scripts

Scripts formulated in a scripting language like the one presented in the previous section can be considered to be "programs" that construct (partial) proofs for

```
1    script prove_transitive() {
2      symbex;                          // perform symbolic execution of the program
3      foreach { heapSimplification; }  // simplify heap terms
4      cases {
5        case matchSeq
6          'seqPerm(?Res0Copy, ?Arr),
7           seqPerm(?Res0Sort, ?Res0Copy),
8           seqPerm(?Res1Copy0, ?Res0Sort),
9           seqPerm(?Res2Copy1, ?Res0Sort) ==>
10          seqPerm(?Res2Copy1, ?Arr)':
11        { SeqPermSym on='seqPerm(?Res0Copy, ?Arr) ==>';        // symmetry rule
12          SeqPermSym on='seqPerm(?Res0Sort, ?Res0Copy) ==>';   // symmetry rule
13          SeqPermSym on='seqPerm(?Res1Copy0, ?Res0Sort)==>';   // symmetry rule
14          SeqPermSym on='seqPerm(?Res2Copy1, ?Res0Sort) ==>';  // symmetry rule
15          SeqPermTrans on='seqPerm(?Res0Copy, ?Arr) ==>';      // transitivity rule
16          SeqPermTrans on='seqPerm(?Arr, ?Res0Sort) ==>'       // transitivity rule
17                       with='seqPerm(?Arr,?Res2Copy1)';        // with specific term
18          SeqPermSym on='seqPerm(?Arr,?Res2Copy1)';
19          auto maxSteps=10000             // automatic strategy with 10000 rule applications
20        }
21        case matchSeq
22          'seqPerm(?Res0Copy, ?Arr),
23           seqPerm(?Res0Sort, ?Res0Copy),
24           seqPerm(?Res1Copy0, ?Res0Sort) ==>
25          seqPerm(?Res1Copy0, ?Arr)':
26        { SeqPermSym on='seqPerm(?Res0Copy, ?Arr)';
27          SeqPermSym on='seqPerm(?Res0Sort, ?Res0Copy)';
28          SeqPermSym on='seqPerm(?Res1Copy0, ?Res0Sort)';
29          SeqPermTrans on='seqPerm(?Res0Copy, ?Arr)';
30          SeqPermTrans on='seqPerm(?Arr, ?Res0Sort)'
31          SeqPermSym On='==> seqPerm(?Res1Copy0, ?Arr)';
32          auto maxSteps=10000
33        }
34        case true: { auto maxSteps=10000 }
35      }
36    }
```

Listing 2. Example proof script for method `transitive()`.

a proof obligation. They take the initial proof goal as input and derive a set of new goals. The input goal is successfully proved if the derived goal set is empty. The similarity between proof scripts and imperative programs allows us to draw an analogy between implementing and debugging programs on the one hand and coming up with proof scripts and analysing failed proof attempts on the other. The main analogies between the two processes are summarised in Table 1.

Note that evaluating a proof script corresponds to executing a *multi-threaded* program because of the proof-forking nature of some proof commands (which implement case distinctions). Proof commands on different open goals can be handled independently and in parallel. In that sense, executing a cases command (see Sect. 4) corresponds to forking threads, which are joined again when the cases command terminates. The proof tree that is built when executing a script corresponds to the set of traces of all threads when executing a program.

However, there is also an important difference between proof scripts and general programs: The result of a successful proof script evaluation is known a priori (the empty set of goals). Since no output object needs to be constructed, in many cases predefined operations lead to success. This is the reason why users

Table 1. Analogies between program debugging and debugging failed proof attempts.

Proof Debugging	↔	Program Debugging
proof script	↔	program source code
script state (incl. proof state)	↔	program state
sources and open proof goal(s)	↔	program input
proof tree	↔	traces of all threads
proof branch	↔	trace of an individual thread
partial proof	↔	trace of an incomplete program run
completed proof	↔	trace of a successfully terminating program run

often at first follow a try-and-error approach: Just using the auto command for automatic proof search works for many simple proof goals – which is not possible for arbitrary simple computation tasks if these differ in their expected outputs.

5.2   Analogy between Debugging and Failed Proof Analysis

Software debugging is the analysis process of understanding unexpected program behaviour, localising the responsible piece of code, and mending it. Typically, a concrete run of the program exposing the bug is analysed using specialised software (a debugger) which supports the user in the process by various means of visualisation and abstraction. The features help the user comprehend and explore both individual program states at various points of the execution and paths through the program taken by the execution. Powerful modern debugging tools also allow the engineer to modify an intermediate system state (e.g., by changing the values of variables) to conduct what-if-analyses which help them understand and explore the system.

When mechanising a formal proof, the user often has the main arguments of an abstract proof plan in mind which (supposedly) lead to a closed proof. However, this plan is often at a high abstraction level such that it cannot be transformed directly and easily into proof script commands; the user has to refine the proof plan first to be able to formulate it as a proof script. Especially in early stages of a proof process, the evaluation of a proof script is likely to fail. The typical reasons for a failed proof attempt include that auxiliary annotations (such as loop invariants) may be insufficient, that there may be defects in the source code or the specification, or that the proof script itself may be misleading or not detailed enough. Eliminating all such deficiencies is an iterative process, which may also affect other proofs of the same overall verification task (since there are interfaces and interdependencies between system components even if they are verified separately).

When the evaluation of a proof script does not lead to a closed proof, the user needs to be able inspect the intermediate and final proof states in order to *understand* the undesired behaviour. This process involves *localising* the responsible part of the proof and identifying the type of failure: Does the underlying verification system require more or better guidance? Is there a defect in the program, the specification, or the proof script?

The same kind of questions arise in conventional program debugging (Are the data as expected at this point? Is the next statement in the program the correct? Are all parameters to a routine call correct?). Hence, the user needs tool support to decide these questions also for debugging proof scripts. Similar inspection possibilities are required to come up with actions in the proof process. It must be, in particular, possible to link proof states to commands in the proof script and to the user's mental proof plan. To find a suitable course of action, the user needs to have means to *explore* the proof state and to test hypotheses about the cause of failure and about effects of next steps to the proof.

5.3   Adoption of Program Debugging Methods for Proof Debugging

The analogy between proof scripts and programs and the similarities between the software debugging process and the process for the analysis of failed proof attempts allow us to adopt well-known techniques from software debugging to the debugging of (failed) proofs. We focus on user support for the activities of localisation, comprehension, and exploration. Additionally, we adapt the presentation of program states for script states, allowing a detailed inspection.

A screenshot of our early prototype[1] (based on the KeY system) realising these concepts is shown in Fig. 3.

State Presentation. Program states in software debugging may be very complex. To support the user in inspecting and understanding a state, debugging systems present the state's information in a structured manner.

Our concept for proof states includes a structured presentation and functionalities for inspecting the state similar to program debugging systems. For this, we have identified the following parts of a state that should be visualised in isolation: (a) the proof tree with a visual highlight of the current node (i.e., the node containing the open goal to which the currently active proof command is being applied), (b) sequent of the current node (i.e., the current open goal), (c) the currently active proof command in the script, (d) the path in the program that corresponds to the currently selected proof branch, and (e) the values of all local variables in the script state.

Localisation. To support the user in localising the cause of a defective behaviour, debugging systems provide *breakpoints*. These allow the user to inspect the program execution in detail when a program location is reached.

In the setting of program verification, defective behaviour corresponds to a proof with open goals, and the user is mostly interested in understanding these. In our concept, using point-and-click interaction with the explicit proof object, users have the flexibility to navigate in the proof tree in both directions: from the root to the open goals (leaves) and backwards from the leaves to the root. The user can follow two possible strategies: (a) Inspecting an open goal that contains unexpected formulas or terms and performing a backwards search to

---

[1] http://formal.iti.kit.edu/key-psdebugger

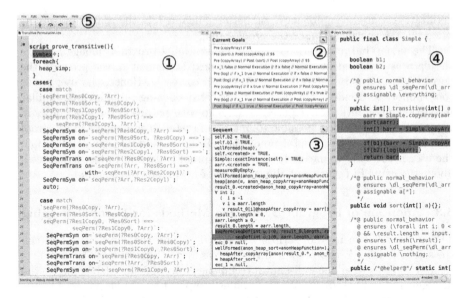

Fig. 3. Screenshot of our proof debugger prototype based on the KeY system. On the left (1) is the proof script editor (in this case containing the script from Listing 2); the currently active proof command is highlighted in blue. In the middle (2), the open goals of the current proof state are listed; here, the last goal is selected. Below, the sequent of the selected goal is shown (3). The source code panel (4) shows the Java program and highlights the symbolic execution path traversed for the selected sequent. The toolbar (5) shows UI elements for stepping through the proof script.

localise where this information was introduced into the proof. (b) Starting from a familiar and expected state and tracing the proof in a forward fashion. In order to support these strategies, we adopt the idea of breakpoints in two ways: *regular breakpoints* and *(reverse) conditional breakpoints*.

A *regular breakpoint* is a syntactical marker that represents a location in the proof script. If, in debug mode, execution of the proof script reaches the breakpoint, execution is stopped and the current proof state is presented to the user. Similar to program debugging, breakpoints may be conditional. Such *conditional breakpoints* include boolean expressions indicating that execution shall only stop if conditions on the state are true when the breakpoint is reached.

For backwards search, we provide *reverse conditional searchpoints*, which consist of a boolean condition and a goal node. While breakpoints are the endpoint of a search, searchpoints are the starting point. The backwards search in the (partial) proof – from the searchpoint towards the root node – stops at the first intermediate proof node for which the condition is evaluated to true.

Conditions in breakpoints and searchpoints can be boolean expression from the script language, in particular all matching conditions can be used here. This design allows the user to find states where certain formulas are introduced into the sequent or nodes in the proof tree where certain rules are applied. Breakpoints can also be used to select states where the complexity or number of formulas in the sequent reaches a certain threshold.

Stepping, Tracing, and Comprehension. Once the user has located an entry point from where to perform a detailed inspection, the next activity is to stepwise retrace what state changes are made by the proof script. To simplify this process, the proof debugger allows the user to limit the inspection to interesting parts of the script (step-into) and to omit the details of subscripts that are deemed irrelevant (step-over). This stepwise retracing allows the user to comprehend the effects of proof commands and subscripts and the creation of proof goals.

Expression Evaluation. Software debugging systems support the task of forming hypotheses about the cause of a defect by allowing the evaluation of user-provided expressions in the current state. A functionality for proof debugging corresponding to expression evaluation is to allow the user to provide a set of formulas, which may or may not be a subset of formulas present in the proof state, and to evaluate whether these formulas are derivable in the context of a node in the proof tree.

One may use external solvers or verification systems to determine whether the set of formulas is satisfiable or not and to get a model in the first case. This is particularly helpful in cases where the size of the sequent prevents the underlying proof system from finding a counterexample.

Changing the State: "What-if"? We adopt the idea of allowing the user to explore the behaviour of the proof script by actively changing the proof state in debug mode. Thus, the user may gain information about which changes are necessary to advance the proof search. In a second step, this knowledge may then be used to, e.g., analyse whether the origin of the part of state that was changed (e.g., the precondition of the program) has to be adapted.

Hot-Swapping. A further element of the proof debugging concept is to allow *hot swapping*, i.e., the user can change parts of the proof script while the script is executed in debug mode, in order to explore hypotheses about how the proof construction can proceed in a successful way.

6   Conclusion and Future Work

We have presented an interaction concept for deductive program verification systems that combines point-and-click interaction with the use of a proof scripting language. This concept introduces a flexible and concise proof scripting language tailored to the needs of program verification. In this domain, proofs often consist of many structurally and/or semantically similar cases which are syntactically large but of small intrinsic complexity. Using matching mechanisms, the language provides means taylored to this type of proofs.

Further, we have explored the correspondences between program debugging and proof debugging and introduced a concept for analysing failed proof attempts, which leverages well-established concepts from software debugging.

A prototypical implementation using the KeY system and a case study is currently work in progress. It remains for future work to evaluate the effectiveness of the concepts by performing usability studies.

Acknowledgements. Special thanks go to Alexander Weigl who provided valuable comments concerning the proof debugging concept, the realisation of the script language, and the prototype.

References

1. Hähnle, R., Huisman, M.: Deductive software verification: From pen-and-paper proofs to industrial tools. In: LNCS 10000. (2017)
2. Ahrendt, W., Beckert, B., Bubel, R., Hähnle, R., Schmitt, P.H., Ulbrich, M., eds.: Deductive Software Verification - The KeY Book: From Theory to Practice. Volume 10001 of LNCS. Springer (2016)
3. Beckert, B., Grebing, S., Böhl, F.: How to put usability into focus: Using focus groups to evaluate the usability of interactive theorem provers. In Benzmüller, C., Woltzenlogel Paleo, B., eds.: UITP 2014. Volume 167 of EPTCS. (July 2014) 4–13
4. Beckert, B., Grebing, S., Böhl, F.: A usability evaluation of interactive theorem provers using focus groups. In Canal, C., Idani, A., eds.: 12th International Conference on Software Engineering and Formal Methods (SEFM 2014) – Collocated Workshops: Human-Oriented Formal Methods (HOFM 2014). Volume 8938 of LNCS., Springer (September 2014) 3–19
5. Leavens, G.T., Baker, A.L., Ruby, C.: Preliminary design of JML: A behavioral interface specification language for Java. SIGSOFT/SEN **31**(3) (2006) 1–38
6. Nipkow, T., Paulson, L.C., Wenzel, M.: Isabelle/HOL — A Proof Assistant for Higher-Order Logic. Volume 2283 of LNCS. Springer (2002)
7. Bertot, Y., Castran, P.: Interactive Theorem Proving and Program Development: Coq'Art The Calculus of Inductive Constructions. 1st edn. Texts in Theoretical Computer Science An EATCS Series. Springer-Verlag Berlin Heidelberg (2004)
8. Wenzel, M.: Isar - a generic interpretative approach to readable formal proof documents. In: Proceedings of the 12th International Conference on Theorem Proving in Higher Order Logics. TPHOLs '99, London, UK, UK, Springer-Verlag (1999) 167–184
9. Matichuk, D., Murray, T., Wenzel, M.: Eisbach: A proof method language for isabelle. Journal of Automated Reasoning **56**(3) (Mar 2016) 261–282
10. Ziliani, B., Dreyer, D., Krishnaswami, N.R., Nanevski, A., Vafeiadis, V.: Mtac: A monad for typed tactic programming in coq. SIGPLAN Not. **48**(9) (September 2013) 87–100
11. Obua, S., Scott, P., Fleuriot, J.: Proofscript: Proof scripting for the masses. In Sampaio, A., Wang, F., eds.: Theoretical Aspects of Computing – ICTAC 2016: 13th International Colloquium, Taipei, Taiwan, ROC, October 24–31, 2016, Proceedings, Cham, Springer International Publishing (2016) 333–348
12. Lin, Y., Le Bras, P., Grov, G.: Developing and debugging proof strategies by tinkering. In: Proceedings of the 22nd International Conference on Tools and Algorithms for the Construction and Analysis of Systems - Volume 9636, New York, NY, USA, Springer-Verlag New York, Inc. (2016) 573–579
13. Hentschel, M.: Integrating Symbolic Execution, Debugging and Verification. PhD thesis, Technische Universität Darmstadt (January 2016)

PRuning Through Satisfaction*

Marijn J.H. Heule[1], Benjamin Kiesl[2], Martina Seidl[3], and Armin Biere[3]

[1] Department of Computer Science, The University of Texas at Austin
[2] Institute of Information Systems, TU Wien
[3] Institute for Formal Models and Verification, JKU Linz

Abstract. The classical approach to solving the satisfiability problem of propositional logic prunes unsatisfiable branches from the search space. We prune more agressively by also removing certain branches for which there exist other branches that are more satisfiable. This is achieved by extending the popular conflict-driven clause learning (CDCL) paradigm with so-called PR-*clause learning*. We implemented our new paradigm, named *satisfaction-driven clause learning* (SDCL), in the SAT solver LINGELING. Experiments on the well-known pigeon hole formulas show that our method can automatically produce proofs of unsatisfiability whose size is cubic in the number of pigeons while plain CDCL solvers can only produce proofs of exponential size.

1 Introduction

Conflict-driven clause learning (CDCL) [11] is the leading paradigm for solving the satisfiability problem of propositional logic (SAT). It is well-known that CDCL solvers are able to generate resolution proofs but this useful ability comes at a price because it means that CDCL solvers suffer from the same restrictions as the resolution proof system. For instance, there are seemingly simple formula families that admit only exponential-size resolution proofs, implying that solving these formulas with CDCL takes exponential time [14].

To deal with the limitations of resolution, stronger proof systems have been proposed [19]. Popular examples of such proof systems are *extended resolution* [18] and an even more general system based on blocked clauses [10]. These systems extend resolution by allowing the introduction of short definition clauses over new variables. As shown by Cook [3], the introduction of these clauses already suffices to obtain short proofs of the famous pigeon hole formulas—a class of formulas known for admitting no short resolution proofs [4]. But the introduction of new variables has a downside: The search space of possible variables is infinite in general, which complicates the search for useful definition clauses. This may explain the limited success of GLUCOSER [1], a CDCL solver that uses extended resolution. To cope with this drawback, we recently introduced a proof system, called PR (short for *propagation redundancy*), that allows for short proofs of the pigeon hole formulas without the need to introduce new variables [6].

* Supported by the National Science Foundation under grant CCF-1526760 and by the Austrian Science Fund (FWF) under projects S11409-N23 and W1255-N23.

O. Strichman and R. Tzoref-Brill (Eds.): HVC 2017, LNCS 10629, pp. 179–194, 2017.
https://doi.org/10.1007/978-3-319-70389-3_12

In this paper, we enhance the CDCL paradigm by extending it in such a way that it can exploit the strengths of the PR proof system. To do so, we introduce *satisfaction-driven clause learning* (SDCL), a SAT solving paradigm that extends CDCL as follows: If the usual unit propagation does not lead to a conflict, we do not immediately decide for a new variable assignment (as would be the case in CDCL). Instead, we first try to prune the search space of possible truth assignments by learning a so-called PR clause.

Intuitively, a PR clause is a clause that might not be implied by the current formula but whose addition preserves satisfiability. As we show in this paper, deciding whether a given clause is a PR clause is NP-complete. We therefore use an additional SAT solver for finding such clauses. Finding useful PR clauses is a non-trivial problem as it is not immediately clear which clauses should be added to improve solver performance. To gain further insight, we develop a strong theory that relates our SAT encoding for finding PR clauses with two concepts from the literature: *autarkies* [9] and *set-blocked clauses* [8].

The main contributions of this paper are as follows: (1) We introduce satisfaction-driven clause learning, a paradigm that extends CDCL by performing the addition of PR clauses. (2) We prove that the problem of deciding whether a given clause is a PR clause is NP-complete. (3) We use a SAT solver for finding PR clauses and show that the corresponding SAT encoding is strongly related to the concepts of autarkies and set-blocked clauses. (4) We implement SDCL as an extension of the award-winning SAT solver LINGELING [2], which is developed by the last author of this paper. An experimental evaluation shows that our approach can generate proofs for much larger pigeon hole formulas than two existing tools based on extended resolution.

2   Preliminaries

Below we present the most important background concepts related to this paper.

Propositional logic. We consider propositional formulas in *conjunctive normal form* (CNF), which are defined as follows. A *literal* is either a variable x (a *positive literal*) or the negation $\bar{x}$ of a variable x (a *negative literal*). The *complementary literal* $\bar{l}$ of a literal l is defined as $\bar{l} = \bar{x}$ if $l = x$ and $\bar{l} = x$ if $l = \bar{x}$. Accordingly, for a set L of literals, we define $\bar{L} = \{\bar{l} \mid l \in L\}$. A *clause* is a disjunction of literals. A *formula* is a conjunction of clauses. We view clauses as sets of literals and formulas as sets of clauses. For a set L of literals and a formula F, we define $F_L = \{C \in F \mid C \cap L \neq \emptyset\}$. For a literal, clause, or formula F, $var(F)$ denotes the variables in F. For convenience, we treat $var(F)$ as a variable if F is a literal, and as a set of variables otherwise.

Satisfiability. An *assignment* is a function from a set of variables to the truth values 1 (*true*) and 0 (*false*). An assignment is *total* w.r.t. a formula if it assigns a truth value to all variables occurring in the formula; otherwise it is *partial*. A literal l is *satisfied* (*falsified*) by an assignment α if l is positive and $\alpha(var(l)) = 1$

$(\alpha(var(l)) = 0$, resp.) or if it is negative and $\alpha(var(l)) = 0$ $(\alpha(var(l)) = 1$, resp.). We often denote assignments by sequences of literals they satisfy. For instance, $x\,\overline{y}$ denotes the assignment that assigns 1 to x and 0 to y. For an assignment α, $var(\alpha)$ denotes the variables assigned by α. Further, α_L denotes the assignment obtained from α by flipping the truth values of the literals in L. A clause is satisfied by an assignment α if it contains a literal that is satisfied by α. Finally, a formula is satisfied by an assignment α if all its clauses are satisfied by α. A formula is *satisfiable* if there exists an assignment that satisfies it.

Formula simplification. We denote the empty clause by $\bot$ and the satisfied clause by $\top$. Given an assignment α and a clause C, we define $C\,|\alpha = \top$ if α satisfies C; otherwise, $C\,|\alpha$ denotes the result of removing from C all the literals falsified by α. For a formula F, we define $F\,|\alpha = \{C\,|\alpha \mid C \in F$ and $C\,|\alpha \neq \top\}$. We say that an assignment α *touches* a clause C if $var(\alpha) \cap var(C) \neq \emptyset$. Given an assignment α, the clause $\{x \mid \alpha(x) = 0\} \cup \{\overline{x} \mid \alpha(x) = 1\}$ is the clause that *blocks* α. A *unit clause* is a clause with only one literal. The result of applying the *unit clause rule* to a formula F is the formula $F\,|l$ where (l) is a unit clause in F. The iterated application of the unit clause rule to a formula, until no unit clauses are left, is called *unit propagation*. If unit propagation yields the empty clause $\bot$, we say that it derived a *conflict*.

Formula relations. Two formulas are *logically equivalent* if they are satisfied by the same assignments. Two formulas are *satisfiability equivalent* if they are either both satisfiable or both unsatisfiable. Given two formulas F and F', we denote by $F \vDash F'$ that F implies F', i.e., all assignments satisfying F also satisfy F'. Furthermore, by $F \vdash_1 F'$ we denote that for every clause $(l_1 \vee \cdots \vee l_n) \in F'$, unit propagation on $F \wedge (\overline{l}_1) \wedge \cdots \wedge (\overline{l}_n)$ derives a conflict. If $F \vdash_1 F'$, we say that F implies F' through unit propagation. For example, $(x) \wedge (y) \vdash_1 (x \vee z) \wedge (y)$, since unit propagation of the unit clauses $(\overline{x})$ and $(\overline{z})$ derives a conflict with (x), and unit propagation of $(\overline{y})$ derives a conflict with (y).

Conflict-driven clause learning (CDCL) in a nutshell. To evaluate the satisfiability of a formula, a CDCL solver iteratively performs the following operations: First, the solver performs unit propagation. Then, it tests whether it has reached a conflict, meaning that the formula is falsified by the current assignment. If no conflict has been reached and all variables are assigned, the formula is satisfiable. Otherwise, the solver chooses an unassigned variable based on some decision heuristic, assigns a truth value to it, and continues by again performing unit propagation. If, however, a conflict has been reached, the solver learns a short clause that prevents it from repeating similar (bad) decisions in the future ("clause learning"). In case this clause is the (unsatisfiable) empty clause, the unsatisfiability of the formula can be concluded. In case it is not the empty clause, the solver revokes some of its variable assignments ("backjumping") and then repeats the whole procedure again by performing unit propagation.

3 Searching for Propagation-Redundant Clauses

As already mentioned in the introduction, the addition of so-called PR clauses (short for *propagation-redundant clauses*) to a formula can lead to short proofs for hard formulas without the introduction of new variables. In this section, we present an approach for finding PR clauses. Although PR clauses are not necessarily implied by the formula, their addition preserves satisfiability [6]. The intuitive reason for this is that the addition of a PR clause prunes the search space of possible assignments in such a way that there still remain assignments under which the formula is as satisfiable as under the pruned assignments. In the following definition, assignments can be partial with respect to the formula [6]:

Definition 1. *Let F be a formula, C a clause, and α the assignment blocked by C. Then, C is* propagation redundant (PR) *with respect to F if there exists an assignment ω such that ω satisfies C and $F|\alpha \vdash_1 F|\omega$.*

The clause C can be seen as a constraint that prunes from the search space all assignments that extend α. Since $F|\alpha$ implies $F|\omega$, every assignment that satisfies $F|\alpha$ also satisfies $F|\omega$, meaning that F is at least as satisfiable under ω as it is under α. Moreover, since ω satisfies C, it must disagree with α on at least one variable. We refer to ω as the *witness*, since it witnesses the propagation-redundancy of the clause. Consider the following example [6]:

Example 1. Let $F = (x \vee y) \wedge (\overline{x} \vee y) \wedge (\overline{x} \vee z)$, $C = (x)$, and let $\omega = x\,z$ be an assignment. Then, $\alpha = \overline{x}$ is the assignment blocked by C. Now, consider $F|\alpha = (y)$ and $F|\omega = (y)$. Clearly, unit propagation on $F|\alpha \wedge (\overline{y})$ derives a conflict. Thus, $F|\alpha \vdash_1 F|\omega$ and so C is propagation redundant w.r.t. F. □

Most known types of redundant clauses are PR clauses [6]. This includes *blocked clauses* [10], *set-blocked clauses* [8], *resolution asymmetric tautologies* (RATs) [7], and many more. As a new result, we show next that deciding whether a given clause is a PR clause is NP-complete, which complicates the search for PR clauses.

Definition 2. *The* PR problem *is the following decision problem: Given a formula F and a clause C, decide if C is propagation-redundant w.r.t. F.*

Theorem 1. *The* PR *problem is* NP-*complete.*

Proof. MEMBERSHIP IN NP: Let α be the assignment blocked by C. To decide whether or not C is propagation-redundant with respect to F, just guess an assignment ω and check if $F|\alpha \vdash_1 F|\omega$.

NP-HARDNESS: We present a polynomial reduction from the SAT problem. Let F be an input formula (in CNF) for the SAT problem and let v be a fresh variable that does not occur in F. Now, let $C = \overline{v}$ and obtain the formula F' from F by adding to each clause the literal v. We show that F is satisfiable if and only if C is propagation-redundant with respect to F'.

For the "only if" direction, assume that F is satisfied by some assignment ω and let $\alpha = v$ be the assignment blocked by C. Now, obtain a new assignment

ω' from ω by extending it as follows: $\omega'(x) = \omega(x)$ if $x \in var(F)$ and $\omega'(v) = 0$. Then, ω' disagrees with α on v. Moreover, since ω satisfies F, it satisfies F'. Hence, $F'|\omega' = \emptyset$ and thus $F'|\alpha \vdash_1 F'|\omega'$ trivially holds. It follows that C is propagation-redundant with respect to F'.

For the "if" direction, assume that C is propagation-redundant with respect to F' and let $\alpha = v$ be the assignment blocked by C. Then, there exists an assignment ω' such that $F'|\alpha \vdash_1 F'|\omega'$ and ω' disagrees with α, meaning that $\omega'(v) = 0$. Since every clause in F' contains v, it follows that α satisfies F' and so it must be the case that ω' satisfies F'. Since $\omega'(v) = 0$ and $F'|\overline{v} = F$, it follows that ω' satisfies F. □

Since the identification of PR clauses is NP-hard, we use a SAT solver to search for PR clauses. We thus next introduce a SAT encoding which, for a given formula F and an assignment α, tries to find a witness ω that certifies the propagation redundancy of the clause that blocks α. We obtain the encoding, which we call the *positive reduct*, by selecting only a subpart of F:

Definition 3. *Let F be a formula, α an assignment, and C the clause that blocks α. The* positive reduct $p(F, \alpha)$ *of F with respect to α is the formula $G \wedge C$, where G is obtained from F by first removing all clauses that are not satisfied by α and then removing from the remaining clauses all literals that are not assigned by α.*

Example 2. Let $F = (x \vee \overline{y} \vee z) \wedge (w \vee \overline{y}) \wedge (\overline{w} \vee \overline{z})$ and $\alpha = x\,y\,\overline{z}$. Then, the positive reduct $p(F, \alpha)$ of F w.r.t. α is the formula $(x \vee \overline{y} \vee z) \wedge (\overline{z}) \wedge (\overline{x} \vee \overline{y} \vee z)$. □

We next show that the positive reduct is satisfiable if and only if the clause blocked by α is a set-blocked clause [8] (see Definition 4 below), meaning that it is also a PR clause [6] (note that deciding set-blockedness of a clause is also NP-complete [8]). We show later that we can usually shorten this set-blocked clause and thereby turn it into a PR clause that might not be set-blocked anymore.

Definition 4. *A clause C is* set-blocked *by a non-empty set $L \subseteq C$ in a formula F if, for every clause $D \in F_{\overline{L}}$, the clause $(C \setminus L) \cup \overline{L} \cup D$ contains two complementary literals.*

We say that a clause is set-blocked in a formula F if it is set-blocked by some of its literals in F. Consider the following example [8]:

Example 3. Let $C = (x \vee y)$ and $F = (\overline{x} \vee y) \wedge (x \vee \overline{y})$. Then, C is set-blocked by $L = \{x, y\}$: Clearly, $F_{\overline{L}} = F$ and $C \setminus L = \emptyset$. Therefore, for $D_1 = (\overline{x} \vee y)$ we get that $(C \setminus L) \cup \overline{L} \cup D_1 = (\overline{x} \vee \overline{y} \vee y)$ contains two complementary literals and the same holds for $D_2 = (x \vee \overline{y})$, for which we get $(C \setminus L) \cup \overline{L} \cup D_2 = (\overline{x} \vee \overline{y} \vee x)$. □

Assume we are given a clause C which blocks some assignment α. Our new result given in the following theorem implies that C is set-blocked in a formula F if and only if the positive reduct $p(F, \alpha)$ is satisfiable. Recall that for an assignment α and a set of literals L, α_L denotes the assignment obtained from α by flipping the truth values of the literals in L:

Theorem 2. *Let F be a formula, α an assignment, and C the clause that blocks α. Then, C is set-blocked by $L \subseteq C$ in F if and only if α_L satisfies the positive reduct $p(F, \alpha)$.*

Proof. For the "only if" direction, assume that C is set-blocked by L in F. We show that α_L satisfies $p(F, \alpha)$. Clearly, α_L satisfies C since α_L is obtained from α by flipping the truth values of the literals in L. Now, let D be a clause in $p(F, \alpha)$ that is different from C. We show that D is satisfied by α_L. By the definition of $p(F, \alpha)$, D is satisfied by α and thus, if D contains no literals of $\overline{L}$ (i.e., $D \notin F_{\overline{L}}$), it is also satisfied by α_L. Assume therefore that $D \in F_{\overline{L}}$. Then, since C is set-blocked by L in F, the clause $(C \setminus L) \cup \overline{L} \cup D$ contains two complementary literals.

Since C cannot contain two complementary literals (because it blocks the assignment α), there must be a literal $l \in D$ such that one of the following holds: (1) $\bar{l} \in D$, (2) $\bar{l} \in C \setminus L$, (3) $\bar{l} \in \overline{L}$. In the first case, D is clearly satisfied by α_L. In the second case, since α_L differs from α only on literals in L and since α falsifies C, it follows that α_L falsifies $\bar{l}$ and thus it satisfies l. Finally, in the third case, it follows that $l \in L$ and so α_L satisfies l since it satisfies all the literals in L. It follows that D is satisfied by α_L. Therefore, α_L satisfies $p(F, \alpha)$.

For the "if" direction, assume that α_L satisfies $p(F, \alpha)$. We show that L set-blocks C in F. Let $D \in F_{\overline{L}}$. Since α falsifies C, it falsifies L. Therefore, α satisfies $\overline{L}$ and thus $p(F, \alpha)$ contains the clause D', obtained from D by removing all literals that are not assigned by α. By assumption, α_L satisfies D' and since it falsifies $\overline{L}$, it must satisfy some literal $l \in D' \setminus \overline{L}$. But then $\bar{l} \in C \setminus L$ and thus the clause $(C \setminus L) \cup \overline{L} \cup D$ contains two complementary literals. Hence, C is set-blocked by L in F. ▢

Thus, if the SAT solver finds an assignment α for which the positive reduct with respect to F is satisfiable, then the clause that blocks α is a set-blocked clause and so its addition to F preserves satisfiability. Even better, when using a CDCL solver, we can usually add a shorter clause: If α is the current assignment of the solver, it consists of two parts—a part α_d of variable assignments that were decisions by the solver and a part α_u of assignments that were derived from these decisions via unit propagation. This means that $F|_{\alpha_d} \vdash_1 F|_\alpha$. Since C is set-blocked—and thus propagation-redundant—with respect to F, we know that there exists some assignment ω such that $F|_\alpha \vdash_1 F|_\omega$. But then $F|_{\alpha_d} \vdash_1 F|_\omega$ and so the clause that blocks α_d, which is a subclause of the clause that blocks α, is a PR clause with respect to F. We conclude:

Theorem 3. *Let C be a PR clause w.r.t. a formula F and let $\alpha = \alpha_d \cup \alpha_u$ be the assignment blocked by C. Assume furthermore that the assignments in α_u are derived via unit propagation on $F|_{\alpha_d}$. Then, the clause that blocks α_d is propagation-redundant w.r.t. to F.*

We can thus efficiently find short PR clauses by using an additional SAT solver for finding a set-blocked clause and then shortening the clause by removing literals that are not decision literals.

4   Conditional Autarkies

We have seen that the positive reduct can be used to determine whether a clause is set-blocked with respect to a given formula. As we show in this section, searching for satisfying assignments of the positive reduct is actually the same as searching for certain kinds of partial assignments [12]:

Definition 5. *A partial assignment ω is an* autarky *for a formula F if ω satisfies every $C \in F$ for which $var(\omega) \cap var(C) \neq \emptyset$.*

In other words, an autarky is a (partial) assignment that satisfies every clause it touches. For example, if a literal l is pure in a formula (i.e., $\bar{l}$ does not occur in the formula), then the assignment $\omega = l$ is an autarky for the formula. But also the empty assignment as well as every assignment that satisfies the whole formula are autarkies. If we are given an autarky ω for a formula F, we can use ω to simplify F because $F|\omega$ and F are satisfiability equivalent, although they are not necessarily logically equivalent [12]. Autarkies yield PR clauses as follows:

Theorem 4. *Let F be a formula and ω an autarky for F. Then, every clause C such that ω satisfies C and $var(C) \subseteq var(\omega)$ is a PR clause with respect to F.*

Proof. Let α be the assignment blocked by C. We show that $F|\alpha \vdash_1 F|\omega$. Let $D|\omega \in F|\omega$ for $D \in F$. Since D is not satisfied by ω, it follows that D is not touched by ω and thus—since $var(\alpha) \subseteq var(\omega)$—it is also not touched by α. Hence, $D|\alpha = D|\omega = D$ is contained in $F|\alpha$ and so $F|\alpha \vdash_1 D|\omega$. It follows that C is a PR clause with respect to F.   □

Suppose a SAT solver has found a partial assignment ω_{con} for some formula F. We can then try to search for autarkies in the simplified formula $F|\omega_{\mathrm{con}}$. Given an autarky ω_{aut} for $F|\omega_{\mathrm{con}}$, we call $\omega = \omega_{\mathrm{con}} \cup \omega_{\mathrm{aut}}$ a *conditional autarky* for F:

Definition 6. *A partial assignment ω is a* conditional autarky *for a formula F if there exists a subassignment $\omega_{\mathrm{con}} \subset \omega$ such that ω is an autarky for $F|\omega_{\mathrm{con}}$. We call ω_{con} the* conditional part *of ω.*

If $\omega \setminus \omega_{\mathrm{con}}$ assigns exactly one variable, we call the literal satisfied by $\omega \setminus \omega_{\mathrm{con}}$ a *conditional pure literal with respect to ω_{con}.*

Example 4. Consider the formula $F = (x \vee y) \wedge (\bar{x} \vee z) \wedge (\bar{y} \vee \bar{z})$. The assignment $\omega = \bar{y}\,z$ is a conditional autarky with conditional part $\omega_{\mathrm{con}} = \bar{y}$: By applying ω_{con} to F, we obtain the formula $F|\bar{y} = (x) \wedge (\bar{x} \vee z)$. The only clause of $F|\bar{y}$ that is touched by ω is the clause $(\bar{x} \vee z)$, which is satisfied ω. The literal z is a conditional pure literal with respect to ω_{con}.   □

Note that every autarky ω is a conditional autarky where ω_{con} is the empty assignment. However, as illustrated by Example 4, the converse does not hold: Although the assignment $\omega = \bar{y}\,z$ is a conditional autarky for F, it is not an autarky for F because the clause $(x \vee y)$ is touched but not satisfied by ω. The following theorem shows that satisfying assignments of the positive reduct are nothing else than conditional autarkies:

Theorem 5. *Let F be a formula and α a partial assignment. Then, an assignment ω over $var(\alpha)$ satisfies the positive reduct $p(F, \alpha)$ if and only if ω is a conditional autarky for F with $\omega_{con} = \alpha \cap \omega$.*

Proof. For the "only if" direction, assume that ω is a satisfying assignment of $p(F, \alpha)$. First, note that ω disagrees with α on at least one variable since ω satisfies the clause that blocks α. Therefore, $\omega_{con} \subset \omega$. It remains to show that ω is an autarky for $F|_{\omega_{con}}$. Let $D|_{\omega_{con}}$ be a clause in $F|_{\omega_{con}}$ such that $D \in F$ and assume that $D|_{\omega_{con}}$ is touched by ω. Since $var(\omega) = var(\alpha)$, it follows that $D|_{\omega_{con}}$ is also touched by α. Now, if α does not satisfy $D|_{\omega_{con}}$, then ω satisfies $D|_{\omega_{con}}$ since ω disagrees with α on all variables in $var(\alpha) \setminus var(\omega_{con})$. In contrast, if α satisfies $D|_{\omega_{con}}$, then the clause D', which contains only those literals of D that are touched by α, is contained in $p(F, \alpha)$. Hence, ω satisfies D' and thus it satisfies $D|_{\omega_{con}}$. It follows that ω is a conditional autarky for F.

For the "if" direction, assume that ω is a conditional autarky for F with $\omega_{con} = \alpha \cap \omega$ and let $D' \in p(F, \alpha)$. If D' is the clause that blocks α, then ω satisfies D' since ω disagrees with α (note that by definition $\omega_{con} \subset \omega$). Assume thus that D' is not the clause that blocks α. Then, there exists a clause $D \in F$ such that α satisfies D and D' is obtained from D by removing all literals that are not assigned by α. Assume now that ω_{con} does not satisfy D'. Then, $D|_{\omega_{con}} \in F|_{\omega_{con}}$ (note that ω_{con} cannot satisfy D since the literals in $D \setminus D'$ are not assigned by α and thus also not by ω). Since α satisfies D, it satisfies $D|_{\omega_{con}}$. Hence, $D|_{\omega_{con}}$ is touched by α and thus also by ω. But then ω satisfies $D|_{\omega_{con}}$ since it is a conditional autarky for F. Hence, since D' contains all literals of D that are assigned by α (and thus by ω), ω satisfies D'. It follows that ω satisfies $p(F, \alpha)$. $\square$

Combining Theorem 5 with Theorem 2, which states that a clause C is set-blocked by $L \subseteq C$ in a formula F if and only if α_L satisfies $p(F, \alpha)$, we obtain the following relationship between conditional autarkies and set-blocked clauses:

Corollary 1. *Let F be a formula, C a clause, and α the assignment blocked by C. Then, C is set-blocked by $L \subseteq C$ in F if and only if α_L is a conditional autarky for F with conditional part $\alpha_L \cap \alpha$.*

This correspondence between set-blocked clauses and conditional autarkies reveals an interesting relationship between set-blocked clauses and PR clauses:

Theorem 6. *Let $C \vee L$ be a clause that is set-blocked by L with respect to a formula F. Any clause $C \vee l$ with $l \in L$ is a PR clause with respect to F.*

Proof. Let α be the assignment that is blocked by $C \vee l$. We need to show that there exists an assignment ω such that ω satisfies $C \vee l$ and $F|_\alpha \vdash_1 F|_\omega$. Let ω be α_L. Clearly, ω satisfies $C \vee l$ on l. Moreover, we know from Theorem 1 that ω is a conditional autarky for F with conditional part $\omega_{con} = \alpha \cap \omega$. Now, let $F' = F|_{\omega_{con}}$, $\alpha' = \alpha \setminus \omega_{con}$, and $\omega' = \omega \setminus \omega_{con}$. Then, $F|_\alpha = F'|_{\alpha'}$ and $F|_\omega = F'|_{\omega'}$. Since $var(\alpha') \subseteq var(\omega')$ and ω' is an autarky for F' (Lemma 4), it follows that $F'|_{\alpha'} \vdash_1 F'|_{\omega'}$. But then $F|_\alpha \vdash_1 F|_\omega$ and thus $C \vee l$ is a PR clause w.r.t. F. $\square$

```
SDCL (formula F)
1     α := ∅
2     forever do
3         α := Simplify (F, α)
4         if F|α contains a falsified clause then
5             C := AnalyzeConflict ()
6             if C is the empty clause then return unsatisfiable
7             F := F ∪ {C}
8             α := BackJump (C, α)
9         else if p(F, α) is satisfiable then
10            C := AnalyzeWitness ()
11            F := F ∪ {C}
12            α := BackJump (C, α)
13        else
14            l := Decide ()
15            if l is undefined then return satisfiable
16            α := α ∪ {l}
```

Fig. 1. Pseudo-code of the SDCL procedure

This basically means that if a clause $C \vee L$ is set-blocked by L in a formula F, we can add any clause $C \vee l$ such that $l \in L$ to F without affecting its satisfiability.

Example 5. Consider the formula $F = (x \vee y \vee z) \wedge (\overline{x} \vee \overline{y} \vee z) \vee (x \vee \overline{y} \vee \overline{z})$. The clause $(\overline{x} \vee y \vee z)$ is set-blocked by $\{\overline{x}, y\}$ in F and so $(\overline{x} \vee z)$ and $(y \vee z)$ are PR clauses w.r.t. F as both $\alpha = x\,\overline{y}\,\overline{z}$ and $\omega = \overline{x}\,y\,\overline{z}$ are autarkies for F. Therefore, the addition of $(\overline{x} \vee z)$ or $(y \vee z)$ to F preserves satisfiability.   □

We have seen different approaches to finding and adding PR clauses to a formula. In the following, we make use of these approaches when introducing our extension of conflict-driven clause learning.

5   Satisfaction-Driven Clause Learning

Our *satisfaction-driven clause learning* (SDCL) paradigm extends the CDCL paradigm in the following way: Whenever the CDCL solver is required to pick a new decision, we first check whether the current assignment and all its extensions can be *pruned* from the search space by learning the clause which contains the negation of all previous decisions. As explained in Section 3, such a learned clause can be obtained by searching for a satisfying assignment of the positive reduct with respect to the formula and the current assignment of the solver.

Figure 1 shows the pseudo code of the SDCL procedure. Removing lines 9 to 12 would result in the classical CDCL algorithm, which consists of three phases: *simplify*, *learn*, and *decide*. The simplify phase uses unit propagation to extend the current assignment α (line 3). The main reasoning of CDCL is performed in the learn phase, which kicks in when a *conflict* is reached, i.e., when a clause is falsified by the current assignment α (i.e., when the if condition in line 4 is true). In this case, a so-called *conflict clause* is computed by the AnalyzeConflict procedure (line 5). A conflict clause serves as a constraint that should prevent the solver from investigating unsatisfiable parts of the search space in the future by encoding the reasons for the current conflict. The naive approach for this is to use the clause that blocks α as conflict clause. A stronger conflict clause can be obtained by computing the conflict clause that blocks only the decision literals of α. In practice, there are several approaches for learning even smaller clauses [11,17].

If the conflict clause is the empty clause, then the solver can conclude that the formula is unsatisfiable (line 6); otherwise, the clause is added to the formula (line 7). After adding the conflict clause to the formula (*clause learning*), the solver backjumps (line 8) to the level where the conflict clause contains a literal that is not falsified. Finally, the decide phase (lines 14 to 16) extends α by selecting a literal and making it true. In case all variables are assigned and no clause is falsified, the formula is identified as satisfiable (line 15).

The SDCL related lines (9 to 12) work as follows: If the current assignment α does *not* lead to a conflict (i.e., the if condition on line 4 fails), we check (optionally in a limited way) whether the positive reduct $p(F, \alpha)$ is satisfiable. If not, a new decision is made (line 14). Otherwise, we conclude that the clause that blocks α is set-blocked and thus redundant with respect to F. Similar to the AnalyzeConflict procedure, which shortens conflict clauses in practice, we can learn a clause that is smaller than the one that blocks α. This is done in the AnalyzeWitness procedure, which analyzes the assignment that satisfies the positive reduct (the witness). As shown in Theorem 3, we can add the clause that blocks only the decision literals of α since it is a PR clause. Alternatively, we can add PR clauses based on conditional autarkies as described in Theorem 6. After the clause addition, we backjump by unassigning all variables up to the last decision (line 12) and continue with a new iteration of the procedure.

A crucial part of the algorithm is the underlying decision heuristic of the Decide procedure. Most practical implementations of CDCL use the so-called *VSIDS* (*Variable State Independent Decaying Sum*) [13] heuristic which selects the variable that occurs most frequently in recent conflict clauses. In our early experiments, VSIDS turned out to be a poor heuristic for SDCL. A possible explanation is that VSIDS can select variables as early decisions that occur in different parts of the formula, thereby making it impossible to satisfy the resulting positive reduct.

In order to select variables in the same part of the formula, we propose the *autarky decision heuristic*: Given a formula F and the current assignment α, the autarky decision heuristic selects the variable that occurs most frequently in clauses in $F|\alpha \setminus F$ (i.e., in the clauses of F that are touched but not satisfied by α). Occurrences are weighted based on the length of clauses—the smaller the clause, the larger the weight. If $F|\alpha \setminus F$ is empty, then α is an autarky for F, hence the name. So this heuristic tries to guide the solver to an autarky.

We expect that this heuristic helps with finding conditional autarkies—and thus with satisfying the positive reduct formulas—more efficiently.

The autarky heuristic can only be used for non-empty assignments. We therefore need a special heuristic for the first decision. This turned out to be challenging and is still part of current research. A heuristic that works really well for the pigeon hole formulas is to select the variable x that is least constrained, i.e., either x or $\overline{x}$ occurs least frequently in the formula. The rationale behind this heuristic is that it creates an initial positive reduct with as few unit clauses as possible: Notice that a clause which is satisfied by the first decision becomes a unit clause in the positive reduct unless unit propagation assigns other literals in that clause. Such a unit clause makes it impossible to satisfy the positive reduct for the first decision. Also, this heuristic finds pure literals and fixes them using a PR clause: The positive reduct has only the clause that blocks the current assignment and can thus be trivially satisfied. However, it is unlikely that this heuristic is effective for a wide spectrum of benchmark families.

In the next section, we illustrate how short proofs of the pigeon hole formulas can be produced manually by combining the addition of set-blocked clauses with resolution. With this we want to illustrate why short proofs can be found automatically by our implementation of SDCL.

6   Solving Pigeon Hole Formulas using SDCL

A pigeon hole formula PHP_n intuitively encodes that $n+1$ pigeons have to be assigned to n holes such that no hole contains more than one pigeon. In the encoding, a variable $x_{i,k}$ denotes that pigeon i is assigned to hole k:

$$PHP_n := \bigwedge_{1 \le i \le n+1} \overbrace{(x_{i,1} \vee \cdots \vee x_{i,n})}^{P_i} \wedge \bigwedge_{1 \le i < j \le n+1} \bigwedge_{1 \le k \le n} \overbrace{(\overline{x}_{i,k} \vee \overline{x}_{j,k})}^{H_{i,j}^k} \quad (1)$$

Clearly, pigeon hole formulas are unsatisfiable. Following Haken [4], we use array notation for clauses: Every clause is represented by an array of $n+1$ columns and n rows. An array contains a "+" ("−") in the i-th column and k-th row if and only if the variable $x_{i,k}$ occurs positively (negatively, respectively) in the corresponding clause. The representation of PHP_n in array notation has for every clause $(x_{i,1} \vee \cdots \vee x_{i,n})$, an array in which the i-th column is filled with "+". Moreover, for every clause $(\overline{x}_{i,k} \vee \overline{x}_{j,k})$, there is an array that contains two "−" in row k—one in column i and the other in column j. For instance, PHP_4 in array notation looks as follows:

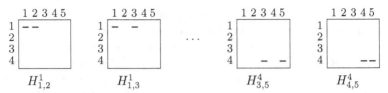

We use array notation to describe a method for learning binary clauses. For the explanation, we pick $(\overline{x}_{1,5} \vee \overline{x}_{4,1})$ in PHP_4 as it allows an easy formulation of the proof of pigeon hole formulas. The proof idea is similar to that of Cook: We reduce a pigeon hole formula PHP_n to the smaller formula PHP_{n-1}. The main difference is that in our case PHP_{n-1} still uses the same variables as PHP_n.

Again, we pick the clause $C = (\overline{x}_{1,5} \vee \overline{x}_{4,1}) \in PHP_4$. Let $\alpha_d = x_{1,5}\, x_{4,1}$ be the assignment blocked by C. Then, $\alpha = \overline{x}_{1,1}\, \overline{x}_{1,2}\, \overline{x}_{1,3}\, \overline{x}_{1,4}\, x_{1,5}\, x_{4,1}\overline{x}_{4,2}\, \overline{x}_{4,3}\, \overline{x}_{4,4}\, \overline{x}_{4,5}$ is obtained from α_d by applying unit propagation. Let C' be the clause that blocks α. The clauses and assignments in array notation are as follows:

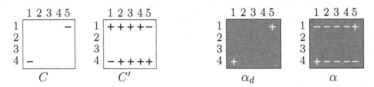

Next, we construct the positive reduct $p(PHP_4, \alpha)$. The positive reduct contains C' and all clauses of PHP_4 that are satisfied by α, which are the following 22 clauses: $P_1, P_5, H_{1,2}^1, \ldots, H_{4,5}^1, H_{1,2}^4, \ldots H_{4,5}^4$. From these clauses, we remove the literals that are not assigned by α and obtain the positive reduct $p(PHP_4, \alpha)$:

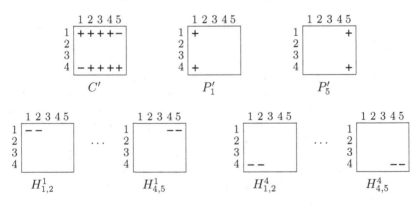

The positive reduct is satisfied by the following witness and conditional autarky:

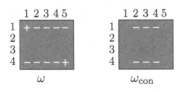

According to Theorem 3, we can learn clause C and, according to Theorem 6, we can learn the clauses A_1, A_2, A_3, and A_4:

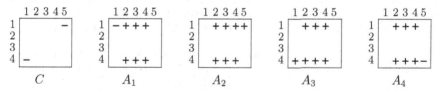

After learning $(\overline{x}_{1,5} \vee \overline{x}_{4,1})$, we can learn the clause $(\overline{x}_{2,5} \vee \overline{x}_{4,1})$ in a similar way. Now the assignment $\alpha_d = x_{4,1}$ can be extended using unit propagation to obtain $\alpha = \overline{x}_{3,1} \overline{x}_{3,2} \overline{x}_{3,3} \overline{x}_{3,4} x_{3,5} x_{4,1} \overline{x}_{4,2} \overline{x}_{4,3} \overline{x}_{4,4} \overline{x}_{4,5}$ The positive reduct of the extended formula, $p(PHP_4 \wedge (\overline{x}_{1,5} \vee \overline{x}_{4,1}) \wedge (\overline{x}_{2,5} \vee \overline{x}_{4,1}), \alpha)$, is satisfiable, allowing us to learn the unit clause $(\overline{x}_{4,1})$. By repeating the same procedure three times, we can learn the clauses $(\overline{x}_{4,2})$, $(\overline{x}_{4,3})$, and $(\overline{x}_{4,4})$ in a similar way. Now the clauses P_1 to P_4 can be shortened because their last literal is falsified. We have thus reduced PHP_4 to PHP_3.

7   Evaluation

We implemented a prototype[4] of SDCL on top of the plain LINGELING solver [2] (no pre- or inprocessing), including proof-logging support in the PR proof format [6]. We focus on solving large pigeon hole formulas efficiently and automatically, although we envision that the paradigm will be broadly applicable.

Apart from the standard encoding of the pigeon hole formulas, we ran experiments on two alternative, more compact, encodings. Both encodings replace the at-most-one constraint $\leq_1(x_{1,k}; \ldots; x_{n+1,k})$, i.e., the $H^k_{i,j}$ clauses in formula (1): The first alternative replaces the direct encoding by a sequential counter encoding [15]. The second alternative, the minimal encoding, iteratively replaces three literals of the at-most-one constraint with a new literal and adds an at-most-one constraint between the three replaced literals and the new literal.

We compared our method with two tools that can reason using extended resolution: EBDDRES [16] and GLUCOSER [1]. Both tools can refute pigeon hole formulas efficiently compared to CDCL solvers. EBDDRES solves a given formula using BDDs and optionally converts the BDD proof into an extended-resolution proof, linear in the number of BDD nodes, which in turn can be checked using the TraceCheck tool [5]. GLUCOSER is an extension of the GLUCOSE solver that allows *extended learning*—a method that adds definitions based on conflict clauses. Proof logging is not supported by GLUCOSER, but it could in theory be added with reasonable effort.[5]

Table 1 shows the results of our experiments. Each benchmark was executed on a compute node with two Intel(R) Xeon(R) E5-2620 v4 @ 2.10GHz CPUs and 128 GB of main memory, running Ubuntu 16.04.2 64-bit.

---

[4] The tools and files are available at http://fmv.jku.at/prune/
[5] Because we were unable to compile the sources, we could not add proof logging. Instead, we used a statically compiled binary.

Table 1. The number of variables and clauses of pigeon hole formulas—standard (-std), sequential counter (-seq), and minimal (-min)—as well as the runtime (in seconds) and proof size (in BDD nodes or lemmas) for solving the formulas with EBDDRES, GLUCOSER, and our SDCL variant of LINGELING. "TO" means a timeout after 9000 seconds and "OF" means 32-bit index overflow ($\geq 2^{30}$ cache lines) for EBDDRES.

	input		EBDDRES		GLUCOSER		LINGELING (PR)	
formula	#var	#cls	time	#node	time	#lemma	time	#lemma
PHP_{10}-std	110	561	1.00	3,182,495	22.71	329,470	0.07	329
PHP_{11}-std	132	738	3.47	9,493,302	146.61	1,514,845	0.11	439
PHP_{12}-std	156	949	10.64	27,351,195	307.29	2,660,358	0.16	571
PHP_{13}-std	182	1,197	30.81	76,513,832	982.84	6,969,736	0.22	727
PHP_{20}-std	420	4,221	OF	——	TO	——	1.61	2,659
PHP_{30}-std	930	13,981	OF	——	TO	——	13.45	8,989
PHP_{40}-std	1,640	32,841	OF	——	TO	——	67.41	21,319
PHP_{50}-std	2,550	63,801	OF	——	TO	——	241.14	41,649
PHP_{10}-seq	220	311	OF	——	1.62	25,712	0.07	327
PHP_{11}-seq	264	375	OF	——	6.94	77,747	0.10	437
PHP_{12}-seq	312	445	OF	——	19.40	174,084	0.14	569
PHP_{13}-seq	364	521	OF	——	172.76	1,061,318	0.18	725
PHP_{20}-seq	840	1,221	OF	——	TO	——	1.05	2,657
PHP_{30}-seq	1,860	2,731	OF	——	TO	——	6.55	8,987
PHP_{40}-seq	3,280	4,841	OF	——	TO	——	27.10	21,317
PHP_{50}-seq	5,100	7,551	OF	——	TO	——	86.30	41,647
PHP_{10}-min	180	281	28.60	81,490,141	0.64	15,777	0.06	329
PHP_{11}-min	220	342	143.92	399,014,970	1.82	34,561	0.10	439
PHP_{12}-min	264	409	OF	——	9.87	121,321	0.13	571
PHP_{13}-min	312	482	OF	——	57.66	483,789	0.18	727
PHP_{20}-min	760	1,161	OF	——	TO	——	1.03	2,659
PHP_{30}-min	1,740	2,641	OF	——	TO	——	6.30	8,989
PHP_{40}-min	3,120	4,721	OF	——	TO	——	26.65	21,319
PHP_{50}-min	4,900	7,401	OF	——	TO	——	85.00	41,649

Our version of LINGELING is the only tool that can solve pigeon hole formulas with 20 or more pigeons. Over 99% of the learned clauses ("lemmas") produced by LINGELING are PR clauses; the remaining ones are conflict clauses. The number of lemmas for PHP_n is cubic in n, while the number of variables and the size of the formula are at least quadratic in n. All PR clauses that are found by LINGELING are also added to the proofs. The size of the automatically produced PR proofs is similar to that of our manual proofs [6]. For the proofs returned by LINGELING, we observed that between around 5 % and 40 % of the clauses are not required for proving unsatisfiability. Moreover, our approach is robust: Performance varies only minimally across the different encodings of the pigeon hole formulas.

If we turn off our SDCL code, LINGELING requires exponential runtime on PHP_n formulas. Runtimes are similar but in all cases larger than for GLUCOSER, e.g., 153 seconds for PHP_{13}-min. We also want to highlight that the autarky decision heuristic is essential for proving the unsatisfiability of the pigeon hole formulas—without this heuristic, LINGELING could not find proofs within the given time limit.

8   Conclusions

We proposed a theoretical and a practical approach to searching for PR clauses. First, we showed that searching for a PR clause is an NP-complete problem. As a consequence, a SAT solver that performs the addition of PR clauses has to solve multiple NP-complete problems instead of only one. To make this approach feasible and efficient, we turned the problem of finding a PR clause into a SAT encoding that is significantly easier than the original problem. We called this encoding the *positive reduct* and showed that satisfying the positive reduct yields a set-blocked clause, or, equivalently, a conditional autarky. We also demonstrated how this set-blocked clause can be shortened. Based on our theoretical results, we introduced SDCL—a new SAT-solving paradigm that generalizes CDCL so that it produces not only conflict clauses but also PR clauses. Finally, we implemented SDCL in the solver LINGELING and performed preliminary experiments with the pigeon hole formulas that are very promising.

In future work, we want to focus on making the SDCL approach effective on a wide spectrum of formulas. There are several challenges ahead. First and foremost, a heuristic needs to be developed that facilitates finding PR clauses with few decisions. Our autarky decision heuristic appears to be a useful first step. Second, experiments should be performed to find out which PR clauses prune the search space most effectively. In our evaluation, we selected PR clauses based on decisions. An alternative is to use PR clauses based on conditional autarkies. It is also not yet clear when and how often an SDCL solver should search for PR clauses to achieve the best performance. Moreover, it could make sense to restrict the time spent on solving the positive reduct. Finally, we observed that although the computational costs for solving the positive reducts are low, the costs of generating the reducts are very high. Reducing the generation costs could thus improve the performance significantly.

References

1. Audemard, G., Katsirelos, G., Simon, L.: A Restriction of Extended Resolution for Clause Learning SAT Solvers. In: Proc. of the 24th AAAI Conference on Artificial Intelligence (AAAI 2010). pp. 15–20. AAAI Press (2010)
2. Biere, A.: Splatz, Lingeling, Plingeling, Treengeling, YalSAT Entering the SAT Competition 2016. In: Proc. of SAT Competition 2016 – Solver and Benchmark Descriptions. Dep. of Computer Science Series of Publications B, vol. B-2016-1, pp. 44–45. University of Helsinki (2016)
3. Cook, S.A.: A short proof of the pigeon hole principle using extended resolution. SIGACT News 8(4), 28–32 (Oct 1976)
4. Haken, A.: The intractability of resolution. Theoretical Computer Science 39, 297–308 (1985)

5. Heule, M.J.H., Biere, A.: Proofs for satisfiability problems. In: All about Proofs, Proofs for All (APPA), Math. Logic and Foundations, vol. 55. College Pub. (2015)
6. Heule, M.J.H., Kiesl, B., Biere, A.: Short proofs without new variables. In: Proc. of the 26th Int. Conference on Automated Deduction (CADE-26). LNCS, vol. 10395, pp. 130–147. Springer (2017)
7. Järvisalo, M., Heule, M.J.H., Biere, A.: Inprocessing rules. In: Proc. of the 6th Int. Joint Conference on Automated Reasoning (IJCAR 2012). LNCS, vol. 7364, pp. 355–370. Springer, Heidelberg (2012)
8. Kiesl, B., Seidl, M., Tompits, H., Biere, A.: Super-blocked clauses. In: Proc. of the 8th Int. Joint Conference on Automated Reasoning (IJCAR 2016). LNCS, vol. 9706, pp. 45–61. Springer, Cham (2016)
9. Kleine Büning, H., Kullmann, O.: Minimal unsatisfiability and autarkies. In: Handbook of Satisfiability, pp. 339–401. IOS Press (2009)
10. Kullmann, O.: On a generalization of extended resolution. Discrete Applied Mathematics 96-97, 149–176 (1999)
11. Marques Silva, J.P., Sakallah, K.A.: GRASP: A search algorithm for propositional satisfiability. IEEE Trans. Computers 48(5), 506–521 (1999)
12. Monien, B., Speckenmeyer, E.: Solving satisfiability in less than 2^n steps. Discrete Applied Mathematics 10(3), 287–295 (1985)
13. Moskewicz, M.W., Madigan, C.F., Zhao, Y., Zhang, L., Malik, S.: Chaff: Engineering an efficient SAT solver. In: Proceedings of the 38th Design Automation Conference (DAC 2001). pp. 530–535. ACM (2001)
14. Nordström, J.: On the interplay between proof complexity and SAT solving. SIGLOG News 2(3), 19–44 (2015)
15. Sinz, C.: Towards an optimal CNF encoding of boolean cardinality constraints. In: Proc. of the 11th Int. Conference on Principles and Practice of Constraint Programming (CP 2005). LNCS, vol. 3709, pp. 827–831. Springer (2005)
16. Sinz, C., Biere, A.: Extended Resolution Proofs for Conjoining BDDs. In: Proc. of the 1st Int. Computer Science Symposium in Russia (CSR 2006). LNCS, vol. 3967, pp. 600–611. Springer (2006)
17. Sörensson, N., Biere, A.: Minimizing learned clauses. In: Proc. of the 12th Int. Conference on Theory and Applications of Satisfiability Testing (SAT 2009). LNCS, vol. 5584, pp. 237–243. Springer (2009)
18. Tseitin, G.S.: On the complexity of derivation in propositional calculus. In: Automation of Reasoning: 2: Classical Papers on Computational Logic 1967–1970. pp. 466–483. Springer, Heidelberg (1983)
19. Urquhart, A.: The complexity of propositional proofs. In: Current Trends in Theoretical Computer Science, pp. 332–342. World Scientific (2001)

LRA Interpolants from No Man's Land

Leonardo Alt, Antti E. J. Hyvärinen and Natasha Sharygina

Università della Svizzera italiana, Lugano, Switzerland
leonardoaltt@gmail.com, antti.hyvaerinen@usi.ch, natasha.sharygina@usi.ch

Abstract. Interpolation is becoming a standard technique for over-approximating state spaces in software model checking with Satisfiability Modulo Theories (SMT). In particular when modelling programs with linear arithmetics, the standard state-of-the-art technique might provide either interpolants that are too specific or too generic to be useful for a given application. In this work we introduce the SI-LRA interpolation system for linear real arithmetics that allows the tuning of interpolants based on shifting between the primal and dual interpolants. We prove a strength relation between the interpolants constructed by SI-LRA, and integrate SI-LRA into a propositional interpolator in an SMT solver. Our evaluation, performed using a state-of-the-art software model checker, reveals that correct tuning with SI-LRA can reduce the number of needed refinements by up to one third and provide lower runtimes.

1 Introduction

Many modern software verification techniques rely on satisfiability modulo theories (SMT) solvers which accept as input instances of the propositional satisfiability problem (SAT) where some of the Boolean variables are interpreted as equalities in some first-order theory. Satisfiability in linear real arithmetics (LRA) consists of determining whether a set of linear equalities defined over real variables has a solution. Most LRA solvers use highly efficient variants of the Simplex algorithm [9], making LRA ubiquitous in model checking and as an intermediary solving step for non-linear real arithmetics (NRA), linear integer arithmetics (LIA), and other techniques.

One of the core tasks in software verification is to find invariants that prove the absence of bad behavior and are inductive with respect to a program loop. In many powerful verification approaches the invariants are synthesized as generalizations of simple examples produced by SMT solvers on short loop-free fragments of program executions. In this work we consider the problem of proving that a set of linear equalities over real variables does not have a solution, and how these inequalities can be relaxed while still preserving the property of not having solutions. In particular in model checking this problem is known as *interpolation* over LRA. For clarity we present the *strength-controlled interpolation system for LRA* (SI-LRA), a novel interpolation algorithm based on computing a primal and a dual interpolant and constructing the final interpolant from the area between these two (hence the *No Man's Land* in the title). We present the

© Springer International Publishing AG 2017
O. Strichman and R. Tzoref-Brill (Eds.): HVC 2017, LNCS 10629, pp. 195–210, 2017.
https://doi.org/10.1007/978-3-319-70389-3_13

system as an extension of [17] which allows the use of a *strength factor* control the strength. Our experimental results on the interpolating model checker HiFrog [2] suggest that mid-range strengths result in high-quality interpolants as indicated by fewer required refinements, and surprisingly that this does not correlate with the algorithm runtime.

Given the central role of interpolation in program verification, it is natural to search for LRA interpolants that meet the needs of different model checkers. Such needs include efficiency in generating interpolants, simplicity of the formulas representing the interpolants, and how they integrate with SMT solvers. Nevertheless the flexibility of LRA interpolation approaches is still an issue, and many existing techniques do not allow the interpolation-based application to interfere with the interpolant generation. To the best of our knowledge, this paper presents the first flexible interpolation system for LRA capable of generating an infinite amount of interpolants for a given interpolation problem.

Related work. The Propositional Labeled Interpolation System (LIS-PROP), introduced in [7] and further developed in [21,20,3,24], provides a framework for adjusting Craig interpolants with respect to their strength and, to some extent, size for a particular application. LIS-PROP is extended to interpolation of equalities over uninterpreted functions in [4], while this work presents a way of controlling the strength of interpolants in linear real arithmetics.

The pioneering work in LRA interpolation was presented in [19] and then used in [17], where inference rules are given and extended to accommodate the interpolation algorithm of [19]. A more practical approach is taken in [9], where LRA interpolation is done inside an SMT solver by extracting the proof of unsatisfiability from the Simplex algorithm. Both [9] and [17] are only capable of computing a single interpolant, while our SI-LRA is able to generate an infinite amount of interpolants.

In [1] the authors construct convex interpolants for $A \wedge B$, where A and B are disjunctions of constraints, leading potentially to general and simple interpolants. A similar smoothing approach is followed in [5]. SI-LRA is orthogonal to both these approaches, since we aim at creating interpolants of different strength. The techniques can be used together, with the algorithms from [1,5] using SI-LRA to generate interpolants for specific subsets of A and B.

Interpolants can be generated by first solving a constraint problem in linear arithmetics, and then applying a linear programming solver as a black box [23]. However, since most SMT solvers already use the Simplex algorithm for LRA solving, the use of a black-box solver introduces an extra overhead. The algorithm from [23] is also not able to generate multiple interpolants for a given problem, and does not provide strength control as SI-LRA does. A similar approach is presented in [25] for computing shared interpolants for a maximal number of conflicts by minimizing the number of linear equations in the interpolant with respect to computing an interpolant from a single theory conflict. The approach suffers from the same overhead as [23], and does not provide control over the strength of the generated interpolants.

An approach related to the interpolation system discussed in this work is presented for Nonlinear Real Arithmetics in [10]. This work is also able to provide interpolants of different strength, controlled by a labeling function. The interpolation system from [10] uses the proof of unsatisfiability generated by a decision procedure based on Interval Constraint Propagation. In a high level, their system is similar to [19].

Finally, [22] constructs interpolants based on program semantics. Applying semantics to the real equations would provide a powerful heuristic for LRA interpolation.

This work is organized as follows. We present our notation in Sec. 2 and the SI-LRA interpolation framework in Sec. 3. Section 4 presents an experimental evaluation using a model checker and conclusions are drawn in Sec. 5.

2   Preliminaries

This section introduces the quantifier-free theory of Linear Real Arithmetic (LRA) and interpolation. We refer the reader to [16] and [9] for an in-depth discussion on decision procedures for linear real arithmetics as used by modern SMT solvers.

An LRA instance is a conjunction of *linear constraints* of the form $c \bowtie a_1x_1 + \ldots + a_nx_n$ where $\bowtie \in \{<, \leq\}$, constants a_i are rational numbers, and the *problem variables* x_i assume rational values from $\mathbb{Q}$. The *General Simplex* is an algorithm that takes as input an LRA instance and determines whether there are values for the problem variables such that the set of constraints is satisfiable. In case there are values for the problem variables that satisfy the constraints the algorithm provides one such concrete valuation. If the set of constraints is unsatisfiable the algorithm returns an unsatisfiable subset Γ of the constraints as an explanation for the unsatisfiability. In standard SMT solving the explanations are used for guiding the SAT solver underlying the SMT solver to avoid similar conflicts. In practice this is done by adding the *explanation clause* $C_{\mathrm{LRA}} = \neg(\bigwedge_{c \in \Gamma})$ to the SAT solver. In the context of interpolation they have a further use for constructing safe overapproximations of search spaces.

Given an unsatisfiable first-order formula $A \wedge B$, a *Craig interpolant* [6] for A is a first-order formula I_A such that $A \rightarrow I_A$, $I_A \wedge B$ is unsatisfiable, and I_A is defined over the non-logical symbols shared between A and B. Given an interpolation algorithm $Itp(A, B)$, the *dual interpolant* for A is the negation of the interpolant computed by $Itp(B, A)$.

2.1   LRA Interpolation

An explanation Γ is a minimal unsatisfiable subset of the constraints of a query. The explanation can be used to create a proof of unsatisfiability which in turn can be used to compute an interpolant. A straightforward but inflexible approach to create LRA interpolants is presented in [17]. The idea is to create a tree that represents the proof of unsatisfiability and annotate the nodes with partial

Table 1. LRA proof system for BI-LRA [17].

Hyp	Comb
$\dfrac{\quad}{\phi} \ \phi \in \Gamma$	$\dfrac{0 \leq t \quad 0 \leq u}{0 \leq t + u}$
Taut	Mult
$\dfrac{\quad}{0 \leq c} \ c \in \mathbb{Q}, c \geq 0$	$\dfrac{0 \leq c \quad 0 \leq t}{0 \leq ct} \ c \in \mathbb{Q}, c > 0$

interpolants. We present this system here and will extend it using the duality of interpolants to create the SI-LRA in Sec. 3. To clarify the difference, we call the system from [17] the *basic interpolation system for LRA* (BI-LRA).

A *term* in BI-LRA is a linear combination $c_0 + c_1 x_1 + \ldots + c_n x_n$, where $x_1 \ldots x_n$ are distinct variables and $c_0 \ldots c_n$ are constants. This proof system accepts constraints of the form $0 \leq term$. The rules for deriving a proof in BI-LRA are given in Table 1, where t and u are terms, and Γ is the explanation for unsatisfiability.

Example 1. Consider the unsatisfiable formula $(3 \leq x_1 + x_2) \wedge (0 \leq -x_2) \wedge (0 \leq 2x_2 - x_1)$. Once the constraints have been transformed into the form accepted by the proof system, we can compute the following proof using the rules in Table 1:

(a) $0 \leq -3 + x_1 + x_2$ (c) $0 \leq -x_1 + 2x_2$ (d) $0 \leq 3$ (b) $0 \leq -x_2$

(e) $0 \leq -3 + 3x_2$ (f) $0 \leq -3x_2$

(g) $0 \leq -3$

Applying the *Hyp* rule to the constraints (a)-(c) is straightforward. We then apply rule *Comb* to (a) and (c) to infer (e). We apply rule *Taut* to obtain the tautology (d) $0 \leq 3$ and then *Mult* to multiply (b) by (d) and infer (f) $0 \leq -3x_2$. Now we can apply *Comb* to combine (e) and (f) to finally infer (g) $0 \leq -3$, a contradiction.

An LRA interpolation problem is a 3-tuple $P = (A, B, R)$, where A and B are two sets of LRA constraints such that they are unsatisfiable when conjoined, and R is the proof of unsatisfiability for $A \wedge B$. The intuition behind BI-LRA is to use the contribution from the constraints from A to the sum that leads to the contradiction. The contribution from A is then effectively the interpolant, since (i) it is implied by A; (ii) summing the contribution with B leads to a contradiction; and (iii) summing all the contributions from A removes the symbols local to A, therefore leaving only the common symbols from A and B to the interpolant.

The interpolation rules of BI-LRA are given in Table 2, where x, y, x' and y' are terms, and $[\phi]$ is the annotated term such that $0 \leq \phi$ is the partial interpolant for that node.

Table 2. Interpolation system from [17].

Hyp-A	Hyp-B
$\dfrac{}{0 \le x \; [x]} \; (0 \le x) \in A$	$\dfrac{}{0 \le x \; [0]} \; (0 \le x) \in B$
Comb	Mult
$\dfrac{0 \le x \; [x'] \quad 0 \le y \; [y']}{0 \le x + y \; [x' + y']}$	$\dfrac{0 \le c \quad 0 \le x \; [x']}{0 \le cx \; [cx']}$

Example 2. Continuing Example 1, suppose $A = \{0 \le -3 + x_1 + x_2, 0 \le -x_1 + 2x_2\}$ and $B = \{0 \le -x_2\}$. The interpolant for A is computed by BI-LRA as follows. Using the *Hyp-A* and *Hyp-B* rules we can infer the partial interpolants

$$\frac{}{(a) \; 0 \le -3 + x_1 + x_2 \; [-3 + x_1 + x_2]} \; (0 \le -3 + x_1 + x_2) \in A \, ,$$

$$\frac{}{(c) \; 0 \le -x_1 + 2x_2 \; [-x_1 + 2x_2]} \; (0 \le -x_1 + 2x_2) \in A \, , \text{ and}$$

$$\frac{}{(b) \; 0 \le -x_2 \; [0]} \; (0 \le -x_2) \in B \, .$$

Following the proof from Example 1, we apply the *Comb* rule on (c) and (a) to infer (d)

$$\frac{0 \le -3 + x_1 + x_2 \quad 0 \le -x_1 + 2x_2}{(d) \; 0 \le -3 + 3x_2 \; [-3 + 3x_2]} \, .$$

We now apply the *Taut* rule to use the tautology (e) $0 \le 3$ and then *Mult* rule on (e) and (b) to infer (e) $0 \le -3x_2 \; [0]$. By applying *Comb* on (d) and (f) we infer (g) $0 \le -3 \; [-3 + 3x_2]$. The annotated proof of unsatisfiability is

(a) $0 \le -3 + x_1 + x_2$ (c) $0 \le -x_1 + 2x_2$ (b) $0 \le -x_2$ (e) $0 \le 3$
$[-3 + x_1 + x_2]$ $[-x_1 + 2x_2]$ $[0]$

(d) $0 \le -3 + 3x_2$ (f) $0 \le -3x_2$
$[-3 + 3x_2]$ $[0]$

(g) $0 \le -3$
$[-3 + 3x_2]$

and the final interpolant for A is $0 \le -3 + 3x_2$.

2.2 Propositional Interpolation

In our experiments in Sec. 4 we combine SI-LRA with the propositional inter-polation interpolation system (LIS-PROP) from [8,3]. We briefly introduce the system here; for lack of space we assume familiarity with propositional resolution (see, e.g., [3]).

A resolution refutation is a directed, acyclic tree where the leaves are *source clauses*, the inner nodes are *resolvent clauses*, and the root is the empty clause. LIS-PROP takes as input two propositional formulas A, B in conjunctive normal form, a resolution refutation R of $A \wedge B$, and a *labeling function* $L(p, C) \mapsto \{a, b, ab\}$, where (p, C) is an occurrence of a variable p in a clause C, of the refutation R, and a, b, ab are *labels*. The system returns an interpolant I for A such that the shape of I depends on L. For all variable occurrences (p, C) in R, $L(p, C) = a$ if p is local to A; and $L(p, C) = b$ if p is local to B. However, the label can be freely chosen for the shared variables, allowing in practice a significant amount of flexibility in constructing interpolants. The label of a variable occurrence in a resolvent C is determined by the labels of the variables in its antecedents: If a variable occurs in both its antecedents with different labels, the label of the new occurrence is ab; and in all other cases the label is equivalent to the label in its antecedent or both antecedents.

An interpolation algorithm based on LIS-PROP [3] computes an interpolant with a dynamic algorithm by annotating each clause of R with a *partial interpolant* starting from the source clauses. The partial interpolant of a source clause C is

$$I(C) = \begin{cases} \bigvee\{l \mid l \in C \text{ and } L(var(l), C) = b\} & \text{if } C \in A, \text{ and} \\ \bigwedge\{\neg l \mid l \in C \text{ and } L(var(l), C) = a\} & \text{if } C \in B, \end{cases} \tag{1}$$

The partial interpolant of a resolvent clause C with pivot p and antecedents C^+ and C^-, where $p \in C^+$ and $\neg p \in C^-$, is

$$I(C) = \begin{cases} I(C^+) \vee I(C^-) & \text{if } L(p, C^+) = L(p, C^-) = a, \\ I(C^+) \wedge I(C^-) & \text{if } L(p, C^+) = L(p, C^-) = b, \text{ and} \\ (I(C^+) \vee p) \wedge (I(C^-) \vee \neg p) & \text{otherwise.} \end{cases} \tag{2}$$

The final interpolant can be obtained as $I(\bot)$ where $\bot$ is the empty clause, i.e., the root of the refutation.

LIS-PROP allows ordering interpolants partially with respect to their logical strength based on the labeling function. In Sec. 4 we use six propositional interpolation algorithms based on LIS-PROP: The algorithms M_s and M_w that are known as the strong and the weak McMillan interpolants [18]; the Huang [12] Krajíček [15] Pudlák [19] interpolation algorithm (P), and the proof-sensitive interpolation algorithms PS, PS_s, and PS_w from [3]. Given an ordering $\leq$ for logical strengths of formulas, where the least element is the strongest, one can show that $M_s \leq I \leq M_w$ for any LIS-PROP-based interpolation algorithm I, and that $PS_s \leq PS \leq PS_w$.

The interpolation algorithms from LIS-PROP can be combined with the algorithm BI-LRA, and later with SI-LRA, by first computing the interpolants I_{LRA} for the explanation clauses C_{LRA} of LRA, and then using these interpolants as the partial interpolants $I(C_{\mathrm{LRA}})$.

Table 3. The dual interpolation system

Hyp-A	Hyp-B
$\dfrac{}{0 \leq x \; [0]}\,(0 \leq x) \in A$	$\dfrac{}{0 \leq x \; [x]}\,(0 \leq x) \in B$

Comb	Mult
$\dfrac{0 \leq x \; [x'] \quad 0 \leq y \; [y']}{0 \leq x+y \; [x'+y']}$	$\dfrac{0 \leq c \quad 0 \leq x \; [x']}{0 \leq cx \; [cx']}$

3   The LRA Interpolation System SI-LRA

The intuition of the interpolation system SI-LRA is to apply the duality of interpolants to the interpolation algorithm BI-LRA to obtain two interpolants and construct new interpolants by a shift transformation that lie between the interpolant and its dual. Let Itp_M be the interpolation algorithm of BI-LRA. We define its dual Itp_D to be $Itp_D(A, B, R) = \neg Itp_M(B, A, R)$. To formalize the presentation we first prove an ordering between Itp_M and Itp_D in Lemma 2 and then define what we mean by interpolant shifting in Theorem 1.

We start the presentation with an example illustrating the dual interpolant.

Example 3. Recall Example 2, where we had $A = \{0 \leq -3 + x_1 + x_2, 0 \leq -x_1 + 2x_2\}$ and $B = \{0 \leq -x_2\}$. The interpolant Itp_D is given by the annotated proof

$$
\begin{array}{cccc}
0 \leq -3 + x_1 + x_2 & 0 \leq -x_1 + 2x_2 & 0 \leq -x_2 & 0 \leq 3 \\
[0] & [0] & [-x_2] & \\
\end{array}
$$

$$
\begin{array}{cc}
0 \leq -3 + 3x_2 & 0 \leq -3x_2 \\
[0] & [-3x_2]
\end{array}
$$

$$
0 \leq -3 \\
[-3x_2]
$$

where the dual interpolant is $\neg(0 \leq -3x_2)$.

Formally, the dual interpolation algorithm works as shown in Table 3, where x, y, x' and y' are terms, and $[\phi]$ is the annotated term such that $0 \leq \phi$ is the partial interpolant for that node.

Let $[\gamma]$ be the annotation in the root of the proof tree and the inequality $0 \leq \gamma$ an interpolant for B. By duality of interpolants, we can assert that $\neg(0 \leq \gamma)$ is an interpolant for A. Furthermore, we can state the following relationship between the primal and dual interpolants Itp_M and Itp_D:

Lemma 1. *Let $P = (A, B, R)$ be an interpolation problem. Let the inequality $c_1 \leq x$ be the interpolant generated by Itp_M, where c_1 is a constant and x is an LRA term. Then Itp_D generates an interpolant of the form $\neg(c_2 \leq -x)$, where c_2 is a constant.*

Proof. Let R be a proof tree that proves the unsatisfiability of $A \wedge B$, annotated with partial interpolants. By Table 1 we know that R is constructed by summing the inequalities from A and B, and by multiplying by a constant. The proof can be seen as a way to parenthesize these operations. Using associativity of sum, we can rearrange any arbitrary proof such that the contradiction is inferred via an application of the *Comb* rule on two inequalities

$$0 \le -c_1 + x \tag{3}$$

$$0 \le -c_2 - x \tag{4}$$

such that (i) $0 \le -c_1 + x$ is inferred only using inequalities from A; and (ii) $0 \le -c_2 - x$ is inferred only using inequalities from B, where x is an LRA term and $-c_1 - c_2 < 0$. From (i), the partial interpolants for Eq. (3) and Eq. (4), when computing Itp_M are, respectively, $[-c_1 + x]$ and 0; from (ii) follows that the partial interpolants for Eq. (3) and Eq. (4), when computing Itp_D are, respectively, 0 and $[-c_2 - x]$. Therefore, we can see that the term annotated with the contradiction node is $[-c_1 + x]$ when computing Itp_M and $[-c_2 - x]$ when computing Itp_D. Because of that, we know that the interpolant Itp_M is $c_1 \le x$ and the interpolant Itp_D is $\neg(c_2 \le -x)$.   □

Lemma 2. *Let $c_1 \le x$ and $\neg(c_2 \le -x)$ be the interpolants generated for a fixed interpolation problem by Itp_M and Itp_D, respectively. The interpolants generated by Itp_M and Itp_D represent lower bounds for x, where $-c_2 < c_1$.*

Proof. In $Itp_M(P)$, c_1 is clearly a lower bound for x. Transforming $Itp_D(P)$ shows that $\neg(c_2 \le -x) \equiv \neg(-c_2 \ge x) \equiv -c_2 < x$. By Eq. (3) and Eq. (4), $-c_1 - c_2 < 0$, and therefore it follows that $-c_2 < c_1$.   □

3.1   The Strength Factor

By Lemma 2 we have established the strength relation between Itp_M and Itp_D, and are ready to introduce SI-LRA. Our idea is based on the observation that Itp_M and Itp_D represent lower bounds for the same term (Lemma 2), which means that any constant c such that $-c_2 < c \le c_1$ can substitute c_1 in $Itp_M = c_1 \le x$, to create a new interpolant $Itp_c = c \le x$.

Lemma 3. *Let $c_1 \le x$ and $\neg(c_2 \le -x)$ be the interpolants generated for the same interpolation problem P by Itp_M and Itp_D, respectively. Let c be a constant such that $-c_2 < c \le c_1$. Then $Itp_c = c \le x$ is an interpolant for P.*

Proof. Because $c \le c_1$, $Itp_M(P) \rightarrow Itp_c(P)$. Because $-c_2 < c$, $Itp_c(P) \rightarrow Itp_D(P)$. Therefore Itp_c is an interpolant for P.   □

Algorithm 1 SI-LRA

```
1: procedure ITP(P = (A, B, R, α))
2:     Requires 0 ≤ α ≤ 1.
3:     if α = 1 then
4:         return Itp_D(P)
5:     if α = 0 then
6:         return Itp_M(P)
7:     c_1 ≤ x ← Itp_M(P)
8:     ¬(c_2 ≤ −x) ← Itp_D(P)
9:     return c_1 − α(c_1 + c_2) ≤ x
```

Since the bounds c_1 and $-c_2$ change from problem to problem, it is easier to normalize this interval and apply a *strength factor*. Let P be an interpolation problem such that $Itp_M(P) = c_1 \leq x$ and $Itp_D(P) = -c_2 \leq -x$. Given a factor α such that $0 \leq \alpha \leq 1$, we can create a new interpolant $Itp_\alpha \equiv c_\alpha \leq x$, where $c_\alpha = c_1 - \alpha(c_1 + c_2)$.

We extend the LRA interpolation problem to include the strength factor, $P = (A, B, R, \alpha)$ and for clarity present SI-LRA in the form of an algorithm in Alg. 1. In case $-c_2 < c_1$ it is possible to generate infinitely many interpolants of different strength for a given interpolation problem, giving a very fine-grained control over the strength of the generated interpolants.

Theorem 1. *Let α and α' be two strength factors such that $0 \leq \alpha < \alpha' \leq 1$. Then $Itp(A, B, R, \alpha) \to Itp(A, B, R, \alpha')$.*

Proof. Analogous to the proof of Lemma 3. □

Theorem 1 shows that the strength of the LRA interpolants can be controlled by the strength factor. The interpolation algorithm Itp_M from [17] is represented by the strength factor 0, and generates the strongest interpolants among SI-LRA. The dual interpolation algorithm Itp_D generates the weakest interpolants.

The main advantage of SI-LRA can be visualized when it is combined with propositional interpolation in an SMT solver.

Example 4. Let $A = x \leq 1 \land y \leq 1$ and $B = (y \geq 4 \land x \geq 0 \land x \leq 3) \lor (x \geq 3 \land y \geq 0)$ be two Boolean formulas such that the atoms are LRA terms. Notice that we cannot decide satisfiability of $A \land B$ using Simplex only. To achieve this task we can, for instance, use an SMT solver. The formula $A \land B$ is unsatisfiable, proven by two unsatisfiable queries to the LRA solver, where each query consists of a conjunction of LRA constraints and is solved using the Simplex algorithm. The LRA interpolants that are generated by these queries are then used in propositional interpolation. Using a fixed propositional interpolation algorithm we get the following interpolants for A when changing the LRA interpolation algorithm:

$$Itp_M : \quad I_M = x \leq 1 \land y \leq 1$$
$$Itp_D : \quad I_D = \neg x \geq 3 \land \neg y \geq 4$$
$$Itp_{0.5} : \quad I_{0.5} = x \leq 2 \land y \leq 2.5$$

Notice that $I_M \to I_{0.5} \to I_D$. Fig. 1 shows the graphical representation of the problem. The blue region is A and the red region is B. We can see graphically that they are unsatisfiable when conjoined. The interpolant I_M happens to be the same as A. Interpolants $I_{0.5}$ and I_D are represented, respectively, by the light and dark green areas of the graph.

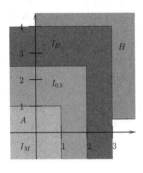

Since the strength of the LRA interpolants is given in the level of the theory interpolants, if a propositional interpolation algorithm from the Labeled Interpolation Systems is used, the strength of the final interpolant is maintained.

Theorem 2. *Let* $P = (A, B, R)$ *be an interpolation problem. Given two LRA interpolation algorithms* $Itp_\alpha, Itp_{\alpha'}$ *from SI-LRA such that* $0 \leq \alpha < \alpha' \leq 1$, *and a fixed propositional interpolation algorithm* Itp_{prop} *from LIS-PROP, the interpolants* I, I' *computed by the combination algorithm* Itp_{prop}, Itp_α *and* $Itp_{prop}, Itp_{\alpha'}$, *respectively, are ordered such that* $I \leq I'$.

Fig. 1. LRA problem and different interpolants.

Proof. Eq. (1) and Eq. (2) show how an interpolation algorithm from LIS-PROP creates interpolants from the leaves to the root. Eq. (1) is only applied to Boolean clauses and not to theory clauses, so can be disregarded in this context. Let n be a non-leaf node of R that has as children two theory leaves, t_1 and t_2. Let $x_1 = Itp_\alpha(t_1)$, $x_2 = Itp_\alpha(t_2)$, $y_1 = Itp_{\alpha'}(t_1)$ and $y_2 = Itp_{\alpha'}(t_2)$. By Theorem 1, $x_1 \rightarrow y_1$ and $x_2 \rightarrow y_2$.

We now analyze the three possibilities to build the partial interpolant for n in Eq. (2):

- The first is a disjunction of the partial interpolants of t_1 and t_2. We know that $((x_1 \rightarrow y_1) \wedge (x_2 \rightarrow y_2)) \rightarrow ((x_1 \vee x_2) \rightarrow (y_1 \vee y_2))$, so the strength is maintained.
- The second is a conjunction of the partial interpolants of t_1 and t_2. We know that $((x_1 \rightarrow y_1) \wedge (x_2 \rightarrow y_2)) \rightarrow ((x_1 \wedge x_2) \rightarrow (y_1 \wedge y_2))$, so the strength is maintained.
- The third is a conjunction of two disjunctions, formed by the partial interpolants of t_1 and t_2 and the pivot of the resolution rule which is an arbitrary variable. It is also true that $((x_1 \rightarrow y_1) \wedge (x_2 \rightarrow y_2)) \rightarrow (((x_1 \vee p) \wedge (x_2 \vee \neg p)) \rightarrow ((y_1 \vee p) \wedge (y_2 \vee \neg p)))$, so the strength is maintained.

The case where n has as children a theory leaf and a Boolean leaf clearly holds. Since the annotation of the propositional part of R is not affected, the Theorem holds.   □

Note that the proof of Theorem 2 allows choosing different strength factors for different theory leaves in the refutation proof, giving the application even more possibilities to generate suitable interpolants.

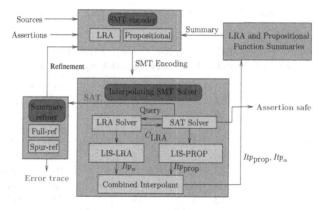

Fig. 2. Components of HiFrog relevant to our experiments

4   Experimental Evaluation

We implemented and integrated SI-LRA into the existing propositional interpolation in OpenSMT2 [14]. Often software verification can be done in a level
which ignores arithmetic overflows. In this case LRA can be used in software
model checking to abstract the heavy-weight bit-precise propositional encoding
to gain speed-up due to the higher-level theory. If a model checker reports that
a certain property is true when using LRA, it is also true for the propositional
model. However, if a property is determined unsafe in LRA, the generated counterexample might be spurious and introduced by the LRA abstraction. There
are several *refinement strategies* a model-checker can recover from such cases
(see, e.g., [13]). For simplicity we study two strategies in the experiments: one
where a bit-precise solver needs to be invoked for every counterexample (*Full-
ref*), and another where the bit-precise solver is invoked only for the spurious
counterexamples (*Spur-ref*).

HiFrog applies interpolation-based techniques to create function summaries
that are stored and reused while checking incrementally different assertions in
a program. Our set of benchmarks consists of C code originating both from the
industry and from SV-COMP (https://sv-comp.sosy-lab.org/) where this
approach is relevant.

Figure 2 describes the main components of the HiFrog model-checking environment relevant to our experiments. The Source files and assertions are given
as input to the system which either (i) reports that an assertion is safe and
produces a summary for a function in the form of an interpolant, or (ii) outputs
an error trace witnessing an execution that breaks an assertion. The SMT encoding can be either in combination of propositional logic and LRA, or purely
in propositional logic, possibly using previously computed function summaries
(*top* of Fig. 2). The encoding is then inserted to the Interpolating SMT Solver
which determines the satisfiability of the encoding. In case of unsatisfiability the

Table 4. Comparison between propositional and LRA encoding in HiFrog.

	LRA Results			LRA Time (s)			
Name (# asserts)	Correct	SAT	Spurious	LRA	Spur-ref	Full-ref	Bool
floppy1 (21)	16	5	5	27.5	193	193	192
tcas_asrt (162)	162	132	0	65.5	65.5	144	86.0
kbfiltr1 (10)	10	0	0	5.30	5.30	5.30	4.12
diskperf1 (14)	10	4	4	609	667	667	194
cafe (115)	105	95	10	4.75	5.90	14.8	19.2
s3 (131)	126	109	5	1.77	1.82	3.00	1.50
mem (149)	146	52	3	106	106	125	44.6
ddv (152)	56	105	96	12.5	123	124	260
disk (79)	62	72	17	800	1200	8710	8190
total (833)	693	574	140	1630	2370	9990	8900

solver reports that an assertion is safe, produces a Combined Interpolant using both SI-LRA and LIS-PROP, and stores the summary for future use. In case of satisfiability, the trace is provided to the Summary Refiner, which uses a refinement strategy to classify the trace either as spurious, triggering a re-check, or concrete, resulting in an error trace.

We first compare LRA-based incremental software verification using function summaries to the corresponding approach using propositional logic. To then develop a more in-depth understanding of the performance of SI-LRA we study different interpolants that HiFrog can construct during its search.

Modelling in LRA and propositional logic. Table 4 reports experimental results on how LRA can help the propositional solver in speeding up function-summary-based model-checking. The column *Name* reports the name and the number of assertions for each benchmark, while the columns *LRA Results* and *LRA time* report the results and the runtimes for the LRA-based model-checker. The column *Bool* reports the runtime on the purely propositional model.

The column *Correct* reports how many of the assertions could be immediately solved in the LRA model without refinement; the column *SAT* reports how many potential error traces could be found in the LRA model; and the column *Spurious* reports how many of these error traces were spurious in the end. Surprisingly many of the assertions can be checked only using LRA logic, as indicated by the big numbers in *correct*. However, in the current implementation, especially when resorting to the *Full-ref* mode, we see that the spuriousness checks result in a significant overhead. In the *Spur-ref* mode where a more intelligent strategy for refinement is used, the use of LRA in encoding provides almost a three-fold speed-up for the solving.

In general the experiments implicate that modelling with LRA can provide big speed-ups with respect to propositional models and that the LRA interpolation algorithms are not forming a bottleneck for the solver performance.

Table 5. Number of function refinements for HiFROG using different combinations of propositional and LRA interpolation algorithms.

Alg	floppy1	tcas_asrt	kbfiltr1	diskperf1	cafe	s3	mem	ddv	disk	Σ
M_s,Itp_M	27100	**53800**	**5120**	39900	**6400**	0	25600	**7940**	47600	214000
$M_s,\text{Itp}_{0.5}$	25100	**53800**	**5120**	39200	**6400**	0	25100	**7940**	41500	204000
M_s,Itp_D	24800	**53800**	5380	39200	**6400**	0	25600	**7940**	64000	227000
P,Itp_M	27100	**53800**	**5120**	39700	**6400**	0	25600	**7940**	47600	213000
$P,\text{Itp}_{0.5}$	25100	**53800**	**5120**	39200	**6400**	0	25088	7940	41500	204000
P,Itp_D	24800	**53800**	5380	39200	**6400**	0	25600	**7940**	64000	227000
M_w,Itp_M	27100	**53800**	**5120**	41500	**6400**	0	25600	**7940**	47600	215000
$M_w,\text{Itp}_{0.5}$	25100	**53800**	**5120**	**37400**	**6400**	0	25100	**7940**	41500	**20200**
M_w,Itp_D	**24600**	**53800**	5380	39200	**6400**	0	25600	**7940**	64000	227000
PS,Itp_M	27100	**53800**	**5120**	40200	**6400**	0	25600	**7940**	47600	214000
$PS,\text{Itp}_{0.5}$	25100	**53800**	**5120**	39200	**6400**	0	25088	**7940**	41500	204000
PS,Itp_D	**24600**	**53800**	5380	38100	**6400**	0	25600	**7940**	64000	226000
PS_w,Itp_M	27100	**53800**	**5120**	39700	**6400**	0	25600	**7940**	47600	213000
$PS_w,\text{Itp}_{0.5}$	25100	**53800**	**5120**	39200	**6400**	0	25088	**7940**	41500	204000
PS_w,Itp_D	24800	**53800**	5380	39900	**6400**	0	25600	**7940**	64000	228000
PS_s,Itp_M	27100	**53800**	**5120**	39200	**6400**	0	25600	**7940**	47600	213000
$PS_s,\text{Itp}_{0.5}$	25100	**53800**	**5120**	39200	**6400**	0	25088	**7940**	41500	204000
PS_s,Itp_D	**24600**	**53800**	5380	39200	**6400**	0	25600	**7940**	64000	227000

The SI-LRA evaluation. We compare the different combined interpolation algorithms using in total 18 combinations, where the propositional interpolation algorithms range over M_s, M_w, P, PS, PS_s, PS_w of LIS-PROP and the LRA interpolation algorithms range over Itp_M, Itp_D, and $\text{Itp}_{0.5}$, i.e., the strong and weak LRA interpolation algorithms and the interpolation algorithm with strength factor $\alpha = 0.5$, from SI-LRA.

One way to compare the behavior of different interpolation algorithms is to observe how many summary refinements are needed in model-checking a set of assertions. The lower the number of refinements is, the more relevant summaries the interpolation algorithm created. Table 5 reports the number of function refinements needed when running different interpolation algorithms for the instances in Table 4. We note that on most instances the interpolation algorithm does affect the required refinements, providing clear evidence that the choice of the interpolation algorithm can significantly affect the work flow of the model checker, resulting in the most extreme case (**disk**) in 35% difference in number of refinements between the extremes. Interestingly the SI-LRA interpolation algorithm $\text{Itp}_{0.5}$ provides most of the low refinement numbers, showing that neither one of the straightforward interpolation algorithms provides the most relevant interpolants for our benchmarks. It is also interesting to note that the strength

Table 6. Verification time for HiFrog using different combinations of propositional and LRA interpolation algorithms.

Alg	floppy1	kbfiltr1	diskperf1	mem	disk	Σ
M_s,Itp$_M$	28.2	5.23	604	106	809	1550
M_s,Itp$_{0.5}$	33.8	5.42	561	136	988	1720
M_s,Itp$_D$	28.2	5.28	476	107	1203	1820
P,Itp$_M$	28.0	5.38	587	104	**799**	**1520**
P,Itp$_{0.5}$	34.1	5.15	548	135	998	1720
P,Itp$_D$	28.1	5.38	**440**	106	1290	1870
M_w,Itp$_M$	**27.5**	5.30	609	106	800	1550
M_w,Itp$_{0.5}$	34.1	5.16	607	137	977	1760
M_w,Itp$_D$	27.9	5.45	475	106	1250	1860
PS,Itp$_M$	28.1	5.44	666	105	804	1610
PS,Itp$_{0.5}$	34.1	5.10	558	135	1000	1730
PS,Itp$_D$	28.0	5.57	473	107	1240	1850
PS$_w$,Itp$_M$	27.8	5.51	616	**104**	826	1580
PS$_w$,Itp$_{0.5}$	34.1	5.28	535	136	998	1710
PS$_w$,Itp$_D$	28.1	5.57	453	106	1250	1840
PS$_s$,Itp$_M$	28.1	5.49	604	105	815	1560
PS$_s$,Itp$_{0.5}$	34.2	5.12	549	136	996	1720
PS$_s$,Itp$_D$	27.8	5.62	446	107	1290	1880

of the LRA interpolants that led to the least number of refinements was not the strongest nor the weakest, showing that a fine strength tuning may lead to fast convergence in interpolation-based model checkers.

We report in Table 6 in addition the verification times for HiFrog using different combinations of propositional and LRA interpolation algorithms for the cases where the number of refinements was not constant over different interpolation algorithms. The average runtimes for the remaining instance **tcas_asrt**, **cafe**, **s3**, and **ddv** were 66.0, 4.70, 1.77, and 12.8 seconds, respectively, with small variance. Interestingly the per-instance winning algorithms are almost evenly distributed, making it hard to predict which algorithm provides the lowest run time on our benchmarks, the exception being the strong propositional algorithms M_s and PS$_s$, which score no wins. Inside each propositional algorithm Itp$_M$ scores in total 18 wins compared to five wins of Itp$_{0.5}$ and 11 wins of Itp$_D$. However, for certain instances a given LRA algorithm is consistently better: in particular for **kbfiltr1** Itp$_{0.5}$ almost always wins, and for **diskperf1** Itp$_D$ always wins. Finally we note that there is little correlation between the number of refinements and the run times, suggesting that the run time invested in the solving phase may pay off in higher quality interpolants in applications where convergence is the dominating performance criterion as opposed to run time.

In general our preliminary results suggest that there are interesting and non-trivial choices to be made when designing an efficient LRA interpolation algorithm that call for further analyses.

5 Conclusions

This work presents an interpolation system for linear real arithmetics, proves its correctness and orders the produced interpolants with respect to their logical strength, integrates the interpolation system to a propositional interpolation system, and provides experimental evaluation when used in a model-checking application. The system is based on computing an interpolant and its dual, and obtaining by shifting arbitrary "intermediary" interpolants that lie between the two extremes.

Experimental results in model checking suggest that the choice of the interpolant affects both run time and number of refinements, and mid-strength interpolants, i.e., $\alpha = 0.5$, result in small number of refinements. In the future we plan to apply SI-LRA in domains such as software model checking based on the PDR algorithm [11], as well as approaches for adapting the strength, starting with $\alpha = 0.5$, and tuning the factor depending on whether the generate interpolants are too precise or too abstract.

Acknowledgements. This work was supported by the SNF grants 200020_163001 and 200020_166288.

References

1. Albarghouthi, A., McMillan, K.L.: Beautiful interpolants. In: Proc. CAV 2013. pp. 313–329. No. 8044 in LNCS, Springer (2013)
2. Alt, L., Asadi, S., Chockler, H., Even-Mendoza, K., Fedyukovich, G., Sharygina, N.: HiFrog: SMT-based function summarization for software verification. In: Proc. TACAS 2017. pp. 207–2013. No. 10206 in LNCS, Springer (2017)
3. Alt, L., Fedyukovich, G., Hyvärinen, A.E.J., Sharygina, N.: A proof-sensitive approach for small propositional interpolants. In: Proc. VSTTE 2015. pp. 1–18. No. 9593, Springer (2016)
4. Alt, L., Hyvärinen, A.E.J., Asadi, S., Sharygina, N.: Duality-based interpolation for quantifier-free equalities and uninterpreted functions. In: Proc. FMCAD (2017), to appear.
5. Bogomolov, S., Frehse, G., Giacobbe, M., Henzinger, T.A.: Counterexample-guided refinement of template polyhedra. In: Proc. TACAS 2017. LNCS, vol. 10205, pp. 589–606 (2017)
6. Craig, W.: Three uses of the herbrand-gentzen theorem in relating model theory and proof theory. The Journal of Symbolic Logic 22(3), 269–285 (1957)
7. D'Silva, V.: Propositional interpolation and abstract interpretation. In: Proc. ESOP 2010. pp. 185–204. No. 6012 in LNCS, Springer (2010)
8. D'Silva, V., Kroening, D., Purandare, M., Weissenbacher, G.: Interpolant strength. In: Proc. VMCAI 2010. pp. 129–145. No. 5944 in LNCS, Springer (2010)

9. Dutertre, B., de Moura, L.: A fast linear-arithmetic solver for DPLL(T). In: Proc. CAV 2006. pp. 81–94. No. 4144 in LNCS, Springer (2006)

10. Gao, S., Zufferey, D.: Interpolants in nonlinear theories over the reals. In: Proc. TACAS 2016. pp. 625–641. No. 9636 in LNCS, Springer (2016)

11. Gurfinkel, A., Kahsai, T., Komuravelli, A., Navas, J.A.: The SeaHorn verification framework. In: Proc. CAV 2015. pp. 343–361. No. 9206 in LNCS, Springer (2015)

12. Huang, G.: Constructing craig interpolation formulas. In: Proc. COCOON 1995. LNCS, vol. 959, pp. 181–190. Springer (1995)

13. Hyvärinen, A.E.J., Asadi, S., Even-Mendoza, K., Fedyukovich, G., Chockler, H., Sharygina, N.: Theory refinement for program verification. In: Proc. SAT 2017. LNCS, vol. 10491, pp. 347–363. Springer (2017)

14. Hyvärinen, A.E.J., Marescotti, M., Alt, L., Sharygina, N.: OpenSMT2: An SMT solver for multi-core and cloud computing. pp. 547–553. No. 9710 in LNCS, Springer (2016)

15. Krajíček, J.: Interpolation theorems, lower bounds for proof systems, and independence results for bounded arithmetic. Journal of Symbolic Logic 62(2), 457–486 (1997)

16. Kroening, D., Strichman, O.: Decision Procedures: An Algorithmic Point of View, Second Edition. Texts in Theoretical Computer Science. An EATCS Series, Springer (2016)

17. McMillan, K.L.: An interpolating theorem prover. Theor. Comput. Sci. 345(1), 101–121 (2005)

18. McMillan, K.L.: Interpolation and SAT-based model checking. In: Proc. CAV 2003. pp. 1–13. No. 2725 in LNCS, Springer (2003)

19. Pudlák, P.: Lower bounds for resolution and cutting plane proofs and monotone computations. Journal of Symbolic Logic 62(3), 981–998 (1997)

20. Rollini, S.F., Alt, L., Fedyukovich, G., Hyvärinen, A.E.J., Sharygina, N.: PeRIPLO: A framework for producing effective interpolants in SAT-based software verification. In: Proc. LPRA-19. pp. 683–693. No. 8312, Springer (2013)

21. Rollini, S.F., Sery, O., Sharygina, N.: Leveraging interpolant strength in model checking. In: Proc. CAV 2012. pp. 193–209. No. 7358 in LNCS, Springer (2012)

22. Rümmer, P., Subotic, P.: Exploring interpolants. In: Proc. FMCAD 2013. pp. 69 – 76. IEEE (2013)

23. Rybalchenko, A., Sofronie-Stokkermans, V.: Constraint solving for interpolation. In: Proc. VMCAI 2007. pp. 346–362. No. 4349 in LNCS, Springer (2007)

24. Schlaipfer, M., Weissenbacher, G.: Labelled interpolation systems for hyper-resolution, clausal, and local proofs. Journal of Automated Reasoning 57(1), 3–36 (2016)

25. Scholl, C., Pigorsch, F., Disch, S., Althaus, E.: Simple interpolants for linear arithmetic. In: Proc. DATE 2014. pp. 1–6. European Design and Automation Association (2014)

Tool Papers

ACAT: A Novel Machine-Learning-Based Tool For Automating Android Application Testing

Ariel Rosenfeld[1,†], Odaya Kardashov[2], and Orel Zang[2]

[1] Dept. of Computer Science and Applied Mathematics,
Weizmann Institute of Science, Rehovot, Israel
[2] Dept. of Computer Science, Bar-Ilan University, Ramat-Gan, Israel
[†] Corresponding author, arielros1@gmail.com

Abstract. Mobile applications are being used every day by more than half of the world's population to perform a great variety of tasks. With the increasingly widespread usage of these applications, the need arises for efficient techniques to test them. Many frameworks allow automating the process of application testing, however existing frameworks mainly rely on the application developer for providing testing scripts for each developed application, thus preventing reuse of these tests for similar applications. In this demonstration, we present a novel tool for the automation of testing Android applications by leveraging machine learning techniques and reusing popular test scenarios. We discuss and demonstrate the potential benefits of our tool in an empirical study where we show it outperforms standard methods in realistic settings.

Keywords: Android Application Testing, Mobile Testing Automation, Activities Classification, Demonstration

1 Introduction

Mobile devices become a key component in our lives, with more than five million applications developed so far [1], making them the main productivity feature of these devices. As mobile devices become more popular, arise the need for efficient techniques for testing their applications. The large fragmentation of the Android market, as well as the diverse set of scenarios in which a mobile application can be used, make testing new applications an expensive, time-consuming and a complex process. Recently, test automation became the standard, with many solutions and frameworks that allow automating the process of application testing [2]. The main limitation of these frameworks is that tests are hand-coded for *each application and scenarios*, and each new application or new functionality requires spending many resources to reuse these tests.

In this demonstration, we present a novel tool for automatic testing of Android applications in order to find as many functional bugs as possible. Our tool is based on the premise that different activities in an Android application share a similar structure. In order to use this similarity to our benefit, we use machine learning techniques to classify each activity in the application into one of

© Springer International Publishing AG 2017
O. Strichman and R. Tzoref-Brill (Eds.): HVC 2017, LNCS 10629, pp. 213–216, 2017.
https://doi.org/10.1007/978-3-319-70389-3_14

seven pre-defined activity types. For each classified activity, we can run specific tests, at user interface level, that were coded to utilize the fact that we know its general structure and desired behavior. We have implemented this approach and developed an add-on in the Java programming language for the TestProject[1] test automation framework. The platform includes hundreds of add-ons for Web, Mobile and API testing which are freely available to anyone wishing to accelerate the automation development project. Our developed add-on is named ACAT, standing for "Activities Classification for Application Testing". The add-on will be available to install via TestProject Add-ons store.

To evaluate our add-on, we conducted an experiment in which we ran it on different applications while evaluating their performance. We found that the ACAT add-on shows great ability, compared to the standard random-testing method, in exploring the application's state space and testing its key components without prior knowledge about the application. This lets the developer focus on the development of the application and not on writing tests. The use of machine learning in application testing tools is, to the best of our knowledge, a novel method which has yet to be fully explored.

2 Demonstration

In this demonstration we are going to illustrate a common scenario in testing an Android application with the ACAT add-on. Before executing the ACAT, the developer provides basic information using a textual input file which includes technical parameters which are required for the TestProject framework to communicate with the mobile device. Then, the developer can provide specific information in the input file, such as a username and a password, which the add-on will later utilize during the test in the correct context.

During the test, for each new reached activity in the application, the ACAT classify it using our machine learning model into one of seven pre-defined activities types. Then, it executes a series of test cases designed for the predicted activity type. The ACAT keeps classifying activities and deploying tests until the main activity of the application has been classified and tested (e.g., mail activity, browser activity, etc) or when its configured time is up.

Finally, after executing the test, the ACAT creates a textual report file which includes comprehensive information about the test. This includes some various statistics about the test, such as the number Of discovered activities and a list of all the actions executed by the add-on which allows the developer to track the steps of the test. The most important part of the report is the description of all the bugs that were discovered during the test, either technical real-time crashes or logical defects which reflect in the application's user interface. An example for the bugs section of this report can be found in Figure 3. Figures 1 and 2 depict the results of running the ACAT on Android's default mail application while explaining about the underlying process.

---

[1] http://testproject.io

Fig. 1: The activity was classified as a mail activity. Thus, the ACAT executes the mail activity test cases. It scrolls through the inbox mails and opens a random one from the list. Then, it returns to the inbox screen and opens the compose mail activity.

Fig. 2: The ACAT verifies that a user cannot send a mail without a recipient address and with an invalid address. Finally, the ACAT verifies that a user can send a valid mail through this activity by sending a mail to the same user while filling in a randomly generated ID in the mail's subject. Then, the ACAT refreshes the inbox list and searches for a mail with the ID that was sent before.

Fig. 3: An excerpt from the report which was generated after this test.

3   Evaluation & Discussion

We evaluate our add-on against the Android Application Monkey tool [3]. With the purpose of demonstrating the power of the ACAT, we designed a novel experiment which focuses on applications logical bugs. These bugs are related to the application's logic, meaning unwanted behavior in the application's functionality, as opposed to real-time application crashes which are caused by uncaught exceptions thrown in the code.

We use 2 open source Android applications in which we artificially "plant" various logical bugs. While examining the experiment's results, which we will present at the demonstration as well, we can identify 2 major trends: 1) The ACAT was able to classify correctly the 3 unseen activities; 2) The ACAT managed to discover all of the "planted" bugs while the Android Monkey discovered none.

These trends show an interesting phenomenon. While the Android monkey was not able to detect a single logical bug, the ACAT discovered all of the various bugs implemented in the source code of the applications, *as well as a bug that already existed in the original code*. This is contributed to our activities classification method, which enables this add-on the power to tests an activity against its expected behavior. In addition, our experiment demonstrates that testing an application by a series of single case tests, designed for each activity at its own, may provide an advantage compared to the standard testing of applications which considers the application as a whole unit.

4   Conclusions

This paper introduces a novel add-on for testing Android applications using machine learning techniques. We have tested our add-on on different applications, demonstrating its advantage against other popular Android applications testing tools such as the Android Monkey. The ACAT add-on is shown to find more logical bugs in an application, which opens the possibility for developing more sophisticated testing tools. We are currently working with TestProject in order to integrate the ACAT add-on for the TestProject framework, utilizing their database of thousands of mobile applications patterns. The ACAT add-on will be available to install via TestProject Add-ons store. For more technical details about the approach of the tool see the full publication [4].

References

1. "Number of apps available in leading app stores as of march 2017." https://www.statista.com/statistics/276623/number-of-apps-available-in-leading-app-stores/.
2. J. Gao, X. Bai, W.-T. Tsai, and T. Uehara, "Mobile application testing: a tutorial," *Computer*, vol. 47, no. 2, pp. 46–55, 2014.
3. S. R. Choudhary, A. Gorla, and A. Orso, "Automated test input generation for Android: Are we there yet?," in *Automated Software Engineering (ASE), 2015 30th IEEE/ACM International Conference on*, pp. 429–440, IEEE, 2015.
4. A. Rosenfeld, O. Kardashov, and O. Zang, "Automation of Android Applications Testing Using Machine Learning Activities Classification," *ArXiv e-prints*, Sept. 2017.

MicroTESK: Specification-Based Tool for Constructing Test Program Generators

Mikhail Chupilko[1], Alexander Kamkin[1,2,3],
Artem Kotsynyak[1], and Andrei Tatarnikov[1]

[1] Ivannikov Institute for System Programming of the Russian Academy of Sciences
[2] Lomonosov Moscow State University
[3] Moscow Institute of Physics and Technology
{chupilko, kamkin, kotsynyak, andrewt}@ispras.ru

Abstract. The paper presents MicroTESK, a tool that automates construction of test program generators for microprocessors. A constructed generator consists of the core that implements architecture-independent generation methods and the model that holds information required to generate tests for the corresponding architecture. The tool extracts this information from formal specifications of the instruction set architecture. The extracted information is used in multiple ways: (1) to get the assembly format of the instructions; (2) to build the coverage model of the instruction set architecture; (3) to construct the instruction set simulator used as a reference model. Test programs are created on the basis of test templates provided by users. Flexible architecture of the tool facilitates integration of new test generation engines. MicroTESK has been applied to the ARMv8, MIPS64, PowerPC, RISC-V, and x86 architectures.

Keywords: microprocessors, functional verification, test program generation, instruction set architectures, formal specifications

1 Introduction

Test program generation and analysis of test execution traces is the most widely used approach to *functional verification* of microprocessors. To generate test programs, special tools called *test program generators* (TPGs) are used. They implement various test generation methods to exercise behavior of a microprocessor in "all possible" situations. An important requirement for modern TPGs is applicability to a wide range of *instruction set architectures* (ISAs). This implies that information on the ISA must be separated from the implementation of the test generation methods. Such approach is referred to as *model-based testing*.

Industrial TPGs such as Genesys-Pro [1] and RAVEN [2] follow the model-based approach. The main idea is that a TPG consists of the *core* that implements architecture-independent test generation methods and the *model* that stores all information required to create test programs for a specific ISA. Generation is performed on the basis of *test templates*, which describe high-level properties of test programs.

O. Strichman and R. Tzoref-Brill (Eds.): HVC 2017, LNCS 10629, pp. 217–220, 2017.
https://doi.org/10.1007/978-3-319-70389-3_15

In this paper, we present MicroTESK, an open-source tool for constructing model-based TPGs [3]. It provides the reusable core and constructs models by processing *formal specifications* of ISAs. Formal specifications are described in nML, a simple architecture description language [4]. This simplifies development and maintenance of TPGs. Test templates used by MicroTESK-based TPGs are written in a Ruby-based language [5]. The use of a well-tried programming language significantly decreases the learning effort.

2   MicroTESK Approach

MicroTESK is divided into two main parts: (1) the *modeling framework* that processes formal specifications and constructs a microprocessor model; (2) the *testing framework* that generates test programs on the basis of the model and test templates provided by users, i.e. verification engineers. The architecture of MicroTESK is shown in Figure 1.

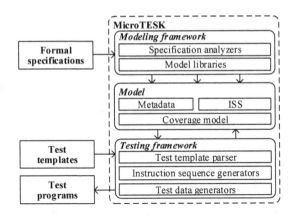

Fig. 1. The MicroTESK architecture

The model consists of the following components: (1) the *metadata* that provides a catalogue of supported instructions; (2) the *instruction set simulator* (ISS) that serves as a reference model; (3) the *coverage model* that holds constraints describing execution paths of individual instructions.

The modeling framework includes components that analyze formal specifications, extract the necessary information, and construct the model. ISA specifications are developed manually in nML language [4]. They describe data types, registers, memory, addressing modes, and instructions. There is a language extension called MMUSL aimed at specifying *memory management units* (MMUs): address types, segments, buffers, tables, and overall load/store logic [6]. Here is an nML specification of MIPS64's ADD instruction.

```
op add(rd: R, rs: R, rt: R)
  syntax = format("add %s, %s, %s", rd.syntax, rs.syntax, rt.syntax)
  image  = format("000000%5s%5s%5s00000100000", rs.image, rt.image, rd.image)
  action = {
    if sign_extend(WORD, rs<31>) != rs<63..32> || sign_extend(WORD, rt<31>) != rt<63..32> then
      unpredicted; // Precondition
    endif;
    temp33 = rs<31>::rs<31..0> + rt<31>::rt<31..0>;
    if temp33<32> != temp33<31> then
      exception("IntegerOverflow"); // Coverage item 1
    else
      mark("Normal"); // Coverage item 2
      rd = sign_extend(DWORD, temp33<31..0>);
    endif;
  }
```

The testing framework includes the reusable TPG core that generates test programs for the given model by processing test templates provided by verification
engineers. The generation process consists of the following stages:

1. constructing an abstract instruction sequence (no particular data);
2. solving constraints applied to the instructions and generating data;
3. creating initialization code that prepares the registers and the memory;
4. executing the instructions (including the initialization code) in the ISS;
5. creating self-checks based on the information provided by the ISS (optional);
6. printing the resulting instructions to an assembly file.

Test templates are represented in a special Ruby-based language [5]. ISA-
specific constructs such as instruction wrappers are created on-the-fly by using
the model metadata. Broadly speaking, test templates specify how to combine
instruction sequences and what constraints to apply. For example, the code below
describes all possible pairs of ADD and SUB instructions with "Normal" and
"IntegerOverflow" constraints having been attached.

```
class MyTemplate < Template
  def run
    block(:combinator => 'product') {
      iterate {
        add t0, t1, t2 do situation('Normal') end
        add t0, t1, t2 do situation('IntegerOverflow') end
      }
      iterate {
        sub t3, t4, t5 do situation('Normal') end
        sub t3, t4, t5 do situation('IntegerOverflow') end
      }
    }.run
  end
end
```

MicroTESK allows constructing complex instruction sequences by combining smaller parts. To solve constraints, the tool utilizes a number of built-in
and external SAT- and SMT-solvers. Supported types of constraints include:
(1) constraints on instruction operands; (2) constraints related to control flow;
(3) floating-point constraints; (4) MMU-related constraints. The tool architecture facilitates integration of custom components for sequence processing and
constraint solving (test data generation).

3 Practical Application

MicroTESK has been applied to create TPGs for several ISAs including ARMv8, MIPS64, PowerPC, RISC-V, and x86. The created TPGs are shipped together with formal specifications and basic test templates. Some of TPGs (including the ISA specifications) are open source (licensed under the Apache License, Version 2.0), while others are closed and distributed on a commercial basis. Details on the MicroTESK-based TPGs are provided in Table 1.

Table 1. TPGs constructed with the help of MicroTESK

Architecture	Project Type	Public/Closed	Supported Version
ARMv8	Industrial	Closed	AArch64 v8.2
MIPS64	Industrial	Open Source	Revision 6.04
PowerPC	Research	Closed	e500mc
RISC-V	Research	Open Source	Version 2.2
x86	Research	Open Source	x86-16, partially x86-64

The TPG development is reduced to specifying the corresponding ISA. The labor costs are approximately 2–5 instructions per person-day (depending on the ISA complexity). It should be noted that specifications can be reused when describing other designs of the same family. The nML and MMUSL languages allow marking specification elements with revisions, which makes it possible to enable/disable those elements depending on the ISA version.

The bug-finding ability depends on test templates created by verification engineers. Experience shows that with a properly organized verification process, a MicroTESK-based TPG can serve as a primary means of chip-level verification.

References

1. A. Adir, E. Almog, L. Fournier, E. Marcus, M. Rimon, M. Vinov, A. Ziv. *Genesys-Pro: Innovations in Test Program Generation for Functional Processor Verification.* Design & Test of Computers, 21(2), 2004. pp. 84–93.
2. *RAVEN Test Program Generator* – http://www.slideshare.net/DVClub/introducing-obsidian-software-andravengcs-for-powerpc
3. *MicroTESK Page* – http://forge.ispras.ru/projects/microtesk
4. M. Freericks. *The nML Machine Description Formalism.* Technical Report TR SM-IMP/DIST/08, TU Berlin CS Department, 1993.
5. A. Tatarnikov. *Language for Describing Templates for Test Program Generation for Microprocessors.* Proceedings of ISP RAS, 28(4), 2016. pp. 81–102.
6. M. Chupilko, A. Kamkin, A. Kotsynyak, A. Protsenko, S. Smolov, A. Tatarnikov. *Specification-Based Test Program Generation for ARM VMSAv8-64 Memory Management Units.* Workshop on Microprocessor Test and Verification, 2015. pp. 1–6.

Embedded functions for test design automation

George B. Sherwood[1][0000-0003-0865-1679]

[1] Testcover.com LLC, 41 Clover Hill Road, Colts Neck NJ 07722, USA
sherwood@testcover.com

Abstract. Testcover.com introduced an embedded functions feature into its combinatorial test design service. The feature allows functionally dependent relations among test factors to be defined as functions in a general purpose programming language, PHP. These relations enforce constraints among test factor values and insure that all valid combinations of determinant factors are considered for the test design. Resulting usability improvements enable automated pairwise test designs to meet novel objectives: Cover equivalence classes of expected results; verify univariate and multivariate equivalence class boundaries; verify corners among intersecting boundaries and edges. The demonstration illustrates how embedded functions can improve automation, accuracy, control and flexibility in the test design process.

Keywords: automated test design, boundary testing, combinatorial testing, constraints, embedded function, equivalence class, functional dependence, interaction testing, PHP, software test design, test case generation.

Introduction

Recent concerns about engineering the Internet of Things (IoT) include conflicting requirements and inadequate analysis and verification. Diomidis Spinellis observes: "No doubt, a paradigm shift from balkanized IoT applications to an integrated infrastructure in which individual IoT nodes are first-class citizens raises formidable challenges... when multiple IoT nodes and applications get integrated, diverse requirements will interfere with each other..." [1]

Similarly, Vinton Cerf writes: "Concerns for safety, security, privacy, and control must be assuaged by systematic analysis of increasingly complex use scenarios. It might even be argued that these analyses will need to be carried out automatically just to keep up with the non-linear growth in potential use cases and device interactions as the devices proliferate." [2]

This demonstration of embedded functions (EFs) illustrates the automated design of software tests to conform to requirements and meet test objectives. Embedded functions define and enforce required constraints among test factors (e.g. configurations and inputs). [3, 4] They can insure that required test factor combinations (e.g. for system states or equivalence classes) appear in test cases, and that invalid combinations do not. The EF feature resolves composite relations among test factors so that test cases conform to the chains of functional dependence.

© Springer International Publishing AG 2017
O. Strichman and R. Tzoref-Brill (Eds.): HVC 2017, LNCS 10629, pp. 221–224, 2017.
https://doi.org/10.1007/978-3-319-70389-3_16

When equivalence class factors or boundary value factors are included in the design, additional test objectives can be met automatically, as needed:

- Cover equivalence classes of expected results [4-6]
- Pair equivalence classes with nondeterminant factor values [4-6]
- Verify univariate and multivariate equivalence class boundaries [4, 6]
- Pair boundary values and edges to verify corner cases [4, 6]

The embedded functions feature represents test design automation progress, leading to improved usability and efficiency for practitioners. It offers significant contributions for testing systems developed in various processes. We anticipate a range of uses from embedded software to agile systems and the IoT. We know of no other automated test design tool that can meet these objectives for practicing software engineers.

Combinatorial testing. Combinatorial testing generates small sets of test cases to cover interactions among test factors in complex systems. These test cases must conform to system constraints to be valid. When a test case has an invalid combination of values, it cannot verify the expected result. If such a test case is omitted, the valid combinations it may have contained might be missing from the remaining test cases. So the test cases must contain all the required combinations and none of the invalid ones.

A second constraint challenge is generating test cases that lead to a particular expected state or class of expected results. Test cases need combinations of factor values that steer the system under test for the behaviors to be verified. Otherwise the test process may be inefficient and time consuming.

Research and development progress has led to tools that conform to constraints, but constraints remain a challenge to the broad adoption of combinatorial testing in practice. [3]

Functional dependence. Constraints in test models can be expressed as functionally dependent relations. For example, test factors for a date input may include Month, Day and Year, with respective values nov, 1 and 2017. The first and last day of each month are boundary values for the Day factor. All months start with Day 1, but the last day of the month depends on the values of Month and Year. The Day value can be determined by a function last_day(Month,Year). With an appropriate definition for the last_day function, the boundary values for Day can be listed as 1 and last_day(Month,Year). In this relation Month and Year are determinant factors, and Day is the dependent factor.

The essential concept for embedded functions is to use simple functions in a well-known language to describe the system and test constraints. Automated evaluation of embedded functions reduces the manual analysis work and yields designs that can meet a variety of test objectives. The analysis is limited to selecting test factors and values, and defining the embedded functions. PHP was selected as the language for this implementation of embedded functions. [7]

Description

Testcover.com provides an online, commercial test design service. [8, 9] The Software as a Service is accessible with a standard browser. It can be used with a variety of development environments, processes and tools.

The embedded functions feature was proposed in 2015. [3] During its development elements of the feature were described and demonstrated at IWCT 2016. [5] Subsequently support for substitution functions (described below) and for the functions editor was included. The EF feature was deployed for controlled introduction June 30, 2017.

Basic Blocks. Reference [6], example 2 illustrates a test design using calendar constraints. There are 5 blocks of factor values (Month, Day and Year) in the test design request. All combinations of factor values in each block are allowed; combinations that do not appear in any blocks are disallowed. Thus the set of allowed combinations is the union of all the blocks' combinations.

Forty test cases are generated, and they cover all allowed pairs of factors. The design covers the Day boundary values also.

Embedded Functions. Reference [6], example 2 also illustrates the calendar design using a single block and the embedded function last_day($month,$year). The $month and $year factors are renamed as PHP variables, so they can be arguments for the last_day function. These factors list all months and years to be included in the design. The Day factor contains the fixed values 1 and 10, and the last_day($month,$year) function.

The last_day function is a wrapper for the PHP internal function cal_days_in_month. [6, 7] When the request is processed, the last_day function is evaluated for all combinations of $month and $year values. These are used to generate the same 40 test cases as with the basic blocks request.

The last_day function is a *combination function* to be evaluated *before* test case generation. [3] Each combination function is called for all combinations of its arguments' values. The function returns a list of one or more allowed values for generating test cases. Combination functions should not return values for invalid combinations of arguments.

Substitution functions are evaluated *after* test case generation. [3] They are used to relax the requirement for pairwise coverage, e.g. when test case values should be random or unique (function fUser in example 6 [6]). In example 5c [4, 6] the $Weight factor value is a test input computed by the substitution function Weight_boundary. Pairing the boundary value with other factors is not an objective for this design, so Weight_boundary is defined as a substitution function.

Substitution functions should return an individual value for each test case (not a list). They also resolve composite relations among test factor values, similarly to those of combination functions.

Equivalence Class Factors and Boundary Value factors. Use of embedded functions, together with equivalence class factors and boundary value factors, enable automated combinatorial test designs to meet the objectives listed above. Test cases can be constrained to cover expected equivalence classes by the inclusion of equivalence class factors. When their factor values are given by combination functions, every expected class determined by the other factors appears in at least one test case. [4-6]

Similarly, test cases can be constrained to compute and cover boundary values automatically, using factors to specify the required boundaries. [4, 6] When multiple boundaries are covered, the intersections cover their respective corner cases. And whether all corners or selected corners are covered can be controlled by the assignment of combination or substitution evaluation to each EF. [4, 6]

Conclusions

The demonstration shows that specifying constraints (including equivalence class and boundary requirements) as simple functions, in a language familiar to software engineers, can automate much of the analysis for software test design. Moreover, functions can be reused for different designs, and they can enhance consistency and accuracy as test factors and values change.

Reference [4], sections 4-6 illustrate in detail the control and flexibility offered by embedded functions. They show different test design choices, based on various test objectives, leading to different patterns of coverage.

Test designs must accommodate system complexity and size, as well as diverse objectives. The embedded functions feature offers improvements in automation, accuracy, control and flexibility, for advances in test efficiency and quality.

References

1. Spinellis, D.: Software-engineering the Internet of Things. IEEE Software 34(1), 4-6 (2017).
2. Cerf, V. G.: A brittle and fragile future. Communications of the ACM 60(7), 7 (2017).
3. Sherwood, G. B.: Embedded functions in combinatorial test designs. In: IEEE Eighth International Conference on Software Testing, Verification and Validation Workshops (ICSTW), pp. 1-10. IEEE, Graz, Austria (2015).
4. Sherwood, G. B.: Test design automation: equivalence classes, boundaries, edges and corner cases. 2016/7/3. http://testcover.com/pub/background/ecbecc.pdf, last accessed 2017/7/27.
5. Sherwood, G. B.: Embedded functions for constraints and variable strength in combinatorial testing. In: IEEE Ninth International Conference on Software Testing, Verification and Validation Workshops (ICSTW), pp. 65-74. IEEE, Chicago, IL, USA (2016).
6. Testcover.com embedded functions examples (2017), http://testcover.com/pub/background/examples2017.php, last accessed 2017/7/27.
7. M. Achour, F. Betz, A. Dovgal, et al.: PHP Manual. http://php.net/manual/en/index.php, last accessed 2017/7/27.
8. About Testcover.com, http://testcover.com/pub/about.php, last accessed 2017/7/27.
9. Testcover.com performance, http://testcover.com/pub/performance.php, last accessed 2017/7/27.

KERIS: A CT Tool of the Linux Kernel with Dynamic Memory Analysis Capabilities

Bernhard Garn[1], Fabian Würfl[2], and Dimitris E. Simos[1]

[1] SBA Research, 1040 Vienna, Austria
{bgarn, dsimos}@sba-research.org
[2] FH Campus Wien, 1100 Vienna, Austria
fabian.wuerfl@stud.fh-campuswien.ac.at

Abstract. We present KERIS, a configurable, non-centralized server-based framework which enables the combinatorial testing of the Linux kernel's system call interface. The tool constitutes an improvement over our previously developed tool called ERIS by incorporating dynamic memory analysis capabilities among other improvements. The testing framework is designed to offer large-scale automation and requires only minimal high-level input from the user. Several experiments performed with KERIS demonstrate the capabilities of finding and reproducing Linux kernel bugs in an automated manner.

Keywords: combinatorial testing, Linux kernel, system call, tool

1 Introduction

In this paper, we introduce KERIS, the KASAN Enhanced ERIS, which is based on our combinatorial testing tool ERIS presented in [1]. We created a new test oracle by integrating an intra-kernel dynamic memory analysis feature called KASAN, which results in an automated fine-grained test oracle for real-world experiments.

Combinatorial testing (CT) is a generic test case generation strategy which is focused on interactions between values of modelled parameters [2]. Mathematical objects called covering arrays (CAs) guarantee these demanded interactions and are subsequently translated into software artifacts to be used as test sets. KERIS employs the widely-used ACTS tool[3] for generating CAs.

2 KERIS

KERIS' features cover the complete testing cycle: modelling, test case generation, test case execution, log archiving and subsequent post-processing of the results stored in an SQL database for use-case specific analysis queries.

---

[3] http://csrc.nist.gov/groups/SNS/acts/download_tools.html

© Springer International Publishing AG 2017
O. Strichman and R. Tzoref-Brill (Eds.): HVC 2017, LNCS 10629, pp. 225–228, 2017.
https://doi.org/10.1007/978-3-319-70389-3_17

ERIS: Linux System Call Testing. For testing Linux system calls, it is necessary to specify the version, the system call and some abstract test model. The ERIS framework offers *automated large-scale testing* capabilities, requiring only these three mentioned inputs and then populates or creates the necessary data for each test run independently. The framework accepts lists or ranges for kernel versions or system calls as input for test runs.

The ERIS framework is built upon loops where for each given kernel version, for each given system call, for each chosen modelling strategy, and for each chosen interaction strength of the test set, it executes the following core function as described in Algorithm 1, and considers these parameters jointly as parameters of a *system under test* (SUT). The framework makes use of the Xen virtualization technology to boot a virtual machine (VM) created from the previous SUT specification and stores various data parsed out of the VM's system log file into an SQL database for further analysis. Although the framework and the Linux kernel support many different hardware architectures, the test executions are currently focused on running with a guest image of the x86_64 architecture.

Algorithm 1 Architectural Design of the Core ERIS Framework

---

    function ERISCORE(*version, syscall, t*)
Require: *version, syscall*   ▷ SUT: Kernel version and system call
Require: *t*   ▷ Interaction strength of CA - test set
        Mount copy of guest image
        Copy latest version of ERIS into guest image
        Generate CA of strength *t* for *syscall*   ▷ The CA is translated to a test set
        if precompiled kernel available **then**
           Use precompiled kernel
        else
           Compile kernel
        end if
        Compile kernel modules
        Install kernel and modules into guest image
        Finalize guest image for testing operations
        Boot guest image using Xen hypervisor
        Execute test set for *syscall* in dedicated VM
        End testing cycle by shutting down the VM and **perform** clean-up
        Import test results into SQL database for further analysis
    end function

KASAN: A Kernel Address Sanitizer adopted to ERIS. The KernelAddressSANitizer (KASAN) is a dynamic memory error detector for the Linux kernel. It uses compile-time instrumentation for checking every memory access and is especially useful for finding use-after-free and out-of-bounds bugs[4].

KERIS is an enhanced version of ERIS, including various bug fixes and other improvements to the runtime efficiency and usability which were made during its development. KERIS' overall architectural design is shown in the figure below. We give a concise overview of the most important improvements. Large-scale testability was mainly achieved by precompiling kernel images. Previously, each kernel version was compiled on demand and deleted after test execution finished. To solve this issue, all kernel versions (git tags) from v3.2 to v4.10-rc6, including all release candidates and stable releases, were precompiled (1007 in total; 248 additional with a KASAN-enabled configuration). Now, whenever a test is run

---

[4] https://www.kernel.org/doc/html/latest/dev-tools/kasan.html

with a specific kernel version and configuration, the respective precompiled kernel image is used. This saves about six minutes for each SUT in one test run, reducing the total test execution time by ten hours for just 100 SUTs.

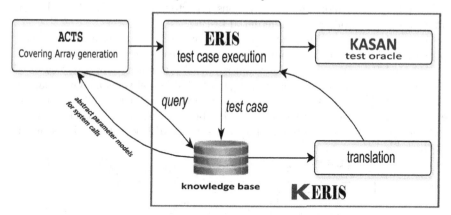

KERIS also supports "named" kernel configurations and images, which allows to have several precompiled kernel images of the same version, but with a different configuration - a necessity to utilize kernels with and without KASAN. Finally, usability was greatly improved by enhancing the management-scripts to also support regular expressions, for example when specifying the list of kernel versions to test.

Additional Improvements to ERIS. In addition, post-processing was improved by various scripts. One script parses the main log file of the guest image to generate an overall report for inclusion in the SQL database on (a) how many test cases should have been executed, (b) how many test cases were actually executed, (c) how many test cases succeeded or failed, and (d) a more detailed listing of why some test cases could have failed. Moreover, we have implemented various sophisticated sanity checkers (e.g., whether the guest image booted correctly) to enable a more fine-grained analysis of the test results.

3   Automated Large-Scale Kernel Testing

For this work we tested with KERIS 23 different system calls with 134 kernel versions each (a total of 3082 SUTs) in roughly 102 hours. Furthermore, processing and analyzing all test runs' log output took less than two minutes. The KERIS test environment is currently hosted on a machine running OpenSUSE 13.2 (Harlequin) with kernel version 3.16.7-48-xen (64-bit), CPU Intel (R) Core (tm) i7-4770 with eight cores running at 3.4 GHz and has 22.2 GB of RAM.

Of the 3082 SUTs, the test execution of 77 SUTs failed. Further analysis showed that 69 of those failures were due to three malfunctioning kernel images (v4.0-rc1, v4.1.28, v4.2-rc2) which crashed before KERIS could be started. The remaining eight failures were due to Xen not being able to start the guest image.

The kernel versions tested were in the range of v4.0 up to v4.6. For each kernel version, the final release, all release candidates and a selection of stable releases were tested. Every kernel was compiled with KASAN enabled. As none of the SUTs triggered memory access violations reported by KASAN, the following analysis employs concepts of differential testing.

For each system call individually, we performed a comparison of the discrepancies in the number of accepted (i.e., system call execution returned zero) vs. rejected (i.e., system call execution returned a non-zero value) test cases of the same test set, across the entire range of tested kernel versions. Our analysis showed that for most system calls, these numbers stayed the same across the entire range of tested kernel versions. By far the largest deviations between different kernel versions were found for the **settimeofday** system call, as shown in the table below.

Count kernel versions	# of test cases	# of accepted	# of rejected
72	100	0	100
43	100	45	55
15	100	30	70
1	100	34	66

Detecting Dynamic Memory Errors. With KERIS' capability of utilizing KASAN-enabled kernels, we are able to assess and detect errors that are caused by memory access violations among other reasons. Recently, Google's Project Zero team discovered a vulnerability in Linux' networking stack[5], also with the help of KASAN. We used the characteristics of this particular vulnerability for a fine-tuned combinatorial model of a network configuration setup together with assigning parameter values to the **sendto** system call, in order to demonstrate that KERIS is capable of detecting such vulnerabilities. Already in the first test execution batch, two kernels crashed with a kernel `Oops`, which was subsequently detected by our KASAN-based test oracle. A snippet of one of the resulting error messages encountered by KERIS is shown below.

```
[30.605462] BUG: unable to handle kernel paging request at ffff880007a60b28
[30.605500] IP: [<ffffffff818baf55>] prb_fill_curr_block.isra.62+0x15/0xc0
[30.605525] PGD 1e0c067 PUD 1e0d067 PMD ffd4067 PTE 8010000007a60065
[30.605550] Oops: 0003 [#1] SMP KASAN
```

Acknowledgements. The research presented in the paper has been funded in part by the the Austrian COMET Program (FFG).

References

1. Garn, B., Simos, D.E.: Eris: A tool for combinatorial testing of the linux system call interface. In: Software Testing, Verification and Validation Workshops (ICSTW), 2014 IEEE Seventh International Conference on. pp. 58–67. IEEE (2014)
2. Kuhn, D., Kacker, R., Lei, Y.: Introduction to Combinatorial Testing. Chapman & Hall/CRC Innovations in Software Engineering and Software Development Series, Taylor & Francis (2013)

---

[5] https://googleprojectzero.blogspot.com/2017/05/exploiting-linux-kernel-via-packet.html

RATCOP: Relational Analysis Tool for Concurrent Programs

Suvam Mukherjee[1], Oded Padon[2], Sharon Shoham[2], Deepak D'Souza[1], and
Noam Rinetzky[2]

[1] Indian Institute of Science, India
[2] Tel Aviv University, Israel

Abstract. In this paper, we present RATCOP, a static analysis tool for efficiently
computing relational invariants in race free shared-variable multi-threaded Java
programs. The tool trades the standard sound-at-all-program-points guarantee for
gains in efficiency. Instead, it computes sound facts for a variable only at program
points where it is "relevant". In our experiments, RATCOP was fairly precise
while being fast. As a tool, RATCOP is easy-to-use, and easily extensible.

1 Introduction

Writing efficient and correct multi-threaded programs is an onerous task, since a multi-
threaded program admits a large set of possible behaviors. As a result, such programs
provide fertile ground for many insidious defects: the bugs are difficult to detect, difficult to reproduce, and can result in unpredictable failures. Thus, developers are greatly
aided by tools which can automatically report such defects.

Unfortunately, designing algorithms which can automatically reason about behaviors of concurrent programs is also a very hard problem. Key to the difficulty lies in ac-
counting for the large set of inter-thread interactions. Static analysis algorithms, based
on the abstract interpretation framework [3], compute sound approximations of the set
of "concrete states" arising at each program point. With this notion of soundness, a
precise static analyzer does not usually scale, whereas a fast analysis is usually quite
imprecise [2].

In this paper, we describe RATCOP [3]: **R**elational **A**nalysis **T**ool for **CO**ncurrent
Programs, a tool to efficiently compute relational invariants in shared-memory data
race free multi-threaded Java programs. RATCOP does not handle procedure calls or
dynamic memory allocation. The abstract analyses implemented in RATCOP are based
on a novel *thread-local* semantics, called *L-DRF* [7]. Here, each thread maintains a local
copy of the global state. When a thread t executes a non-synchronization command (an
assignment or an `assume`), it operates on its local state alone. Each `release` instruction
is associated with a "buffer". When t executes a `release(m)` command, it stores a copy
of its local state in the corresponding buffer. When a thread t' subsequently acquires m,
it is allowed to observe the states stored at a set of "relevant" buffers. t' then performs
a mix of these states to create a fresh local state. As [7] shows, for data race free (DRF)
programs, each trace in the standard semantics corresponds to some trace in the *L-DRF*

---

[3] The source code of RATCOP is available at https://bitbucket.org/suvam/ratcop

© Springer International Publishing AG 2017
O. Strichman and R. Tzoref-Brill (Eds.): HVC 2017, LNCS 10629, pp. 229–233, 2017.
https://doi.org/10.1007/978-3-319-70389-3_18

semantics, and vice versa. Thus, the *L-DRF* semantics is a precise description of the behaviors of DRF programs.

The *L-DRF* semantics allows one to rapidly port existing sequential analyses to analyses for race free programs. Such analyses operate on a program graph called sync-CFG (first introduced in [4]), which is a collection of the control-flow graphs of each thread, augmented with synchronization edges between the release of a lock m, and an acquire of m. Consequently, the sync-CFG restricts inter-thread propagations to synchronization points alone. The resulting analyses satisfy a non-standard notion of soundness: the computed facts for a variable are sound only at program points where it is *accessed*. A more precise analysis is obtained by parameterizing *L-DRF* with a user-defined partitioning of the program variables, resulting in a semantics called *R-DRF*. Each partition is also called a "region". Assuming that the input program is free from *region races* [7], which is a stronger notion than data races,

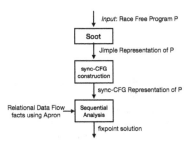

Fig. 1. High-level overview of RATCOP

the resulting abstract analyses are more precise than those derived from *L-DRF*.

In RATCOP, we instantiate abstractions of *L-DRF* and *R-DRF* to create several relational analyses with varying degrees of precision. Our objective was two-fold: (i.) to investigate the ease of porting a sequential relational analysis to an analysis for race free concurrent programs (ii.) to investigate the efficiency and precision of the resulting analysis. The base-line is an interval analysis derived from an earlier work [4]. RATCOP makes use of the Soot [8] and Apron [5] libraries. RATCOP intelligently leverages the race freedom property of the input program to minimize the number of inter-thread data flow propagations, while retaining a fair degree of precision. As shown in [7], on the benchmarks, RATCOP was able to prove upto 65% of the assertions, in comparison to 25% achieved by the base-line analysis. On a separate set of benchmarks, RATCOP was upto 5 orders of magnitude faster than Batman, a recent static analyzer for concurrent programs [6]. Finally, RATCOP is easy-to-use, quite robust, and easily extensible. In this paper, we detail the architecture of RATCOP.

2   Architecture of RATCOP

RATCOP comprises around 4000 lines of Java code, and implements a number of relational analyses with varying degrees of precision and scalability. Through command line arguments, the tool can make use of the following three abstract domains provided by Apron: convex polyhedra, octagons and intervals. It takes only a few lines of code to extend RATCOP to use additional numerical abstract domains.

RATCOP assumes that the input program is free from data races, and does not perform any explicit checks for the same. To detect region-level races, RATCOP implements the scheme outlined in [7], which reduces the problem of checking for region-level races to that of checking for data races on specific "auxiliary" variables.

R-DRF	L-DRF	Value-Set	Thread t₁	Thread t₂	Value-Set	L-DRF	R-DRF
$0=x=y=z$	$0=x=y=z$	$0=x=y$ $=z$			$0=x=y=z$	$0=x=y=z$	$0=x=y=z$
			1: acquire (m);	8: z++;			
$x=y,$ $0\le y,$ $0\le z\le1$	$0\le x,$ $0\le y,$ $0\le z\le1$	$0\le x,$ $0\le y,$ $0\le z\le1$			$x=0,$ $y=0,$ $0\le z\le1$	$0=x=y,$ $z=1$	$0=x=y,$ $z=1$
			2: x := y;	9: assert (z = 1);			
$x=y,$ $0\le y,$ $0\le z\le1$	$x=y,$ $0\le y,$ $0\le z\le1$	$0\le x,$ $0\le y,$ $0\le z\le1$			$x=0,$ $y=0,$ $0\le z\le1$	$0=x=y,$ $z=1$	$0=x=y,$ $z=1$
			3: x++;	10: acquire (m);			
					$0\le x,$ $0\le y,$ $0\le z\le1$	$0\le x,$ $0\le y,$ $0\le z\le1$	$x=y,$ $0\le y,$ $0\le z\le1$
			4: y++;	11: assert (x = y);			
$x=y,$ $1\le y,$ $0\le z\le1$	$x=y,$ $1\le y,$ $0\le z\le1$	$1\le x$ $1\le y,$ $0\le z\le1$			$0\le x,$ $0\le y,$ $0\le z\le1$	$0\le x,$ $0\le y,$ $0\le z\le1$	$x=y,$ $0\le y,$ $0\le z\le1$
			5: assert (x = y);	12: release (m); 13:			
$x=y,$ $1\le y,$ $0\le z\le1$	$x=y,$ $1\le y,$ $0\le z\le1$	$1\le x$ $1\le y,$ $0\le z\le1$					
			6: release (m); 7:				

Fig. 2. An example from [7] illustrating the relational analyses implemented in RATCOP. The *sync*-CFG representation of the program is given at the center: *inter*-thread communication is restricted to synchronization points alone. All the variables are shared and initialized to 0. The Value-Set column shows the facts computed using an interval analysis derived from [4]. The *L-DRF* and *R-DRF* columns show the facts computed by polyhedral abstractions of the thread-local semantics, and its region-parameterized version. The *R-DRF* analysis is able to prove all the 3 assertions, the *L-DRF* proves 2, while the Value-Set analysis only proves 1 assertion.

RATCOP re-uses the code to construct the *sync*-CFG representation of a program from the implementation of [4]. The *sync*-CFG construction makes use of a pointer-analysis, coupled with a may-happens-in-parallel analysis.

The tool now performs a *sequential* analysis, with the only additional operator being the inter-thread join. Once the fixpoint is reached, RATCOP automatically tries to prove the assertions in the program, which amounts to checking whether the computed facts at a program point imply the condition being asserted. If the tool fails to prove the implications, the assertion condition and the corresponding data flow fact is logged for further manual investigation.

For the non-synchronization instructions, RATCOP performs some light parsing, followed by re-using the existing sequential transformers exposed by Apron. The only operator we define afresh is the *inter*-thread join, which is used at the acquire points. However, this turns out to be simple as well, being a combination of operations provided by Apron. Thus, porting a sequential relational analysis based on Apron to an analysis for a race free concurrent program, using our framework, turns out to be quite straightforward. Fig. 1 summarizes the set of operations in RATCOP.

RATCOP implements 5 relational analyses: **A1** − **A4**, are derived from the *L-DRF* and *R-DRF* semantics, and use the octagon domain. The fifth, **A5** (which is also our baseline), is an interval analysis derived from [4]. The analyses differ in the degree of abstraction from the *L-DRF* and *R-DRF* semantics, with **A4** using the most precise abstract domain, and **A5** being the least.

3   Experiments

We illustrate the operation of RATCOP on a simple program from [7], shown in Fig. 2. The program is free from data races. If the regions are defined to be $\langle \{x, y\}, \{z\} \rangle$, then the program is free from region races as well [4]. The results of **A5** are shown under the column "Value-Set". Since an interval based analysis is the best we can do using [4], the resulting analysis is quite imprecise: it is only able to prove the assertion at line 9. The analysis cannot track any relational properties. We do better with **A2**, derived from *L-DRF*, which uses octagons. This analysis *does* track the correlation between x and y, which allows it to be additionally prove the assertion at line 5. However, the inter-thread mixing (at the `acquire` points) is done at the granularity of individual variables. This keeps **A2** from inferring $x = y$ at line 12, for example, even though the two incoming edges clearly maintain this invariant. The analysis **A4** performs this mixing at the granularity of the specified regions. Thus, it is able to prove all 3 assertions.

In our experiments in [7], we used a subset of concurrent programs from the SV-COMP 2015 suite [1], after porting them to Java and introducing locks appropriately to remove races. We ran our experiments in a virtual machine with 16GB RAM and 4 cores which, in turn, ran on a machine with 32 RAM and a quad-core Intel i7 processor. Unsurprisingly, **A4** was the most precise, being able to prove 65% of the assertions. It was also the slowest, the average time being 406ms. **A5** was the least precise, having proved 25% of the assertions with an average time of 204ms.

We compared RATCOP with a current abstract interpretation based tool for multi-threaded programs [6], called Batman. Unlike RATCOP, which handles a large subset of multi-threaded Java programs, Batman handles a toy language with limited constructs. Moreover, Batman does not automatically check the validity of assertions, which renders it difficult to use with even small programs. We evaluated the two tools on multi-threaded programs with little inter-thread communication. RATCOP leveraged the lack of inter-thread communication intelligently to perform up to 5 orders of magnitude faster than Batman. The key difference between the two tools is that Batman tries to compute sound facts at *every* program point, whereas RATCOP computes sound facts for variables only at program points where they are *accessed*.

4   Conclusion

In this paper, we presented RATCOP: a static analysis tool which efficiently computes relational invariants for race free concurrent programs, with a non-standard notion of soundness. We hope that RATCOP will serve as a stepping stone for future static analyses for the class of race free programs.

---

[4] The interested reader may refer to [7] for the exact definition of region races.

References

1. Dirk Beyer. Software verification and verifiable witnesses. In *International Conference on Tools and Algorithms for the Construction and Analysis of Systems*, pages 401–416. Springer, 2015.
2. Ravi Chugh, Jan Wen Voung, Ranjit Jhala, and Sorin Lerner. Dataflow analysis for concurrent programs using datarace detection. In *Proceedings of the ACM SIGPLAN 2008 Conference on Programming Language Design and Implementation*, pages 316–326, 2008.
3. Patrick Cousot and Radhia Cousot. Abstract interpretation: a unified lattice model for static analysis of programs by construction or approximation of fixpoints. In *Proceedings of the 4th ACM SIGACT-SIGPLAN Symposium on Principles of Programming Languages*, pages 238–252. ACM, 1977.
4. Arnab De, Deepak D'Souza, and Rupesh Nasre. Dataflow analysis for datarace-free programs. In *Programming Languages and Systems - 20th European Symposium on Programming, ESOP 2011*, pages 196–215, 2011.
5. Bertrand Jeannet and Antoine Miné. Apron: A library of numerical abstract domains for static analysis. In *International Conference on Computer Aided Verification*, pages 661–667. Springer, 2009.
6. Raphaël Monat and Antoine Miné. Precise thread-modular abstract interpretation of concurrent programs using relational interference abstractions. In *International Conference on Verification, Model Checking, and Abstract Interpretation*, pages 386–404. Springer, 2017.
7. Suvam Mukherjee, Oded Padon, Sharon Shoham, Deepak D'Souza, and Noam Rinetzky. Thread-local semantics and its efficient sequential abstractions for race-free programs. In *Static Analysis - 24th International Symposium, SAS 2017, New York, NY, USA, August 30 - September 1, 2017, Proceedings*, pages 253–276, 2017.
8. Raja Vallée-Rai, Phong Co, Etienne Gagnon, Laurie Hendren, Patrick Lam, and Vijay Sundaresan. Soot-a java bytecode optimization framework. In *Proceedings of the 1999 conference of the Centre for Advanced Studies on Collaborative research*, page 13. IBM Press, 1999.

Posters

More adaptive does not imply less safe
(with formal verification)

Luca Pulina[1] and Armando Tacchella[2] *

[1] POLCOMING, Università degli Studi di Sassari, Viale Mancini 5 – 07100 Sassari – Italy
[2] DIBRIS, Università degli Studi di Genova, Via Opera Pia, 13 – 16145 Genova – Italy
lpulina@uniss.it — armando.tacchella@unige.it

Abstract. In this paper we provide a concise survey of our work devoted to applying formal methods to check the safety of adaptive cyber-physical systems.

1 Introduction

In the past few years, the notion of cyber-physical system (CPS) emerged to define complex systems intertwining physical processes, hardware, software and communication networks. With respect to "classical" embedded systems, CPSs add elements of complexity including different spatial and temporal scales among components, multiple and distinct behavioral modalities, and context-dependent interaction patterns [1]. When considering *adaptive* (also *reconfigurable*) CPSs, we refer to implements capable of modifying their internal parameters to achieve and maintain a prescribed quality of service even in the face of a partially unknown and mutating environment. The addition of "adaptive" remarks the sharp distinction we draw between systems which only react according to prescribed control policies and systems which can learn and/or update their control policies. While adaptation is a desirable requirement for CPSs in many circumstances, most CPSs are deployed in applications where misbehavior can cause serious damage to the surrounding environment, which makes their safety a mandatory requirement. Unfortunately, adaptivity and safety are two conflicting propositions: safety can be increased by reducing the amount of automatic reconfiguration, while changing internal parameters during operation may yield unsafe control policies.

The vision behind our research is that the trade-off between safety and adaptivity could be reduced substantially by resorting to model-based design (MBD) techniques and formal methods. While MBD tools represents a steadily growing area in CPSs the application of formal methods is still confined to a niche. In our view, the availability of abstract system models from MBD tools is an enabler for analyzing those models in a precise way, and since it is impossible to foresee all the potential adaptations of a system in advance, formal verification is the only practical way to increase confidence in the correct adaptive behavior of the final implement. The research question is thus whether verification techniques conceived with non-adaptive systems in mind, can be borrowed and/or extended to verify (industry-scale) CPSs.

In the following, we divide our attempts to answer such question in two families. In Section 2 we consider the safety of *stateless* models, i.e., models whose purpose is to

---

* The authors wish to thank their collaborators and colleagues Erika Ábrahám, Nils Jansen, Joost-Pieter Katoen, Francesco Leofante, Giorgio Metta, Lorenzo Natale, Shashank Pathak and Simone Vuotto, who contributed to the research herewith presented.

O. Strichman and R. Tzoref-Brill (Eds.): HVC 2017, LNCS 10629, pp. 237–240, 2017.
https://doi.org/10.1007/978-3-319-70389-3_19

approximate functional implements. Our main contributions along this research stream involve safety of artificial neural networks [2,3,4] and kernel-based machines [5]. In Section 3 we consider *modal* models, i.e., representations of dynamical systems. Here we consider both hybrid systems [6] augmented with adaptive capabilities, and probabilistic systems [7,8,9,10], wherein models of environments and control policies are acquired through approximate dynamic programming.

2   Stateless models

In applications of CPSs, it is often the case that functional relationships between system variables are to be approximated and possibly updated to maintain optimal performances. Consider, for instance, the relationship between fuel and air intake in electronic injection systems. While interpolation of a fixed look-up table might suffice to determine the correct air intake, an adaptive approach might seek to find the best relationship based, e.g., on fuel quality, air relative humidity, and exhaust gas emissions. Both neural networks and kernel-based machines — see [4,5] for references — have been proved very successful in fulfilling these tasks by "learning" accurate mappings from data. However, in spite of some exceptions, their application is confined to non-safety related implements. The main reason is the lack of general, automated, yet effective safety assurance methods for learning systems.

Introduced for the first time in our work [4], verification of neural networks known as Multi-Layer Perceptrons (MLPs) can be carried out using abstraction-refinement techniques and Satisfiability Modulo Theory (SMT) solvers. The same approach was later extended to consider several safety-related conditions in [2], and to consider kernel-based machines in [5]. The key idea of the approach is that both MLPs and kernel-based machines are linear combinations of non-linear functions. Therefore, it is sufficient to abstract non-linear elements in order to obtain abstract machines whose input-output properties can be checked using quantifier-free linear arithmetic over reals (QF-LRA). Abstract machines are conservative over-approximations of concrete ones. Therefore, safety of abstract machines implies safety of concrete ones, whereas abstract counterexamples must be checked for realization — a process branded Counter-Example Triggered Abstraction Refinement (CETAR) in [4]. To a certain extent, spurious counterexamples can also be used to *repair* the network, i.e., improve its safety. To the best of our knowledge, this is the only contribution in the literature where formal methods are leveraged to improve the quality of a functional approximation.

The results obtained in [2] and [5] show that CETAR based on SMT solvers is applicable to small-to-medium sized networks. However, recent advancements in the machine learning community command for much larger and complex networks known as *Deep Neural Networks*. While the performances of such networks in terms of predictive power on a variety of tasks are impressive, they also feature some unexpected behaviors. For instance, in [1] it is shown that very small perturbations on input instances can cause dramatic effects on output results. This "instability" of deep neural networks was the inspiration behind recent contributions, see, e.g., [11,12]. In spite of these recent advancements, the problem of verifying large and complex networks is still an open question worth of further investigation.

3   Modal models

Modeling CPSs as a whole usually requires modal models. Furthermore, due to the interaction with physical processes, discrete-time finite-state models are not sufficient to capture all the subtleties of a CPS. Hybrid and/or probabilistic models are to be considered instead. With respect to the classical tasks of controller verification and synthesis, such models introduce additional computational issues which might make formal approaches untenable in practical applications. Adaptivity, i.e., learning parameters and/or control strategies, thickens the plot even further. Our research has focused on applicable formal methods for verification, synthesis and repair of controllers, considering the robotic domain as benchmarks for realistic, yet reasonably sized CPSs.

In [6] we considered a robot learning to play defense in the air hockey game. This setup is paradigmatic since the robot must see, decide and move fastly, but, at the same time, it must learn and guarantee that the control system is safe throughout the process. The (multi-agent) control system is comprised of a *vision* agent devoted to visual perception, a *motion control* agent sending position commands to the manipulator and a *coordination* agent converting stimuli into commands. The parameters of the coordination agent change over time, possibly improving on the robot's ability to intercept the puck. The system is unsafe if the manipulator moves too close to the table's edges. Agents are modeled as hybrid automata, and execution traces are checked for safety with HYSAT [13]. Because of learning, the whole system must be (re)verified eventually. The key idea is to preserve safety at all times by keeping safe – and possibly ineffective – parameters of the coordination agent in place, until a more effective – and definitely safe – setting is available. Experimental analysis in the air hockey setup shows that this approach can yield safety without heavily compromising on effectiveness.

In a series of papers started with [9], we considered the problem of synthesizing safe controllers using probabilistic models. In these works, we assume that the interaction between the robot and the environment can be modeled as a Markov Decision Process (MDP), and that a control strategy for the task at hand can be acquired by approximate dynamic programming — also known as Reinforcement Learning (RL). Here, the focus is on safety at the deliberative level, enabling a discrete-time, discrete state abstraction of the problem domain, where probabilistic effects account for noise in sensing and acting.[3] Since RL acquires (an implicit) system model and an (explicit) control strategy by trial and error, we postulate that learning is performed in a simulator and then the control strategy is deployed on the actual robot. The key idea is that, given a control strategy, an MDP becomes a Markov chain so that safety properties can be expressed using probabilistic temporal logic and verified using model checkers. In [9] we consider a task wherein a humanoid should grasp some object while avoiding others, whereas in [8] we consider a standing-up task for a small (19 degrees-of-freedom) robot. In both contributions we consider both the problem of verifying that a learned control strategy fulfills some requirements, and the problem of repairing it until it does. Moreover, in [8], we consider also the problem of monitoring that the (verified, repaired) control strategy maintains its properties once deployed on the actual robot.

---

[3] It is however assumed that the state can be detected with sufficient precision, i.e., we postulate full observability.

References

1. Edward A. Lee. Cyber physical systems: Design challenges. In *11th IEEE International Symposium on Object-Oriented Real-Time Distributed Computing (ISORC 2008), 5-7 May 2008, Orlando, Florida, USA*, pages 363–369, 2008.
2. Luca Pulina and Armando Tacchella. Challenging SMT solvers to verify neural networks. *AI Commun.*, 25(2):117–135, 2012.
3. Luca Pulina and Armando Tacchella. NeVer: a tool for artificial neural networks verification. *Ann. Math. Artif. Intell.*, 62(3-4):403–425, 2011.
4. Luca Pulina and Armando Tacchella. An Abstraction-Refinement Approach to Verification of Artificial Neural Networks. In *Computer Aided Verification, 22nd International Conference, CAV 2010, Edinburgh, UK, July 15-19, 2010. Proceedings*, pages 243–257, 2010.
5. Francesco Leofante and Armando Tacchella. Learning in Physical Domains: Mating Safety Requirements and Costly Sampling. In *AI*IA 2016: Advances in Artificial Intelligence - XVth International Conference of the Italian Association for Artificial Intelligence, Genova, Italy, November 29 - December 1, 2016, Proceedings*, pages 539–552, 2016.
6. Giorgio Metta, Lorenzo Natale, Shashank Pathak, Luca Pulina, and Armando Tacchella. Safe and effective learning: A case study. In *IEEE International Conference on Robotics and Automation, ICRA 2010, Anchorage, Alaska, USA, 3-7 May 2010*, pages 4809–4814, 2010.
7. Shashank Pathak, Luca Pulina, and Armando Tacchella. Evaluating probabilistic model checking tools for verification of robot control policies. *AI Commun.*, 29(2):287–299, 2016.
8. Francesco Leofante, Simone Vuotto, Erika Ábrahám, Armando Tacchella, and Nils Jansen. Combining Static and Runtime Methods to Achieve Safe Standing-Up for Humanoid Robots. In *Leveraging Applications of Formal Methods, Verification and Validation: Foundational Techniques - 7th Int.l Symp., ISoLA 2016, Imperial, Corfu, Greece, October 10-14, 2016, Proceedings, Part I*, pages 496–514, 2016.
9. Shashank Pathak, Luca Pulina, Giorgio Metta, and Armando Tacchella. Ensuring safety of policies learned by reinforcement: Reaching objects in the presence of obstacles with the iCub. In *2013 IEEE/RSJ International Conference on Intelligent Robots and Systems, Tokyo, Japan, November 3-7, 2013*, pages 170–175, 2013.
10. Shashank Pathak, Luca Pulina, and Armando Tacchella. Verification and Repair of Control Policies for Safe Reinforcement Learning. *To appear in Applied Intelligence*, 2017.
11. Xiaowei Huang, Marta Kwiatkowska, Sen Wang, and Min Wu. Safety verification of deep neural networks. *arXiv preprint arXiv:1610.06940 – To appear as invited paper at CAV 2017*, 2016.
12. Guy Katz, Clark Barrett, David Dill, Kyle Julian, and Mykel Kochenderfer. Reluplex: An efficient smt solver for verifying deep neural networks. *arXiv preprint arXiv:1702.01135 – To appear in the proc. of CAV 2017*, 2017.
13. Martin Fränzle and Christian Herde. Hysat: An efficient proof engine for bounded model checking of hybrid systems. *Formal Methods in System Design*, 30(3):179–198, 2007.

APSL: a Light Weight Testing Tool for Protocols with Complex Messages

Tom Tervoort and I.S.W.B. Prasetya[0000−0002−3421−4635]

Dept. of Inf. and Comp. Sciences, Utrecht University, the Netherlands
s.w.b.prasetya@uu.nl

Abstract. Many real world communication protocols exchange complex messages, consisting of multiple nested fields, some could have values that depend on other fields. To properly test an implementation, it is not sufficient to only explore different orders of message exchanges. We also need to test if the implementation produces correctly formatted messages, and responds correctly when it receives different variations of every message type. This paper presents a light weight model based testing tool called APSL. Models are described as labelled transitions systems, from which abstract test sequences can be generated. APSL's main contribution is in its language for describing complex message formats, text-based or binary, allowing APSL to automatically concretize abstract test sequences, and check incoming messages for their type and format conformance. Testing works out thus of the box: developers do not need to first write a dedicated concretization layer, which would otherwise require substantial investment.

Keywords: model based testing of protocols

1 Introduction

Communication protocols are often quite complex. Implementing one is always tricky and error prone. An implementation should thus be thoroughly tested. Model-based testing (MBT) has been widely used to do this [1]. In this approach we first model the behavior of a protocol, from which test sequences can be systematically derived to test the conformance of an implementation.

The complication modern protocols lies however not only in the interaction between the communicating parties, but also in the *formats* of the messages that they exchange. A message can be a quite complex record structure with multiple fields, some could be optional, or have delicate dependencies, which in turn are prone to errors. Existing languages to model protocols, e.g. SDL, Estelle, or UML's MSC, mostly focus on describing the interaction part. These languages can enumerate different message types, but are not refined enough to describe the formats of the messages. MBT tools for protocols, e.g. TorX [6] and TGV [3] follow the same trend. When the above languages or tools are used for MBT, the generated test sequences are abstract in the sense that each step in a sequence specifies which message type is to be sent or received to/from the Implementation Under Test (IUT), but it does not specify how to *concretize* the step. It does not tell us how to generate a correctly formatted instance of

© Springer International Publishing AG 2017
O. Strichman and R. Tzoref-Brill (Eds.): HVC 2017, LNCS 10629, pp. 241–244, 2017.
https://doi.org/10.1007/978-3-319-70389-3_20

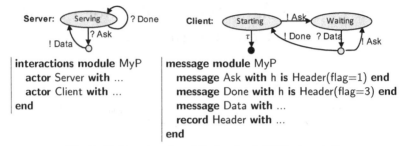

Fig. 1. MyP protocol and its top level APSL description.

the message type to be sent to the IUT, nor how to determine if an incoming message from the IUT is correctly formatted. Consequently, to actually use them developers still need to build a separate layer that performs the concretization steps. The needed effort is substantial. Traditionally, Abstract Syntax Notation One (ASN.1) [4], introduced in 1984, is used by the industry for describing complex formats. However ASN.1 has has grown to be large and complex. For example, it has more than 10 different string types, many intended for legacy character encodings. It also has ten expansive standards. These make building an ASN.1-based tool expensive.

This short paper presents APSL (A Protocol Specification Language): a language and tool for specifying protocols for the purpose of MBT. As in e.g. TorX, each actor in a protocol is modeled by a labelled transition system (LTS). However, APSL allows the formats of messages, both text-based and binary, to be described. Once the formats are defined, APSL can automatically do the concretization of abstract test sequences. This means that MBT with APSL works out of the box: there is no need for developers to first build a concretization layer. Although much lighter than ASN.1, APSL is expressive enough to express the formats of various real world protocols e.g. NTP, BSON, DNS, WebSocket, and IMAP —these examples, and APSL source code, can be found in [5].

2   Describing Protocols in APSL

Consider a hypothetical protocol called MyP shown in Figure 1, consisting of two actors: a server and a client, interacting as visually shown by the corresponding LTS's. A transition in the LTS of an actor represents either an action by the actor to send a message (!m, where m is the type of the message to send), or the receipt of a message (?m), or a non-observable internal action (τ).

To describe a protocol in APSL we define: (1) an *interaction module*, describing which *actors* participate in the protocol and the LTS of each, and (2) a *message module*, describing different types of messages in the protocol and how they are formatted. Figure 1 shows MyP's top level interaction and message modules. There are three types of messages in MyP. Data are sent by the server to the client, carrying payload. The client sends an Ask to the server to ask for an instance of Data, or a Done if it has enough. Messages are basically records, composed from *fields*. In the example, the message types Ask and Done are both defined to have a single field named h of a type called Header.

Specifying complex messages Each field in a record has a name and a type, e.g. Integer or Text. In typical specification languages, e.g. OCL or Z , we do not have to care about how 'types' are implemented. In protocol engineering we need to: a protocol may insist on a specific way with which values are encoded in bits. E.g. it may require a certain integer field to be represented in a 4-bits big-endian, while another integer field should be 32-bits, and so on. So in addition to specifying the type of a field, in APSL we also need to specify a so-called *codec* to describe how instances of the type should be represented in bitstrings. As an example, below we define the record type Header (used in the Ask and Done messages), which has two fields:

```
record Header with
    flag is Integer as BigEndian(signed=false,length=2)
    reserved is Binary(value=b'000000') end
```

The field flag is an integer, but furthermore, its BigEndian codec says that it will be represented by two bits in the unsigned big-endian format. APSL comes with a range of common codecs, e.g. to format texts, in various ways, into bitstrings —see the documentation in [5]. The field reserved is of type Binary, which means that it is simply a bitstring. For such, no codec is required.

APSL supports *dependent types*: types that are parameterized by value-level expressions used to specify a subset of a base type. E.g., the type expression Binary(value=b'000000') above specifies a subset consisting of a single value: the bitstring 000000 (so, this is the only allowed value of the field reserved). As another example, Integer(min=0, max=500) specifies a subset of integers, from 0 up to 500.

An important design principle is that a receiver should be able to efficiently determine when each field within a message ends. One way to achieve this is by using a codec that adds a specific bit pattern to mark the end of a field. Another common convention is to have a field that specifies the length of the next field or fields. Dependent types are essential to capture such dependency, which can be quite complex. This is shown by the example below:

```
record DataItem with
    n is Integer(min=0,max=500) as BigEndian(signed=false,length=32)
    data is Binary(length=8*n)
    padding is Binary(length=8*(4 − n%4), char8_pattern=/\0*\1/) end
```

The field data is used to hold binary payload. Its type parameter says that its length is $8n$ bits. Notice that n is another field, whose type parameter says that it is an integer between 0 and 500. The field padding is more complicated. Suppose that the total length of a DataItem should be a multiple of 32 bits. The field padding is used to pad it if that was not the case. The type parameter length $= 8 * (4 - n\%4)$ specifies how long the padding should be. The type Binary can also be parameterized by a *regular expression* to specify allowed bitstrings. Above, the regular expression in char8_pattern $= /\0 * \1/$ specifies that a bitstring of zero or more 0's closed by a 1 should be used as the padding.

For MyP, we still have to define the message type Data. The definition below shows an example of a message type containing list and optional fields. It says that any instance of Data consists of a header h, payload containing a list of DataItem, and an optional field called foot.

```
message Data with
   h is Header(flag=0)
   payload is List(elem=DataItem,max_length=4) as ... some codec
   hasfoot is Bool as BoolBits(falsehood_string=X'00',truth_string=X'ff')
   foot is Optional(is_empty=!hasfooter,subject=Text) as ... some codec end
```

Specifying interactions The example below shows how to describe the LTS of MyP's client (Figure 1) in APSL:

```
actor Client with
   init state Starting where anytime do send Ask next Waiting or do quit end
   state Waiting where on Data do send Ask continue
                     or do send Done next Starting end end
```

3   APSL's Model Based Testing

With APSL we can test if an implementation of an actor conforms its model. A TCP/IP channel is provided to connect APSL to an implementation under test (IUT). Then, we can proceed with testing, Each test case is generated by generating a traversal through the actor's LTS. The test engine allows a strategy to be specified to guide a traversal. Whenever the traversal has to be extended with a send or receive action, the engine consults the strategy. A basic random strategy, a strategy that steers towards some specified states, and operators to combine strategies are provided. More sophisticated strategies can be programmed in Haskell (the implementation language of APSL). During a traversal, whenever a message of type M has to be sent to the IUT, APSL generates a random and correctly formatted instance of M, then sends it to the IUT through the TCP/IP channel. Whenever the IUT sends a message m, the engine checks for two kinds of errors: m has an invalid format, or m is, according to the LTS, of a wrong type. There is no need to build any concretization layer. A description of the engine's algorithm can be found in [5], including details on how it handles non-deterministic models. Utilities are provided to inspect the obtained transition and message coverage. For debugging, test case reduction e.g. by removing idempotent transitions a la [2] is provided.

References

1. Belinfante, A., Frantzen, L., Schallhart, C.: Tools for test case generation. In: Model-Based Testing of Reactive Systems, LNCS, vol. 3472. Springer (2005)
2. Elyasov, A., Prasetya, I.S.W.B., Hage, J., Nikas, A.: Reduce first, debug later. In: 9th Int. Workshop on Automation of Software Test. pp. 57–63. ACM (2014)
3. Fernandez, J.C., Jard, C., Jéron, T., Viho, C.: Using on-the-fly verification techniques for the generation of test suites. In: Int. Conf. on CAV. Springer (1996)
4. ITU: ASN.1 Project, http://www.itu.int/en/ITU-T/asn1
5. T. Tervoort: APSL, https://git.science.uu.nl/prase101/apsl
6. Tretmans, J., Brinksma, E.: TorX: Automated model-based testing. In: 1ST European Conf. on Model-Driven Software Engineering (2003)

Towards Verification of Robot Design for Self-localization

Ryo Watanabe[†], Kozo Okano[‡], and Toshifusa Sekizawa[§]

† Graduate School of Engineering, Nihon University, Japan
‡ Faculty of Engineering, Shinshu University, Japan
§ College of Engineering, Nihon University, Japan

Abstract. CPS plays important roles along with popularization. In this study, we handle an autonomous robot which estimates its position by observations in discrete two-dimensional field. Probabilistic behaviors are modeled in MDPs, and model checking results validate robot's design.

Keywords: probabilistic model checking, self-localization, autonomous robot

1 Introduction

Cyber-physical systems (CPSs) are widely spread among society and play important roles. Ensuring properties of such systems is vital, and model checking [3] has successfully been applied from the design phase to implementation.

As an application of CPS, we focus on the design of a robot's self-localization in which the robot estimates its position based on observations and a given map. In robotics, self-localization is often required, using values obtained by observations of an external environment. A simple example is a robot running on a maze, where it does not know its initial position. For such a case, it is necessary to design movements, for the robot, since estimation depends on arrangement of structures on a map. In this study, we fix movements of the robot. We then show verification results, using a probabilistic model checker PRISM [4], to see if the robot can determine its position for a given map.

The roadmap of this paper is as follows. Section 2 describes the target system and our settings. In Section 3, we build models and show verification results. Section 4 offers brief discussion, and Section 5 provides a concluding summary.

2 Target System and Our Settings

Probabilistic robotics [6] handles autonomous mobile robots that motions are determined by uncertain observations of an external environment. The position is estimated by matching observation values and a given map. One key concept is *belief* that represents existence probabilities for all possible positions.

We consider a robot that runs on a two-dimensional array, as a concrete example. We assume that a map is a discrete finite space that has periodic boundary conditions, and the robot moves in discrete time. Specifically, let a map M

© Springer International Publishing AG 2017
O. Strichman and R. Tzoref-Brill (Eds.): HVC 2017, LNCS 10629, pp. 245–248, 2017.
https://doi.org/10.1007/978-3-319-70389-3_21

Algorithm 1 Deterministic Markov Localization

Input: $bel(M(x_{t-1}, y_{t-1})), u_t, z_t, M$
Output: $bel(M(x_t, y_t))$
  for all x_t, y_t **do**
    $\overline{bel}(x_t, y_t) = bel\left((x_{t-1} - u_t + N_x)\%N_x, y_{t-1}\right)$
    $bel(x_t, y_t) = \eta\, p(z_t \mid M(x_t, y_t), M)\, \overline{bel}(x_t, y_t)$
  end for

---

be a two-dimensional array, and denote an element as $M(x_t, y_t)$. Then periodic boundary conditions are given as $M(N_x, y) = M(0, y), M(x, N_y) = M(x, 0)$, where N_x and N_y are the maximum numbers of rows and columns, respectively. We then set two kinds of structures, *door* (0) and *wall* (1). *i.e.*, $M(x_t, y_t) \in \{0, 1\}$. A *movement* is changing position in a computational time. We design the directions of movements as follows. Let the current position be $M(x, y)$. i) if the observation value is 0, then moves to $M(x + 1, y)$, ii) if the observation value is 1, then moves to $M(x, y + 1)$. These movements are deterministic, since non-deterministic movements potentially cause round trip and no convergence. We consider that these limitations are naturally required in the design phase. An *observation* is reading a structure. Then the next movement is decided by the read value. As probabilistic behaviors, we only consider read error of an observation. In these settings, if the robot misdetects a wall, then the robot obtains a door.

We adopt the Markov localization algorithm [6] to calculate the beliefs, as shown in Algorithm 1. Algorithm 1 takes belief bel_{t-1}, movement u_t and observation z_t, and a map M as input, and returns belief bel_t for all positions $M(x_t, y_t)$. We assign $p(z_t | M(x_t, y_t), M) = (M(x_t, y_t) + 1)\,\%2$ if $z_t = 0$, otherwise $M(x_t, y_t)$. This assignment does not accurately represent a probabilistic observation. Such uncertainty is handled as probabilistic transition in modeling. Note that, η is the normalization coefficient.

3   Modeling and Verification

We build a model using Markov decision process (MDP) $\mathcal{M} = (S, s_0, \mathcal{A}, \mathcal{T})$ representing robot behaviors defined in Algorithm 1, and verify using probabilistic model checker PRISM [4]. We assign all beliefs, bel_t and $\overline{bel}_t$, to states S. According to the algorithm, bel_t is memoryless and satisfies the Markov property. The initial state is bel_0 in which existence probability is uniform distribution. Movements and observations are assigned to transitions $\mathcal{T}$. We add an action *move* to $\mathcal{A}$ that corresponds to a movement. Next, our observations. The robot non-deterministically observes either a wall or a door. We also add *wall* and *door* to the set of actions A. Then, $\mathcal{A} = \{move, wall, door\}$, lastly. For each observation, there is a possibility of error detection, therefore a transition probability $p < 1.0$ is assigned to a transition for observing the structure, *i.e.*, another transition has probability $1 - p$ for the observation failure. We also consider improbable

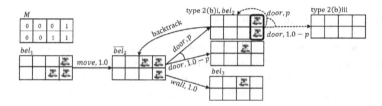

Fig. 1. Modeling of Self-localization

observation. That is, if all the structures are the same at positions where existence probability is not 0, the action is decided deterministically to the value of the structure, but error detection is still considered.

Before specifying formulas, let an *observation sequence* be a sequence of observation values. For a given map, one of the purposes of verification is validating whether the position of the robot converges for all observation sequences. This property is express as a PCTL formula as $\mathbb{P}_{\geq 1.0}\left[\textbf{FG} \bigvee_{i,j}\left(bel(i,j) \neq 1\right)\right]$. If this property does not hold for the given map, the robot can uniquely estimate its position. Additionally for the cases of no convergence, we verify a property $\mathbb{P}_{\geq 1.0}\left[\textbf{FG} \bigvee_{i,j}\left(bel(i,j) = 1\right)\right]$ to validate whether the position converges for some observation sequences. According to the verification results, we are able to classify maps as three types, 1, 2a and 2b, as follows.

1. The robot can uniquely estimate its position for all observation sequences.
2. The robot cannot estimate its position. This type of maps can be further classified as the following two types.
   (a) Essentially impossible to estimate its position uniquely.
   (b) Cannot uniquely estimate because of some observation sequences.
       i. The doors are lining up vertically, *i.e.*, $M(x,y) = M(x,y+1) = 1$, and there is at least one another door which enables estimation.
       ii. $M(x,y) = M(x+1,y) = M(x+2,y+1) = 1$ and otherwise 0.
       iii. When the structure is uniquely judged as wall or door at potential positions, but observation obtains the opposite value.

Types 2(b)i and 2(b)ii are caused by limitations of robot movements. However, the position cannot be estimated by exhaustive searching even if the limitations are removed. Type 2(b)iii induces existence probability 0 for all positions.

We adopt backtracking to achieve verification of type 2b. Specifically, if the observation value is obtained nondeterministically, store the value and $\overline{bel}_t$. After that, if type 2(b)i or 2(b)ii occurs by referring the map at calculating bel_{t+1}, then back to $\overline{bel}_t$. After that, adopt another observation value and continue searching. Figure 1 shows a case of type 2b in which a backtrack occurs. Note that this approach enables verification of type 2(b)iii caused by misdetection. We set the size of the map as $N_x = 4$ and $N_y = 2$. All 256 combinations are verified according to the approach. Verification results show the robot can uniquely estimate its position, except for the type 2a.

4 Brief Discussion and Related Work

The size of the map is fixed in this study. We have tried some experimental verification of larger maps. So far, the results indicate that larger maps contain similar characteristics of structure arrangement. Therefore, it would be possible to reduce the size of state space by considering such arrangements.

There have been a number of studies about autonomous robotics associated with verification. Many of them focus on analyzing behaviors of a multi-robot system, such as [1]. One similar study is motion planning and control [5]. This study handles one autonomous robot exploring a field divided into discrete regions. However, this study aims verification of the entire system, not motions of the robot. Embedded systems often consist of continuous and discrete dynamics, or hybrid systems. Another considerable approach is co-simulation using a model checker and a simulator. The Modana framework [2] provides useful reference, since it analyzes probabilistic behaviors of CPSs based on co-simulation using functional mock-up interface.

5 Conclusion

We have studied self-localization by an autonomous robot and verification to ensure its motion design. Our experimental results suggest usefulness of model checking for the design of robot motions. In this study, we considered probabilistic observations and adopted Markov localization in discrete two-dimensional systems. The modeling and verification results showed possibilities of probabilistic model checking to motion designs of an autonomous robot.

Although still in a preliminary stage, we hope to extend this study to analyses and design methods of various robot vehicles. Future work includes extension of time-related properties or hybrid systems to handle continuous dynamics, as these characteristics are important in the design phase in general. In that process, combining model checking and simulation seem to be effective.

This study was supported by JSPS KAKENHI Grant Number 17K00111.

References

1. Brambilla, M., Pinciroli, C., Birattari, M., Dorigo, M.: Property-driven design for swarm robotics. In: AAMAS. pp. 139–146. IFAAMAS (2012)
2. Cheng, B., Wang, X., Liu, J., Du, D.: Modana: An integrated framework for modeling and analysis of energy-aware CPSs. In: COMPSAC. pp. 127–136. IEEE (2015)
3. Clarke, E.M., Grumberg, O., Peled, D.: Model Checking. MIT Press (1999)
4. Kwiatkowska, M., Norman, G., Parker, D.: PRISM 4.0: Verification of probabilistic real-time systems. In: CAV'11. LNCS, vol. 6806, pp. 585–591. Springer (2011)
5. Lahijanian, M., Wasniewski, J., Andersson, S.B., Belta, C.: Motion planning and control from temporal logic specifications with probabilistic satisfaction guarantees. In: ICRA. pp. 3227–3232. IEEE (2010)
6. Thrun, S., Burgard, W., Fox, D.: Probabilistic Robotics. Intelligent robotics and autonomous agents, MIT Press (2005)

Probabilistic Model of Control-Flow Altering based Malicious Attacks

(Poster submission)

Sergey Frenkel

Federal Reserach Center "Computer Science and Control " Russian Academy of Sc.,
Moscow, Russia, fsergei51@gmail.com

Introduction. The system designers need in various design tools which could help them both for estimation of possible threats to the security and select one or another ways of their neutralization. There are many approaches to the evaluation (verification) of the degree of protection of programs against possible attacks. First of all, this is fault Injection (FI) simulation techniques [1]. Main drawback of the FI is necessity to have different expensive software that can be not used to solve other design problems, in particular for functional verification and testing. Also, due to the similarity between system failures because of intentional attacks and those due to accidental component failures, reliability/availability-like models to evaluate system survivability are used in the security design [2]. But they are based on Continuous Time Markov Chain (CTMC), identification of which deals with some technical difficulties.

This paper considers a probabilistic approach to estimation of security risks of the programs due to malicious attacks which try to change the control flow of the program to corrupt the program behavior, the system calls sequence in particular. It is shown the possibility to use a Markov model with two absorbing states defined on direct product of the spaces of two finite state machines (FSM), one of which is a program finite automaton model that is running under normal conditions, and second is the same FSM in which at some point in time (depending on the considered temporal discreteness) there was a failure due to external attacks (e.g., within the time of a single operation, or a program's block execution). Previously this model was suggested for hardware fault-tolerance analysis [6]. However, in contrast to the previously considered model, in which the effect of an erroneous state change was considered as a result of the damage of one or another bit of the status codeword, here we consider an altering of the program control flow (or system calls sequence) as a cause of the attack malicious effect.

Model of Program under Attacks. The application program model considered is the Finite State Machine (FSM) of Mealy type, corresponding to the algorithm implemented by this program. This FSM can be built either from a program source or from system calls sequences. We consider the attacks effect (that is the malicious codes action) as the *control-data attack* which alter the target program's control data, say, as data that are loaded to processor program counter at some point in program execution.

© Springer International Publishing AG 2017

O. Strichman and R. Tzoref-Brill (Eds.): HVC 2017, LNCS 10629, pp. 249–252, 2017.

https://doi.org/10.1007/978-3-319-70389-3_22

Malicious behavior model : $\{(a_i,a_j) \rightarrow (a_i, a_k)\}$, where (a_i,a_j) is an inter-state transition in the FSM, represented the program with normal behavior, which was changed to the transition in the state a_k due to an attack. No new states arise.

Note, that such assumption is coordinated with the flow graph altering model.

Let us a program which may be subjected to an attack is represented by an Mealy automaton (FSM) $s_{t+1} = \delta (x_{t+1}, s_t)$, where δ is a transition system, x and s are input and state vectors correspondingly. The automaton clock t corresponds to execution of each of the program operator, or each of system call execution. A way of the FSM building from a system calls sequences see, e.g., in [4,5]. Note, that the program on the system calls level (parametrized, in general) can be also modeled by such FSM. [4].

Let us assume, that all components of the input vector x are independent random variables. This independence can be provide by a specific choice of the FSM inputs (see, for example, in [7]).

Let $\{M_t, t \geq 0\}$ is Markov chain (MC) describing the target behavior of target FSM with n states under random input, that is, functioning without effect of any faults caused by an attack (altering the flow graph, corresponding to the transition function δ) and $\{F_t , t \geq 0\}$ is the MC based on the same FSM but exposed by some altering transition. Let $Z_t = \{(M_t, F_t, t \geq 0\}$ corresponding to behavior of the MCs pairs that is MC with state space $S^2 = S \times S$ of pairs (a_i, a_j), $a_i, a_j \in S$. The size of the MC is $n(n-1)+2$. The matrix of transition probabilities of these MCs are calculated from the given FSM transitions table, and the probabilities of Boolean input binary variables of the FSM as well. Along with the states, Z_t has two absorbing states A_0 and A_1, where A_0 is the event "by the moment the FSM's trajectory has been restored and the output is not were distorted", A_1 is "malfunctioning has already manifested itself in the output signal". The pairs of (a_i, a_j) states enables representation of any transient faults as "the FSM instead of the state a_i, in which it should be on this clock after the transition at the previous time cycle, as a result of the malfunction was in the state a_j".

We characterize the security regarding an malicious attack as the probability of event that the trajectories (states, transitions and outputs) of M_t and F_t will be coincided after the termination the attack causing a flow graph deviation, before a clock t when outputs of both FSMs (underlying these MCs) become mismatched. This probability that the FSM returns to correct functioning after some number t of time slots can be computed as probability to get in one an absorbing states, using Chapman-Kolmogorov equation expressing the probability vector $\vec{p}(t)$ of the states into which the falls the Z_t (and corresponding FSM as well, which is the product of these two FSMs) after t transitions in terms of initial distribution $\vec{p}(0)$ of the MC states. $\vec{p}(0)$ is determined by the initial states of the fault-free and faulty FSMs, and the state transition probability matrix of this Markov chain. The components of the vector $\vec{p}(t)$ are the probabilities $p_0(t)$, $p_1(t)$ of getting into the absorbing state A_0 and A_1 mentioned above, and the probability of transitions to the rest (transient) states of the MC, in the sum equal to $1 - p_0(t) - p_1(t)$. If the fault-free FSM at the initial moment 0 is in the state i_0, and the faulty state (say, due to an attack effect) is in the state $j_0 \neq i_0$, then $p_{i_0,j_0}(0) = 1$, and the remaining coordinates of the vector $\vec{p}(0)$ are zero.

An example of the model application. Here this method for an example of a program from [5] is demonstrated.

Let's consider a program with control flow graph (Fig.2), where the original control-flow is depicted as solid-lined arrows, and altering of the program execution under a malicious action (attack), which completely bypassing basic block 2, is depicted as a dashed-lined arrow. The branching in the node 2 is a computational condition presented in the program.

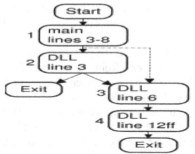

Fig. 1. The program flow graph and its altering due to attack

In order to build the Mealy automaton, the program block diagram of the Fig, 2 is rewritten as "Algorithmic State Machine" [3,6] in Fig. 2, where each vertex Y1,..Y5 are some abstractions of the operations which corresponding blocks of the program Fig.1 execute (e.g., call of the DLL in the line 3), the results of which are represented by output variables y1,..y5. Note, that function of vertex Y5 in this representation is to synchronize the condition checking (x1, corresponding to the conditional vertex 2 in the program (Fig.1)) only and the result to form.   The (ai,yi) pairs are the states and the automaton output variables of the FSM (Fig.2(a)), and x1", is the input variable of the automaton.

A_n	A_n	X	Y
a1	a4	1	y5
a2	a1	1	y2
a3	a2	x1	y3
a3	a1	~x1	y1
a4	a3	1	y4

(a)

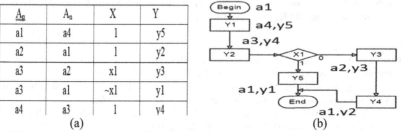

(b)

Fig. 2. States transition table ((a)) and "Algorithmic State Machine" ((b)) of the program Fig.1 corresponding to the FSM.

Then, in accordance with definition of malicious behavior by an attack mentioned above, this attack altering the program flow graph (Fig.2) is described in terms of this automaton transitions as {(4,3)→(4,2)}.

The authors of the program [5] explain that this attack works and stays undetected because it takes advantage of a specific characteristic of the late binding technique (dynamic dispatch) when the affected variables are stored on the heap. But, on the other hand, if in the normally functioning program takes place the condition "Go To Exit" and if the program variable that controls this "Go To" act is checkable by an built-in checker (which, suppose, convoys the program execution), the attack can be detected in a point corresponding to the node "Exit" (Fig.2), e,g., if the program's code contains "return 1". Then, we could characterize the possibility to detect the attack using this path by the probability of its activation. Obviously, this probability depends on the probability of variable x1. That is the program's input data also play a role in the abstraction of the program behavior by affecting the branching choice probability, that is the probability that input data provide the choice just a given branch.

For example, let's Prob (x1=1)=0.9, which is the probability that result of block 2 Fig. 1 (which a DLL returns) activates the exit from the module. Then, probabilities that the output values (say,y2) of the program has already manifested itself to the given clock t as corrupted, what means the attack detection, can be obtained by the solution of the above Markov chain is the following vectror: P_D = (0,0, 0.09, 0.091, 0.093, 0.1629, 0.1638), where the number of each position corresponds to the clock number minus 1 (the first element corresponds to the moment of failure and is considered a zero index). It means, that to the fourth clock of the automaton work, when the Exit will be achieved the attack can be detected with probability about 0.09 only, that may be turned out rather small, from the point of view sequrity requirements to this program. But If the probability of the condition Prob(x1=1)=0.4. this probability is about 0.3, that is has essentially more chances to be detected.

Thus, the model reflects the dynamic of the program behavior.

Note, that as we deal with high abstraction level of the design description, the number of the FSM states are usually not very large. Thus, taking into account that the Markov chain size is n(n-1)+2, n is the number of states, and complexity of the probabilities vector computation is quadratic, we can consider this model as rather efficient.

Acknowledgment. This work was partially supported by the Russian Foundation for Basic Research under grants RFBR 15-07-05316 .

References

1. Darbari, A., Al Hashimi, B., Harrod, P., and Bradley, D., A New Approach for Transient Fault Injection using Symbolic Simulation, IOLTS 2008: pp. 93-98, 2008

2.Hai Wang, Peng Liu, Modeling and evaluating the survivability of an intrusion tolerant database system, Proceeding of ESORICS'06, pp. 207-224, Hamburg, 2006

3. Baranov, S.: ASMs in high level synthesis of EDA tool Abelite. In: DESDes'09 Int. IFAC Workshop Proceedings. – Valensia, Spain, pp. 195–200 (2009)

4. Jacob, G., Debar,H., Eric Filiol, Behavioral detection of malware: from a survey towards an established taxonomy, J Comput Virol (2008) 4:251–266

5. Seeger, M. M., Using control-flow techniques in a security context: A survey on common prototypes and their common weakness. In *Network Computing and Information Security (NCIS), 2011 International Conference on*, volume 2, pages 133–137, May 2011.

6.Frenkel, S., Frenkel, S.: Some measures of self-repairing ability for fault-tolerant circuits design. In: Second Workshop MEDIAN 2013, Avignon, France, pp. 57–60, May 30–31, 2013

7. Frenkel, S., et al.: Technical report of FRC "Computer Science and Control" of RAS, Moscow, Russia (2017), http://www.ipiran.ru/publications/Tech_report.pdf

Author Index

Printed in the United States
By Bookmasters